Mozart's Ghosts

Mozart's Ghosts

HAUNTING THE HALLS OF MUSICAL CULTURE

Mark Everist

OXFORD
UNIVERSITY PRESS

OXFORD
UNIVERSITY PRESS

Oxford University Press is a department of the
University of Oxford. It furthers the University's objective
of excellence in research, scholarship, and education
by publishing worldwide

Oxford   New York
Auckland   Cape Town   Dar es Salaam   Hong Kong   Karachi
Kuala Lumpur   Madrid   Melbourne   Mexico City   Nairobi
New Delhi   Shanghai   Taipei   Toronto

With offices in
Argentina   Austria   Brazil   Chile   Czech Republic   France   Greece
Guatemala   Hungary   Italy   Japan   Poland   Portugal   Singapore
South Korea   Switzerland   Thailand   Turkey   Ukraine   Vietnam

Oxford is a registered trade mark of Oxford University Press
in the Uk and certain other countries

Published in the United States of America by
Oxford University Press
198 Madison Avenue, New York, NY 10016

Library of Congress Cataloging-in-Publication Data
Everist, Mark.
Mozart's ghosts : reception and renown, 1791–present / by Mark Everist.
p.   cm.
Includes bibliographical references and index.
ISBN 978-0-19-538917-3 (hardcover : alk. paper)   1. Mozart, Wolfgang
Amadeus, 1756–1791—Criticism and interpretation.   I. Title.
ML410.M9E946   2012
780.92—dc23   2012015749

1 3 5 7 9 8 6 4 2

Printed in the United States of America
on acid-free paper

{ CONTENTS }

{ PREFACE }

There's a certain generation of academics whose early careers were marked by the publication of David Lodge's *Small World* (1984), and the efflorescence of the campus novel.[1] In his kaleidoscopic parody of the various tints of contemporary literary criticism, Lodge finds space for the redoubtable but ridiculous Siegfried von Turpitz, who is introduced to Lodge's readers "in a sleekly functional hotel room on the Kurfürstendamm";[2] his hand is sheathed in black kid, apparently hiding some hideous deformity, "the original...having been crushed and mangled in the machinery of the Panzer tank which Siegfried von Turpitz commanded in the later stages of World War II."[3] Turpitz is a professor at the fictional University of Baden-Baden, with ambitions and an interest in *Rezeptionsästhetik*.

Ambitions hardly characterize the main protagonist of Lodge's novel, Persse McGarrigle, a graduate student from Limerick, except perhaps in his dissertation title, "T. S. Eliot's Influence on Shakespeare," with its obvious resonances with von Turpitz's professional interests.[4] Constantly misunderstood as "Shakespeare's influence on T. S. Eliot" by the more cruelly parodied members of Lodge's cast, McGarrigle's subject goes right to the heart of what is understood by reception in literary studies: not, as its intellectual leader in the 1960s and 1970s Hans Robert Jauss suggested, the place in a hotel where you picked up your keys, but an acknowledgment, an understanding, that works of literature, music, and in other media have a changing after-life. McGarrigle's study of Shakespeare at the hands of T. S. Eliot was—in the early 1980s—a curiously current topic to emerge from what is painted in Lodge's novel as a sleepy backwater.

The depiction of the reception-historian/aesthetician as a German with a doubtful military past, a penchant for large cars, and a way of driving them that had much in common with his military background as a tank commander may well have been a reflection of the way studies in reception were perceived as a particularly German phenomenon in the early 1980s. But in music, perhaps hardly surprisingly, many of the early studies in what in later years would come to be considered studies in reception were published in English and outside German-speaking areas. Two striking examples were Schrade's *Beethoven in France* (1942) and King's

---

[1] David Lodge, *Small World: An Academic Romance* (London: Secker & Warburg, 1984; reprint, Harmondsworth, England: Penguin, 1985) (p. nos. refer to 1985 reprint).
[2] Ibid., 96.
[3] Ibid., 97.
[4] Ibid., 51.

Mozart in Retrospect (1955), both of which were thoroughgoing engagements with the materials of the same type that Jauss and his Konstanz colleagues would handle so much later.[5]

In the mid-1990s, everyone who felt themselves touched by the seismic changes in the study of music—or felt they had to make reference to them in the issues-based university courses that were then so popular—was reevaluating personal approaches to historiography, aesthetics, and scholarship in general. It was an environment that encouraged the experimentation of looking at well-known re-pertories in new and innovative ways. But despite the fact that Jaussian reception theory had become fully embedded in literary criticism and history by the 1990s, music seemed to have passed it by. Certainly there were many studies of the fates of composers' works after their death, but apart from invocations of the terms "reception history" and "reception theory" (almost invariably in the German—*Rezeptionsgeschichte*—with something vaguely unsettling, exciting, about the extra syllable of the word *Rezeption* in German), engagement with the work of Jauss and the Konstanz School was limited.

So to start thinking about music in the 1990s in terms familiar to the Konstanz School of the 1960s was simultaneously innovative and atavistic, and one could begin to publish work that both made use of such modes of thinking and more formally to reflect on it. And as work began to coalesce around Mozart, there came a point at which putting together the fragments of Mozart reception with some new work in a way that made its theoretical and historical intentions clear became an obvious course of action. This book is the result.

One of the dangers of working in such a field as Mozart reception is the speed with which one crosses the boundaries from fields of scholarship in which one is reasonably comfortable into one in which one is definitely not. It is at this point that one is happy to have colleagues worldwide who work on Tchaikovsky, Shaw, and mid-nineteenth-century furniture who are happy to give up their time to answer questions they would be embarrassed to hear posed by their less able undergraduates. An alphabetical list is really the only way of acknowledging them all fairly: Thomas Betzwieser, Rachel Cowgill, Joachim Draheim, Katharine Ellis, Katrina Faulds, Marina Frolova-Walker, Sarah Hibberd, Björn Heile, Stephen Huebner, Lawrence Kramer, Erik Levi, Katherine Massip, Cormac Newark, Robert Pascall, Leon Plantinga, Dorothy Potter, Sabina Ratner, Michael Thomas Roe, William Rosar, Julian Rushton, John Sloboda, Beverly Smith, Marian Smith, Michael Struck, Ingrid Sykes, Stanley Weintraub, Ian Woodfield, and Neal Zaslaw. Karol Berger, Scott Burnham, Cliff Eisen, and Ralph Locke were kind enough to

---

[5] Leo Schrade, *Beethoven in France: The Growth of an Idea* (New Haven: Yale University Press; London: Humphrey Milford and Oxford University Press, 1942); Alec Hyatt King, *Mozart in Retrospect: Studies in Criticism and Bibliography* (London, New York, and Toronto: Geoffrey Cumberledge; Oxford University Press, 1955).

read a draft of the original proposal and to offer suggestions that immeasurably improved the final text. I was lucky to have a number of research assistants who undertook various sorts of work, from preparing a digital edition of the writings on music of Blaze de Bury to negotiating permissions for the book's illustrations; I thank Sarah Boak, Aurélie Branger, Gabriella Firth (née Dideriksen), Austin Glatthorn, Stephen Groves, Francesca Placanica, and Kimberly White.

I was fortunate to have financial support on two occasions for the preparation of this book: Arts and Humanities Research Council, Small Grant, October 2006 (AH/E002668/1), and Arts and Humanities Research Council, Research Leave, July 2009 (AH/H004653/1). The University of Southampton granted me a semester's sabbatical leave in 2009–10 to complete the text, and I am grateful to my colleagues in the Department of Music for giving me a home in such a dynamic environment for the pursuit of scholarship. Parts of chapter 3 appeared in *"L'esprit français" und die Musik Europas—Entstehung, Einfluß und Grenzen einer ästhetischen Doktrin*, ed. Rainer Schmusch and Michelle Biget-Mainfroy, Studien und Materialen zur Musikwisenschaft 40 (Hildesheim: Olms, 2006), 398–411; parts of chapter 6 in *19th-Century Music* 25 (2001), 165–189; and parts of chapter 8 in *Mozart-Jahrbuch 2002 des Zentralinstitutes für Mozartforschung der Internationalen Stiftung Mozarteum Salzburg* (Kassel: Bärenreiter, 2002), 115–134. Many thanks go to Suzanne Ryan, Norman Hirschy, Erica Tucker, and Adam Cohen at Oxford University Press, New York. One day I will get over the embarrassment I suffered— or was it enjoyed?—as my OUP editor prostrated herself in front of me in a moderately prestigious central London restaurant.

Greatest thanks, though, go to those closest to home. My daughter Amelia contributed to the project in its very earliest stages, when she received a present in the shape of a cube that, depending on which side you pressed, played a selection of well-known Mozartiana (thank you, Tim Carter and Annegret Fauser); this priceless site of Mozart reception has been treasured ever since. Jeanice Brooks, the most distinguished musicologist in the household by far, deserves all the blame for the book's creation: it was her idea to develop my ideas on Mozart reception into a monograph, and at an al fresco lunch in the summer of 2007 she came up with (1) the title, (2) the structure, (3) the section titles, and (4) the inspiration for me to take up the challenge. I can never thank her enough.

{ LIST OF MUSIC EXAMPLES }

{ LIST OF TABLES }

{ LIST OF FIGURES }

Mozart's Ghosts

{ 1 }

Introduction

It is not difficult to envisage what "Mozart reception" might be. Mozart's music, and the idea of the composer and his music, were received during his lifetime and throughout the nineteenth and twentieth centuries; Mozart is still received today, perhaps more noticeably than ever. One only has to look at most forms of cultural production—concert halls, opera houses, film, television, imaginative fiction, the advertising industry, just to mention the most obvious—to bear witness to the purchase that the composer's music has on our lives.[1]

Ways of receiving music have been investigated in many different ways in the last half century. Perhaps the best known is the study of composers and their works through the press, especially the musical press, during the nineteenth century; indeed, for much of the last half of the twentieth century, "reception" was almost synonymous with the study of the press.[2] But such a view would have been considered curious by any literary scholar who, ever since the emergence of the "Konstanz School" in the 1960s, with Hans Robert Jauss at its head, has been sensitive

---

[1] For a careful review of this position, see Richard Taruskin, "Why Mozart Has Become an Icon for Today," *New York Times*, 9 September 1990, reprinted with a 1994 postscript, as "An Icon for Our Times," in Taruskin, *Text and Act: Essays on Music and Performance* (New York and Oxford: Oxford University Press, 1995), 263–272.

[2] The study of the nineteenth-century press is by now a widespread industry, led by the Retrospective Index of Music Periodicals project, www.ripmfulltext.org (accessed 10 July 2012), which undertakes the online publication of parts of the specialist music press, and this is reflected in the studies of the press. See, for England, Leanne Langley, "The English Musical Journal in the Early Nineteenth Century," 2 vols. (Ph.D. diss., University of North Carolina at Chapel Hill, 1983); for France, Katharine Ellis, *Music Criticism in Nineteenth-Century France: La revue et gazette musicale de Paris, 1834–80* (Cambridge: Cambridge University Press, 1995). William Robinson, "Conceptions of Mozart in German Criticism and Biography 1791–1828: Changing Images of a Musical Genius" (Ph.D. diss., Yale University, 1974), reads the image of Mozart through the lens of music journalism in German, and Belinda Cannone, *La Réception des opéras de Mozart dans la presse parisienne (1793–1829)* (Paris: Klincksieck, 1991), examines an even narrower range of material through the press.

to the varying domains in which works of literature—and texts frequently held not to be literature—develop meaning.[3] She might quite legitimately ask about the ways Mozart has been embodied in biography, performance, publication, and—perhaps most obviously—in the way his music has been projected across the various literary domains of poetry, drama, short story, romance, and novel.[4] And if she has read her Jauss in a particular way, she might also ask some hard questions about the status of the particular text being received, how it might have been changed, or—to refamiliarize a musical concept—arranged.[5]

In the case of Mozart, biography has been an important element in the study of his reception for a long time. Biographical texts by Niemetschek, Schlictegroll, Nissen, Holmes, and Jahn have all been extensively examined for the ways they have configured and reconfigured the composer's biography and the ways they may have distorted the past.[6] But biographical texts may be considered "sites" of reception: contested locations where the composer and his music are controlled and disciplined; and the nature of that control, that discipline, is an important subject for scholarly inquiry.[7] Viewed in this light, the press becomes just another site of reception, one that can be read according to the ideology of the journalist, the

---

[3] Two useful overviews of the wide range of activity that has been subsumed under the discipline of "reception theory" are Susan R. Suleiman, "Introduction: Varieties of Audience-Oriented Criticism," in Suleiman, *The Reader in the Text: Essays on Audience and Interpretation* (Princeton, N.J.: Princeton University Press, 1980), 3–45; Robert C. Holub, *Reception Theory: A Critical Introduction*, New Accents (London and New York: Routledge, 1984), 53–146. For Jauss and the Constanz School see Hans Robert Jauss, "Was heißt und zu welchem Ende studiert man Literaturgeschichte?," inaugural address at the Celebration of the 60th Birthday of Gerhard Hess (rector of the University of Konstanz), University of Konstanz, 13 April 1967, published as *Literaturgeschichte als Provokation der Literaturwissenschaft*, Konstanzer Universitätsreden 3 (Konstanz: Konstanz Universitätsverlag, 1967; 2nd ed. 1969); reprinted in Jauss, *Literaturgeschichte als Provokation* (Frankfurt am Main: Suhrkamp, 1970), 144–208; reprinted in *Rezeptionsästhetik*, ed. Rainer Warning, Uni-Taschenbücher 303 (Munich: Fink, 1975; 2nd ed. 1979), 126–162; partially translated (chapters 5–12) as "Literary History as a Challenge to Literary Theory," *New Literary History* 2 (1970–71), 7–37; retranslated in full in Jauss, *Toward an Aesthetic of Reception*, trans. Timothy Bahti, Theory and History of Literature 2 (Minneapolis: University of Minnesota Press, 1982), 3–45.

[4] For a review of studies of reception in music and a more sustained investigation of Jauss and the Constanz School, see Mark Everist, "Reception Theories, Canonic Discourses and Musical Value," in *Rethinking Music*, ed. Nicholas Cook and Mark Everist (Oxford: Oxford University Press, 1999), 378–402.

[5] This is in essence the difference between *Wirkung* and *Rezeption*. *Wirkung* (effect) focuses on the textual and musical aspects of the process while *Rezeption* (reception) addresses the reader—in the broadest sense, the recipient of the text. See Holub, *Reception Theory*, xi–xii.

[6] Mozart's early biography provides much of the material for the so-called Mozart Myths discussed in William Stafford, *The Mozart Myths: A Critical Reassessment* (Stanford: Stanford University Press, 1991), which are discussed in various places in this book. Stafford, "The Evolution of Mozartian Biography," in *The Cambridge Companion to Mozart*, ed. Simon P. Keefe (Cambridge: Cambridge University Press, 2003), 200–211, is a useful point of departure for such an inquiry.

[7] See, for example, Ulrich Konrad, "Friedrich Rochlitz und die Entstehung des Mozart-Bildes um 1800," in *Mozart: Aspekte des 19. Jahrhunderts*, ed. Hermann Jung and Imogen Fellerer, Mannheimer Hochschulschriften 1 (Mannheim: Palatium, 1995), 1–22.

political *tinta* of the publication, the musical leanings of the proprietors, all of which will change with time and circumstance. It is however just one among many sites, all of which serve as the subject matter for this book.

Performances of Mozart's works are highly variable in terms of the ease with which they may be reconstructed. For example, productions of the operas at major houses across Europe are by and large easy to track; performances of even large-scale instrumental music much less so (Mozart's accounts of performances during his lifetime in his letters notwithstanding) before the middle of the twentieth century.[8] Publication of Mozart's works, on the other hand, is a domain of the composer's reception that has been and remains central to musical scholarship for at least 150 years.[9] Ludwig Ritter von Köchel's now legendary catalogue of the composer's works was first published in 1862, and a large part of its purpose was the documentation of surviving sources, both print and manuscript; its scope has conditioned the range of sources consulted, for example, in the *Revisionsberichte* of the *Neue Mozart Ausgabe,* the complete critical edition of the composer's works begun in 1956.[10] The most recent edition of Köchel's work is in the final stages of preparation.[11] But Köchel's original concern was largely for the authentic—or at least the contemporary—and the immense range of publications of Mozart's music fell outside his field of vision and has characterized subsequent editions of his work up to the present.[12] However, the digital control of library catalogues—coupled with the sophisticated means for dating printed music via plate numbers, publishers' addresses, and so on—means that the most recherché publications of Mozart's music, whether they are from 1812 or 2012, are relatively easy to track down, date, and analyze.

But in terms of both publication and performance, Mozart's works were subject to massive degrees of variation, arrangement, and transformation. And outside the field of arrangements and transcriptions made by major named composers (Liszt, Busoni, Herz, and Thalberg, perhaps) these are largely relegated to what Carl Dahlhaus notoriously called the "rubble" of music history, and treated with some

---

[8] See, for example, the recent study of Mozart's operas in Prague by Ian Woodfield, *Performing Operas for Mozart: Impresarios, Singers and Troupes* (Cambridge: Cambridge University Press, 2011).

[9] For recent endeavors, see Gertaut Haberkamp, *Die Erstdrucke der Werke von Wolfgang Amadeus Mozart*, 2 vols., Musikbibliographisches Arbeiten 10 (Tützing: Schneider, 1986); Jean Gribenski, *Catalogue des éditions françaises de Mozart, 1764–1825*, Musica Antiquo-moderna: Collection du Centre de Musique Baroque de Versailles 1 (Hildesheim: Olms, 2006).

[10] Ludwig Ritter von Köchel, *Chronologisch-thematisches Verzeichnis sämtlicher Tonwerke Wolfgang Amadé Mozarts* (Leipzig: Breitkopf und Härtel, 1862).

[11] Neal Zaslaw, ed., *Köchelverzeichnis: Chronologisch-thematisches Verzeichnis sämtlicher Tonwerke Wolfgang Amadé Mozarts—Neuausgabe in Zusammenarbeit mit der Internationalen Stift ung Mozarteum'* (Leipzig and Wiesbaden: Breitkopf und Härtel, forthcoming). This new edition will simultaneously be published online and in English on the website of the Salzburg Mozarteum, http://mozarteum.at/wissenschaft.html (accessed 10 July 2012).

[12] Ludwig Ritter von Köchel, *Chronologisch-thematisches Verzeichnis sämtlicher Tonwerke Wolfgang Amadé Mozarts*, 8th ed., ed. Franz Giegling, Alexander Weinmann, and Gerd Sievers (Wiesbaden: Breitkopf und Härtel, 1983) is the most recent published edition of the catalogue.

embarrassment if not contempt by contemporary scholarship.[13] Within the event-dominated world of opera, highly mobile musical and poetic texts are accepted as the norm, and Mozart's own engagement in a world in which the recomposition of stage music, the composition of substitute arias and translation was common, is well known.[14] Perhaps less well known—and perhaps more resisted—is the idea that most large-scale concerted pieces circulated in versions for reduced forces that had immense levels of exposure; in short, the circulation and consumption of the symphony was more frequently in the form of some sort of arrangement.

To show just how critical the arrangement of a work could be, a contemporary arrangement of Mozart's Symphony 38 K. 504 ("Prague") contrasted with what modern scholarship construes as the original of Mozart's score may serve as an example of how different the experience of an instrumental work by Mozart around 1800 might have been to the way it is experienced today. Example 1.1 gives the opening of the work in an arrangement for two violins, two violas, cello and bass (or two cellos), and flute; Example 1.2 gives the same passage from the *Neue Mozart Ausgabe*.[15]

Even in this short example one may see issues not only relating to texture, tessitura, and spacing but also to questions of musical structure.

Giovanni Battista Cimadoro, known as Cimador after his arrival in London from Venice in 1791, was an important agent in the reception of Mozart, not only in London but also, as the example here shows, in Paris.[16] It is reasonably certain

---

[13] Carl Dahlhaus *Grundlagen der Musikgeschichte*, Musiktaschenbücher: Theoretica 13 (Cologne: Hans Gerig, 1977), trans. by J. R. Robinson as *Foundations of Music History* (Cambridge: Cambridge University Press, 1983), 164 (p. nos. hereafter refer to English trans.).

[14] Despite the wide range of understanding of the mobility of the texts of Mozart's stage works, standard accounts of the operas from Dent to Kunze largely ignore such complexities and treat the operas as reified works of music. See Edward J. Dent, *Mozart's Operas: A Critical Study* (London: Chatto and Windus, 1913; 2nd ed., London: Oxford University Press, 1947); Stefan Kunze, *Mozarts Opern* (Stuttgart: Reclam, 1984).

[15] Trois / *Grandes Simphonies* / Composées / par *W. M Mozart* / Arrangées pour / *Deux Violons, Deux Altos, Basse, Contrebasse et Flûte* / La Flûte Obligato ou Ad-libitum / ou *Deux Violons, Deux Altos, Deux Basses et Flûte* / La Flûte toujours Obligato ou Ad-libitum. / par / J. B. Cimador / N.B. *La Contradiction apparente dans les mots Obbligato et Ad-libitum vient de ce que la partie* / *de Flûte quoique fort belle, n'est pas absolument nécessaire* / [1] Suite. *Enregistré à la Bibliothèque Nationale*. Prix 18 fr. / à Paris / Chez IMBAULT, *Professeur & Editeur de Musique, au Mont d'Or Rue S*ᵗ *Honoré N*° *200, près celle des Poulies* / Et Péristile du Théâtre Italien Rue Favart N°.461; Wolfgang Amadeus Mozart, *Sinfonien*, vol. 8, ed. Friedrich Snapp and László Somfai, Neue Ausgabe sämtlicher Werke IV/11/8 (Kassel: Bärenreiter, 1971).

[16] Little is known of Cimador's biography beyond what is given in François-Joseph Fétis, *Biographie universelle des musiciens et bibliographie générale de la musique*, 8 vols., 2nd ed. with supp. in 2 vols. (Paris: Firmin Didot, 1860–65), 2:302. Entries in standard dictionaries do little more than translate Fétis, and, in the case of *Die Musik in Geschichte und Gegenwart*, all but suppress Cimador's work in the dissemination of Mozart. See Rodney Slatford and Marita P. McClymonds, "Cimador, Giambattista," in *Grove Music Online*. Oxford Music Online, www.oxfordmusiconline.com/subscriber/article/grove/music/05784 (accessed 10 July 2012); Rodney Slatford, "Cimador, *Cimadoro*, Giambattista, *Giovanni Battista, Gian Battista*," in *Die Musik in Geschichte und Gegenwart: Allgemeine Enzyklopädie der Musik*, *Personenteil 4* (Kassel: Bärenreiter; Stuttgart and Weimar: Metzler, 2000), 1125–1127.

EXAMPLE 1.1: *Mozart, Symphony 38 K. 504, ("Prague"), slow introduction, 1–13, from Trois /* Grandes Simphonies / *Composées* / par W. M Mozart / *Arrangées pour* / Deux Violons, Deux Altos, Basse, Contrebasse et Flûte / *La Flûte Obligato ou Ad-libitum* / ou Deux Violons, Deux Altos, Deux Basses et Flûte / *La Flûte toujours Obligato ou Ad-libitum.* / par / *J. B. Cimador /… / à Paris* / Chez *IMBAULT,* Professeur & Editeur de Musique, au Mont d'Or Rue St Honoré No 200 , près celle des Poulies / *Et Péristile du Théâtre Italien Rue Favart Nº. 461.*

EXAMPLE 1.2: *Mozart, Symphony 38 K. 504 ("Prague"), slow introduction, 1–13.*

that the Imbault publication on which Example 1.1 is based dates from between 1799 and 1802;[17] the English edition of the same arrangement by Monzani and Hill is apparently later, and probably published after Cimador's death in 1805. At what

---

[17] The style of the address on the title page clearly places the publication within these dates. See Anik Devriès and François Lesure, *Dictionnaire des éditeurs de musique français*, 2 vols. (vol. 1 in 2 pts.), Archives de l'édition musicale française 4 (Geneva: Minkoff, 1979–88), 1:85.

EXAMPLE 1.2 *continued*

date the arrangement originated is not clear, nor is its provenance. Fétis reports
that Cimador made the arrangements because of his irritation with the fact that
the orchestra of the King's Theatre, Haymarket, refused to play the works because
of their difficulty; if this anecdote is correct, it would argue—together with Cimador's residency in London—for an English provenance.[18] Nevertheless, the publication of the same arrangement in two different European capitals argues for a
wide dissemination of what Fétis again called the product of the arranger's "taste
and intelligence."[19]

Cimador's arrangement of six Mozart symphonies translates the scores into a
form that is at once elaborate and complex. His title page gives alternative scor-
ings for the lower two parts of the texture: either cello and double bass (in which
case the lowest part of the text transposes down an octave) or two cellos (in which
case the music is played at pitch); Mozart's original rarely divides cellos and
basses, however.[20] The effect of this alternative can be seen immediately in the
work, where the register of the bass, if performed by two cellos, means that the

[18] Fétis, *Biographie universelle*, 2:302.
[19] "Cette collection, qui fait honneur au goût et à l'intelligence de Cimador, eut le plus grand succès"
(ibid.).
[20] For example, bars 199–205 in the first movement allegro.

progression ends on a 6–4 chord; this is one place where the lower octave is essential. Furthermore, Cimador's bizarre indication of the flute part as "obligato or ad libitum" is glossed on the title page as follows: "The apparent contradiction in the words 'obligato' and 'Ad libitum' arises from the fact that the flute part, although very beautiful, is not however absolutely necessary." This is hardly true: throughout the entire extract given in Example 1.1 the flute adds a critical higher octave to the texture. The claims for every conceivable variant in the scoring are presumably driven by commercial concerns: omitting the flute to appeal to string ensembles exclusively, and the double bass for those ensembles without the instrument.

In its full scoring for two violins, two violas, cello, double bass, and flute, Cimador's arrangement rewrites the opening tutti in a way that more or less maintains the tessitura and spacing of the original, not difficult for a unison opening. Brass and timpani are missing on the quarter note beats of course, and their omission is the most striking feature of the opening. In the exchanges in bars 4–6, the four-part progression is voiced almost identically in the arrangement as in the original, although using two violins, viola, cello, and bass instead of two violins, viola, and bass. The risks associated with the use of two cellos in this progression have already been signaled, but otherwise the scoring of violin, viola, cello, and bass maintains the spacing of the original harmony. The woodwind response in bar 6 is voiced, albeit with strings, identically to the original (flute 1 = violin 1; oboe 1 = viola 1; oboe 2 = viola 2; bassoon = cello [1]). The same cannot be said about the tutti in bar 4, where the second violin and both violas pick up most of the woodwind parts but cannot, for example, include the descending C#–B in the second flute part, thus leaving a full octave between the top of the texture and the next voice down. Similar compromises are visible in the rest of the extract.

Perhaps the most striking change in the arrangement is the passage beginning in the original at bar 16, which follows on from Example 1.1 and 1.2. In Cimador's arrangement, bars 16–17 and 20–21 are simply omitted, and Mozart's highly chromatic approach to the dominant—reached in bar 28—is shortened in a remarkable way. His original progression is given as Example 1.3, and Cimador's abbreviation as Example 1.4.

Cimador effectively interrupts the dominant in bar 15 onto VI$^\flat$, whereas Mozart simply cadences onto the tonic minor and then moves to the sixth below. Cimador's progression from a B-flat triad to the V$^6_5$ in g minor arguably

EXAMPLE 1.3: *Mozart, Symphony 38 K. 504 ("Prague"), slow introduction. Harmonic summary of 16–28 (based on ex. 1.2).*

EXAMPLE 1.4: *Mozart, Symphony 38 K. 504 ("Prague"), slow introduction, arranged Cimador. Harmonic summary of 16–28 (based on ex. 1.1).*

introduces a bass line (a diminished fourth and a progression foreign if not to Mozart then at least to the introduction of the *"Prague" Symphony*). It is not at all clear what were the motivations for these particular changes; it is tempting to see an attempt at tidying up on Cimador's part—a view that held that Mozart's six statements of the same musical phrase could usefully be compressed into four—or there might, at the other extreme, have been some textual disturbance in Cimador's exemplar.

Be that as it may, Cimador's arrangement of the *"Prague" Symphony* succinctly dramatizes the form in which Mozart's larger-scale concerted works were received. It points not only to modifications of scoring and to the textural dimensions of Mozart's sound-world but also to substantive changes of pitch and duration that alter harmonic rhythm and structure.

However varied the forms in which posterity enjoyed Mozart's music, strictly musical presentations of the composer's works make up only a part of the picture, only a proportion of the sites of reception of Mozart in the nineteenth and twentieth centuries. A further area that has received significant scholarly attention is the presence of Mozart's music in various forms of belles lettres: prose, poetry, staged and unstaged drama, opera libretti, philosophical texts, formally published memoirs, and letter collections. Many of these are very well known: Søren Kierkegaard's chapter "The Immediate Stages of the Erotic" from his 1843 text *Either/Or*,[21] George Bernard Shaw's *Man and Superman* of 1903,[22] Alfred de Musset's *La Matinée de Don Juan* (1833) and *Namouna* (1832–33),[23] as

---

[21] Søren Kierkegaard, *Either/Or*, trans. David F. Swenson and Lillian Marvin Swenson (Princeton, N.J.: Princeton University Press, 1971). For the idea that the philosopher might have reworked ideas from Hoffmann's essay, see Thomas Grey, "Metaphorical Modes in Nineteenth-Century Music Criticism: Image, Narrative and Idea," in *Music and Text: Critical Inquries*, ed. Steven Paul Scher (Cambridge: Cambridge University Press, 1992), 114–116.

[22] *The Complete Plays of Bernard Shaw* (London: Odham, 1934), 332–405.

[23] Maurice Allem, ed., *A. de Musset: Théatre Complet: Comédies et proverbes, théâtre complémentaire, théâtre posthume*, Bibliothèque de la Pleiade 17 (Paris: Gallimard, 1947), 625–629; Allem, ed., *Alfred de Musset: Poésies Complètes*, Bibliothèque de la Pleiade 12 (Paris: Gallimard, 1957), 239–270 (the relevant passage is on p. 261). *Namouna* is found in *Un Spectacle dans un fauteuil*, which bears a publication date of 1833 but was in fact listed in the *Bibliographie de la France* on 18 December 1832 (see ibid., 696).

well as Eduard Mörike's *Mozart auf der Reise nach Prag* (1856).[24] These are just
the most familiar tip of a very large iceberg that has been described by Erdmann
Werner Böhme, in—for German texts at least—great detail.[25]

So if the material that might constitute the reception of Mozart can range
from the press cutting to the philosophical tract, and if it can be acknowledged
that the form in which a work by Mozart might have existed—even for such a
canonical a work as a symphony—might be radically different from the way
the piece is known today, this has resulted in a number of metanarratives of
the composer's reception. Many such metanarratives are well known and
involve in some cases specific works. Early nineteenth-century views of the
composer focused on the demonic, and prized such works as *Don Giovanni*,
the *Requiem,* and the d minor piano concerto above others. Around 1900, the
"Back to Mozart" movement was a clearly orchestrated attack on Wagnerian
hegemony, while the Olympian Classicism of the second half of the twentieth
century had much to do with the recording industry and high modernist ideals
of purity that could efface so much of what the nineteenth century had found
so difficult in the composer's music; it also had much to do with the primacy
of instrumental music over opera. For the late twentieth and early twenty-first
centuries, Mozart has come to represent the embodiment of the critical category of "classical music."

The ways Mozart reception has been studied are highly varied. As in the case of
many studies of reception, much scholarship falls prey to the documentary

---

[24] Eduard Mörike, *Sämtliche Werke*, 2 vols., ed. Helmut Koopman (Düsseldorf and Zurich: Artemis-
Winkler, 1996–97), 1:566–622. The bibliography on Mörike's story is extensive. See Herbert Meyer, "Das
Fortleben Mozarts bei Mörike und seinen Freunden," *Acta Mozartiana* 32 (1985): 29–40. For a discussion
of the emphasis on death in the story, see Hans Joachim Kreutzer, "Die Zeit und der Tod: Über Eduard
Mörikes Mozart-Novelle," in *Obertöne: Literatur und Musik, neun Abhandlungen,* ed. Kreutzer
(Würzburg: Königshausen & Neumann, 1994), 196–216; see also Kreutzer, "Ein Tag aus Mozarts
Jugendleben: Die neapolitanische Pantomime in Mörikes Mozart-Novelle," in *Bericht über den
Internationalen Mozart-Kongreß, Salzburg, 1991,* ed. Rudolph Angermüller, Dietrich Berke, Ulrike
Hofmann, and Wolfgang Rehm, 2 vols. [paginated consecutively], *Mozart-Jahrbuch 1991 des
Zentralinstitutes für Mozartforschung der Internationalen Stiftung Mozarteum Salzburg* (Kassel:
Bärenreiter, 1992), 248–253. For a view of the novel that reads it as covert Wagner criticism, see Gerhard
von Graevenitz, "Don Juan oder die Liebe zur Hausmusik: Wagner-Kritik in Edouard Mörikes
Erzählung *Mozart auf der Reise nach Prag,*" *Neophilologus* 65 (1981): 247–262; for the ambitious claim
that the story is structured around the principles of "sonata form," see Hartmut Kaiser, "Mörike's Use of
Sonata Form in Mozart's Tale of the Neapolitan Water Games," *A Yearbook of Interdisciplinary Studies
in the Fine Arts* 2 (1990), 607–625. Two studies trace substantial parts of Mörike's text to Alexander
Dmitryevich Oulibicheff 1843 *Nouvelle Biographie de Mozart*: Martin Staehelin, "Mozart auf der Reise
nach Prag: Musikhistorisches zu Mörikes Novelle," *Neue Zürcher Zeitung,* 26–27 May 1990, 68; Roye E.
Wates, "Eduard Mörike, Alexander Ulibishev and the 'Ghost Scene' in *Don Giovanni,*" in Wates, *The
Creative Process* (New York: Broude, 1992), 31–48.

[25] Erdmann Werner Böhme, "Mozart in der schönen Literatur (Drama, Roman, Novelle, Lyrik)," in
*Bericht über die musikwissenschaftliche Tagung der Internationalen Stiftung Mozarteum in Salzburg vom
2. bis 5. August 1931* (Leipzig: Breitkopf und Härtel, 1931), 179–297; Böhme, "Mozart in der schönen
Literatur: Ergänzungen und Fortsetzung," *Mozart-Jahrbuch 1959 des Zentralinstitutes für Mozartforschung
der Internationalen Stiftung Mozarteum Salzburg* (1959), 165–187.

impulse, to the attraction of simply recording the existence of sites of reception. And the impulse is understandable, given their vast numbers and—for the most part—the generous survival of material documenting them. The inevitable consequence, however, has been many descriptive rather than analytical accounts of the subject and frequently an atomic view of the field: the study of tiny instances of Mozart reception, frequently treated in a rather short-winded fashion, and then collected into multiauthored volumes.[26]

A developing hagiography around the composer is a characteristic of much nineteenth- and twentieth-century thinking, and in many respects this book is devoted to the analysis of such hagiography. But it is also true that such a hagiography has left its mark on modern scholarship that itself seeks to unmask the works that made up the nineteenth- and early twentieth-century Mozartian canon. This can take one of two forms: a largely uncritical retreading of tropes developed since 1800 as found in the introduction and first two essays in the conference proceedings published in the wake of the 1991 bicentennial celebrations, *On Mozart*. These essays are instructive, since they demonstrate the tenacity of the threads drawn together and analyzed in this book, and how they are projected into the present. How otherwise could one interpret such lines as "What about the Mass in c minor? Is it not a genuinely religious work, and not a function of the Enlightenment? I cannot hear it as a religious work. It seems to me just as secular as *Die Zauberflöte* and to have been produced by transferring to choir stalls and pews the methods of the opera house. There is no sense, in the c minor Mass, of the community that dwells beyond events." Here, subjective reaction based on the well-worn nineteenth-century trope of the theatricality of Mozart's sacred music can be made to stand in for critical prose, and may be productively compared with, for example, the nineteenth- and twentieth-century texts associated with the so-called Twelfth

---

[26] The following collections of essays all appeared in the wake of the 1991 celebrations of the two hundredth anniversary of Mozart's death, and resulted from conferences held that year. Those that do not specifically invoke issues of Mozart reception in the title include large numbers of contributions on the subject: *Mozart: Origines et transformations d'une mythe: Actes du colloque international organisé dans le cadre du Bicentaire de la mort de Mozart, Clermont-Ferrand, décembre 1991*, ed. Jean-Louis Jam (Berne: Lang, 1994); *Mozart: Aspekte des 19. Jahrhunderts*, ed. Hermann Jung and Imogen Fellerer, Mannheimer Hochschulschriften 1 (Mannheim: Palatium, 1995); *Bericht über den Internationalen Mozart-Kongreß, Salzburg, 1991*, ed. Rudolph Angermüller, Dietrich Berke, Ulrike Hofmann, and Wolfgang Rehm, 2 vols., *Mozart-Jahrbuch 1991 des Zentralinstitutes für Mozartforschung der Internationalen Stiftung Mozarteum Salzburg* (Kassel: Bärenreiter, 1992); *Internationaler Musikwissenschaftlicher Kongress zum Mozartjahr 1991, Baden-Wien*, 2 vols., ed. Ingrid Fuchs (Tützing: Schneider, 1993); *On Mozart* (New York: Cambridge University Press; Washington, D.C.: Woodrow Wilson Center for Scholars, 1994); *Das Phänomen Mozart im 20. Jahrhundert: Wirkung, Verarbeitung und Vermarktung in Literatur, bildender Kunst und den Medien*, ed. Peter Csobádi, Gernot Gruber, Jürgen Kühnel, Ulrich Müller, and Oswald Panagl, Wort und Musik: Salzburg Akademische Beiträge 10 (Anif and Salzburg: Müller-Speiser, 1991). *Mozart in Anglophone Cultures*, ed. Sabine Coelsch-Foisner, Dorothea Flothow, and Wolfgang Görtschacher, Salzburg Studies in English Literature and Culture 4 (Frankfurt-am-Main: Lang, 2009), was a specific response to the 250th anniversary of the composer's birth in 2006, as is *Mozart et la France: De l'enfant prodige au génie (1764–1830)*, ed. Jean Gribenski and Patrick Taïeb (Lyon: Symétrie, forthcoming).

Mass (chapter 5).[27] Similarly, key texts from the nineteenth century may serve as the basis for modern exegesis. So, in a recent collection of essays on *Don Giovanni*, we may read thinly veiled repetitions of E. T. A. Hoffmann's 1813 essay on the work, and a further gloss on Edouard Mörike's *Mozarts Reise nach Prag* of 1855. These articles are evidence of the enduring importance of nineteenth-century texts on modern thinking about the composer, as those texts are served up again with an early twenty-first-century garnish.[28]

A further way the current endeavor differs from previous ones is in its handling of myth and legend. Although the alliterative qualities of such a title as *The Mozart Myths* have an obvious attraction, most of the apocryphal stories surrounding Mozart's biography have at least some sort of origin in truth, eschew the supernatural, and have more in common—strictly speaking—with legend, as in the sense of the *Legenda aurea*, the much-copied series of medieval saints' lives.[29]

To take a single example to stand for many, William Stafford points to two stories from Mozart's early life: the writing out of Allegri's *Miserere* in the Sistine Chapel after a single hearing, and Mozart's completion of the entrance examination for the Accademia Filarmonica in Bologna.[30] In the first case, Stafford shows that many of the elements were overstated: written copies of the work in fact existed, and its contrapuntal style is simple; furthermore, it repeats the same material no less than five times. In the Bolognese example, the surviving autograph and documentary materials show that Mozart's first attempt was less than successful and that Martini modified it in order that the young Mozart should pass. In both cases, Stafford shows how Leopold Mozart enlarged on the stories, thus laying the ground for later biographers.

Modern methods of investigation have quite logically sought to disentangle truth from fiction, to set out clearly where the boundaries between evidence and interpretation lie. And this position is given much weight by Stafford as he closes

---

[27] Denis Donaghue, "Approaching Mozart," in *On Mozart* (New York: Cambridge University Press; Washington, D.C.: Woodrow Wilson Center for Scholars, 1994), 32–33.

[28] The two articles in question are Richard Eldridge, "'Hidden Secrets of the Self': E. T. A. Hoffmann's Reading of *Don Giovanni*," in *The Don Giovanni Moment: Esssays on the Legacy of an Opera*, 33–46, and Hans Rudolf Vaget, "Mörike's Mozart and the Scent of a Woman," 61–74, both in *The Don Giovanni Moment: Esssays on the Legacy of an Opera*, ed. Lydia Goehr and Daniel Herwitz (New York: Columbia University Press, 2006).

[29] Jacobus de Voragine's *Legenda aurea* was compiled in the 1260s and served as a standard text until the sixteenth century. The standard English translation is Jacobus de Voragine, *The Golden Legend: Readings on the Saints*, trans. William Granger Ryan, 2 vols. (Princeton, N.J.: Princeton University Press, 1993). For a critical account of the work, see Sherry L. Reames, *The Legenda Aurea: A Reexamination of Its Paradoxical History* (Madison: University of Wisconsin Press, 1985). See also Geoffrey Stephen Kirk, "On Defining Myths," *Sacred Narrative: Readings in the Theory of Myth*, ed. Alan Dundes (Berkeley: University of California Press, 1984), 53–61.

[30] Stafford, *The Mozart Myths*, 170–171. It should be noted, however, that the sources cited by Stafford for the unmasking of both these legends are hardly impeccable: Ivor Keys, *Mozart: His Music in His Life* (St Albans: Holmes & Meier, 1980), and Alfred Einstein, *Mozart: His Character and His Work*, trans, Arthur Mendel (London: Kassel, 1944); no primary sources are discussed.

The Mozart Myths: "the portrait [of Mozart] can be cleaned, with the aid of a vigorous application of historical method. The myths can be cleared away and the
reality revealed. Above all it is necessary to adopt a critical attitude to the tradition,
and the sources upon which it is based."[31] Admirable sentiments, indeed, and to an
extent ones that are shared by this book, but to an entirely different end. Any
claims here to "a critical attitude" are directed toward understanding the context of
the stories that have been told about Mozart (whether within the domain of poetry
or material culture, drama or performance) rather than debunking them. Reading
this book against the methods of *The Mozart Myths* reveals a fundamental
difference in orientation, purpose, and outcome.

Bringing together a wide range of disparate material in a framework that com-
plements both short independent studies and more general surveys, this book sits
between on the one hand the publication of articles that subject endless sites of
Mozart reception to scrutiny and on the other general and highly distinguished
overviews in which it is difficult to do justice to the cultural texture of the material.[32]
While it does less in terms of coverage than published surveys, this book does
more than smaller separate publications that treat Mozart reception as a series of
unrelated atomic moments. This book cannot claim to escape the charge of
reinscribing some sort of hagiography, given that Mozart is its subject, but its sensitivity to such concerns gives it a distance that other works might perhaps lack. It
is in the domain of myth, however, that this book undertakes radically different
cultural work. Rather than simply pulling the rug out from under stories that have
little basis in fact, and replacing a legend with a documentary "truth," the stories
themselves form the subject of the inquiry (regardless of their implicit or explicit
falseness), and are examined here for evidence of what they reveal of the *mentalités*
of those who uttered them or wrote them down.[33]

The chronological coverage of the book extends from 1791 to the present. This is
in part a response to the disproportionate emphasis given to early nineteenth-century German[34] romanticism in current accounts of Mozart reception, but more

---

[31] Stafford, *The Mozart Myths*, 267–268.

[32] The sorts of general survey that are relevant here are Gernot Gruber, *Mozart und die Nachwelt*
(Salzburg: Residenz Verlag, 1985), trans. by R. S. Furness as *Mozart and Posterity* (London: Quartet,
1991); Alec Hyatt King, "Mozart in Retrospect," in *Mozart in Retrospect: Studies in Criticism and
Bibliography* (London, New York, and Toronto: Geoffrey Cumberledge; Oxford University Press, 1955),
1–54; John Daverio, "Mozart in the Nineteenth Century," in *The Cambridge Companion to Mozart*, ed.
Simon P. Keefe (Cambridge: Cambridge University Press, 2003), 171–184; Jan Smaczny, "Mozart and the
Twentieth Century," in ibid., 185–199.

[33] Such a theoretical standpoint that accepts the equal importance of literary and nonliterary "texts,"
needless to say, invites comparison with much work that marched under the banner of the "New
Historicism" in the 1980s. See H. Aram Veeser, introduction to *The New Historicism*, ed. Aram Veeser
(New York and London: Routledge, 1989), xi, where such ephemeral texts as John Rolfe's conversation
with Pocahontas's father and Nietzsche's "note to self" to the effect that "I have lost my umbrella" are
given weight equal to Shakespeare's tragedies.

[34] See Böhme's concentration on German and Germanophone materials. To take a recent example, of
the twenty-seven "milestones in nineteenth-century Mozart reception" cited in Daverio, "Mozart in the

important, it is a recognition that the subject describes an unbroken continuum from 1791 to today. And while such texts as Peter Schaffer and Milos Foreman's *Amadeus* (1979 and 1984) have received attention from those who lived through them, the earlier twentieth century in particular suffers from neglect.[35] Furthermore, Mozart reception is characterized by historical continua that can range from 1819 to the present (chapter 5), 1856 to 1914 (chapter 6), and 1961 to the present (chapter 9).

The geographical scope of Mozart reception is similarly broad, ranging from such obvious areas as Berlin and Vienna to Paris, the French provinces, London, Birmingham, Manchester, Philadelphia, and New York. Some subjects take the inquiry into geographical areas that are not noted for their reception of Mozart: Scandinavia (Kierkegaard's well-known commentary on *Don Giovanni* is a noteworthy exception) and Italy.[36] The range of works that carry the largest burden of Mozart reception is largely circumscribed by the history of those works in the nineteenth and twentieth centuries. Thus, some works, *Don Giovanni* and *Die Zauberflöte* for example, show up with some regularity, whereas piano concertos make little impression until relatively late in the tale. Such largely problematic genres as the *Konzertarie* feature not at all, but in perhaps the most egregious case in the book, a work not by Mozart at all, the "Twelfth Mass," undertook immense cultural work in the nineteenth and twentieth centuries.

There are similarities of approach between the current undertaking and studies of the reception of Beethoven, Dickens, Shakespeare,[37] and van Gogh.[38] The project

Nineteenth Century," all but six are German, and of those six, three are Russian, one English (Holmes's biography), one Danish (Kirkegaard, naturally) and one barely French: Oulibicheff's' biography.

[35] See, among others, Robert L. Marshall, "Mozart and *Amadeus*," *Sonus* 4 (1983), 1–15; Gabriele Brandstetter and Gerhard Neumann, "Mozart auf der Reise ins 20. Jahrhundert: Mörike's Novelle und Schaffer's Amadeus," *Freiburger Universitätsblatter* 27 (1988), 85–105.

[36] The following texts give a sense of the attention Kierkegaard's writing on Mozart has engendered, and the reason why he is abandoned in favor of Bo Widerberg's alternative Scandinavia in chapter 9 here: Rudiger Gorner, "Zu Kierkegaards Verstandnis der *Zauberflöte*," *Miteillungen der internationalen Stiftung Mozarteum* 28 (1980), 25–31; Gorner, "*Die Zauberflöte* in Kierkegaards *Entweder-Oder*," in *Mozart-Jahrbuch 1980-83 des Zentralinstitutes für Mozartforschung der Internationalen Stiftung Mozarteum Salzburg* (Kassel: Bärenreiter, 1983), 247–257; Gotz Harbsmeier, *Unmittelbares Leben: Mozart und Kierkegaard* (Göttingen: Vandenhoeck und Ruprecht, 1980); Petr Osolsobe, "Kierkegaard's Aethetics of Music: A Concept of the Musical Erotic," *Sborník prací Filozofické Fakulty Brnenské Univerzity. H. Rada hudebnevedná* 27-28 (1992–93), 97–106; Alfons Rosenberg, "Mozart in Kierkegaards Deutung," *Österreichische Musikzeitschrift* 23 (1968), 409–412; Peter Tschuggnall, "Sören Kierkegaards Mozart-Rezeption: Analyse einer philosophisch-literarische Deutung von Musik" (Ph.D. diss., Universität Innsbruck, 1991); Walter Wiora, "Zu Kierkegaards Ideen über Mozarts *Don Giovanni*," *Beiträge zur Musikgeschichte Nordeuropas: Kurt Gudewill zum 65. Geburtstag*, ed. Uwe Haensel (Wolfenbüttel and Zurich: Möseler, 1978), 39–50; Jörg Zimmermann, "Philosophische Musikrezeption im Zeichen des spekulativ-erotischen Ohrs: Sören Kierkegaard hört Mozarts *Don Juan*," in Zimmermann, *Rezeptionsästhetik und Rezeptionsgeschichte in der Musikwissenschaft*, Publikationen der Hochschule für Musik und Theater Hannover 3 (Laaber: Laaber, 1991) 73–103.

[37] Gary Taylor, *Reinventing Shakespeare: A Cultural History from the Restoration to the Present* (London: Hogarth, 1990).

[38] Nathalie Heinich, *The Glory of Van Gogh: An Anthropology of Admiration*, trans. Paul Leduc Browne (Princeton, N.J.: Princeton University Press, 1996).

that has resulted in this study sprang from a dissatisfaction arising from a reading of George Ford's *Dickens and His Readers*;[39] the dissatisfaction lay not so much in the quality of the book—which remains high, even after half a century—but with the questions that it raised that for music seemed to remain unasked. The situation has changed greatly even for such a book as this to be conceivable, not only in terms of the studies of Mozart reception discussed in this introduction but also in terms of the study of the reception of other composers, among whom Beethoven looms large.[40]

Mozart's Ghosts examines the developing and changing reputation of the composer from his death in 1791 to the present. Its title implies two concepts. The first has a respectable theoretical pedigree: reception. The second has a currency among less specialized readers of books on music: renown. The latter is a loose term, related to reputation, significance, and a host of other concepts that attribute value to cultural artifacts and their producers. On the other hand, "reception," in literary studies at least, is a hotly contested concept and—despite the infrequent reference to such studies in writing about music—has its own scholarly markers: key authors, schools, and texts.[41]

The tension between reception, which (as the previous section has suggested) risks simply assembling greater and greater volumes of material with lesser and lesser degrees of theoretical control, and renown, which raises questions—less theoretically grounded, certainly—that are of importance beyond the academy, is central to the contemporary world of audiences, media, and judgments of value. Reception may be taken to mean the multiplicity of readings of the composer's work in the period between the work's composition and the present, and these sites may be considered the principal environment for the development of meaning. Sites of reception have much of the sense of a building site: something currently poorly defined, perhaps with a sense that something might arrive or be built on it, but clearly not a "work" or even an "event." They are confused and contradictory: there is certainly a trace of an original musical work or event, and such sites may very well be covered in Dahlhaus's "rubble"; they urgently call out for analysis but are often treated with contempt. The decoding, interpretation, and explanation of such sites is an essential component of any attempt to speak of the meaning that a cultural artifact might develop over time. So Mozart's reception, for example, in

---

[39] George Ford, *Dickens and His Readers: Aspects of Novel Criticism since 1836* (Princeton, N.J.: Princeton University Press, 1955; reprint, New York: Norton, 1965).

[40] The literature on Beethoven reception is larger than that on Mozart. See, for a tiny sample, Hans Heinrich Eggebrecht, *Zur Geschichte der Beethoven-Rezeption: Beethoven 1970*, Akademie der Wissenschaften und der Literatur: Abhandlungen der Geistes- und Sozialwissenschaftlichen Klasse, Jahrgang 1972, 3 (Wiesbaden: Steiner, 1972); Alessandro Comini, *The Changing Image of Beethoven: A Study in Mythmaking* (New York: Rizzoli, 1987); Scott Burnham, *Beethoven Hero* (Princeton, N.J.: Princeton University Press, 1995).

[41] See above pp. 3–4 for the exact situation of this book in this complex theoretical matrix.

Berlin in the 1840s may be contrasted with the way his works were received in Paris in 1880, or in London in 1920. Opera, sacred music, and instrumental music require treatment as even-handed as the history that supports them; their analysis therefore reflects the changing emphases of these three *genera* over the course of two centuries.

The overarching aim of this book is to explore the idea that modern reverence for the composer—his renown—is conditioned by earlier responses to his music—its reception. It also argues that such earlier responses are more complex than a simple model of production and reception (the composer composes; the audience or critic "receives") allows, and that the outline given in the previous section might imply. It does this by stressing the problematic and indirect nature of much Mozart reception and contrasts this with the more antiquarian, perhaps static, gathering of information about such sites of reception as performances, reviews, and so on.

An obvious corollary to the suggestion that "sites of reception" might be the focus of musical and scholarly inquiry is that the synchronic comes into play in a particularly forceful way. To understand Mozart in London in 1920, for example, presupposes an understanding of music in London in 1920 in all its forms, and an analysis of the relationship between the diachronic trajectory of a work by Mozart across time and of its synchronic impact on a musical culture radically different from the one that supported the work's creation. Another way of looking at this question is to invoke Jauss's *Erwartungshorizont*, the "Horizon of Expectations," a powerful image that serves as a constant reminder of the changing nature of cultures and the shifting relationship between works over time and the cultures that support and will support them.[42] This also means that understanding the reception of Mozart means tracing a route through nineteenth- and twentieth-century music history. In other words, to borrow an example from chapter 3 of this book and to elide it with the title of a well-known text by James Webster, it may be claimed that "to understand Mozart, we must understand Offenbach."[43]

With these aims in mind, this book is divided into three parts: "Phantoms of the Opera," "Holy Spirits," and "Specters at the Feast." "Phantoms of the Opera" is dedicated intensively to music for the stage, and music on the stage. It considers the position Mozart holds in Gaston Leroux's novel *La fantôme de l'Opéra* of 1910 and in the silent-film versions of the tale in the 1920s. While the diagetic musical emphases in his text center on Gounod's *Faust*, there is a subtext that requires the association of Erik (*le fantôme*) with Mozart: the composition of a *Requiem*, a mass to celebrate his wedding, and a work called *Don Juan triomphant*. This Mozartian

---

[42] For Jauss's own view on the *Erwartungshorizont* as it appeared at the end of the 1980s (nearly a quarter century after its first appearance), see Hans Robert Jauss, "Horizon Structure and Dialogicity," *Question and Answer: Forms of Dialogic Understanding*, ed. and trans. Michael Hays, Theory and History of Literature 68 (Minneapolis: University of Minnesota Press, 1989), 197–231.

[43] James Webster's original is "To Understand Verdi and Wagner We Must Understand Mozart," *19th-Century Music* 11 (1987), 175–193.

element is maintained and enhanced in silent film. This is juxtaposed with the chapter on Mozart and Offenbach, to which allusion has already been made, and in which, in order to establish an artistic position that was sufficiently serious to warrant the attention of the aristocratic audiences he was trying to attract, Offenbach explored foreign repertories from the long eighteenth century: Rousseau, Pergolesi, early Rossini, and—most important for the history of early *opérette*—Mozart. This first part concludes with a particular moment in the history of *Don Giovanni*, when there were remarkably no less than three new productions of *Don Giovanni* in Paris in a single year: 1866 saw the appearance of the work at the Paris Opéra, the Théâtre Italien, and the Théâtre-Lyrique. No fewer than fifty arrangements for keyboard of excerpts from *Don Giovanni* were published in 1866 in Paris alone, and this material forms the basis for an examination of the reworking of the opera—in its various forms—for keyboard.

The two chapters in "Holy Spirits" deal with sacred music and tropes of the sacred. For the nineteenth and most of the twentieth centuries, "Mozart's" "Twelfth Mass" was—together with the *Requiem*—the most popular sacred work attributed to Mozart and could rival *Don Giovanni* and *Die Zauberflöte* in nineteenth-century musical affections. The "Twelfth Mass" is key to Mozart reception throughout the Anglophone world, from the early nineteenth century to the present, and chapter 5 diagnoses its impact. "Enshrining Mozart" might seem to be ostensibly about *Don Giovanni*, since Pauline Viardot-Garcia purchased the autograph of *Don Giovanni* in London in 1855; but it was associated with a number of ritualistic discourses comparable with very few such documents before or since, and its treatment rendered *Don Giovanni* as sacred as the treatment of the "Twelfth Mass" made the latter secular. Viardot preserved the document in an artifact that was as close in construction to a reliquary that its nature would allow, and treated it as a shrine. Visitors to her homes in Paris and Baden-Baden behaved exactly as if they were in the presence of a relic: Rossini genuflected, and Tchaikovsky claimed to have been in the presence of divinity.

"Specters at the Feast" returns this book to literature and film. Modern views of French nineteenth-century understandings of Mozart have been colored by access only to the writings of Berlioz, which, however imaginative from a literary viewpoint, represent a highly idiosyncratic and pointed voice; an alternative, and more typical, perspective is given in chapter 7 by examining the changing views on Mozart during the half century that Ange-Henri Blaze (Blaze de Bury; 1813–88) wrote music criticism for the *Revue des deux mondes* (1834–82). Chapter 8 moves us from the press (although via a well-known critic) to imaginative prose. Although George Bernard Shaw's *Man and Superman* has been a recurrent topic in studies of the reception of Mozart's *Don Giovanni*, it was preceded by Shaw's "Don Giovanni Explains" (1887). Shaw humorously argues Don Giovanni's case: the Don is misunderstood and unfairly reviled. Shaw's story parodies E. T. A. Hoffmann's much better known text "Don Juan: Eine fabelhafte Begebenheit," and carefully imitates the pretext, scenario, focus, narrative, and supernatural context of Hoffmann's story, and in doing so contributes a skeptical Victorian's critique of German romantic fiction. This book concludes with a consideration of Mozart in contemporary film. It has been over forty years since Bo Widerberg's *Elvira Madigan* (1967), together with Geza Anda's recording with the Camerata Academica des Mozarteums Salzburg (1961), gave the slow movement of Mozart's C major piano concerto (K. 467) the same celebrity as that enjoyed by the d minor concerto (K. 466) in the early nineteenth century. The elision of the slow movement of K. 467 with a piece of cinema from which it has never subsequently been divorced raises a spectrum of questions concerning the representation of music and image, the status of classic instrumental music, and the reception of Mozart in the last half century.

Driving this book, then, is a fundamental question of to what extent today's views of Mozart—axiological (how his music is valued), aesthetic, and cultural—are direct responses to the genius of the composer and the innate, transcendental, qualities of the works themselves and how much they are reactions to the ways the composer and his music have been viewed during the last two hundred years.[44] Suspicious of the primacy of transcendental value, the book takes as its central task to investigate significant sites of reception that point to ways the composer's past status can be understood as part of today's veneration. It attempts to engage in a dialogue with the idea of a transcendental Mozart and one that is more obviously historically conditioned.

This book, therefore, reflects the unprecedented range of sites of reception to give as great as possible a resonance to the questions it poses. And although the press and performance provide the source material for chapters 7 and 3, respectively, Mozart reception invokes sites as varied as piano transcriptions of opera arias (chapter 3), material culture (chapter 6), tourist literature and technology transfer (chapter 5), short stories (chapter 8) and mass market film of very different periods (chapters 2 and 9); it emphatically does not deal with performance history, which would be a very different type of study. The registral range of the materials treated is similarly wide: comedy, tragedy, ritual, the supernatural, elite-mass and the technical; chapters 5 and 6 deal, for example, with the trope of the sacred while chapters 2, 4, and 9 all address questions of mass culture in different periods.

Rather than simply document various types of "impact" (*Wirkung*), this book takes as it target sites of Mozart reception that are problematic or compromised, and occupies itself not exclusively with the means by which the works were received (*Wirkungsträger*) but as much with the subversive use to which the works were put. These extend from, for example, the willful appropriation of a Mozart opera to enhance the commercial opportunities of a fledgling opera house (chapter 3) to the immense cultural impact of a work that turns out not to be by Mozart at

---

[44] This is a view with a pedigree in the experimental sciences. See Karl E. Weick, David P. Gilfillan, and Thomas A. Keith, "The Effect of Composer Credibility on Orchestra Performance," *Sociometry 36* (1973), 435–462.

all (chapter 5), to the remarkable shift in medium as a Mozart piano concerto profited from its association with film, to the parody of one of the classics of early nineteenth-century writing about music in German (chapter 8). The concept of Mozart reception emerges as a significantly more subtle phenomenon than might be thought from current studies, with the idea of "ghost" developing both the idea of a unmediated reception and the illusory qualities found in the sites of reception given attention here.

There is a danger in talking about "Mozart reception" that separates it from the historiography of nineteenth- and twentieth-century music. This separation leaves traditional histories untrammeled by questions of reception and therefore free to occupy the comfortable ground populated by familiar stories of composers and works; it also risks allowing studies of reception to fall prey to being consigned to a type of scholarly ghetto, from which it is difficult to escape. Although the individual chapters in this book fall clearly into the domain of "Mozart reception," they are at least as much concerned with the history of nineteenth- and twentieth-century musical cultures as they are with understanding the impact that Mozart's music made on its legatees. To set these concerns in the theoretical context in which they originate is to point to the equal emphasis in the book on *Erwartungshorizont* (horizon of expectations) and on sites of reception. Thus, Pauline Viardot's veneration of the autograph of *Don Giovanni* engages with musical cultures as varied as Clara Schumann's visits to Baden-Baden in the 1860s and the early work on the first edition of the Köchel catalogue, while the remarkable history of the "Twelfth Mass" engages—among a host of other contexts, and very much to its disadvantage—with the emergence of a professional musicology in England in the 1950s.

The study of Mozart reception demands a geographical balance between the main linguistic areas that have "received" the composer. Such a balance therefore recognizes the immense power of nineteenth- and twentieth-century views in France and Anglophone countries as at least as important as those from German-speaking areas. The topographical—or linguistic—blocks play off one another throughout the book: Offenbach's reuse of *Der Schauspieldirektor* depends heavily on Viennese and Berlin traditions (chapter 3) while Shaw's "Don Giovanni Explains" rereads Hoffmann's "Don Juan: Eine fabelhafte Begebenheit," from Bamberg, with a satirical twist from Victorian London (chapter 8). Hoffmann again resurfaces in Blaze de Bury's Mozart criticism in French (chapter 7), while chapter 4 juxtaposes practices in London, Berlin, Paris, and Vienna. And while North America figures prominently in chapter 5, German-speaking states ironically figure as *éminences grises* in the same chapter.

This book plays with a number of issues—subversive, counterintuitive, and perhaps perverse—in an attempt to understand some of the stranger pages in the history of nineteenth- and twentieth-century music. It does this in pursuit of an understanding of one of the most powerful cultural icons of our times, and one that—despite the reputed collapse of commercial interests in "classical" music—seems to survive each and every attempt to decry it. "Phantoms of the Opera" is the title of the first substantive chapter of the book, one that picks up the nineteenth-century history of the Paris Opéra and projects it across the early twentieth-century novel, across silent film, and into the present. It could almost serve as an emblem for the survival of Mozart's music itself.

PART I

Phantoms of the Opera

2

Phantoms of the Opera

Gaston Leroux's novel *Le fantôme de l'Opéra* has been at the forefront of the pene-tration of music of the classical Western tradition into popular culture throughout the twentieth and twenty-first centuries. One of the characteristics of the history of reworking the text between 1909 and the present has been the changing for-tunes of the musical repertories represented therein. Indeed, no one familiar with the history of *Le fantôme de l'Opéra* in the second half of the twentieth century will have given a second's thought to any role that Mozart might have played in this text. But, as this chapter will show, in Leroux's original novel, not only is Mozart present, but he represents one of the embodiments of Erik, the protagonist. In his role as a composer of three works: a marriage mass, a requiem mass, and an opera based on the *Don Juan* legend, Erik shares a compositional profile with one com-poser, and one only: Mozart, whose Mass in c minor, K. 427, *Requiem,* K. 626, and *Don Giovanni ossia Il dissoluto punito,* K. 527, are the works in question. Mentioned only incidentally, alongside other casual references to Mozart, first of all, they appear with greater density until all three are brought into alignment toward the end of the novel.

Leroux's novel was first published in installments in the daily newspaper *Le gau-lois* between September 1909 and January 1910, and then published complete by Lafitte in Paris later in 1910.[1] The outline of the story is well known: Christine Daaé is a largely overlooked artist at the Paris Opéra who has been taking lessons with an anonymous—and largely invisible—teacher who turns out to be the so-called *fan-*

---

[1] For the publication history of *Le fantôme de l'Opéra*, see Cormac Newark, "'Vous qui faites l'endormie': The Phantom and the Buried Voices of the Paris Opéra," *19th-Century Music* 33 (2009), 63, note 3. The version referenced in this chapter is Gaston Leroux, *Le fantôme de l'Opéra* (Paris: Livre de Poche, 1983). A machine-readable version of the text is available at "Feedbooks" (although the bibliographical source for this edition is not specified), www.ebooksgratuits.com (accessed 10 July 2012).

tôme of the Opéra, Erik. Christine's ambitions are confused by the attentions of a young aristocrat, Raoul de Chagny, who plays a key role in her rescue after Erik abducts her and removes her to his underground apartments in the Palais Garnier.[2] Raoul shares the task of rescuing Christine with a mysterious Persian (*le persan*) who accompanies him in his travels in the subterranean parts of the Palais Garnier.

Le fantôme de l'Opéra is a remarkable mix of the fictional, the real, and much that falls in between the two. The existence of Erik himself is creation of Leroux's imagination, whereas much of the musical detail is very carefully documented. But many of the apparently fictional characters in the novel allude to real ones in ways Leroux exploits. The figure of Christine Daaé, for example, is modeled on that of Kristina Nilsson, not only in terms of her Swedish origins, so clearly laid out by Leroux in his novel, but also in terms of the rivalry between Christine and La Carlotta, which was also based on the real-life rivalry between Nilsson and Caroline Miolhan-Carvalho.[3]

The chronology set up by Leroux in *Le fantôme de l'Opéra* is complex and detailed. Belying his casual note that the events he records were supposed to have taken place no further in the past than *guère une trentaine d'années*, much of the new music described in this chapter is carefully chosen to have been only just available at the very end of the 1870s. Productions are placed with great care, and even the most incidental details similarly chosen. For example, one of the locations of the sightings of the Fantôme is the third basement, where scenery from Massenet's *Le roi de Lahore* has been abandoned, no longer required.[4] It was here that the body of the stagehand Joseph Buquet is found early in the novel and where, much later, the entrance to the Fantôme's subterranean apartments is discovered.[5] *Le roi de Lahore* received its premiere on 27 April 1877; it was given thirty performances that year, eleven in 1878, and sixteen in 1879 and then consigned to oblivion.[6] Late 1879 or early 1880 were perfectly reasonable dates for the scenery still to be lying around in the third basement to serve now as a prop for the action in Leroux's novel.

The distribution of musical events in *Le fantôme de l'Opéra* strikingly separates out allusions to the three key Mozart works, placing references to what might loosely be called "new" music in the first half of the novel (chapters 1–13) and Mozart almost exclusively in the second half (chapters 13–27), with chapter 13 ("La Lyre d'Apollon") representing both a fulcrum and a turning point. Thus the gala

---

[2] The Palais Garnier was formally opened on 5 January 1875, but had been in construction since 1860. Its opening was triggered by the fire at the old Opéra, the Salle Le Peletier, during the night of 28 October 1873. The construction of the Palais Garnier itself is a critical theme running throughout *Le fantôme de l'Opéra*.

[3] See Newark, "Vous qui faites l'endormie," 76–77.

[4] Massenet's *Le roi de Lahore*, to a libretto by Louise Gallet, was premiered at the Paris Opéra on 27 April 1877.

[5] Leroux, *Le fantôme de l'Opéra*, 32 and 374.

[6] See Albert Soubies, *Soixante-sept ans à l'Opéra en une page du "Siège de Corinthe" à "La Walkyrie" (1826–1893)* (Paris: Fischbacher, 1893).

concert in chapter 2 exposes so much of the music from the second half of the 1870s, and the early parts of Christine and Erik's relationship center on performances of Rossini and Gounod. Hardly any mention of this "new" repertory is made in the second half of the novel: Mozart is the only emblem of musical tradition Leroux employs, and mention of his music requires decoding in some detail.

The Gala Concert and *La Marguerite Nouvelle*

The first set-piece in *Le fantôme de l'Opéra* has a double function within the work's narrative: the gala concert serves as the celebration of the end of the previous directors' tenure (Debienne and Poligny) and, as a result of the indisposition of La Carlotta, Christine's first major role on the stage, on which she has up till now merely taken the minor role of Siebel in Gounod's *Faust*.[7] The evening is given a particular piquancy in the novel because of the discovery of the body of the stage-hand Joseph Buquet by an overexcited part of the corps de ballet just before the beginning of the concert. Leroux frames his entire second chapter as a parenthesis between two announcements of Bouquet's death, including not only the gala concert but also Raoul's first meeting with Christine and the scene in which he overhears—although he does not understand—Christine and Erik speaking on either side of the wall of her dressing room.

Leroux describes the program in greater detail than do many public accounts of concerts of the period. Not only were there works by Gounod, Reyer, Saint-Saëns, Massenet, Guiraud, and Delibes, but the composers in turn took on the responsibility of conducting their own works. The concert marks out the ground for what constitutes new music for Leroux's novel, as the program shows (table 2.1).

The concert consisted of works that were new but in the public domain. Gounod's *La marche funèbre d'une marionette* dated from 1872, but its orchestration had only been published in 1878. Similarly, Saint-Saëns's *Danse Macabre* had been published in 1875. The two numbers from ballets by Delibes dated from 1876 (*Sylvia*) and 1870 (*Coppélia*), respectively, and Guiraud's *Carnaval* is clearly the fourth number in his *Suite d'orchestre en 4 parties*, published in 1872.[8] The second piece by Saint-Saëns, described as "une *Rêverie orientale*"—the indefinite article pointing to a work as yet unknown—was almost certainly the *Rêverie du soir (à Blidah)* from his op. 60 *Suite algérienne* composed in 1879 but not published until 1881.[9] Despite having been begun as long ago as the 1860s, Reyer's *Sigurd* was not

---

[7] Leroux, *Le fantôme de l'Opéra*, 36–39.

[8] A MONSIEUR / JULES PASDELOUP. / SUITE D'ORCHESTRE / EN 4 PARTIES / PAR / E. GUIRAUD / Arrangé pour Piano à 4 mains par l'Auteur /.../ Paris, Maison FLAXLAND / DURAND, SCHŒNWERK & Cⁱᵉ, 32–45.

[9] A Monsieur le Docteur KOPFF / Suite Algérienne / *Impressions pittoresques d'un voyage en Algérie* /.../ PAR / C. SAINT-SAËNS / OP: 60 / PARIS, DURAND, SCHŒNWERK & Cⁱᵉ. / Ancⁿᵉ Maison G. FLAXLAND / 4 Place de la Madeleine, 4.

TABLE 2.1: Program of Christine Daaé's Gala Concert, summarizing *Le fantôme de l'Opéra*

Composer	Title	Notes
Gounod	*La marche funèbre d'une marionette*	1872 (orch. 1878)
Reyer	Overture to *Sigurd*	1884 premiere (Brussels)
Saint-Saëns	*La danse macabre*	1874 (pub. 1875)
Saint-Saëns	*Rêverie orientale* (= *Rêverie arabe*, from *Suite Algérienne* op. 60)	1879 (pub. 1881)
Massenet	*Marche hongroise* (inédit)	Scènes hongroises, suite no. 2, c. 1870 (1880), arr. of "Pièces pour piano à quatre mains," 1869–70
Guiraud	*Carnaval*	?
Delibes	*Valse lent* (*Sylvia*)	1876 Paris Opéra
Delibes	*Pyzzicati* (*Coppélia*)	1870 Paris Opéra
Verdi	*Boléro* (*Les vêpres siciliennes*)	Mlle. Krauss
Donizetti	*Brindisi* (*Lucrèce Borgia*)	Denise Bloch
Gounod	(Quelques passages) *Roméo et Juliette*	Not yet heard at Palais Garner; Christine Daaé
Gounod	Prison act + final trio (*Faust*)	Christine Daaé

premiered at the Paris Opéra until 1884. Massenet's *Marche hongroise* is explicitly noted by Leroux as "inédit," and this concurs exactly with the publication date (1880) of the orchestral arrangement of the "Pièces pour piano à quatre mains" of 1869–70.[10]

Two short vocal numbers provide a clear articulation with the new by reaching back decades. The *boléro* is probably Hélène's *sicilienne* "Merci, jeunes amies" from Verdi's *Les vêpres siciliennes*; this not only dated from 1855 but had not been heard on stage since the fifteen performances of its revival in 1863–64.[11] Donizetti's *Lucrezia Borgia* (premiered at Milan's La Scala theatre in 1833) is an interesting inclusion here, since it was not known at the Paris Opéra at all, but was a familiar landmark at the Théâtre Italien, where it appeared almost every year from 1840 to 1874. At this point, it fell out of the repertory, except for a seven-performance run in 1884, so that—like the Verdi—it did not form part of any current operatic experience for Leroux's fictional audience.[12]

Currency was not an issue for the two key pieces in the concert that featured Christine Daaé. However complex the early textual history of Gounod's *Faust*, by the late 1870s it had been in repertory for a decade and appeared on average once every two weeks at the Paris Opéra.[13] It had taken its place alongside the four

---

[10] A GEORGES BIZET / SCÈNES HONGROISES / 2me Suite d'Orchestre /.../ MUSIQUE DE / J. MASSENET /... PARIS / G. HARTMANN, Editeur, 60, Rue Neuve-St-Augustin, 26–39.

[11] Soubies, *Soixante-sept ans.*

[12] Albert Soubies, *Le Théâtre-Italien de 1801 à 1913* (Paris: Fischbacher, 1913).

[13] For the compositional history of *Faust*, see Steven Huebner, *The Operas of Charles Gounod* (Oxford: Clarendon Press, 1990), 99–132. For its performance history, see Soubies, *Soixante-sept ans.*

grands opéras of Meyerbeer. Leroux explains a good deal about the timeliness of Christine's performance of "certain passages" of Gounod's *Roméo et Juliette*: "It was the first time that the young artist sang this work by Gounod, which among others had not yet been transferred to the Opéra, and that the Opéra-Comique had just taken up a long time after it had been premiered at the old Théâtre-Lyrique by Mme Carvalho."[14] Leroux's description was perfect: *Roméo et Juliette* was premiered at the Théâtre-Lyrique in 1867 and transferred to the Opéra-Comique in 1873; it did not emerge at the Paris Opéra until 1888.[15] Exactly which passages Christine sang is not clear, although Leroux's citation of the two protagonists' closing words "Seigneur! Seigneur! Pardonnez nous!" suggests that one of the extracts must have been the Scène et Duo "Salut! Tombeau! Sombre et silencieux" that ends the opera.[16]

To the program outlined by Leroux should be added a further current work, although its exact context is not as clear as the other works by Gounod. At the very beginning of the account of the gala concert, the dressing room of the prima ballerina La Sorelli is invaded by members of the corps de ballet "qui remontaient de scène après avoir 'dansé' *Polyeucte*." This is clearly Gounod's opera *Polyeucte*, premiered at the Opéra in 1878, and it seems likely that the dancers who so troubled La Sorelli had simply performed the elaborate act 3 *divertissement* from that work, which consisted of no less than seven numbers, as a prelude to the concert described in the next chapter.[17]

While all the music at the Gala Concert is authentic, to the point that it is possible to distinguish between contemporary works that the audience might have known and those that had yet to be released publicly, the personnel involved are more mixed. Two of the performers, Gabrielle Krauss and Jean-Baptiste Faure, are well-documented figures at the Paris Opéra at the period when *Le fantôme* is set: Krauss was employed there from 1875 to 1887, so she never sang *Les vêpres siciliennes* on stage; Faure worked there from 1861 to 1876, but continued to perform away from the stage until much later.[18]

---

[14] "C'était la première fois que la jeune artiste chantait cette œuvre de Gounod, qui, du reste, n'avait pas encore été transportée à l'Opéra et que l'Opéra-Comique venait de reprendre longtemps après qu'elle eut été créée à l'ancien Théâtre-Lyrique par Mme Carvalho" (Leroux, *Le fantôme de l'Opéra*, 36–37).

[15] For the work's compositional history, see Huebner, *Operas of Charles Gounod*, 155–174.

[16] Leroux, *Le fantôme de l'Opéra*, 37.

[17] FORMAT LEMOINE / POLYEUCTE / OPÉRA EN CINQ ACTES / PAROLES DE / JULES BARBIER ET MICHEL CARRÉ / MUSIQUE DE / CH. GOUNOD / DE L'INSTITUT /.../ PARIS / HENRY LEMOINE, ÉDITEUR, RUE PIGALLE, 17. The ballet is 197–237, and includes Le Dieu Pan, La Déesse Bellone, Vénus, Danse de Vénus, Bacchus, Danse de Bacchus, and Bacchanale. Leroux, *Le fantôme de l'Opéra*, 17.

[18] Karl-Josef Kutsch and Leo Riemens, *Großes Sängerlexikon*, 4 vols. (Bern and Stuttgart: Francke, 1987–94); 4th ed., 7 vols. (Munich: Saur, 2003), 4:2501–2502 (Krauss) and 2:1408–1409 (Faure). Faure was Gounod's first Méphistophélès at the Opéra in 1869.

Denise Bloch is perhaps the most interesting inclusion here. *Rosine* Bloch was a distinguished contemporary of Faure's and an older contemporary of Krauss, active at the Paris Opéra from 1865 until 1880, and a favored Leonore in Donizetti's *La favorite* and Fidès in Meyerbeer's *Le prophète* (both very popular in the late 1870s).[19] Thus far, Leroux has either presented his readers with real figures (Faure, Krauss, all the composers in the Gala Concert, Pierre Gailhard)[20] or fictional ones calqued on real figures in the manner of a roman à clef: Christine Daaé on Kirstina Nilsson or La Carlotta on Marie Miolhan-Carvalho. Denise Bloch sits uncomfortably between the two: neither hiding under the pseudo-anonymity of a key nor projected as herself. Needless to say, the central figure in the Gala Concert is Christine Daaé herself. Heard only in extracts from Gounod, she sings in works that are current and much admired (*Faust*) or highly sought-after—the yet-unheard (at the Opéra at least) *Roméo et Juliette*.

With two exceptions—albeit important ones—the Gala Concert projects not just modern music but the most highly sought-after and in some cases unknown music. The work that this scene undertakes, then, is to set out one dimension of the musical landscape of the book, to be set against a second—the classics of the *ottocento*—both of which may then be read against a third: Mozart. This modern dimension has two faces, however: the composers of instrumental music with their new or unheard orchestral compositions, and music by Gounod. The latter is of a decisive importance for the conduct of the novel.

The French *Ottocento* and *Le Fantôme*

When Krauss and Bloch sing extracts from Verdi and Donizetti at the Gala Concert, they set up a further strand of musical discourse within the novel, one that is exclusively related to Erik. In chapter 13, "La lyre d'Apollon," Raoul and Christine take refuge on the roof of the Opéra, and Christine relates the story of her involvement with Erik (who overhears the entire conversation), her arrival in his underground domain, and his unmasking. This, the longest chapter in the book, which also includes much of the key material that identifies Erik with Mozart, has two scenes that align Erik with the character of Otello from Rossini's opera of the same name. Premiered in 1816 in Naples, *Otello* had been an *œuvre-clé* for Paris since its appearance at the Théâtre Italien in 1821. Apart from a dip in popularity in the late 1840s, it was never absent from the theatre, and held its own with middle-period Verdi: *Rigoletto*, *La traviata*, and *La forza del destino*. The reason for its temporary disappearance in the late 1840s was its appropriation by the Opéra itself, in French translation, in 1844; the production staggered on until

---

[19] Ibid., 1:454.
[20] Leroux cites Gailhard as the source of an anecdote (Leroux, *Le fantôme de l'Opéra*, 21, note 1); Gailhard managed the Opéra from 1884 to 1906.

the end of the decade, at which point it was picked up again by the Théâtre Italien. It was a Parisian (not to say worldwide) classic by 1880, the date of the setting of *Le fantôme de l'Opéra*, even more so by the time Leroux began publication of his novel in 1909.[21]

But this is an assimilated *ottocento*: in the same way that Krauss and Bloch perform in French (the original language for *Les vêpres siciliennes* and a translation, presumably, for *Lucrèce Borgia*), what Christine and Erik sing is the 1844 French translation of *Otello* as *Othello*.[22] Thus the *canzone del salice* from act 3 becomes "la romance de Desdémone," and the work and the eponym are described as *Othello* rather than the Italian *Otello* throughout. But despite the large number of changes wrought in the 1844 *Othello*, the third act remains largely untouched in the two versions, and of the four numbers in the act—the *canzone del gondoliero*, the *canzone del salice*, the *preghiera,* and the final *duetto*—two constitute the pillars of the scene in *Le fantôme de l'Opéra*. And readers of Leroux's chapter will not have missed that the performance of the *canzone del salice* is preceded by the near-congruence of the barcarolle (the *canzone del gondoliero*) in the opera and the journey across the subterranean lake in the novel. And it is not hard to read much of the chapter's dialogue between the *canzone del salice* and the closing *duetto* as much akin to the *preghiera* that separates the two numbers in the opera. In a sense, then, Leroux reinscribes all of act 3 of *Otello* into chapter 13 of the novel in ways similar to those in which works by Gounod and Halévy are treated.

With Christine as his visitor in his subterranean home, Erik performs Desdemona's *romance* "Au pied d'un saule" to the harp.[23]

> That evening, we no longer exchanged a word. . . . He took his harp and began to sing to me, with his man's voice, an angel's voice, Desdemona's romance. The memory of having sung it myself filled me with shame. My friend, there is a virtue in music such that there is nothing in the world beyond those sounds which come to strike your heart. My extraordinary adventure was forgotten. Alone the voice revived, and I followed, intoxicated, its harmo-

---

[21] For the 1844 *Othello* and its significance for the politics of genre in mid-1840s Paris, see Mark Everist, "Rossini at the Paris Opéra, 1843–1847: Translation, Arrangement, *Pasticcio*," in *Librettoübersetzung: Interkulturalität im europäischen Musiktheater*, ed. Herbert Schneider and Rainer Schmusch, Musikwisenschaftliche Publikationen 32 (Hildesheim: Olms, 2009), 131–163, "'Il n'y a qu'un Paris au monde, et j'y reviendrai planter mon drapeau!' Rossini's Second *grand opera*," *Music & Letters* 90 (2009), 636–672, and "Partners in Rhyme: Alphonse Royer, Gustave Vaëz, and Foreign Opera in Paris during the July Monarchy," in *Fashions and Legacies in Nineteenth-Century Italian Opera*, ed. Roberta Montemarra Marvin and Hilary Poriss (Cambridge: Cambridge University Press, 2009), 30–52.

[22] *Seule Edition conforme à l'exécution de l'Opéra /—/ OTHELLO / Grand Opéra en trois Actes / Paroles de MM /* Alphonse Royer et Gustave Waez / *Musique* / DE / G. ROSSINI / PRIX 10ᶠ. net / *PARIS* / AU MÉNESTREL, 2 bis rue Vivienne, HEUGEL et FILS / Editeurs-Propriétaires pour tous Pays.

[23] See, for the *Canzone di salice*, Michael Collins, ed., *Otello, ossia, Il moro di Venezia: Dramma per musica in tre atti di Francesco Berio di Salsa, musica di Gioachino Rossini*, Edizione critica delle opere di Gioachino 1/19 (Pesaro: Fondazione Rossini, 1994), 2:786–799, and for the duet "Non arrestar," ibid., 2:840–865.

nious journey; I was part of Orpheus' herd. The voice walked with me in pain, in joy, in martyrdom, in despair, in happiness, in death and in triumphant wedding ceremonies.... I listened.... It sang.[24]

Erik is imbued with several attributes in this scene. In addition to the now familiar "Ange de la musique," he is now also vicariously identified as Orpheus, with Christine as a member of his herd.[25] Claims of musical autonomy are furthermore very strong, claims that lure Christine into forgetting her extravagant adventure, and that allow her to become intoxicated with the music's "harmonious voyage." And this is inevitably bound up with identifying Erik as "La voix," a key element in the confusion engendered by his singing a soprano aria. With Erik equated with "La voix," all personal pronouns become feminine, so when Christine is "led into sadness and into joy," the sentence begins "*Elle* me promena..." And even in the middle of this complex regendering of the aria, Christine's memory of her own performance of the aria in comparison fills her with shame.

If this scene opens up issues of Erik's gender profile (a key issue for most literary critics who have commented on the novel), the second musical performance in this chapter develops other ways he is othered.[26] At the end of the account of Erik's own opera, Erik invites Christine to sing with him:

"Let's sing opera, Christine Daaé."
He said to me:
—"Let's sing opera, Christine Daaé," as if it were an insult.
But I had not the time to dwell on the melody he had given these words. We immediately began the duet from *Othello*, and already catastrophe was upon us. This time, he had left me the role of Desdemona, which I sang with a real despair, real terror that I had never felt even up to today. The proximity of such a partner, rather than annihilate me, inspired in me a magnificent terror. The events of which I was the victim brought me particularly close to the thought of the poet and I found the accents in which the musician had rejoiced. As for him, his voice was thunderous, his vindictive soul figured on each sound, greatly increased its power. Love, jealousy, hatred broke out

---

[24] "Ce soir-là, nous n'échangeâmes plus une parole.... Il avait saisi une harpe et il commença de me chanter, lui, voix d'homme, voix d'ange, la romance de Desdémone. Le souvenir que j'en avais de l'avoir chantée moi-même me rendait honteuse. Mon ami, il y a une vertu dans la musique qui fait que rien n'existe plus du monde extérieur en dehors de ces sons qui vous viennent frapper le cœur. Mon extravagante aventure fut oubliée. Seule revivait la voix et je la suivais enivrée dans son voyage harmonieux; je faisais partie du troupeau d'Orphée! Elle me promena dans la douleur, et dans la joie, dans le martyre, dans le désespoir, dans l'allégresse, dans la mort et dans les triomphants hyménées... j'écoutais.... Elle chantait" (Leroux, *Le fantôme de l'Opéra*, 244).

[25] Strangely, there is a sustained account of the analogy of *Le fantôme de l'Opéra* with the Orpheus legend that completely fails to mention this scene (Michael Grover-Friedlander, "'The Phantom of the Opera': The Lost Voice of Opera in Silent Film," *Cambridge Opera Journal* 11 (1999), 191–192.

[26] Jerrold E. Hogle, *The Undergrounds of "The Phantom of the Opera": Sublimation and the Gothic in Leroux's Novel and Its Progeny* (New York and Basingstoke: Palgrave, 2002), 69.

around us in tearing cries. Erik's black mask made me think of the natural mask of the Venetian moor. He was Othello himself. I believed he was going to strike me, that I would fall under his blows; . . . and yet I made no movement to flee him, to avoid his fury like the timid Desdemona. On the contrary, I came close to him, attracted, fascinated, finding morbid charms at the centre of such a passion; but before dying, I wanted to know, so that I could take the sublime image to my last, these unknown features which the fire of eternal art must transfigure. I wanted to see the face of The Voice, and instinctively, through a gesture of which I was not at all the mistress, since I was no longer in possession of myself, my rapid fingers pulled off the mask.[27]

To a degree, this performance is more straightforward: Christine takes the role of Desdemona and Erik that of Otello; the voices match, and the artists are inspired. Erik's presence encourages "a despair, a real terror that [Christine] had never achieved before," but this brings her close to the thinking of the poet (more Shakespeare than Berio di Salsa) and helps her find an interpretation with which the composer would have been delighted. Erik exhibits a vindictive soul, and "love, jealousy, hatred" erupt around the singers. But for Christine, Erik here becomes the character of Otello; although she fears that he might strike her, she is led to an even greater intimacy, one that persuades her to remove Erik's black mask, turning him back from the embodiment of Otello (the color of the mask is not accidental of course) into Erik, *le fantôme*.

The two scenes based around Rossini's *Otello* serve to emphasize the intimacy between Christine and Erik, perhaps the most counterintuitive element in the novel, but one that is realized almost entirely through musical means. Erik sings to Christine, in the same room rather than through a wall, for the first time,

---

[27] "Chantons l'Opéra, Christine Daaé."

Il me dit:

—"Chantons l'Opéra, Christine Daaé," comme s'il me jetait une injure.

Mais je n'eus pas le temps de m'appesantir sur l'air qu'il avait donné à ses paroles. Nous commençâmes tout de suite le duo d'*Othello*, et déjà la catastrophe était sur nos têtes. Cette fois, il m'avait laissé le rôle de Desdémone, que je chantai avec un désespoir, un effroi réels auxquels je n'avais jamais atteint jusqu'à ce jour. Le voisinage d'un pareil partenaire, au lieu de m'annihiler, m'inspirait une terreur magnifique. Les événements dont j'étais la victime me rapprochaient singulièrement de la pensée du poète et je trouvai des accents dont le musicien eût été ébloui. Quant à lui, sa voix était tonnante, son âme vindicative se portait sur chaque son, et en augmentait terriblement la puissance. L'amour, la jalousie, la haine, éclataient autour de nous en cris déchirants. Le masque noir d'Érik me faisait songer au masque naturel du More de Venise. Il était Othello lui-même. Je crus qu'il allait me frapper, que j'allais tomber sous ses coups; . . . et cependant, je ne faisais aucun mouvement pour le fuir, pour éviter sa fureur comme la timide Desdémone. Au contraire, je me rapprochai de lui, attirée, fascinée, trouvant des charmes à la mort au centre d'une pareille passion; mais, avant de mourir, je voulus connaître, pour en emporter l'image sublime dans mon dernier regard, ces traits inconnus que devait transfigurer le feu de l'art éternel. Je voulus voir le visage de la Voix et, instinctivement, par un geste dont je ne fus point la maîtresse, car je ne me possédais plus, mes doigts rapides arrachèrent le masque" (Leroux, *Le fantôme de l'Opéra*, 251–252).

appropriating her gender for the purpose, and when the two participate in the duet, Christine describes her attraction, her fascination, even finding charms in the death at the center of such a (musical) passion.

Gounod

An important precursor of the appearance of Rossini's *Otello* in *Le fantôme de l'Opéra* is the scene at the end of chapter 10, where Raoul, concealed in Christine's dressing room, overhears Erik singing through the wall and espies Christine's reaction. As in the case of his performance of Desdémone's *romance*, Erik's performance here gives rise to a level of sexual ambiguity. The work in question is introduced obliquely. As Christine listens in a state of rapture to Erik's singing,

> Raoul listened to this voice feverishly and he began to understand how Christine Daaé had been able to appear one night to a stupefied public, with sounds of an unknown beauty, of a superhuman exaltation, no doubt still under the influence of the mysterious and invisible master. And he understood all the more such a considerable event while listening to the exceptional voice that the latter was singing nothing really out of the ordinary.... The banality of the poetry and the easiness and popular near-vulgarity of the melody only appeared further transformed in beauty by a breath that raised them and carried them up into the sky on the wings of passion. Because this angelic voice glorified a pagan hymn.[28]

Leroux's description of the banality of the poetry and the easiness and almost popular vulgarity of the melody leaves wide open the nature of the music Erik is singing, and it comes as a surprise when he identifies the music: "This voice was singing 'Nuit d'hyménée' from *Roméo et Juliette*."[29] Christine's association with Gounod's *Roméo et Juliette* goes back to the Gala Concert, where her knowledge of music unknown at the Paris Opéra was remarked on. Erik's performance is if anything more striking. "Nuit d'hyménée" is the first movement of a multisectional duet for the two lovers from act 4 of Gounod's opera, whose genesis Leroux so carefully detailed in the account of the Gala Concert. Leaving aside the banality of the poetry and the vulgarity of the music, the critical issue becomes what Erik is in

---

[28] "Raoul écoutait cette voix avec fièvre et il commençait à comprendre comment Christine Daaé avait pu apparaître un soir au public stupéfait, avec des accents d'une beauté inconnue, d'une exaltation surhumaine, sans doute encore sous l'influence du mystérieux et invisible maître! Et il comprenait d'autant plus un si considérable événement en écoutant l'exceptionnelle voix que celle-ci ne chantait rien justement d'exceptionnel.... La banalité du vers et la facilité et la presque vulgarité populaire de la mélodie n'en apparaissaient que transformées davantage en beauté par un souffle qui les soulevait et les emportait en plein ciel sur les ailes de la passion. Car cette voix angélique glorifiait un hymne païen" (ibid., 190–191).

[29] "Cette voix chantait 'Nuit d'hyménée' de *Roméo et Juliette*" (ibid., 191).

fact singing. Over a pulsating 9/8 accompaniment, the two soloists sing mostly in sixths and tenths, with Juliette consistently at the top of the texture (ex. 2.1).[30]

EXAMPLE 2.1: *Gounod,* Roméo et Juliette, *act 4 duet (Roméo and Juliette),* "Nuit d'hyménée!" *ROMEO AND JULIET / Opera in Five Acts / Libretto by / J. BARBIER and M. CARRÉ / Music by / CHARLES GOUNOD / The English Version by / DR. THEO. BAKER / With an Essay on / Story of the Opera by / W. J. HENDERSON / G. SCHIRMER, Inc., NEW YORK, 183.*

Sung as a solo, it is impossible to imagine a soloist taking anything other than the soprano line, and this results in the same effect as in the *romance* from *Otello*: he

---

[30] ROMEO AND JULIET / Opera in Five Acts / Libretto by / J. BARBIER and M. CARRÉ / Music by / CHARLES GOUNOD / The English Version by / DR. THEO. BAKER / With an Essay on / Story of the Opera by / W. J. HENDERSON / G. SCHIRMER, Inc., NEW YORK, 183–189.

sings music for the female eponym. The situation is certainly unclear, and unlike the case of the *romance*, there is no mention of music for soprano sung by a male voice in the novel itself (ex. 2.2, although the context would have made such an account difficult), but the ambiguity provides a measure of transition to the performances of Rossini's *romance* three chapters later.

EXAMPLE 2.2: *Reconstruction of Erik's performance of Gounod's "Nuit d'hyménée," adapted from source used in ex. 2.1.*

"Nuit d'hyménée" also brings out a particular emphasis in its performances. Unlike only one other operatic extract in the novel, one line is quoted no less than four times in three pages: "Destiny inexorably chains me to you."[31] "Nothing could render the passion," writes Leroux, with which the voice sang the line, and—given the dramatic circumstances of the novel—the operatic context of the extract develops a great resonance: as Roméo and Juliette reciprocally declare that destiny chains them together, Erik—addressing Christine—can claim that destiny chains her to him. The words speak for themselves, but the ellipses invite the addition of

---

the next, less oblique, lines: "Under your passionate kisses / Heaven shines in me."[32] The "destiny" line occurs again as Raoul hears it through the wall after Christine's inexplicable disappearance, and the line effectively closes the chapter with an open question: "La destinée t'enchaîne à moi sans retour. A moi? A qui?" leaving Raoul alone in Christine's dressing room weeping the tears of a jealous child.

Despite the two occurrences of extracts from *Roméo et Juliette* in *Le fantôme de l'Opéra*, the operatic star of the novel is Gounod's *Faust*. By 1880, *Faust* had been a fixture at the Opéra, both at the Salle Le Peletier, and at the Palais Garnier. Throughout the 1880s and 1890s, it was performed between twenty and thirty times a year—a performance on average every two weeks.[33] Leroux hardly needed any prompt to base his novel on Gounod's opera, but an important new production took place at the Palais Garnier just months before he started work on the novel: 25 January 1908 saw a production starring Lucien Muratore and Jeanne Hatto in the roles of Faust and Marguerite, conducted by Paul Vidal and directed by Paul Stuart, with choreography by Léo Staats.[34] Readers of *Le fantôme* in *Le Gaulois* in the autumn of 1908 would have understood *Faust* both as a recent media phenomenon and a long-standing classic at the Palais Garnier, and would not have been able to have thought of a more suitable operatic context for the events of 1880 related in Leroux's novel.

There is a congruence between Leroux's handling of the extracts from *Othello* and of those from *Faust*. In the case of *Othello*, Leroux's narrative follows the progress of act 3 of Rossini's opera, envoicing two of the four numbers, alluding directly to another and indirectly to a fourth. In the two scenes from *Faust*, he bases the first on Méphistofélès's serenade from act 4: the selection of a single number largely for its suitability for a series of plays on words; but the second is a sustained reinscription of the first two acts and most of the third that occupies no less than fifteen pages of the novel.[35]

The first scene in which *Faust* is found quoted is part of a near-comic narrative by the *ouvreuse*, Mme. Giry, who relates two stories concerning the *Fantôme* and the occupants of Box no. 5, which he considers his personal property. The first describes how a couple, M. and Mme. Maniera, share a box with their friend, Isidore Saack, and how Erik's invisible voice directs M. Maniera's attention to Saack's attempts to kiss Maniera's former wife's hand. The consequences—Maniera striking Saack in full view of the house—are scandalous. Leroux uses extracts from the act 4 serenade wittily to propel both the original story and Mme. Giry's narrative.

---

[32] "Sous tes baisers de flamme / Le ciel rayonne en moi!" (ROMEO AND JULIET / Opera in Five Acts / Libretto by / J. BARBIER and M. CARRÉ / Music by / CHARLES GOUNOD / The English Version by / DR. THEO. BAKER / With an Essay on / Story of the Opera by / W. J. HENDERSON / G. SCHIRMER, Inc., NEW YORK, 184–185).

[33] Soubies, *Soixante-sept ans*.

[34] Jean-Louis Dutronc, "Un siècle de représentations au Palais Garnier," *Gounod: Faust*, L'Avant-Scène Opéra 2 (Paris: L'Avant-Scène Opéra, 1976), 83.

[35] Leroux, *Le fantôme de l'Opéra*, 142–157.

Méphistofélès's opening phrase "You who pretend to sleep / Do you not hear / O
Catherine my friend / My voice and my steps?"[36] is echoed by Erik's invisible voice
as he says to M. Maniera: "Ha! Ha! It is not Julie who is pretending to sleep" (and
Leroux explains that Mme. Maniera's Christian name is Julie), whereupon
M. Maniera looks to see who is speaking and of course sees no one. Then, while
Méphistofélès is singing "Catherine whom I adore / Why do you refuse / The lover
who implores you / Such a sweet kiss?"[37] M. Maniera hears the same voice saying
"Ha! Ha! Julie would not refuse a kiss from Isidore?" which alerts M. Maniera to
the activity to his left and triggers the public altercation. Leroux's presentation
of this scene is characterized by Mme. Giry's singing. She explains the sequence of
events by direct reference to points in the opera, which she sings to the directors of
the Opéra to whom she is relating the story. This enhances her loquaciousness, so
as she asks the directors if they want her to continue (they repeatedly give their
assent), they are explicitly acknowledging her performance.

Almost as a complement to this use of act 4, one of the central musical scenes
in the novel passes through the entire first three acts of the opera (table 2.2).

The scene of the so-called *salle maudite* is triggered by the directors' refusal of
the Fantôme's demand that Carlotta should be removed from cast of *Faust* and
replaced by Christine. The chapter's narrative in part runs parallel to that of the
opera, and on key occasions merges with it. The directors of the Opéra witness a
defensive cabal on behalf of La Carlotta, Christine Daaé's indifferent performance,
the complete onstage collapse of Carlotta at the end of the third act, and the fall of
the chandelier into the auditorium just afterward.

There is a continuity with Mme. Giry's narration of act 4, in that the opening of
the scene plays on words in exactly the same way. As Faust sings his famous opening lines, "Nothing... In vain do I ask, on an ardent night / Nature and the Creator.
/ Not a voice slips in my ear / A consoling word,"[38] Richard turns to his colleague
Moncharmin and asks "And you, has a voice slipped a word in your ear?"[39] It is a
bon mot that well captures the relaxed atmosphere in the Fantôme's box where the
two directors are seated. But exactly this type of play on words characterizes the
cataclysmic end of the scene. It does so twice: the lines over which Carlotta fails,

---

[36] "Vous qui faites l'endormie / [N'entendez-vous pas / Ô Catherine ma mie / Mes voix et mes pas?]"
(ibid., 84). For the music, see FAUST / Opéra en cinq Actes / DE / Jules BARBIER et Michel CARRÉ /
Musique de / CH. GOUNOD / — / Partition Chant et Piano / Transcrite par LÉO DELIBES /—/ Paris,
CHOUDENS, Editeur / 30 Boulevard des Capucines, 30. /—Belgique: Vᵛᵉ MURAILLE, 199. This is the
fourth edition of the work, with Gounod's recitatives for the 1869 production at the Opéra (pl. A.C. 664)
and would be typical of the period at which *Le fantôme de l'Opéra* was set, and indeed at which it was
published.

[37] "Catherine que j'adore / Pourquoi refuser / L'amant qui vous implore / Un si doux baiser?"
(FAUST / Opéra en cinq Actes, 201; Leroux, *Le fantôme de l'Opéra*, 84).

[38] "Rien....En vain j'interroge en une ardente veille / La Nature et le Créateur. / Pas une voix ne
glisse à mon oreille / Un mot consolateur" (ibid., 142; FAUST / Opéra en cinq Actes, 5).

[39] "Et toi, est-ce qu'une voix a déjà glissé un mot "DANS"'ton oreille?" (ibid., 143).

TABLE 2.2: Mapping of acts 1–3 of Gounod, *Faust* onto the *scène de la salle maudite*, Le *fantôme de l'Opéra*

Faust: acts 1–3	Scène de la salle maudite, Le fantôme de l'Opéra
Act 1, no. 1 (5) [Opening lines of opera] Rien…En vain j'interroge en une ardente veille La Nature et le Créateur. Pas une voix ne glisse à mon oreille Un mot consolateur	Richard addresses Moncharmin and asks him "Et toi, est-ce qu'une voix a déjà glissé un mot à ton oreille?"
Act 2, no. 3 (29) [Chorus] Vin ou bière, Bière ou vin Que mon verre Soit plein!	After the *régisseur* has announced the presence of a cabal mounted by Chritine Daaé's supporters, "Mais le rideau se levait sur la Kermesse et le directeur fit signe au régisseur de se retirer"
Act 2, no. 4 (48) [Siebel] [Plus d'un ami fidèle Saura te remplacer à ses côtés!]	Siebel [Daaé] enters. "Cette ovation indiscrète eût été, du reste, d'une maladresse insigne. Elle ne se produisit pas"
Act 2, no. 6 (77–78) [Marguerite] Non messieurs, je ne suis demoiselle ni belle, Et je n'ai pas besoin qu'on me donne la main	Marguerite [Carlotta] enters. "des bravos éclatants accueillirent la Carlotta. C'était si imprévu et si inutile que ceux qui n'étaient au courant de rien se regardaient en se demandant ce qui se passait, et l'acte encore s'acheva sans aucun incident"
Act 3, no. 7 (89–90) [Siebel] Faites-lui mes aveux, Portez mes vœux	Richard and Moncharmin return to the box after the entracte and find a box of *bonbons anglais* and. after leaving to inquire, return to find a lorgnette now next to the box. Siebel [Daaé] enters but sings badly
Continuation (93) C'est en vous que j'ai foi, Parlez pour moi	Raoul, vicomte de Chagny, sits weeping with his head in his hands
Continuation (94) Que la fleur sur sa bouche Sache au moins déposer Un doux baiser	Raoul remembers Christine's letter telling him never to see her again, and continues to weep
Act 3, no. 9 (104) [Chanson du Roi de Thulé]	"Un tonnerre d'applaudissements…C'est la Carlotta qui fait son entrée"
Continuation (107)	"Quand Marguerite eur fini de chanter l'air du Roi de Thulé, elle fut acclamée"
Continuation (117) [Air de bijoux]	"elle le fut encore quand elle eut terminé l'air des bijoux"
Act 3, no. 11 (138–140) [Faust]: Laisse-moi, laisse-moi contempler ton visage Sous la pâle clarté Don't l'astre de la nuit, comem dans un nuage, Caresse ta beauté [Marguerite]: O silence! O bonheur! ineffable mystère! Enivrante langueur! J'écoute!…Et je comprends cette voix solitaire Qui chante dans mon cœur!	The lengthy description of Carlotta's *crapaud* and eventually the fall of the chandelier

and repeats, are "And I understand this solitary voice / Which sings in my heart!"[40] and the exactitude of the use of the words "La voix" is made clear only toward the end of the novel, when Erik explains that he ventriloquized Carlotta to make her sound like she had failed: so when she sings the lines, they have a terrible irony to them.[41] More straightforwardly, as Erik speaks invisibly—and again ironically—to the directors he says "She [Carlotta] is singing tonight so as to unhook the chandelier,"[42] a figurative expression that—without any irony—would mean that she had sung well, but that in the current context triggers the entirely nonfigurative *decrochement* of the chandelier, with the fatal consequences outlined at the very end of the chapter.[43]

During the second act, both Marguerite (sung by La Carlotta) and Siebel (sung by Christine) make their appearances for the first time. Between the first and second acts, the directors are made aware of cabals on behalf of both artists, but are unable to neutralize them. Cleverly, Christine's supporters refrain from acknowledging her first appearance when she sings "Plus d'un ami fidèle" in the second act,[44] which throws into relief the absurdity of the "shattering bravos" that greet Carlotta's appearance in the *Kermesse* scene. It is all the more absurd because of the incidental, almost passing, nature of this first appearance.[45]

During the waltz, toward the end of the act, Marguerite crosses the stage, Faust approaches her and offers his arm, and Marguerite politely refuses and leaves the stage. The moment is renowned for its understatement, and as Leroux comments, the ovation "was so unexpected and so without purpose that those who were not *au courant* with anything looked at each other wondering what was going on."[46]

Act 2 opens with Siebel's flower song "Faites-lui mes aveux / Portez mes vœux." The first two lines are quoted verbatim by Leroux, and as Christine sings them she looks up at Raoul's box, and from then on "it seemed to all that her voice was less assured, less pure, less crystalline than normal. Something unknown muted, freighted down, her singing....There was underneath trembling and fear."[47] The function of this part of the citation is similar to those of the entries of the two sopranos just discussed. But the two further extracts from Siebel's flower song (given in table 2.2) serve little more than milestones marking the passage of the

---

[40] "Et je comprends cette voix solitaire / Qui chante dans mon cœur!" (ibid., 150; FAUST / Opéra en cinq Actes, 139–140).

[41] Ibid., 429–430.

[42] "Elle [Carlotta] chante ce soir à décrocher le lustre" (ibid., 156).

[43] Ibid., 156–157.

[44] Ibid., 146; FAUST / Opéra en cinq Actes, 48. Siebel's first appearance, like Marguerite's, is almost incidental just before the drinking song "Buvons, Trinquons."

[45] Ibid., 77–78 (Leroux, *Le fantôme de l'Opéra*, 146).

[46] "C'était si imprévu et si inutile que ceux qui n'étaient au courant de rien se regardaient en se demandant ce qui se passait" (ibid.).

[47] "Il sembla à tous que sa voix était moins assurée, moins pure, moins cristalline qu'à l'ordinaire. Quelque chose qu'on ne savait pas, assourdissait, alourdissait son chant....Il y avait, là-dessous, du tremblement et de la crainte" (ibid., 147; FAUST / Opéra en cinq Actes, 90).

opera, as Leroux describes Raoul in his box sobbing (again) as he mulls over the note he has received from Christine telling him never to attempt to contact her. Similarly, the opening of act 2 is signaled by verbatim quotation simply in order to mark the end of the discussion of the two sopranos' cabals.

Immediately after the citation of Christine's dismissive letter to Raoul ("There are things in my life. There are things in your life. Your little Christine"),[48] Leroux savagely interrupts Raoul's reverie with "A thunder of applause....Carlotta makes her entrance."[49] Again, Leroux marks the progress of the third act, noting her performance—this time only mentioning titles of numbers—of the *Chanson du Roi de Thulé* and *Air de bijoux* until she reaches the duet with Faust, and Carlotta's collapse and the subsequent elision of the text of the duet with her inability to sing.

Using a number of types of relationship between citation of the libretto and the action of the novel, Leroux sets up a performance of the first three acts of the opera alongside descriptions of action on stage, in the *parterre* as Carlotta's and Christine's supporters manage their enthusiasm, in the now notorious Box no. 5, and in the box shared by the Comte and Vicomte de Chagny. Novelistic time naturally does not match the dramatic time of the opera until the moment of Carlotta's collapse, where from the second she first hesitates on the words "Qui chante dans mon cœur" until the fall of the chandelier, the musical and literary action unfolds in excruciating real time, as she "threw her eyes around her as if to look for a refuge, a protection or rather the spontaneous assurance of her voice's innocence," and then attempts the phrase again with the same catastrophic results.[50]

Mozart-Erik

When Erik adopts the role of Otello as he sings the final duet from Rossini's opera with Christine, he comes close to the normal practice of music: he takes a male role, and whatever the significance of analogies between Erik and the figure of Otello (and they are important), he sings the music largely as Rossini intended it. But this is something of a rarity. In most of his performances, there is something perverse, something unusual: he inhabits the musical bodies of other musicians. The intriguing case of Erik the gondolier and the missing *canzone del gondoliero* already shows Erik appropriating the singing voice of the gondolier, and in her description of his performance of the Willow Song, Christine goes as far as equating him with Orpheus. But the person whose musical body he occupies as he sings the Willow Song is none other than Christine herself. And exactly the same

---

[48] "Il y va de ma vie. Il y a va de la vôtre. Votre petite Christine" (Leroux, *Le fantôme de l'Opéra*, 149).

[49] "Un tonnerre d'applaudissements....C'est la Carlotta qui fait son entrée" (ibid.).

[50] "Elle jeta, éperdue, les yeux autour d'elle comme pour chercher un refuge, une protection, ou plutôt l'assurance spontanée de l'innocence de sa voix" (ibid., 153).

physical colonization takes place as Erik sings Christine's music from the closing duet in *Roméo et Juliette.*

But the most striking, and most sustained, inhabitation of another musician is the way Erik occupies Mozart. The structure of *Le fantôme de l'Opéra* largely silences reference to Mozart in the first half of the novel, only to elevate the composer to the principal point of musical reference in the second. Indeed, the only two references to Mozart in the first thirteen chapters seem entirely accidental, although their effect is to keep the composer in play, as it were, until the change at midpoint. So in the wake of the success of Christine's gala concert, Leroux has the (presumably fictional) critic who signs himself with the letters "X. Y. Z." review her performance at the Comtesse de Zurich's salon: "When she is heard in Hamlet, one asks if Shakespeare has come down from the Elysian Fields to have her rehearse Ophelia.... It is true that, when she puts on the starry diadem of the Queen of the Night, Mozart, for his part, ought to leave eternal dwellings in order to hear her."[51]

Die Zauberflöte appears here, almost incidentally, alongside *Hamlet.* And again, as Carlotta, collapsed on the stage of the Palais Garnier, is unable to sing, the audience's nostalgia for her moments of triumph turns for a second to Mozart:

> Her strident top Fs, her incredible staccatos in *Die Zauberflöte*, could not be forgotten. One remembered *Don Giovanni*, in which she was Elvira and in which she pulled off the most resounding triumph, one night, singing herself the top B♭ that her friend Donna Anna could not.[52]

The references are clearly overshadowed by the enormity of the events on stage, but Leroux deploys Christine's *diadème d'étoiles* in the Queen of the Night's aria and Carlotta's staccatos and top Fs in the same aria from *Die Zauberflöte* to generate a continuity between the two artists and the two fragmentary Mozartian asides. More important, here, as Leroux has his audience remember Carlotta's act of musical bravado in singing Donna Elvira's top B-flats he brings in a work that will be key for the rest of the novel: *Don Giovanni.*

Erik inhabits Mozart via three works: the *Requiem,* K. 626, the Mass in c minor, K. 427, and *Don Giovanni,* K. 527. Allusions in the second half of *Le fantôme de l'Opéra* are to a *messe des morts,* a *messe de mariage,* and an opera *Don*

---

[51] "Quand on l'entend dans *Hamlet,* on se demande si Shakespeare est venu des Champs-Élysées lui faire répéter *Ophélie....* Il est vrai que, quand elle ceint le diadème d'étoiles de la reine de la nuit, Mozart, de son côté, doit quitter les demeures éternelles pour venir l'entendre" (ibid., 93). *Hamlet* is most likely the opera by Ambroise Thomas, premiered in 1868 and very much still in vogue in 1880. The play on words between "The Elysian Fields" and the "Champs-Elysées" hardly bears comment.

[52] "On ne pouvait avoir oublié ses *contre-fa* stridents, ses *staccati* inouïs dans *La flûte enchantée.* On se souvenait de *Don Juan,* où elle était Elvire et où elle remporta le plus retentissant triomphe, certain soir, en donnant elle-même le *si* bémol que ne pouvait donner sa camarade dona Anna" (ibid., 152–153). The most likely place in the score for this moment to have taken place is the adagio section of the act 1 finale at the words "Protegga il giusto cielo" / "Vendichi il giusto cielo" (bars 259–269).

Juan triomphant, all of which are composed by Erik himself. Mozart is never mentioned by name in any of these allusions, in exactly the same way he is never mentioned in much informal writing on music in French of the period: there is no question of the *Requiem* or the *messe des morts* being by any other composer, nor of any sort of *Don Juan* being by anyone else; even commentaries on Molière have to explain that it is not a question of *Don Giovanni*. In the same way, but earlier in the nineteenth century, "les symphonies" referred exclusively to Beethoven's nine symphonies, for example, without mention of the name of the composer. By projecting Erik as the composer of a requiem, a marriage mass, and an opera on the Don Juan legend, Leroux was pointing to an analogy with a single composer: Mozart.

By 1880, Mozart's *Requiem* was an important part of European musical and ritual life. Known as the *Requiem-Streit*, the public disagreements about its authorship and completion—which continue to this day—had added a controversial veneer to a work whose origins were already well enough known and endlessly replicated in print. The work was already known in French through Alexandre Oulibicheff's biography of the composer that had been published in 1843.[53] By the time Leroux came to write *Le fantôme de l'Opéra*, the story had enjoyed legendary status for over a century. The work had also made a significant impact in performance, especially at funerals of musicians and others. Best known are performances at the funerals of Alexandre-Étienne Choron in 1834 and of Frédéric Chopin in 1849, but the work also figured at the funeral of Cardinal François-Nicolas-Madeleine Morlot, bishop of Paris, in 1863.[54] But there were other performances, notably at the Princesse de Belgioioso's salon in 1839 and 1840 and public performances in the 1860s.

The *messe de mariage* has a different pedigree. Unknown before André's publication in 1840, it had very little currency in France in the nineteenth century, and was a relative newcomer to those parts of the Mozart canon known in Paris when Leroux wrote *Le fantôme de l'Opéra*.[55] What is now known about the composition of K. 427 still admits its interpretation as a *messe de mariage*, although modern musical scholarship might take a slightly more circumspect approach than Leroux. From Mozart's own correspondence and from his sister's diary, it is known that Mozart wrote to his father on 4 January 1783 as follows:

---

[53] Alexandre Oulibicheff, *Nouvelle biographie de Mozart suivie d'un aperçu sur l'histoire générale de la musique et de l'analyse des principales œuvres de Mozart* (Moscow: n.p., 1843; reprint, with an introduction by Jean-Victor Hocquard, Paris: Séguier, 1991), 723–728.

[54] Félix Bonafe and André Schuh, *Le cardinal Morlot* (Paris: Orbec, 1983).

[55] André's edition is *Missa* / aux C moll / von / W. A. MOZART / Partitur / *Nach der* / hinterlassenen Original = Handschrift herausgegeben / und / *mit einem* VORBERICHT *begleitet* / *von* / A. André. / *Eigenthum des Verlegens und eingetragen in das Vereins-Archiv* / Offenbach ª/ₘ, bei Johann André. Nothing, however, in the *Vorbericht* relates to the circumstances of composition, as it focuses exclusively on the description of the manuscript on which the edition was based.

It is quite true about my moral obligation and indeed I let the word flow from my pen on purpose. I made the promise in my heart of hearts and hope to be able to keep it. When I made it, my wife was not yet married; yet, as I was absolutely determined to marry her after her recovery, it was easy for me to make it—but, as you yourself are aware, time and other circumstances made our journey impossible. The score of half of a mass, which is still lying here waiting to be finished, is the best proof that I really made the promise.[56]

The promise to which Mozart makes reference is to bring his wife to Salzburg to meet his father. That he was wrapping up a musical composition with this promise—half a mass well describes K. 427—is clear from the letter.[57] And Mozart kept his side of the bargain. He traveled with Constanze later in 1783, and K. 427 was rehearsed in the *Kapelhaus* in Salzburg on 23 October and performed, presumably with the incomplete sections filled out with other compositions, in St. Peter's Church on 26 October.[58] Whether Mozart had written the work before leaving Vienna or during his stay in Salzburg was not clear even to Constanze when she wrote to André in 1800—and she had, according to Mozart's sister, taken part in the 26 October performance.[59]

Whether these details are sufficient for the confident assertion that "Mozart composed K427... as part of a promise to his new bride, Constanze" is not entirely certain,[60] but the work figures in professionally considered French writing on Mozart before 1900. Although there is nothing in Fétis's *Biographie universelle des musiciens* or Wilder's 1880 biography, Oulibicheff related the story more or less as it is known today:

The joy of seeing his father again, after a separation of more than two years, did not make Mozart forget the vow that he found himself obliged to honour.

---

[56] "Wegen der Moral hat es ganz seine Richtigkeit; es ist mir nicht ohne Vorsatz aus meiner feder geflossen—ich habe es in meinem herzen wirklich versprochen, und hoffe es auch wirklich zu halten.—meine Frau war als ich es versprach, noch ledig—da ich aber fest entschlossen war sie bald nach ihrer Genesung zu heyrathen, so konnte ich es leicht versprechen—zeit und umstände aber vereitelten unsere Reise, wie sie selbst wissen;—zum beweis aber der Wirklichkeit meines versprechen kann die spart von der hälfte einer Messe dienen, welche noch in der besten Hoffnung da liegt." Wilhelm A. Bauer and Otto Erich Deutsch, eds., *Mozart: Briefe und Aufzeichnungen Gesamtausgabe*, 6 vols. (Kassel: Bärenreiter, 1962–71), 3:247–248; trans. from Emily Anderson, ed., *The Letters of Mozart and His Family*, 3rd ed. (London and New York: Macmillan, 1985), 834.

[57] The autograph of the Mass in c minor consists of the Kyrie, Gloria, Sanctus, and Benedictus complete, and the first part of the Credo with figured bass only. See Monika Holl and Karl-Heinz Köhler, eds., *Wolfgang Amadeus Mozart: Messe c-moll KV 427 (417a): Faksimile der autgraphen Partitur*, Documenta musicologica 2:9 (Kassel: Bärenreiter, 1983); Holl and Köhler, eds., *17. Missa in c KV 427 (417ᵃ)*, Neue Ausgabe sämtlicher Werke I/1/5 (Kassel: Bärenreiter, 1983).

[58] Bauer and Deutsch, *Mozart: Briefe*, 3:290.

[59] Ibid., 4:356.

[60] Bruce MacIntyre, "Mass," in *The Cambridge Mozart Encyclopedia*, ed. Cliff Eisen and Simon P. Keefe (Cambridge: Cambridge University Press, 2006), 278.

The mass *ex-voto* had already been begun in Vienna; it was finished in Salzburg and performed in St-Peter's Church.[61]

The same story surrounding the composition of K. 427 was well enshrined in a work published just after Leroux's novel, Henri de Curzon's *Mozart*, in the series "Les Maîtres de la musique" (1914). Curzon wrote:

> Mozart had vowed, if it was one day possible to present Constanza to his father as his wife, to have performed at Salzburg a new mass of his composition. He had thus set to work, and written the Kyrie, Gloria, Sanctus and Benedictus. Completed certainly with the help of older masses, the whole thing was performed on 25 August [*sic*] in St-Peter's church, Constanza sang herself the soprano part.[62]

With a text such as this, it is clear that K. 427 was well known to Parisian musical circles around 1900, and the summary title *messe de mariage* was an easy one to give the work. Both Curzon and Leroux were certainly alerted to the existence of K. 427 and the mythology surrounding it, in addition to the long-standing knowledge of the work thanks to Oulibicheff's widely read biography, by the work undertaken by Alois Schmitt and Ernst Lewicki in the years before the publication of *Le fantôme de l'Opéra*.[63] Schmitt's publication of the work in the Breitkopf edition in 1901 and an important commentary by Lewicki published five years later put K. 427 on the map in a way it had not previously enjoyed.[64] The stage was set for Erik's *messe de mariage*.

Don Giovanni, or *l'opéra des opéras*, as French critics loosely translated Hoffmann's descriptor, was a key work in the history of French nineteenth-century stage music, and given its importance elsewhere in this book needs little introduction here.[65] Never really off the boards at the Théâtre Italien after its 1811 Paris

---

[61] "La joie de revoir son vieux père, après une séparation de plus de deux ans, ne fit pas oublier à Mozart le vœu qu'il se trouvait dans le cas de remplir. La messe *ex-voto* avait déjà été commencée à Vienne; elle fut terminée à Salzbourg et exécutée dans l'église de Saint-Pierre" (Oulibicheff, *Novelle biographie de Mozart*, 141).

[62] "Mozart avait fait vœu, s'il obtenait un jour de présenter Constance à son père comme sa femme, de faire exécuter à Salzbourg une nouvelle messe de sa composition. Il s'était même probablement mis aussitôt au travail, et écrivit ainsi le Kyrie, le Gloria, le Sanctus et le Benedictus. Complété sans doute à l'aide de messes plus anciennes, l'ensemble fut exécuté le 25 août en l'église Saint-Pierre, Constance chantant elle-même la partie de soprano"; Henri de Curzon, *Mozart*, Les maîtres de la musique (Paris: Alcan, 1914), 181.

[63] Georg Alois Schmitt, ed., *Grosse Messe in C moll…-Werk 427–Nach Mozartschen Vorlagen vervollständigt von A. Schmitt*, Wolfgang Amadeus Mozart's Werke: Kritische durchgesehene Gesamtausgabe 24:29 (Leipzig: Breitkopf und Härtel, 1901).

[64] Ernst Lewicki, "Die vervollständigung von Mozarts grosser c-moll Messe durch Alois Schmitt in ihrem Werdegang nach authentischen Quellen dargestellt," *Die Musik* (January-February 1906), 3–12 and 168–175.

[65] "L'opéra des operas" (which does not quite translate Hoffmann perfectly) is found in, among many others, reviews by Bénédict Jouvin, *Le Figaro*, 5 April 1866 (where he alludes directly to Hoffmann), and by Ange-Henri Blaze (Blaze de Bury writing as F. de Lagenvais), *Revue des deux mondes*, 15 May 1866.

premiere,[66] it had been premiered at the Opéra in 1805 with limited success;[67] but the 1834 production had a longevity almost without precedent. It figured regularly at the Opéra until 1845 and then again—largely the same version—from 1866 until the end of the century and beyond.[68]

Erik-Mozart

By 1908, the idea of an opera based on the Don Juan myth was so firmly associated with Mozart that when Leroux titled Erik's opera *Don Juan triomphant*, he barely had any need of the discourse on Mozart's opera that immediately follows the scene in which Christine has her first sight of the opera's score (which in the novel she narrates to Raoul), and in which Erik makes clear that his opera is not like Mozart's. *Don Juan triomphant* is Christine's first inkling that Erik is also a composer. "'Yes,' he says, 'I sometimes compose. It is twenty years since I began this work. When it is finished, I shall take it with me into this coffin and I shall not wake up again.'"[69] As will be seen, this anticipated outcome changes by the end of the novel, but at the moment Christine discovers the score of *Don Juan triomphant*, her suggestion that Erik might play something from it is met with a commentary on the difference between Mozart's opera and his own:

> "Never ask me that," he replied in a sombre voice. "That Don Juan was not written to words by a Lorenzo Da Ponte, inspired by wine, flirtation and vice, finally punished by God. I shall play you Mozart if you wish, that will make your beautiful tears run, and inspire honest reflection. But my own Don Juan burns, Christine, and yet he is not at all struck by the fire of heaven."[70]

While Mozart would make Christine cry and inspire "honest reflection," Erik's opera is inspired, so it seems, by Hell itself.

This is the last scene in which any music other than Mozart figures in the novel—the duet from *Othello* that results in Erik's unmasking. And immediately after the unmasking, Leroux returns to *Don Giovanni*. With Christine still knocked

---

[66] Soubies, *Le Théâtre-Italien de 1801 à 1913*.

[67] Laurent Marty, *1805: La création de "Don Juan" à l'Opéra de Paris*, Univers musical (Paris: L'Harmattan, 2005).

[68] Soubies, *Soixante-sept ans à l'Opéra*. The 1866 productions are discussed in chapter 4 and the 1887 centenary production at the Opéra in chapter 6.

[69] "Oui, me dit-il, je compose quelquefois. Voilà vingt ans que j'ai commencé ce travail. Quand il sera fini, je l'emporterai avec moi dans ce cercueil et je ne me réveillerai plus" (Leroux, *Le fantôme de l'Opéra*, 250).

[70] "Ne me demandez jamais cela, répondit-il d'une voix sombre. Ce Don Juan-là n'a pas été écrit sur les paroles d'un Lorenzo d'Aponte, inspiré par le vin, les petites amours et le vice, finalement châtié de Dieu. Je vous jouerai Mozart si vous voulez, qui fera couler vos belles larmes et vous inspirera d'honnêtes réflexions. Mais, mon Don Juan, à moi, brûle, Christine, et, cependant, il n'est point foudroyé par le feu du ciel" (ibid.).

sideways by the appearance of Erik's unmasked face, he taunts her with the hideousness of his appearance. After the direct demand that she "Look at Erik's face, Now you know the face of the Voice," "Feast your eyes, gorge your soul on my cursed ugliness," Erik turns to irony:

> Are you satisfied? Am I not handsome? When a woman has seen me, like you, she is mine. She loves me for ever! I myself am a person in the style of Don Juan.... Look at me! *I am Don Juan triomphant!*[71]

And Erik drags Christine to him by her hair, at which point Raoul, who has been listening to Christine's narrative, insists that she stop.

Don Juan triomphant is then associated with one of the key turns in the novel, when Christine, having described Erik to Raoul as a monster, a reptile, hears Erik playing *Don Juan triomphant* on the organ and begins to understand what he meant when he talked about his opera; she explains that "his *Don Juan triomphant* (since there was no doubt in my mind that he had thrown himself into his masterpiece in order to forget the horror of the immediate minute), his *Don Juan triomphant* first appeared to me as a long, frightful and magnificent sob in which poor Erik had put all his cursed misery."[72] It is a moot point, at this stage in the chapter, whether these sentiments are real, or part of Christine's deception. Certainly, the parts of her narrative that close the chapter, as she tries to convince Erik of her loyalty, are duplicitous, but the rhetoric surrounding her judgement on the intention behind *Don Juan triomphant* gives the impression of sincerity.

During the course of her account of her time in Erik's underground home, given to Raoul under the statue of Apollo on the roof of the Palais Garnier, Christine describes the tour of Erik's apartment. When he shows her his bedroom, she is struck by the presence on the black curtains that adorn the walls of an enormous stave of music with the repeated notes of the Dies Irae; this is the sequence from the proper liturgy of the Mass for the Dead, and the second movement of many polyphonic requiems. This sets up the focus on the *Messe des morts* and its antonym, the *Messe de mariage* that characterizes the Persian's narrative, and the other most important musical episodes in the second half of the novel.[73]

The Persian, unlike any of the other characters in the novel, knew Erik well before the events described by Leroux. He appears at several points throughout the novel in ways that leave his identification mysterious to all; in the second half of

---

[71] " 'Regarde le visage d'Érik Maintenant, tu connais le visage de La Voix'; 'Repais tes yeux, soûle ton âme de ma laideur maudite!' 'Es-tu satisfaite? Je suis beau, hein?... Quand une femme m'a vu, comme toi, elle est à moi. Elle m'aime pour toujours! Moi, je suis un type dans le genre de Don Juan.... Regarde-moi! Je suis *Don Juan triomphant!* " (ibid., 254).

[72] "Son *Don Juan triomphant* (car il ne faisait point de doute pour moi qu'il ne se fût rué à son chef d'œuvre pour oublier l'horreur de la minute présente), son *Don Juan triomphant* ne me parut d'abord qu'un long, affreux et magnifique sanglot où le pauvre Érik avait mis toute sa misère maudite" (ibid., 258).

[73] Ibid., 249.

the novel, however, he accompanies Raoul into the subterranean parts of the Palais Garnier, and shares his adventures there. In chapter 22, the Persian summarizes his attempts to gain access to Erik's underground apartments, and his exchanges with him. As the Persian makes this speech, Erik's Mozartian composition projects are revealed both to the Persian and to Leroux's readers.

After demonstrating his abilities to move around underground and under water to the Persian (whom he calls Daroga), Erik makes clear that the Persian should never attempt to go there on his own: "Daroga, go and dry yourself, if you do not want to catch a head cold! And don't ever get into my boat...and especially do not try to enter my house...I am always there...Daroga! And I would be pained to dedicate *my Messe des Morts* to you!" (emphasis added).[74] Erik's death threat is neatly encapsulated in the idea of dedicating his *Requiem* to the Persian, and having made the threat Erik moves on to other subjects. Although uncertain from the context, it seems likely—given the reference to dedication—that Erik's *Requiem* is at this point complete.

Similarly, when the Persian shortly afterward declares that it is Erik's obligation to allow Christine to leave, he replies:

"My obligation, immense novice! (*verbatim*). It is my choice...my choice to let her leave, and she will return...because she loves me! All that, I tell you, will finish with a marriage...a marriage at the Madeleine, immense novice (*verbatim*). Do you finally believe me? When I say that my *messe de mariage* is already written....You will see this 'Kyrie.'" He tapped his fingers on the wood of the boat, in a sort of rhythm that he accompanied half singing: 'Kyrie!...Kyrie!...Kyrie Eleison![75]

This is the first mention of a *messe de mariage*, and it is clear—as in the case of the *Requiem*—that this is a composition of Erik himself, and that to the extent that he is capable of singing the "Kyrie," it is also complete. He also—just like Mozart—has a clear occasion for its use: his own marriage, in the Madeleine, to Christine Daaé.

Finally, the Persian's narrative brings in the third Mozartian element: *Don Juan triomphant*. After waiting for several days behind the abandoned set for *Le Roi de Lahore* in the third basement, the Persian finally opens the door and hears Erik in the act of composing—or working on, as the Persian has it—*Don Juan triomphant*, complete with the obligatory moments of breaking off and walking around the

---

[74] "Daroga, va te sécher, si tu ne veux pas attraper un rhume de cerveau!...et ne remonte jamais dans ma barque...et surtout n'essaie pas d'entrer dans ma maison...je ne suis pas toujours là....Daroga! Et j'aurais du chagrin à te dédier *ma Messe des morts!*" (ibid., 389).

[75] "Mon devoir, immense niais!—(textuel).—C'est ma volonté...ma volonté de la laisser partir, et elle reviendra...car elle m'aime!...Tout cela, je te dis, finira par un mariage...un mariage à la Madeleine, immense niais! (textuel). Me crois-tu, à la fin? Quand je te dis que ma messe de mariage est déjà écrite...tu verras ce Kyrie...' Il tapota encore ses talons sur le bois de la barque, dans une espèce de rythme qu'il accompagnait à mi-voix en chantant: 'Kyrie!...Kyrie!...Kyrie Eleison!'" (ibid., 395–396).

apartment, and of the manic words "It must be finished *before*! Certainly finished!"[76] "Before what?" is a question that is left unresolved in the Persian's narrative, but its emphasis certainly leaves open the possibility of ultimate catastrophe.

With Raoul and the Persian in the *Chambre des supplices*, Leroux has the opportunity not only to have them overhear Erik and Christine in the adjacent room, an exchange that makes allusion to Mozart, but also—once Erik has left—to have them conduct a conversation, largely related to the mechanics of escape, that repeats exactly the same allusion to the composer. What Raoul and the Persian overhear first are the words "It is to be accepted or rejected! The *messe de mariage* or the *messe des morts*."[77] And once the two have realized that they can overhear conversations in Erik's apartment without his knowing, they hear his gloss on these words:

> The *messe des morts*, there is no happiness there! continued Erik's voice, although the *messe de mariage*, that really is magnificent! You need to make your mind up and know what you want! I myself find it impossible to live like that, below ground, in a hole, like a mole![78]

In these declarations, Erik's two compositions, the marriage mass and the requiem mass, shadowed by the two Mozart works—the c minor Mass K. 427 and the *Requiem* K. 626, are brought into alignment for the first time, and this is followed immediately by the association of *Don Juan triomphant* with the two masses as Erik says "*Don Juan triomphant* is complete; now I wish to live like the rest of the world."[79] Here, for the first and only time in the novel, are all three Mozart works brought into play for dramatic purposes. The completion of *Don Juan triomphant* signals the end of Erik's underground existence, and the two masses represent the choice Christine has to make. Raoul and the Persian have already overheard Erik's presentation of Christine's choice (cited above), but four pages later, as Christine speaks though the wall to her two would-be saviors, she explains how she has to choose "between the *messe de mariage* and the *messe des morts!*"[80]

Epilogue

Among the wide range of musical references in *Le fantôme de l'Opéra* are many where the Phantom, Erik, inhabits the personae of other musicians. Of these, the most striking is that of Mozart, whose Mass in c minor, *Requiem,* and *Don*

---

[76] "Il faut que tout cela soit fini *avant*! Bien fini!" (ibid., 399).

[77] "C'est à prendre ou à laisser! La *messe de mariage* ou la *messe des morts*" (ibid., 410).

[78] "La messe des morts, ce n'est point gai! reprit la voix d'Érik, tandis que la messe de mariage, parlez-moi de cela! c'est magnifique! Il faut prendre une résolution et savoir ce que l'on veut! Moi, il m'est impossible de continuer à vivre comme ça, au fond de la terre, dans un trou, comme une taupe!" (ibid.).

[79] "*Don Juan triomphant* est terminé, maintenant je veux vivre comme tout le monde" (ibid., 411).

[80] "Entre la messe de mariage et la messe des morts!" (ibid., 414).

Giovanni are reattributed to Erik in the guise of his *messe de mariage, messe des morts,* and *Don Juan triomphant.* But in the immense exposure that Leroux's novel has received as it exchanges media for silent film, talking picture, ballet, megamusical both on stage and screen, the Mozartian element has almost completely disappeared. Tracing this disappearance is an important codicil to Erik's testament in Leroux's novel.[81]

Perhaps even better known than Leroux's novel, Carl Laemmle's silent film *The Phantom of the Opera* was first screened in 1925 and starred Lon Chaney and Mary Philbin. Despite the enormous amount of ink spilt on the film—and its musical implications—little interest has been shown in the music that accompanied it.[82] This is largely because of the severe difficulty with its surviving sources. The oldest document to survive is a Universal cue sheet dated 12 November 1929 that accompanied a partially talking version of the 1925 silent from 1929. This is an immensely problematic source to analyze, and clearly has nothing necessarily to do with the music envisaged for the 1925 silent film.[83] Nevertheless, taken together with the visual material that can be securely linked to 1925, the 1925 pressbook, and the "5th Revised Shooting Script," permit some comments to be made about the music that was used, and the position Mozart holds in the film.[84]

Working purely visually, and supported by the pressbook and the "5th Revised Shooting Script," it is clear that the sections in Leroux's novel dedicated to Gounod's *Faust* triggered the large-scale diagetic episodes in the 1925 film. Indeed, with the exception of the scenes based around the abandoned set for *Le Roi de Lahore,*[85] all sources agree on the exclusive use of Gounod's *Faust*; reference to the composer's *Roméo et Juliette* is omitted, as is any mention of the other works analyzed at the beginning of this chapter.[86] As might be expected, as a five-hundred-page novel is

---

[81] See, for the cinematographic tradition, Isabelle Casta-Husson, "Les fortunes paraculturelles du *Fantôme de l'Opéra,*" in *De l'écrit à l'écran: Littératures populaires—mutations génériques, mutations médiatiques,* ed. Jacques Migozzi (Limoges: Presses Universitaires de Limoges, 2000), 695–704, and for the later tradition, Casta-Husson, *Le travail de l'obscure clarté' dans "Le fantôme de l'Opéra."* Archives des lettres modernes 268 (Paris: Lettres Modernes, 1997), 75.

[82] Scott MacQueen, "The 1926 Phantom of the Opera," *American Cinematographer* 70/9 (September 1989), 34–40; MacQueen, "Phantom of the Opera," *American Cinematographer* 70/10 (October 1989), 34–40.

[83] "List of the Compositions Recorded in Connection with the Photoplay entitled THE PHANTOM OF THE OPERA / Production no. 5019, Erpi no. 1-Uwc-17," n.d., American Society of Composers, Authors and Publishers.

[84] The pressbook is PUBLICITY SECTION / 2nd edition / CARL LAEMMLE / presents / The / Phantom of the Opera / . . . / A UNIVERSAL Production; facsimile in Philip J. Riley, *The Making of "The Phantom of the Opera,"* Classic Silents series 1 (Absecon, N.J.: MagicImage Filmbooks, 1999), 211–254. The "5th Revised Shooting Script," facsimile in ibid., 80–175, under the heading "THE PHANTOM OF THE OPERA" / BY / GASTON LEROUX / ADAPTATION AND SCENARIO / BY / RAYMOND L. SCHROCK / AND / ELLIOT CLAWSON, is in fact paginated from 1 to 173 (with pages in different formats), with the first seven pages unpaginated and page 98 duplicating page 97.

[85] "5th Revised Shooting Script," facsimile in ibid., 23.

[86] Ibid., [4], 30, and 36.

distilled into less than two hours of action, the musical range of Leroux's novel is signficantly restricted.

But two traces of the importance of Mozart in the novel remain in the 1925 "5th Shooting Script," one of which is retained in the film as it found its way into the commercial cinema. In approximately the same place in the film's narrative as in the novel, Erik describes unequivocally his complete "Marriage Mass":

> Erick [*sic*] now drops his sardonic mood which caused the last title. As he releases her he tells her:
> "COME, I WILL PLAY YOU OUR WEDDING MASS. YOU CAN TAKE MY WORD FOR IT! IT IS MAGNIFICENT."
>
> BACK: From this point, Erick seems to forget Christine's presence, so absorbed is he in his new purpose. Erick turns away from her toward the organ.[87]

The uppercase text—so designated to be rendered as a textual dialogue in the film itself—never appeared in the film, and so this Mozartian trace disappeared for ever as a result of the editorial cleansing that followed the shooting.

By contrast, the second Mozartian trace in the 1925 film significantly amplifies the impact of one of Erik's other works that owes a debt to Mozart: *Don Juan triomphant*. Only slightly earlier than the scene just described, Christine is in her room adjacent to Erik's music room:

> INT. ERICK'S MUSIC ROOM AMBER
>   Erick is sitting at the organ in half silhouette, playing the organ. There must be something weird and wild in the picture. Perhaps some of the objects surrounding this can lend to the effect.
>   INT. CHRISTINE'S BEDROOM...AMBER
>   Christine is calm, hypnotized by the powerful music she is hearing. She is marvelling at the genius of this man and is touched by his music.
>   IT WAS THE STRANGEST MOST BEAUTIFUL MUSIC SHE HAD EVER HEARD. IT WAS A SYMPHONY OF LOVE TRIUMPHANT
>   BACK: PRIZMA—Fascinated by the music. Christine opens the door and steps out into the drawing room.
>   INT. ERICK'S MUSIC ROOM PRIZMA
>   MED. CLOSE UP ERICK PLAYING THE ORGAN FROM HIS MANU-SCRIPT
>   Upon the organ side rack is another thick manuscript open. This is enti-tled "Don Juan Triumphant"....Christine enters back of Erick and stands spellbound.[88]

---

[87] Ibid., 147.
[88] Ibid., 97.

The script then turns to the unmasking of Erik, and the film follows its sequence with some precision, although the descriptive text ("IT WAS THE STRANGEST MOST BEAUTIFUL MUSIC") is replaced by two pieces of dialogue, both pronounced by Erik:

"SINCE FIRST I SAW YOUR FACE, THIS MUSIC HAS BEEN SINGING TO ME OF YOU AND OF—LOVE TRIUMPHANT!"

and

"YET LISTEN—THERE SOUNDS AN OMINOUS UNDERCURRENT OF WARNING!"[89]

However, the key visual element is the score, fully notated, on Erik's music stand, which gives the title of the work and its opening (ex. 2.3).

There is enough in this fragment to recognize a fully functioning score, with a piano (the *una corda* marking makes this clear) and transposing instrument in B-flat

EXAMPLE 2.3: *Transcription of Erik's autograph score of* Don Juan Triumphant

---

[89] Ibid.

(clarinet or trumpet), the key of D-flat with dynamics (*pianissimo*), and a tempo indication: "Andante sostenuto." It immediately distances itself from any organ music, although at first sight the three linked staves might be thought to be an organ score, and this might well have been the reason for this music's selection in the first place. What the music might turn out to be, if it is ever identified, is less important than the status of the document itself—Erik's manuscript. Christine's obsession with, and description of, the manuscript as "all messed up with red notes"[90]—even as "written in blood"[91]—evokes comparison with the fetishism of Pauline Viardot's real-life elevation of the manuscript of *Don Giovanni* to the status of a relic and the creation of its accompanying liturgy. Leroux was in Paris in 1892 when the formal handover of the *Don Giovanni* autograph took place (see chapter 6) and must have been aware of this particular tradition. Although there is no indication of any wish on Christine's part to possess the autograph of *Don Juan Triumphant* in the film, nor any ambitions toward *Don Juan triomphant* in Leroux's novel, there is more than a suggestion—a female opera singer in a complex triangular relationship—that Christine, Raoul, and Erik might just echo the similar relationship (whatever that might have been) between Pauline Viardot, her husband Louis, and Ivan Turgenev (also discussed in chapter 6). Hardly surprisingly, the 1925 film reduces the volume of all musical elements of Leroux's novel: that is the nature of the process of reworking the novel to a script and then shooting it, but the equal balance between Mozartian elements—the marriage mass, *Don Juan triomphant*—and other stage music (almost exclusively Gounod) is in the film commensurate with the original novel.

Critically, though, in the 1925 version and its various manifestations before 1930, Mozart is absent from the music that may be associated with the film. Gounod, however, is present both in the 1929 cue sheet and in the Hendricks and Winkler score, with extracts from *Faust* (the ballet, the prison scene, the Jewel Song, and the *Chanson du Roi de Thulé*, among others) figuring large.[92] But this is entirely in keeping with the status Mozart enjoyed in the first quarter of the twentieth century; there was no need for the music of *Don Giovanni* to figure in the film because reference to it was allusive: *Don Juan triomphant*, while still Erik's composition, constantly and ineluctably alludes to Mozart.

But such allusiveness had its risks, and by the 1943 remake, with voices and in Technicolor, not only is the diagetic music that had since the beginning been Gounod's *Faust* changed to Flotow's *Martha*, but any reference to Mozart is completely gone. The only exception concerns a shot of a poster for *Don Giovanni* with the word "Cancelled" superimposed, as the Opéra closes in the wake of Erik's threats.

---

[90] "Tout barbouillé de notes rouges" (Leroux, *Le fantôme de l'Opéra*, 250).

[91] "Écrite avec du sang" (ibid., 258).

[92] "List of the Compositions Recorded in Connection with the Photoplay entitled THE PHANTOM OF THE OPERA." See also the undated piano score PIANO / MUSIC SCORE / Compiled by / G. HINRICHS and M. WINKLER / Original Compositions (except Love Theme) by G. Hinrichs / for / PHANTOM OF THE OPERA / … / BELWIN INC. / NEW YORK, U.S.A.

Mozart and *L'impresario*

In terms of reputation at least, *Don Giovanni* rates as Mozart's most substantial opera. Whether *Der Schauspieldirektor* rates as the least substantial might be open to debate, but there is no doubt that it must come into the reckoning. And if *Don Giovanni* figures as a key element in chapter 2, its more slender fellow plays the same role in this chapter. Similar relationships are in play in the institutions involved as well: the opulence of the Palais Garnier in chapter 2 gives way to the Salle Lacaze and Salle Choiseul here.

Mozart's *Der Schauspieldirektor* has been a severely problematic work for over two hundred years.[1] Subject to a variety of modifications throughout the nineteenth and twentieth centuries, it took a form in mid-1850s Paris that placed it at the intersection of two key trajectories in nineteenth-century music history: the reception of Mozart's stage music and the birth of operetta. Jacques Offenbach found in his production of *Der Schauspieldirektor* as *L'impresario* in May 1856 a work that would give his Théâtre des Bouffes-Parisiens the authority of eighteenth-century classicism that would be so essential both for the cultural location of his company and for his personal artistic positioning.

When the curtain went down on *Der Schauspieldirektor* on 7 February 1786— as part of a double bill with Salieri's *Prima la musica e poi le parole*—Mozart might

---

[1] The work is edited as Gerhard Croll, ed., *Der Schauspieldirektor*, Neue Mozart-Ausgabe II/5/15 (Kassel: Bärenreiter, 1958; 2nd ed. 1990); the critical report to this edition is Elisabeth Föhrenbach, ed., *Der Schauspieldirektor: Kritische Berichte*, Neue Mozart-Ausgabe II/5/15 (Kassel.: Bärenreiter, 2001). Difficulties with the work reached their apogee when it was removed from the canon as defined by such a work as Gustav Kobbé's *Complete Opera Book* in its 10th edition in 1987; Gustav Kobbé, *Complete Opera Book*, 10th edn (London: Bodley Head, 1987). All previous editions up to the 9th had included an account of *Der Schauspieldirektor* that was clearly based on *Mozart und Schikaneder* (see below), a not unreasonable premise for a work that was originally published in 1922; (*Kobbe,, Complete Opera Book*, 9th ed. (London: Bodley Head, 1976), 90.)

well have thought that the future of the work was doubtful.[2] Although *Der Schauspieldirektor* was a work that dated from the same period as the two Mozart operas that made the greatest impact on the nineteenth century—*Le nozze di Figaro* and *Don Giovanni*—its construction made it almost impossible to remove it from its original celebratory and occasional context and to integrate it into the repertory of European music drama.[3] *Der Schauspieldirektor* consisted of an overture, most of the spoken play, and four musical numbers compressed at the very end of the drama, separated by very little spoken dialogue. Put simply, an overture, spoken dialogue, and four numbers only did not make what the world of stage music after 1786 considered an opera.

Two early attempts to turn Mozart's legacy into something that could take its place in the repertory followed conventional practices of the period around 1800, and amalgamated Mozart's music with the music of others. Given the subject matter of the original—the trials and tribulations of a theatrical manager—it was hardly surprising that no less a figure than Goethe should attempt to elide Mozart with the other most illustrious work on the subject, Cimarosa's *L'impresario in angustie*.[4] The result was *Das theatralischer Abenteuer*, which was premiered in Weimar in 1791 as part of Goethe's campaign to mount Italian and French opera in German.[5] A quarter century later, a further attempt was made for the 1816 carnival season in Vienna. This attempt, by Mathäus Stegmayer, retained Mozart's title but fleshed out his music with compositions by Dittersdorf and others. The evidence for this work is patchy, but it seems that it represented an attempt to retain the action of the original, since the dramatis personae are the same. The arrangement ran for six performances that season and seems not to have been revived.[6]

The nineteenth-century German-speaking world knew Mozart's *Der Schauspieldirektor* through a third version, this time prepared for Berlin by Louis Schneider and Wilhelm Taubert in 1845. Entitled *Mozart und Schikaneder*, it took Mozart's music, added five orchestrations of his *Lieder*, and adapted this material to a libretto whose plot was set during the composition and rehearsals of *Die Zauberflöte* in 1791; the dramatis personae included Mozart and his librettist themselves.[7]

---

[2] The generic title *Gelegenheitsstück* on the title page of the libretto makes explicit the occasional nature of the work, and the unlikely nature of any further performance ; (*Der / Schauspieldirektor / Ein / Gelegenheitsstück / in / einem Aufzuge / WJEN, / bei Joseph Edlen von Kurzbek k.k. Hofbuchdrucker / Groß= und Buchhändler. / 1786.*).

[3] While *Der Schauspieldirektor* and *Don Giovanni* were composed in successive years, the proximity of the former with *Le nozze di Figaro* is even more striking; dates of completion in the *Verzeichniss* are 3 February and 29 April 1786, and those of first performance are 7 February and 1 May 1786 respectively.

[4] Otto Jahn, *W. A. Mozart*, 4 vols (Leipzig: Breitkopf und Härtel, 1856–,1859) 4:157.

[5] An outline of the contents of *Das theatralischer Abenteuer* is in Johann August Diezmann, *Goethe-Schiller-Museum* (Leipzig: Baumgärtner, 1858), 13.

[6] Rudolf Hirsch, *Mozart's Schauspieldirektor: Musikalische Reminiscenzen* (Leipzig: Heinrich Matthes, 1859), 18–21.

[7] The *Lieder* were all taken from the Breitkopf und Härtel complete edition, a borrowing that was acknowledged in the libretto (see below): *XXX Gesänge mit Begleitung des Pianoforte von W. A. Mozart*, Œuvres complettes de Wofgang Amadeus Mozart 5 (Leipzig: Breitkopf und Härtel, 1798–1806).

This was the guise in which Mozart's opera was preserved in German-speaking states until well into the twentieth century.[8]

In 1856, Jacques Offenbach inherited Schneider and Taubert's arrangement of *Der Schauspieldirektor* and commissioned a new libretto from Léon Battu and Ludovic Halévy entitled *L'impresario* for his new Théâtre des Bouffes-Parisiens.[9] While the libretto retained the narrative context of the difficulties of theatrical management, it shifted its focus away from practical concerns and toward those of the heart, and in doing so created an important registral shift that had as much to do with the cultural and aesthetic positioning of Offenbach's theater company as it approached its second year of existence as with the ongoing project of the sacralization of Mozart's work.

L'impresario, therefore, stands in a tradition of reworking an operatic theme that had already gone through earlier incarnations. In addition to being understood in terms of its diachronic history, it requires being understood in the context of mid-nineteenth-century *opérette*. Offenbach's ambitions for the institution he founded in 1855, the Théâtre des Bouffes-Parisiens may be paralleled with his interest in, and exploitation of, the music of the long eighteenth century. In turn, this interest is to be explored via Offenbach's reviews in the journal *L' artiste*, his music for *Le carnaval des revues* and in his manifesto for the future of *opéra comique* as expressed in the advertisement for his 1856 competition (the *concours*) for new *opéras comiques* by young composers.

The Théâtre des Bouffes-Parisiens

The mid -1850s were a time of significant change in the culture of music drama in Paris. The three traditional opera houses continued to dominate the field: the Opéra and the Opéra-Comique were still reeling under the onslaught of two recent Meyerbeer successes—*Le prophète* and *L'étoile du nord*, respectively, while the Théâtre Italien was introducing Parisian audiences to middle-period Verdi (1855 saw Verdi's first original work for the Académie Impériale de Musique [the

---

[8] Despite the work's ubiquity in the nineteenth and twentieth centuries, sources for *Mozart und Schikaneder* are rare. For this study, the following libretto was used: Der / Schauspieldirektor /—/ Komische Operette von L. Schneider. /—/ Musik von W. A. Mozart. /—/ Officielle Bearbeitung für die Leipziger Bühne / Leipzig, / Druck und Verlag von Breitkopf und Härtel. The copyist's score of this version is Der Schauspiel-Direktor / Komische Operette in 1 Act / von / Schneider / Musik von W. A. Mozart / comoponiert in February 1786, Mozartem, (Bibliotheca Mozartiana, Internationale Stiftung (Salzburg, *A-Sm*, Rara 486/1).

[9] The work was published as RÉPERTOIRE DES BOUFFES-PARISIENS / L'IMPRESARIO / Opérette bouffe / PAR / MM. LÉON BATTU ET LUDOVIC HALÉVY / MUSIQUE DE / MOZART / - / REPRÉSENTÉE POUR LA PREMIÈRE FOIS SUR LE THÉÂTRE DES BOUFFES-PARISIENS, LE 20 MAI 1856 /.../ PARIS / G. BRANDUS, DUFOUR ET Cᵉ, ÉDITEURS .../ MICHEL LÉVY FRÈRES ÉDITEURS .../ 1856. This edition prefaces the piano-vocal score with the libretto (3–15).

Opéra]: *Les vêpres siciliennes*).[10] But alongside these institutions, the Théâtre Lyrique had been opening up the Parisian repertory since 1851, with new works, older *opéra comique*, and—as the decade progressed—works by foreign composers.[11] More strikingly, perhaps, 1855 had seen the birth of two institutions that dedicated themselves to *opérette*: Hervé's Théâtre des Folies-Nouvelles and Offenbach's Théâtre des Bouffes-Parisiens.[12]

Offenbach saw little to concern himself with at the Théâtre Italien. But the two other main opera houses were important points of reference for him. The Opéra was the antithesis of the Bouffes-Parisiens: the one was large, the other small; the Opéra was the recipient of massive state subsidy, the Bouffes-Parisiens of none; Meyerbeer and his colleagues enjoyed international reputations, while Offenbach and his contemporaries were either unknown or too young to have attracted attention. This antithesis was a critical feature of Offenbach's work at the Bouffes-Parisiens because it gave a logical and easy subject for parody, and right from its opening night, the repertory of the Opéra was the target of Offenbach and his librettists' mordant wit.[13]

The Opéra-Comique was a particular source of interest to the emerging opera house and its manager. When he launched his competition for new composers of *opéra comique* shortly after the premiere of *L'impresario*, he couched the invitation to contribute in terms of a manifesto for comic opera that severely took the Opéra-Comique to task for drifting closer and closer to the style of *grand opéra*, with Meyerbeer's *L'étoile du nord* directly in the firing line.[14]

But it was Hervé's Théâtre des Folies-Nouvelles that was Offenbach's greatest problem. Here were two theaters trying essentially to do the same thing. Whether they were consciously attempting to revert to the lighter style of eighteenth-century *opéra comique* or simply responding to the taste of, and opportunities generated by, the Boulevard audiences, the two institutions had licenses that looked remarkably similar. They were both granted permission to play operetta in one act with

---

[10] Still the best study of the Académie Impériale de Musique during the Second Empire is Genevieve Chinn, "The Académie Impériale de Musique: A Study of Its Administration and Repertory from 1862–1870" (Ph.D. diss., Columbia University, 1969), but this does not cover the period that overlaps with the beginnings of the Bouffes-Parisiens.

[11] Thomas Joseph Walsh, *Second Empire Opera: The Théâtre Lyrique, Paris, 1851–1870*, The History of Opera (London: Calder; New York: Riverrun, 1981).

[12] For the Folies-Nouvelles, see Eugène Woestyn and Eugène Moreau, *Les Folies-Nouvelles*, Les théâtres de Paris (Paris: Martinon, [1855]), and Louis-Henry Lecomte, *Les Folies-Nouvelles*, Histoire des théâtres de Paris 4 (Paris: Daragon, 1909).

[13] The final number of Offenbach's *Les deux aveugles* for Patachon and Giraffier (1855) is a parody of the sicilienne in the act 1 finale "O fortune, à ton caprice" from Meyerbeer's *Robert le diable* (1831), where the aristocratic and military games of dice in the *grand opéra* are translated into a game of dice to decide who keeps the mendicant's pitch on a Parisian bridge.

[14] The announcement of the "Concours pour une opérette en un acte" was published in the *Revue et gazette musicale de Paris*, 20 July 1856, 230–231. It was also printed in *Le Ménestrel*, 27 July 1856, with minimal introduction, and the *articles* only in *La France musicale*, 20 July 1856. The text is discussed below.

severe restrictions on the number and function of the characters on stage, and—perhaps more importantly—their licenses were modified in step with each other.[15]

The Théâtre des Bouffes-Parisiens opened in 1855 under less than ideal circumstances for its composer-manager.[16] Offenbach was restricted by his license to the performance of music drama in a single act with no more than four singing characters on stage.[17] Furthermore, Hervé's Théâtre des Folies-Nouvelles could have been a direct competitor for the same audiences, composers, and librettists as the Bouffes-Parisiens, despite the fact that such competition was what the licensing system itself had been designed to avoid.[18] Finally, the artistic space between the *opérette* that Offenbach was permitted to produce and the works of the subsidized theaters—the Académie Impériale de Musique, Opéra-Comique and Théâtre Italien—had largely been filled five years previously by the Théâtre Lyrique.[19] However, Offenbach held the lease on two theaters, one on the Champs-Elysées and one—sufficiently far from the boulevard home of the Folies-Nouvelles to reduce direct competition—in the Passage Choiseul; he also enjoyed the support of important state officials connected to the aristocracy and the imperial family, and of a bourgeois audience developed during his time as a salon musician.

Offenbach's artistic and professional aims were clear: he wanted to develop the Bouffes-Parisiens into a theater with a radically different mission and profile from that of the Folies-Nouvelles. He could do this by developing the bourgeois rather than the popular elements of his audience—easy at the Salle Choiseul and the Salle Lacaze—and by setting himself two more complex objectives: to support young composers, especially Prix de Rome laureates returning to the capital, and to position the Bouffes-Parisiens and its emergent genre of *opérette* squarely within the tradition of the international comic opera of the past and specifically within that of eighteenth-century *opéra comique*. His first objective tapped into a tradition of

[15] See Nicole Wild, *Dictionnaire des théâtres parisiens au xixe siècle: Les théâtres et la musique* (Paris: Amateurs des Livres, 1989), 63 (for the Bouffes-Parisiens) and 153–15 (for the Folies-Nouvelles).

[16] For an introduction to the early years of the Théâtre des Bouffes-Parisiens, see Jean-Claude Yon, "La création du Théâtre des Bouffes-Parisiens (1855–1862) ou La difficile naissance de l'opérette," *Revue d'histoire moderne et contemporaine* 39 (1992,: 575–600; see also Yon,, *Jacques Offenbach* (Paris: Gallimard, 2000), 128–165. For the repertory of, and other material concerning, the Bouffes-Parisiens, see Annie Ledout, "Le théâtre des Bouffes-Parisiens, historique et programmes, 1855–1880" (Ph.D. diss., Université de Paris IV, 2001).

[17] The earliest version of Offenbach's license restricted him to three singing characters; (4 June 1855, Archives Nationales, Paris, (hereafter *F-Pan*) F[21] 1136),; see Yon, *Jacques Offenbach*, 137); the loosening of this limitation to four was accomplished in the revision of Offenbach's contract, 22 October 1855; Nicole Wild, *Dictionnaire des théâtres parisiens au xixe siècle: les théâtres et la musique* (Paris: Amateurs des Livres, 1989), 63.

[18] For Florimond Ronger (Hervé) and the Théâtre des Folies-Nouvelles, see Eugène Woestyn and Eugène Moreau, *Les Folies-Nouvelles, Les théâtres de Paris* (Paris: Martinon, [1855]) and Louis-Henry Lecomte, *Les Folies-Nouvelles*, Histoire des théâtres de Paris 4 (Paris: Daragon, 1909).

[19] Walsh, *Second Empire Opera*.

aspirant opera managers claiming that their new enterprises would support young composers that dated back at least to the beginning of the licensing system in 1806/7: it was a claim well known to anyone who remembered the attempts to promote music drama at the Odéon in the 1820s or at the Théâtre de la Renaissance in the 1830s.[20] Offenbach's second objective—to return to the music of the past—was an ambitious and idiosyncratic undertaking that had a significant impact on the success of the Théâtre des Bouffes-Parisiens in its first phase.[21]

Offenbach and *L'artiste*

Between 1850 and 1860, Offenbach engaged with earlier music in a variety of ways. As conductor at the Comédie-Française, he was involved in Arsène Houssaye's attempts to revive Molière in ways that might have been familiar to the seventeenth century by removing two centuries of musical tradition.[22] In his articles published in the journal *L' artiste* in the early part of 1855, and in the announcement of his competition for a new *opéra-bouffe* the following year, he exploited the music of the past for his own ends. In addition to attempting to mount productions of largely eighteenth-century comic opera (with variable degrees of success), he used composers from the past to pillory aspects of contemporary musical culture in his *Le carnaval des revues* of 1860.

Offenbach wrote four *causeries musicales* in the journal *L' artiste* in the six months before the Théâtre des Bouffes-Parisiens opened in the Salle Lacaze.[23] One of the tasks they accomplished was to appease those Offenbach considered to be key players in the world of stage music in the mid-1850s. Accordingly, revivals of Halévy's *La juive* and Auber's *La muette de Portici* are praised without reserve, as is the Parisian premiere of Verdi's *Il trovatore*;[24] Émile Perrin's joint direction of the Opéra-Comique and Théâtre Lyrique comes in for approving comments; and Offenbach throws his weight behind the contemporary vogue for the works of

---

[20] See Mark Everist, *Music Drama at the Paris Odéon, 1824–1828* (Berkeley: University of California Press, 2002), 210–211 and "Theatres of Litigation: Stage Music at the Théâtre de la Renaissance, 1838–1840," *Cambridge Opera Journal* 16 (2004), 136.

[21] Despite its title, Gerard Loubinoux, "Le chercheur d'esprit, ou Offenbach et la mémoire du xviiie," in *Retour au xviiie siècle*, ed. Roland Morier and Hervé Hasquin, Études sur le xviiie siècle 22 (Brussels: Éditions de l'Université de Bruxelles, 1994) 63–76, addresses none of the sources or repertories discussed in this article. It reads those libretti of Offenbach's *opérettes* that depend on eighteenth-century settings: *Le chanson de Fortunio* (1861) and *La Foire Saint-Laurent* (1877), *Mesdames de la Halle* (1858; but wrongly assigned by Loubinoux to 1868), and *Madame Favart* (1878), and attributes the interest in the eighteenth century to Offenbach alone rather than to his librettists.

[22] Yon, *Jacques Offenbach*, 101, 107, and 111. In his bid for the management of the Théâtre Lyrique in 1854, however, Offenbach made no mention of any interest in the music of the seventeenth or eighteenth centuries or (pace Wild, *Dictionnaire*, 238–239) in the fate of Prix de Rome laureates. See Offenbach to Camille Doucet [directeur de l'administration des théâtres], 3 July 1854, *F-Pan* F^{21} 1120/2.

[23] *L' artiste*, 14 January 1855, 4 February 1855, 25 February 1855, 25 March 1855.

[24] Halévy:, 25 March 1855, 178, Auber: *L' artiste*, 14 January 1855, 39, Verdi: *L' artiste*, 39–40.

Adolphe Adam.[25] Berlioz is praised for his *L'enfance du Christ*, offered sympathy
for being beaten by Louis Clapisson in the competition for the most recent musical
nomination to the Institut, and praised vicariously by allusions to the shortcom-
ings of the recent revival of *Der Freischütz*—in Castil-Blaze's 1824 version as *Robin
des bois*—at the Théâtre Lyrique.[26] Such attempts to curry favor need to be read
alongside the production of such works as the *Décaméron dramatique: Album du
Théâtre-Français*, published in October 1854, in which each of the major actresses
at the Comédie-Française was presented with a dance for piano composed by Offenbach, a portrait by Hermann Raunheim, and a quatrain by a noted poet of the
day: Gautier, Dumas, Musset, and others.[27] The articles in *L' artiste* also undertook
significant cultural work by praising smaller scale contemporary *opéras comiques*
in terms that stressed their similarities to eighteenth-century classics of the genre.
In doing so, they contributed to a view of contemporary *opéra comique* that set it
apart from more ambitious contemporary works: the eighteenth-century was
made to contribute to Offenbach's aesthetic position as he tried to promote his
own artistic program.

A year after the publication of the articles in *L' artiste* and during the first
year of operation of the Bouffes-Parisiens, Offenbach advertised a "Concours
pour une opérette en un acte" for the composition of an *opéra bouffe* aimed at
composers who had not been performed on any Parisian stage. As part of the
announcement for the "Concours," he published what amounted to a history of
opéra comique that was slanted so as to throw into relief his own activities at
the Bouffes-Parisiens. The announcement constituted not only a partial view
of the history of *opéra comique* up to the present but also a manifesto for the
artistic ambitions of the Bouffes-Parisiens, and its manager and principal composer.

Supported by a series of carefully placed allusions to the music of the past, Offenbach could cast about for works that fell within the limitations of his license,
could amplify the repertory of his theater, and could contribute to its cultural
capital. He identified four comic operas from the previous century—Rousseau's *Le
devin du village*, Pergolesi's *La serva padrona*, Mozart's *Der Schauspieldirektor* and
Rossini's *Il signor Bruschino*–that might be of use to the Bouffes-Parisiens.[28]

---

[25] Perrin: L' artiste 4 February 1855, 78 and 25 March 1855, 178, Adam: 14 January 1855, 40.

[26] L' artiste, 14 January 1855, 4 February 1855.

[27] Yon, *Jacques Offenbach*, 131–132.

[28] The inclusion of Rossini's *Il signor Bruschino* (1813) raises the issue of what repertories Offenbach considered appropriate to his definition of the past. The concept of the "long" eighteenth century does not perhaps allow a sufficiently finely textured view of Offenbach's position, conditioned as it was by his view of the history of *opéra comique* (for which see below). Although Rossini's early *farse* clearly fall into this category—and perhaps Weber too—the music of the 1820s is much more closely contested, as the discussion of both *opéra comique* and *opera semiseria* in the "Concours" article suggests; ibid, 230, 1:5–8 (reference to the "Concours" article is via page, section:paragraph number as published in the *Revue et gazette musicale de Paris*).

Of these, *Le devin du village* and *La serva padrona* fell foul of the controls placed on the theater's license and were never performed (although the Rousseau may well have got as far as rehearsal) *Der Schauspieldirektor* and *Il signor Bruschino*, however, served as important parts of the repertory and key aesthetic statements for Offenbach and the Bouffes-Parisiens in the second half of the 1850s.

Parodying the Long 18th Century

If putting words into the mouths of dead composers was one of the tricks Offenbach was using in his manifesto on *opéra comique* that accompanied the advertisement for the "Concours," it was a short step to having composers of the past speak on stage. Offenbach, together with his collaborators Eugène Grangé and Philippe Gilles, took his chance in his *Le carnaval des revues* of 1860, a review of the previous year's events.[29] One of the main musical targets was the series of concerts Wagner had mounted at the Théâtre Italien—feet from Offenbach's own Salle Choiseul in the Salle Ventadour—but there were three other targets: the inquiry into pitch whose committee had reported during 1859, Meyerbeer's continuing success, and—close to Offenbach's heart—the question of the fate of young composers. The sixth tableau of *Le carnaval des revues* begins in the musical corner of the Elysian Fields; a neat classical allusion to *Orphée aux enfers* that would have been missed by no-one.[30] Grétry enters humming the aria "Et zig et zog" from one of the works Offenbach had endorsed four years earlier in his articles in *L' artiste* (see below), *Richard, cœur de lion*. From the other side of the stage enters Gluck, singing "J'ai perdu mon Eurydice." The resulting banter encompasses the revival of Gluck's *Orphée et Eurydice* at the Théâtre Lyrique and the contralto who took the title role (Pauline Viardot); the two then propose a game of dominos. Before they can start, Mozart enters, and Grétry and Gluck greet him by singing "Mon cœur soupire"— the French version of "Voi che sapete." Before they can start their three-way game of dominos, Weber arrives, and the other three welcome him with a performance of "Chasseur diligent," the French version of the Huntsmen's chorus from *Der Freischütz*. This quartet of posthumous composers—Grétry, Gluck, Mozart and Weber—serves as the commenting chorus against which the objects of Offenbach's satire are projected.

Apart from the attention given to the *compositeur de l'avenir* in *Le carnaval des revues*—almost too easy a target—Offenbach's most important victims were Meyerbeer and the quartet of commenting composers themselves. All served as impor-

---

[29] Eugène Grangé and Philippe Gilles, *Le carnaval des revues: revue de carnaval en 2 actes et 9 tableaux; Les souper de mardi-gras, prologue, Paris, Bouffes-parisiens, le 10 février 1860...Musique de Jacques Offenbach* ([Paris]: Michel Lévy frères, [1860]).

[30] Ibid, 14–17.

tant means of promoting Offenbach's own aesthetic agenda, especially the support to young composers and the appeal to the musical and dramatic values of the past, exactly those elements he was trying to develop at his own institution. Offenbach's quartet of composers served here as a fixed point of reference to whom he could have recourse in his constant invocation of earlier values.

Towards a New Opéra Comique

Offenbach's competition to encourage recent laureates of the Prix de Rome was launched in July 1856, and at face value sought to develop the mission to help young composers that he had set forth in his requests to open a theater the previous year.[31] To have chosen Georges Bizet and Charles Lecocq as winners can be, with hindsight, considered a successful outcome. But when the "Concours" was advertised, Offenbach gave it a context that was no less than the entire history of *opéra comique*; he took advantage of the opportunity to produce a manifesto for the aesthetic project hosted by his own theatre and the music drama supported there. Offenbach's view of the history of *opéra comique* was neatly encapsulated in his attempt to sum up toward the end of his introduction to the "Concours":

> One may easily follow the progress of *opéra comique* from its origins to the present. At first, a little brook with limpid water, with new banks it develops little by little as it advances, until it becomes what we see today, a wide river, with imposing waves on its vast surface.[32]

His metaphor draws an unbroken teleological line from Philidor's *Blaise, le sauvetier* of 1759 to Meyerbeer's *L'étoile du nord* of 1854; in this context, Offenbach outlined three phases in the history of the genre.

Phase 1 of Offenbach's history ran from Philidor—or from Pergolesi and Duni, since Offenbach was anxious to stress the Italian origins of the genre—to Dalayrac and Grétry.[33] But Offenbach proposed a clear distinction between pre- and post revolutionary works, and pointed to a sudden enlargement of the genre after 1789

---

[31] There is a tension in all of Offenbach's comments on young composers between Prix de Rome laureates and those novice composers trained outside the Conservatoire, and therefore not eligible to enter the state competition. These included Offenbach himself, not to mention such competitors as Clapisson or Gevaërt. Such a tension is clear in the "Concours" text itself (Offenbach, "Concours," 231, 3:1–3 and 7).

[32] "On peut suivre aisément la marche de l'opéra comique depuis son origine jusqu'à nos jours. D'abord petit ruisseau aux eaux limpides, au frais rivage, il s'étend peu à peu, à mesure qu'il avance, jusqu'à devenir, ce que nous le voyons aujourd'hui, un large fleuve, roulant dans son vaste lit ses ondes imposantes" (ibid, 2:12).

[33] The account of Offenbach's 1856 *Concours* is developed at greater length in Mark Everist, "Jacques Offenbach: The Music of the Past and the Image of the Present," in *Music, Theater and Cultural Transfer: Paris, 1830–1914.*, ed. Mark Everist and Annegret Fauser (Chicago: Chicago University Press, 2009), 77–84.

that was only accomplished "*en se dénaturant*";[34] he saw this as the product of the influence of ideas of "political and artistic renovation." While this gave a neat point of articulation between his first and second phases, it also gave him the chance to point to works by Dalayrac and Grétry—"the two most illustrious representatives of *opéra comique*"[35]—and accuse them of abjuring the genre that had served them so well, with the result that they had embarked on the composition of *Camille, ou Le souterrain* and *Pierre le grand* and *Guillaume Tell*, respectively. The works of his first phase that Offenbach pointed to with real approval were Monsigny's *Le déserteur*, Gossec's *La fête du village*, three works by Dalayrac (*Adolphe et Clara, Maison à vendre*, and *Picaros et Diego*), and Gretry's *Le tableau parlant, Zémire et Azor, L'amant jaloux*, and *Richard, cœur de lion*. The last of the four works by Grétry came in for special praise as "applauded every day as if it were written yesterday, although it dates from 1785 [*sic*; actually 1784]," and in Offenbach's discourse on the eighteenth century *Richard, cœur de lion* takes on the role of a signature work for its composer.[36]

Offenbach called the second phase of his history of *opéra comique* "the reign of the *harmonistes*," those he said exhibited "a sovereign contempt for *la petite musique*"—a term that recalled the language (*petites ouvrages, petites pièces*) of his articles in *L' artiste* the previous year.[37] Monarchs in this reign were Nicolo, Berton, Méhul, Catel, Boïeldieu, Lesueur, Cherubini, and both Hérold and Halévy in their early works. As he attempts to steer a course between avoiding antagonizing the musical establishment and promoting his own cause, his argument runs the risk of collapse. Having chastised the generation of his second phase, he then turns to his audience and claims that these "masters...have no less created works of which the French stage can justly be proud."[38] Hérold, however, is held up as a figure of transition, with his *Le pré aux clercs* and *Zampa*, representing "the transition... between *opéra comique* of a light allure and musical drama of lugubrious effect."[39] At this moment, for Offenbach, the original genre of *opéra comique* disappeared in favor of larger works; this was not yet *grand opéra* but a mixed genre along the lines of Italian opera *semiseria* and the German-language works that Offenbach thought derived from it: Weber's *Der Freischütz, Oberon*, and *Euryanthe*; Mozart's *Die Zauberflöte*; and Weigl's *Die Schweizerfamilie*.

---

[34] Ofenbach, Concours, , 1:2.

[35] "Les deux plus illustres représentants de l'opéra comique" (*ibidem*, 1:2).

[36] "que nous applaudissons tous les jours, comme s'il était d'hier, bien qu'il date de 1785" (ibid, 231,1:1).

[37] "Le règne des *harmonistes* .....un souverain mépris pour la *petite musique*" ((ibid., 230, 1:2). In his approving comments on the current repertory of one-act *opéras comiques* at the Théâtre Lyrique and Opéra-Comique, Offenbach alludes to "les petites pieces," "petits opéras comiques," and "ce *repertoiricule* charmant et amusant" (*L' artiste*, 25 March 1855, 178).

[38] "Maîtres...n'en ont pas moins créé des œuvres dont la scène française doit justement s'enorgueillir" (Offenbach, "Concours," 230, 1:4).

[39] "Une transition...entre l'opéra comique aux allures légères et le drame musicales aux lugubres effets" (ibid, 2301:5).

Offenbach reserves his greatest censure for works of his third phase: those of Auber, Halévy, Thomas, Reber, some works of Massé and Grisar, Gevaërt, and Meyerbeer. He declares:

> The scores of many of our contemporary composers resemble elegant women on the boulevard: they wear too much crinoline. In the daylight, they constitute quite a substantial outfit, and beautifully coloured. Close up, *en déshabillé*, at the piano, they are phantoms inflated by wind and sound.[40]

The overuse of crinoline echoes one of Offenbach's recurring views on contemporary music: that it is overblown beyond the appropriate confines of its genre, especially in the case of *opéra comique*, and it seems clear from his refusal to extend this particular polemic to works at the Académie Impériale de Musique that it is *opéra comique* at both the Théâtre Lyrique and the Opéra-Comique itself that is his target.

In the articles in *L' artiste*, in the "Concours" text, and even in his commentary on the music of the past in *Le carnaval des revues*, Offenbach subtly rewrote the history of *opéra comique* in a way that threw his own work into relief, and gave a logical context for comic opera from German-speaking and Italian traditions. With this construction of history in place, Offenbach was able to situate the activities of the Théâtre des Bouffes-Parisiens within it as he sought to justify his announcement of the "Concours." His theater's task was, he said, "to resuscitate the original and true genre" of *opéra comique*.[41]

In his account of the French eighteenth-century tradition of *opéra comique*, Offenbach was not only subtly (re)writing history but also reconfiguring the present for his own ends by pointing to the betrayal of true *opéra comique* by his colleagues and their immediate predecessors, and by praising works that seemed to embody the characteristics he considered representative of the true nature of *opéra comique*. In practical terms, he was forbidden to mount productions of classic *opéra comique*, but that did not stop him from attempting to produce an eighteenth-century French classic: Rousseau's *Le devin du village*.

Many of Offenbach's attempts to engage the Théâtre des Bouffes-Parisiens in the music of the eighteenth century were doomed to failure. Rousseau's *Le devin du village* failed because of a perceived conflict of interest with the Opéra, and the production was banned by the Ministry.[42] Similarly, Offenbach's attempt to present a translation of Pergolesi's *La serva padrona* as *La servante maîtresse* fell foul of similar difficulties with the Opéra-Comique.[43] Of

---

[40] "les partitions de beaucoup de nos compositeurs du jour rassemblent aux élégantes du boulevard, elles portent trop de crinoline. A la lumière, elles forment un ensemble assez substantiel et d'un beau coloris. De près, en déshabillé, au piano, ce sont des fantômes gonflés de vent et de son" (*L' artiste*, 14 January 1855, 40).

[41] "De ressusciter le genre primitif et vrai," Offenbach, "Concours," (231, 3:5).

[42] Everist, "Jacques Offenbach: The Music of the Past and the Image of the Present," 86–89.

[43] Ibid, 90.

the two successful productions from the long eighteenth century, Rossini's *Il signor Bruschino* was a worthy counterpart to the reworking of *Der Schauspieldirektor*.[44]

While the fiftieth anniversary of Mozart's death in 1841 and the centenary of his birth in 1856 were celebrated at immense length all over the German-speaking world, they elicited little reaction in Paris. That is not to say that they were not observed. The Parisian music press paid plenty of attention to events beyond the Rhine, but there was almost no institutional response to them.[45] True, there was a revival of *Don Giovanni* at the Théâtre Italien, but it failed to live up to what many Parisians were expecting. Pier-Angelo Fiorentino, writing under his pseudonym, De Rovray, in the *Moniteur universel*, complained the revival had missed Mozart's exact birthday and spoke for many when he complained that "It was on that day [27 January 1856] that one ought to have given an extraordinary and solemn performance of the greatest lyric works as had been done in Stuttgart and in all German opera houses."[46]

In a city that felt that the centenary of Mozart's birth still had a certain status but mostly only knew Mozart the opera composer from *Le nozze di Figaro* and *Don Giovanni*, the emergence of a further opera from exactly the same period in Mozart's compositional maturity was an event of some significance, especially and remarkably when it came from the newcomer, Offenbach's Bouffes-Parisiens. *Der Schauspieldirektor* was barely known in Paris. Never performed before 1856, it had a liminal place in Schlesinger's complete edition of Mozart's stage works, only in

---

[44] Ibid, 91–98.

[45] "The centenary of Mozart's birth was celebrated with enthusiasm throughout Germany. In Vienna, the celebration took place in the great auditorium of La Redoute, in the presence of the entire imperial family, and under the direction of Franz Liszt. In Berlin, the centenary was marked in the Grand Théâtre. In the evening, in the Salle Médor was a great dinner for 300, at which the ministers and all the notable figures in music. Frankfurt was by no means behind the great capitals. In the opera house, *Le nozze di Figaro* was given; in the museum, there was a monster concert; at the church of Saint-Paul, 500 artists or amateurs performed the Davidde penitente and the Requiem. Everywhere, in Dresden, Munich, Darmstadt, Hannover, Braunschweig, Cologne, Mainz, Magdeburg, Bonn, Königsberg etc., the same demonstrations of enthusiasm were found. It is certain that never has Germany been witness to an event more grandiose and more sincerely national." "Le centième anniversaire de la naissance de Mozart a été fêté avec enthousiasme dans toute l'Allemagne. A Vienne, la célébration a eu lieu dans la grande salle de la Redoute, en présence de toute la famille impériale, et sous la direction de Franz Liszt. À Berlin, la fête a été célébrée au Grand Théâtre." Le soir, dans la salle Médor, a eu lieu un grand souper de trois cents couverts, où ont paru les ministres et toutes les notabilités de la musique. Francfort n'est pas restée en arrière des grandes capitales. Au théâtre, on a donné les *nozze di Figaro*; au Musée, on a donné un concert monstre; à l'église Saint-Paul, cinq cents artistes ou amateurs ont exécuté *David Pénitent* et le *Requiem*. Partout, à Dresde, à Munich, à Darmstadt, à Hanovre, à Brunswick, à Cologne, à Mayence, à Magdebourg, à Bonn, à Koenigsberg, etc., ont éclaté les mêmes manifestations enthousiastes. On peut assurer que jamais l'Allemagne n'avait été témoin d'un spectacle plus grandiose et plus sincèrement national" (*Le Ménestrel*, 17 February 1856).

[46] "C'est ce jour-là [27 January 1856] qu'on aurait dû donner une représentation extraordinaire et solennelle du plus grand des chefs d'œuvre lyriques comme on l'a fait à Stuttgard et sur tous les théâtres d'Allemagne" (*Le moniteur universel*, 10 February 1856).

the appendix, and a few extracts—most obviously the overture—had been published separately.[47]

L'IMPRESARIO

Mozart und Schikaneder had been a logical response to earlier attempts to rehabilitate *Der Schauspieldirektor*, and it was an obvious springboard for Offenbach's operetta. The relationships between Mozart's original, the Schneider-Taubert reworking of 1845, and Battu/Halévy-Offenbach's *L'impresario* are given in table 3.1. On the left are the numbers as they appear in *L'impresario*, in the middle the outline of the 1845 *Mozart und Schikaneder*, and on the right the sources both from *Der Schauspieldirektor* and the *Lieder* and other works used by Schneider and Taubert. Apart from giving the detail of the sources for *Mozart und Schikaneder* and *L'impresario*, the table also shows the very close relationship between Offenbach's version and Schneider and Taubert's. The use and sequence of material in the two versions are almost identical, the only exception being the *Lied* "Männer suchen stets zu naschen" which comes before the trio in *Mozart und Schikaneder* and after it in *L'impresario*. The alternation of spoken dialogue and music is commensurately similar. In musical and dramatic terms, *L'impresario* fitted in perfectly with the physiognomy of works permitted by the theater's license and the musical patterns that were emerging during its first year of work. The overture and eight numbers were exactly in line with such works as Adolphe Adam's *Les pantins de Violette* and Offenbach's own *Ba-ta-clan* and *Tromb-Alcazar*; its use, furthermore, of four characters only exactly matched those works and the legal limitations put on the theater's activity.[48]

As Offenbach sought to bring Mozart's new opera within the ambit of the Bouffes-Parisiens, the construction of the libretto was as taxing as the musical revisions were straightforward. The technical details of opera production that form so much a part of the wit of both the later parts of *Der Schauspieldirektor* and all of *Mozart und Schikaneder* were unlikely to work at the Bouffes-Parisiens; on the other hand, to write a libretto for this music that distanced itself too much from the original subject matter would run the risk of undercutting the value of the Mozartian imprimatur. *Mozart und Schikaneder* is set during the preparations for *Die Zauberflöte* and involves, for example, comic scenes around the working out of rhymes for "In diesen heil'gen Hallen" while the theater director's nephew attempts to get his girlfriend hired as the second *prima donna* by having her impersonate Caterina Cavalieri.[49] Real personalities are confused with stage ones, and the whole work contributes to the development of Mozart's reputation—it can with profit be analyzed as a site of Mozart reception. *L'impresario* also involves

---

[47] *Collection complète des opéras de W. A. Mozart*, 9 vols. (Paris: Schlesinger, 1822). Vol. 8 includes the *Requiem* and *Der Schauspieldirektor*.

[48] Adam's *Les pantins de Violette* was premiered at the Bouffes-Parisiens on 29 April 1856; Offenbach's *Ba-ta-clan* on 29 December 1855 and *Tromb-Alcazar* on 3 April 1856.

[49] Der / Schauspieldirektor /—/ Komische Operette von L. Schneider, 8.

impersonation, but this time the tenor and *prima donna* of the San Carlo theater of Naples impersonate the king and his sister in order to dupe the gullible new director. It is clear from the contemporary press that the libretto succeeded in producing something that maintained the authority of a new work by Mozart while adhering to the still-emerging conventions of operetta.[50]

The aesthetic consequences of the reworkings of *Der Schauspieldirektor* were far-reaching, both for the resulting stage works and for the meanings of the original numbers and the *Lieder* that supplemented them. As *Der Schauspieldirektor* metamorphosed into *Mozart und Schikaneder*, five of the eight texts remained almost identical, one was completely rewritten, and two were lightly modified.[51] The dramatic contexts for all the numbers from *Der Schauspieldirektor* were inevitably changed, and works from the *XXX Gesänge* acquired them where that had not previously existed. While the massive dramatic and poetic shifts required in *L'impresario* changed Mozart's original music and poetry out of all recognition, even there some reflections of the original work did remain. These general principles may be exemplified by reference to one number from *Der Schauspieldirektor* and one work from the *XXX Gesänge* (table 3.1).

The *ariette* "Da schlägt die Abscheidsstunde" is the first item in the opera scene in *Der Schauspieldirektor*, and its poetry has almost no relation to the surrounding drama.[52] It is introduced by M. Herz as an audition piece for his wife. In *Mozart und Schikaneder*, the text of the aria is claimed by Schikaneder to be of his own composition, but Mozart demonstrates it in fact to be by Christian Hofmann von Hoffmanswaldau (1616–1679) by reference to a book on Schikaneder's table; Mozart mentions that he has changed the character Damon to Tamion (a logical move given that the aria is to be sung by Pamina and addressed to Tamino).[53] Paradoxically, the *ariette*—or *air* as it becomes in *L'impresario*—takes on an appropriately tragic dramatic context when it is sung by Zerline as she accuses Lélio of treachery; the tragedy is undermined, however, by the fact that Lélio sleeps throughout the opening *Larghetto* and only wakes up at the beginning of the second section of the two-tempo aria.[54] Battu and Halévy's poetry follows the structure of Stephanie's original, to the extent of even mimicking the word-repetitions "um grausam uns zu trennen" / "pitié pour ma souffrance" and in some cases simply translating emphatic words and phrases: "Und du" becomes "Et toi" (bars 26–28), "Doch nein" becomes "Mais non" (bar 32); musical phrases prompt near-identical poetry: the phrase setting "Ach nein" is rendered as "Hélas" in the French version. But for many of the larger text repetitions, Battu and Halévy write new

---

[50] This was made all the more simple when the original artists (Cavalieri and Aloysia Lange) could be made to mediate between Mozart and Offenbach. See Paul Scudo's review in the *Revue des deux mondes*, 1 June 1856, 673–674.

[51] The similarities and differences are noted in table 3.1.

[52] Croll, *Der Schauspieldirektor*, 27–33.

[53] Der / Schauspieldirektor /—/ Komische Operette von L. Schneider, 25–26.

[54] RÉPERTOIRE DES BOUFFES-PARISIENS / L'IMPRESARIO / Opérette bouffe, 11–12 and 31–35.

TABLE 3.1 Comparison of *L'impresario*, *Mozart und Schikaneder*, and Their Sources

L'Impresario (1856)	Der Schauspieldirektor / Mozart und Schikaneder (1845)	Source
Ouverture	[Overture]	*Der Schauspieldirektor* K. 486: Overture
1. *Couplets* (E-♭ major; bass [Rosignuolo] 2 stanzas) "Mon front grisonne"	1. *Lied* (G major, tenor [Schikaneder]; one stanza) "Wenn nur die Verse, prächtig klingen." Text is newly composed except for the two-line refrain, which is retained.	*Die betrogene Welt* K. 474 [Christian Felix Weiße] (G major, soprano; 3 stanzas) "Der reiche Tor, mit Gold geschmükket"
2. *Air* (D major; soprano [Silvia]; two-tempo [but no tempo change marked]) "Sa figure"	2. *Arie* "Bester Jüngling" (E-♭ major; soprano [Uhlich]; two-tempo [Andante–Allegretto]). Text identical to original.	*Der Schauspieldirektor* K. 486: no. 2 Rondò (E-♭ major; soprano [Silberklang]; two-tempo [Andante–Allegretto]) "Bester Jüngling"
3. *Romance* (F major; tenor [Lélio]; 4 through-composed stanzas only) "Mon cœur bat"	3. *Lied* (E-♭ major; tenor [Mozart]; 4 through-composed stanzas only) "Wenn mein Bild aus deinen blauen." Text has close links with original but is substantially reworked.	*An Chloe* K. 524 [Georg Jacobi] (E-♭ major; soprano; 4 through-composed stanzas x 3); "Wenn die Lieb aus deinen blauen"
4. *Trio* (G major; soprano, tenor and bass; thorugh-composed) "Lélio celui que j'aime"	4. *Lied* "Männer suchen stets zu naschen" (F major; tenor; two stanzas + coda). Text identical to source.	"Männer suchen stets zu naschen" K. 433 (416c) [text anonymous; character is Wahrmund] (F major; bass; two stanzas + coda)
5. *Couplets* (A major; soprano [Silvia] two stanzas) "Ce matin j'ai vu mon père"	5. *Terzett* (G major; soprano, tenor and bass; through-composed) "Liebes Mandel." Text has close links with original but is substantially reworked.	*Das Bandel* K. 441 [Mozart in Viennese dialect] (G major; soprano, tenor and bass; through-composed) "Liebes Mandel, wo ist's Bandel," known to Schneider and Taubert through a piano reduction only. "Männer suchen stets zu naschen" K. 433 (416c). See above.
6. *Air* (F minor; soprano [Zerline] two-tempo [Larghetto–Allegro Moderato]) "Hélas toi qui peux faire."	6. *Arie* (G minor; soprano [Lange]; two-tempo [Larghetto–Allegro Moderato]) "Da schlägt die Abschiedstunde." Text identical to original.	*Der Schauspieldirektor* K. 486: no. 1 Arietta (G minor; soprano [Herz]; two-tempo [Larghetto–Allegro Moderato]) "Da schlägt die Abschiedstunde"
	6 1/2. *Lied* (f minor; soprano [voce]; first section only.) "text reads?"	*Das Lied der Trennung* K.519 [Klamer Eberhard Karl Schmidt] (F minor; soprano; 15 stanzas)
7. *Grand Trio* (B-♭ major; 2 sopranos and tenor; through-composed) "Mon Lélio c'est moi"	7. *Terzett* (B-♭ major; 2 sopranos and tenor [Uhlich, Lange, Mozart]; through-composed) "Ich bin die erste Sängerin." Text identical to original.	*Der Schauspieldirektor* K. 486: no. 3 Terzett (B-♭ major; 2 sopranos and tenor [Silberklang, Herz, Vogelsang]; through-composed) "Ich bin die erste Sängerin"
8. *Final* (C major; 2 sopranos and tenor; through-composed) "Notre craintive faiblesse." Only one chorus, and number cut accordingly.	8. *Finale* (C major; 2 sopranos and tenor [Uhlich, Lange, Mozart + Schikaneder; through-composed) "Jeder Künstler." Text identical to original except the final passage for Buff (now Schikander), which is rewritten.	*Der Schauspieldirektor* K. 486: no. 4 Schlußgesang (C major; 2 sopranos and tenor [Silberklang, Herz, Vogelsang, Buff]; through-composed [*vaudeville*]) "Jeder Künstler strebt nach Ehre"

text so that, at the beginning of the allegro moderato (bars 44–50), Mozart has "Ein Herz, das so der Abschied kränket, / Dem ist kein Wankelmut bekannt! / Kein Wankelmut bekannt" whereas in Battu and Halévy the repetition is omitted (but another smaller one introduced) to give "Cruel amant qui me délaisse / Lorsque ma voix, ma voix, te presse / Vois ma tristesse."

The appropriation of *An Chloë* from the *XXX Gesänge* is a more complex undertaking.[55] In *Mozart und Schikaneder*, the number is sung by Mozart to Mlle. Uhlich in a flirtatious response to her performance of "Bester Jüngling."[56] The central conceit of the admiration of the beloved's eyes is set up in the preceding dialogue, when Mozart says "Hören's, Sie sind ein herziger Schatz! Und wissen's'—Ihre Augen–an denen kann ich mich gar nicht satt sehen."[57] But Schneider's reworking of Johann Georg Jacobi's original poem, while retaining the beloved's eyes as a subject, tones down the sexually high-octane character of the poem to something more suitable to the dramatic context of inconsequential flirtation. This is strikingly clear in the third stanza where Jacobi has his narrator grasp his beloved to his breast "der im lezten Augenblicke / *sterbend* nur dich von sich läßt [emphasis added]";[58] Schneider's more publicly acceptable lover offers as the explanation of the burning fire in his lover's eyes "die Klänge meiner Leier." Taubert's setting of Schneider's revised text follows Mozart's word-repetitions carefully insofar as that is possible (see bars 23–28 for example), and manages to substitute for the very careful original underscoring of the word "Sterbend" (bars 36–37) a similar emphasis on the word "Sehnsucht," an example of text-setting about which Mozart would have been unlikely to complain.[59] However, Mozart's original setting of the line "eine düstre Wolke mir" (bars 42–47), brilliantly characterized with a turn to the supertonic and back to the dominant via an *ombra* harmony, sets—in Taubert's arrangement the line "Und das Herz schlägt höher mir"; Mozart's careful characterization is not only now ignored, but his *ombra* harmonies now appear redundant and out of place.[60]

The version of this number worked out by Battu and Halévy for the Bouffes-Parisiens follows similar general practices to those employed in "Da schlägt die Abscheidsstunde."[61] At this point in the drama, Lélio has arrived in Rosignuolo's house with a double objective: he has been commissioned to convey the contract for the license of the San Carlo theater to Rosignuolo (the impresario of the title), and with the resultant good will hopes to claim the hand of Rosignuolo's daughter Sylvia.[62] Battu's and Halévy's text is built around this dramatic point, and Jacobi's

---

[55] Ernst August Ballin, ed., *Lieder*, Neue Mozart-Ausgabe III/8 (Kassel.: Bärenreiter, 1963; 2nd ed. 1987; 3rd ed. 2003); the critical report to this edition is Ernst August Ballin, ed., *Lieder*, Neue Mozart-Ausgabe III/8 (Kassel: Bärenreiter, 1964), 46–49.

[56] Der / Schauspieldirektor /—/ Komische Operette von L. Schneider, 19–20.

[57] Ibid, 19.

[58] Ballin, ed., *Lieder*, 47–48.

[59] *A-Sm* Rara 486/1, 25.

[60] Ibid, 26.

[61] RÉPERTOIRE DES BOUFFES-PARISIENS / L'IMPRESARIO / Opérette bouffe, 14–17.

[62] Ibid, 6.

and Schneider's second person appeals to the beloved are swept away. Mozart's word repetitions are frequently replaced with newly composed poetry, but the ABAC structure of the music for the first stanza elicits from Halévy and Battu a response that matches a repeat of the first line of poetry to the repeat of the musical phrase. Schneider's casual approach to Mozart's setting of "eine düstre Wolke mir" is reflected catastrophically by Battu and Halévy where they respond to Jacobi's clouds with the line "Sous le soleil de beaux jours," a moment in the aria that leaves the listener gasping for mimetic breath.[63]

In his selection of artists for *L'impresario*, Offenbach consciously distanced himself from the teams he had used so far in work at the Bouffes-Parisiens. He abandoned the artists who had invested such works as *Les deux aveugles* and *Le violoneux* with some of the most comic moments seen on the lyric stage and replaced them with recent graduates of the Conservatoire. Jean Berthellier had already been headhunted by the Opéra-Comique, and the other half of the comic team, Étienne Pradher, had no role in *L'impresario*; even Hortense Schneider, as early as 1856 a veteran of operetta, was forsaken.[64] Central to Mozart's original version of *Der Schauspieldirektor* and to all arrangements of it were the two competing sopranos, sung originally by Aloysia Lange and Caterina Cavalieri. For these roles, Offenbach already had Marie-Denise-Victoire Dalmont, who had created the role of Fe-an-nich-ton in *Ba-ta-clan*, and he recruited Adèle-Claire Courtois as the second soprano. Both artists were in their mid twenties, and had won first and second prizes, respectively, at the Conservatoire the previous year.[65]

Dalmont had already demonstrated her suitability for such a role as that of Silvia in *L'impresario*; this corresponded to the role of Mlle. Silberklang in Mozart's original, which had been sung by Caterina Cavalieri. In his last opera, Adam had written the title role of *Les pantins de Violette* especially for Dalmont, and had availed himself of her virtuosity in two numbers in that work.[66] Courtois, the new recruit, was able to benefit from her Conservatoire background in the role of Zerline (Mozart's original Mme. Herz).

But Offenbach's choice of artists was not solely based on the fit between vocal expertise and repertory. In pursuit of his goal of enhancing the status of his theater with such a classic as a version of *Der Schauspieldirektor*, he was able to develop this status with the presentation of the two most successful young sopranos in the capital—a success that had been proven in the most traditional environment, the Conservatoire, and by the simplest means: winning the first and second prizes for singing.

---

[63] Ibid, 16.

[64] Karl-Josef Kutsch and Leo Riemens, *Großes Sängerlexikon*, 4 vols (Bern and Stuttgart: Francke, 1987–94; 3rd ed., 7 vols, Bern: Saur, 1997–2002), 4:3127–3128.

[65] Pierre Constant, *Le Conservatoire National de Musique et de Déclamation: Documents historiques et administratives* (Paris: Imprimerie Nationale, 1900), 255.

[66] Dalmont took the role of Violette in the work, and sang in six of the eight numbers (nos. 5 and 7 were a dance number and *musique de scène*, respectively). The most striking *air*, from the point of view of its virtuosity, was number 1, "Canari, mon chéri."

The coupling of a work by a composer more familiar from the Théâtre Italien and Académie Impériale de Musique with artists who might be expected to develop their careers at those establishments enabled Offenbach to distance his production of *L'impresario* from the rest of his repertory, and from his artistic competitors.

Local contexts meant that that *L'impresario* was not merely desirable for the adjustment of the status of Offenbach's theater, it was almost essential. In May 1856, Offenbach was coming to the end of his first full season and contemplating a return to the Salle Lacaze for the summer. This was a dangerous moment, for when he had left his summer location for the Passage Choiseul at the end of 1855, he had been profiting from the large crowds attending the Grand Exposition at the adjacent Palais de l'Industrie. In the early summer of the following year, this advantage had disappeared, and the theater now had to succeed in its own terms.

A further pressure on Offenbach in the early summer was the fact that he was about to launch his competition for new operettas, and it would be severely disadvantageous, if not a deterrent, if recent Prix de Rome laureates were to view the Bouffes-Parisiens as equal in frivolity to, for example, the Folies-Nouvelles. Furthermore, Offenbach's announcement of the competition was coupled to his self-justificatory manifesto based on the history and contemporary state of *opéra comique*, and a credible eighteenth-century context for that manifesto was critical. *L'impresario* could provide a physical embodiment of that context at just the right moment.

If the beginning of the new season and the imminent presentation of his manifesto were prospective reasons for the importance of *L'impresario*, there were retrospective ones as well. The theater's credibility had been badly damaged by the press reaction to *Le thé de Polichinelle*, premiered two months previously. The work was clearly seen as one that brought the Bouffes-Parisiens too closely into alignment with the Folies-Nouvelles for the taste of Offenbach's bourgeois audiences, and by May 1856 there was a need to redress the registral balance of the theater's repertory that could be fulfilled by such a work as *L'impresario*.[67]

---

[67] For an example of a statement of the possibilities of what the Théâtre des Bouffes-Parisiens might become, and the threats that it faced, the following review by Jules Réal is instructive: "The Bouffes-Parisiens, in order to avoid denying the truth to the their name, must provoke gaiety, but without ever falling into that triviality that paints the vulgar, the low side of things; if they seek out licentious laughter, the spirit of the streets, or daring expressions, they will soon see themselves abandoned by the fine society who have taken them under their patronage. For us, in order for this opera house to succeed, there must be as much good taste on the stage as is found in the auditorium; its music must be, while not pretentious, stand apart from the *ponts-neufs* and the *flons-flons* who knows? More than one musician, after leaving the Bouffes-Parisiens, will go perhaps knocking on M. Perrin's door, since, we thing that the stage in the Passage Choiseul could become a fourth lyric theatre." "Les *Bouffes-Parisiens* doivent, à peine de mentir à leur dénomination, provoquer la gaieté, mais sans tomber jamais dans cette trivialité qui peint le vulgaire, le bas côté des choses; s'ils recherchaient le rire graveleux, l'esprit de carrefour, ou les expressions osées, ils se verraient bientôt abandonnés par la bonne société qui les a pris sous son patronage. Selon nous, pour que ce théâtre continue à réussir, il faut, autant que possible, qu'il y ait sur la scène le bon goût qui se trouve dans la salle; il faut que sa musique, sans afficher de grandes prétentions, sorte de la routine des *ponts-neufs* et des *flons-flons*; qui sait? plus d'un musicien, en quittant les *Bouffes-Parisiens*, ira, peut-être, frapper à la porte de M. Perrin, car, dans notre pensée, la salle du passage Choiseul peut devenir un quatrième théâtre lyrique" (*Le Ménestrel*, 9 March 1856).

The impact of *L'impresario* was everything Offenbach could have wanted. It filled the theater and its bank account, and reviews of the production came close to eulogy. But this was only part of the success of the work from Offenbach's point of view. The Bouffes-Parisiens became the locus of a public discussion of a new work by Mozart, one that became one of the central intellectual debates in the middle of 1856. For such a theater to achieve this status, usually reserved for the Opéra or Théâtre Italien, this was an achievement indeed.

Offenbach was much praised in the Parisian press for having traveled to Vienna, "discovered" Mozart's score, and brought it back to Paris.[68] What he actually brought back was the arrangement made by Schneider and Taubert a decade earlier. There is no evidence of any attempt on Offenbach's part to disabuse the press of this misunderstanding, and the scholarly enterprise he was thought to have undertaken remained an important thread in the public understanding of the opera.[69]

The public commentaries on *L'impresario* continued this scholarly thread by allusion to two recent works that had a bearing on the opera. Alexandre Oulibicheff's 1843 biography of Mozart was frequently cited for what was considered its error in describing *Der Schauspieldirektor* as consisting of an overture and four numbers whereas journalists had heard—so they thought—with their own ears that it had eight.[70] This suggests that the origins of Offenbach's *L'impresario* in Schneider's and Taubert's *Mozart und Schikaneder* were unknown to the press, but also that the journalists were convinced that they were listening to and critiquing a one-act opera by Mozart that had never been performed in Paris before.

---

[68] "[Offenbach] spent six months searching throughout Germany for the complete score of *Der Schauspieldirektor*, or if you prefer, of *L'Impresario* or *The Theater-Director*, since in the collected words of Mozart there are only five pieces in this score, including the overture. Of the four sung items, he only kept three, and procured four others, as they are performed especially on the Viennese stage." "Il a passé six mois à chercher par toute l'Allemagne la partition complète du *Schauspiel-Director*, ou si vous l'aimez mieux, de l'*Impresario*, du *Directeur de Spectacle*, car dans la collection de Mozart, il n'y avait que cinq morceaux de cette partition, y compris l'ouverture. Des quatre morceaux de chant, il n'en a gardé que trois, et s'en est procuré quatre autres, tels qu'on les exécute au théâtre de Vienne notamment" (*Revue et gazette musicale de Paris*, 25 May 1856).

[69] The thread could be woven in fanciful ways. See for example *Le Figaro* (25 May 1856): "Not only has *L'Impresario* not been engraved, but it is also as unknown in Germany as it is in Paris. Buried in a manuscript score in the library in Vienna, its sole existence has been established by scholars and consigned to M. Fétis's *Dictionnaire des musiciens*." "Non seulement l'*Impresario* n' pas été gravé, mais il était aussi inconnu en Allemagne qu'à Paris. Enfouie en partition manuscrite dans la bibliothèque de Vienne, son existence seule avait été constatée par les érudits et consignée dans le *Dictionnaire des Musiciens* de M. Fétis."

[70] See, for example, *Revue et gazette musicale de Paris*, 25 May 1856; *La France musicale*, 25 May 1856; *La revue française* 2/5 (1856), 293–294. Oulibicheff's text is *Nouvelle biographie de Mozart suivie d'un aperçu sur l'histoire générale de la musique et de l'analyse des principales œuvres de Mozart* (Moscow: Sener, 1843) *reprinted* as *Mozart* with an introduction by Jean-Victor Hocquard (Paris: Séguier, 1991), 147 (page nos. refer to the 1991 reprint).

A second text that was a frequent *point d'appui* for the press was Paul Scu-do's 1850 *Critique et littérature musicales*, which was recruited by several jour-nalists to support their view of Mozart's work.[71] Jules Réal's review in *Le Mé-nestrel* is a case in point. Here he quotes Scudo verbatim in his review of *L'impresario*:

> Mozart is as much a great muscian as sublime poet. He sings the grace and
> the exquisite sensations of superior beings, the mysterious sorrows of the
> soul who glimpse infinite horizons, the woes and pleasures of an advanced
> civilization. He has the elegance, the depth and the personality of the patri-
> cian.[72]

This is generic praise that could be heaped as much on Mozart in general as on *L'impresario* in particular. But in fact Scudo, here quoted by Réal, is not talking about *Der Schauspieldirektor* at all but specifically about *Don Giovanni*: Réal is appropriating this discourse on genius for the benefit of a much more modest work whose textual history was more complicated than he knew. The direct bene-ficiary is *L'impresario* and vicariously Offenbach and his theater. *L'impresario* was not just associated with *Don Giovanni* in this way, but also with *Le nozze di Figaro* via a not implausible comparison of the two overtures.[73] It is difficult to imagine a more successful response to the work than elision with what were known as Mo-zart's two most important works, especially since productions of *Don Giovanni* and *Le nozze di Figaro* were forbidden to the Bouffes-Parisiens. This was enhanced by the fact that the press, thanks to Oulibicheff's commentary, knew that *Der Schauspieldirektor* had been composed only a few months before *Le nozze di Figaro*.[74]

---

[71] Paul Scudo, *Critique et littérature musicales* (Paris: Amyot, 1850).

[72] "Mozart est aussi grand musicien que poète sublime. Il chante la grâce et les sentiments exquis des natures supérieures, les douleurs mystérieuses de l'âme qui entrevoit des horizons infinis, les trist-esses et les voluptés d'une civilisation avancée. Il a l'élégance, la profondeur et la personnalité des patriciens." *Le Ménéstrel*, 25 May 1856.

[73] "I will leave you to guess at the surprise, the enchantment of the audience, right form the over-ture, twin sister to that of *Le nozze di Figaro*, charming little composition, full of Italian melody, but lightly enhanced by that harmonic genius that Mozart could not deny himself even in fun; and in the following pieces, in the aria for the director, in that of Sylvia, in Lelio's, in the two trios, the same exqui-site sweetness, the same melodic smoothness, the same instinct for sonority in the orchestra." "Je vous laisse à deviner la surprise, l'enchantement du public, à partir de l'ouverture, sœur jumelle de celle des *nozze di Figaro*, petite composition charmante, toute remplie de mélodie italienne, mais légèrement relevée par ce génie harmonique, dont Mozart ne pouvait se priver même en badinant ; et dans les mor-ceaux qui viennent ensuite, dans l'air du Directeur, dans celui de Sylvia, dans celui de Lelio, dans les deux trios, même douceur exquise, même suavité de cantilènes, même instinct des sonorités de l'orchestre" (*Revue et gazette musicale de Paris*, 25 May 1856).

[74] "When Mozart wrote *Der Schauspieldirektor*, he had arrived at the period of talent when his inspiration, purified by work and enlarged by reflection, was only going to produce masterpieces: the composer was mature enough for *Le nozze di Figaro* and for *Don Giovanni*." "Lorsque Mozart l'écrivit

The impact of *L'impresario* on Parisian music-theatrical circles was immense. That was nothing, however, to the effect that it had on the reputations of Offenbach and his theater. It succeeded in bringing the Bouffes-Parisiens to the attention of the serious musical public with a work by a composer whose music was still considered challenging and elusive; the cachet, furthermore, of any Austro-German composer was a significant prize for any theater (the Théâtre Lyrique was in the process of capitalizing on their productions of Weber, and the Opéra only five years away from flirting with Wagner).

But it was less the nationality of the composer of *L'impresario* that was important for Offenbach than the classic status of the composer. Here, Mozart formed part of a view of comic opera that Offenbach was to develop in his manifesto, published only eight weeks later, and probably written during the first run of *L'impresario*. His interest in the eighteenth century extended to encompass the works he mounted at the Bouffes-Parisiens themselves. He had opened up the possibility of a production of Rousseau's *Le devin du village* in March 1856 (flatly refused by the Minister of the interior) and would mount a successful reworking of Rossini's *Il signor Bruschino* at the very end of 1857, (This is classic Rossini from 1813, not the composer of *Guillaume Tell*). Furthermore, the antagonists of *Le compositeur de l'avenir* and Meyerbeer in Offenbach's *Le carnaval des revues* of 1860 are Grétry and Gluck, who are joined by Mozart and Weber. There was also talk of a production of Pergolesi's *La serva padrona*.[77] And this attempt at mediation between eighteenth-century classics and the mid-nineteenth century is perfectly embodied in the physical location of the Salle Choiseul itself, positioned midway between the eighteenth-century social center of the Palais-Royal and the nineteenth-century boulevards.

L'impresario represents an important part of a process of self-positioning on Offenbach's part during the early years of the Bouffes-Parisiens existence. Its task had been to use the prestige of a work by Mozart to identify the theater as the home of more serious, musically ambitious, operetta. It succeeded beyond Offenbach's wildest dreams.

[*Der Schauspieldirektor*], il était arrivé à cette période de talent où son inspiration, épurée par le travail et grandie par la réflexion, n'allait plus donner que des chefs-d'œuvre : le compositeur était mûr pour les *Noces de Figaro* et pour *Don Juan*" (*Le Figaro*, 25 May 1856). Scudo, in his own review, was struck by the immaturity of the writing, whatever the work's date: "Although this sketch of the *Impresario* comes from the same year as *Le nozze di Figaro*, one would have dated it much earlier, and almost to Mozart's childhood, but gods do not have childhoods and always speak of gold." "Bien que cette esquisse de *l'impresario* soit de la même année que *les nozze di Figaro*, on la dirait d'une date beaucoup plus antérieure et presque de l'enfance de Mozart; mais les dieux n'ont pas d'enfance et parlent toujours d'or" (*Revue des deux mondes*, 1 June 1856).

[77] See Mark Everist, "Jacques Offenbach: The Music of the Past and the Image of the Present."

{ 4 }

The Commendatore and the Clavier (Quadrille)

If the preceding two chapters have shown how Mozart may be embodied in serialized novel and in silent film, and how his opera may be subject to the vicissitudes of changing fashions and cultural politics, this chapter addresses what might be thought to be more conventional sites of reception—the presentation of the composer's operas through the medium of keyboard arrangement.

Keyboard arrangements of opera excerpts are a largely nineteenth-century phenomenon, largely misunderstood and mostly reviled. But they were an important part of musical culture, a key means of repeatedly hearing works, both new and old, and of both intervening in and partially fixing the textual traditions of stage works, so unstable, for the most part, throughout the nineteenth century. It was a pan-European tradition, although one that largely excluded Italy. A list, for example, of keyboard arrangements of numbers from Mozart's operas from the late eighteenth century to around 1900 reveals versions appearing with every publisher on the continent in varying arrangements, of which those for solo keyboard are but one—admittedly very large—subset.[1] So within a very few years of Mozart's death, one could obtain such works for example as "Non più andrai" from *Le nozze de Figaro* arranged for keyboard, published by Longman and Broderip in London and called *The Duke of York's New March, as performed by His Royal Highness's new Band in the Coldstream Reg[imen]t of Guards,* or, still arranged for keyboard, published by André in Offenbach as *Deux Airs de Mozart variés,* "*Dort vergiss leises Flehn*," no. 62 in his *Journal de musique pour les dames.* Both publications date from 1795.[2]

---

[1] See the listing in Gabriella Dideriksen and Mark Everist, "Patterns of Mozart Reception in the Nineteenth Century," www.soton.ac.uk/~me/pmr/pmr.html (accessed 30 June 2012).

[2] THE DUKE of YORK'S / NEW MARCH *as performed by* / HIS ROYAL HIGHNESS'S NEW BAND / *in the Coldstream Regt. of Guards* / *Composed, and Arranged for the* / *PIANO FORTE or HARPSICHORD* / *by* C. H. *Eley* / . . . / LONDON / Printed by Longman and Broderip No. 26 Cheapside and No. 13 Hay Market.

These were simple arrangements of well-known tunes from well-known operas, but by the middle of the nineteenth century, such works as Liszt's *Réminiscences de Don Juan* were central not just to Liszt's own performances but to those of other ambitious performers.[3] Liszt's *Réminiscences de Don Juan* give a dangerously misleading picture, however, of piano works based on operatic subjects by other composers; for the most part the pieces are much simpler, although they exploit as wide a range of material as Liszt, and their performative contexts are much wider. A glance at the two dozen or so compositions based on *Don Giovanni* in the same decade as Liszt's (1840–50) issued by publishers in German-speaking lands alone shows just how much this is the case.[4]

As ever, the capital of the nineteenth century took matters to excess, and every premiere of a Parisian *grand opéra* sparked off a range of keyboard works based on its themes. The only scholarly study of such a constellation showed how the premiere of Meyerbeer's *Le pardon de Ploërmel* (1859) triggered forty-three arrangements of various of its numbers, of which twenty-four were for solo keyboard and bear comparison with the works discussed in this chapter.[5] Mozart's *Don Giovanni* enjoyed the status, from this perspective, of a native French opera, so any production might be expected to result in a similar constellation of keyboard arrangements. But Mozart's status was in a state of flux, so the influential 1834 production of *Don Giovanni*, as *Don Juan*, resulted in a couple of works only.[6] This chapter takes a new production of *Don Giovanni* at the Paris Opéra as its subject, but in the year in question there was not one new production in Paris but three, and the resulting excitement generated large numbers of arrangements of the work, of which nearly thirty were for keyboard alone.[7]

The target for this chapter is the collection of keyboard arrangements of *Don Giovanni* resulting from the three new productions in Paris in 1866. The discussion

---

[3] Liszt's *Don Juan Réminiscences* have received a disproportionate level of attention given the size and scope of the repertory. See Sieghart Döhring, "Réminiscences: Liszts Konzeption der Klavierparaphrase," in *Festschrift Heinz Becker zum 60. Geburtstag am 26. Juni 1982*, ed. Jürgen Schläder and Reinhold Quandt ([Laaber]: Laaber, 1982), 131–151; Jürgen Hunkemüller, "Mozart als Medium: Réminiscences de Don Juan von Franz Liszt," in *Mozart: Aspekte des 19. Jahrhunderts*, ed. Hermann Jung and Imogen Fellerer, Mannheimer Hochschulschriften 1 (Mannheim: Palatium, 1995), 145–159. See also the comments in Kenneth Lawrie Hamilton, "The Opera Fantasias and Transcriptions of Franz Liszt: A Critical Study" (D.Phil. diss., University of Oxford, 1989), and Jonathan Kregor, "Franz Liszt and the Vocabularies of Transcription, 1833–1865" (Ph.D. diss., Harvard University, 2007).

[4] Dideriksen and Everist, "Patterns of Mozart Reception," www.soton.ac.uk/~me/pmr/dggerman.html (accessed 30 June 2012).

[5] Herbert Schneider, "Die Bearbeitung des *Pardon der Ploërmel* von G. Meyerbeer im Jahre der Uraufführung," in Schläder and Quandt, *Festschrift Heinz Becker*, 152–161.

[6] For the 1834 Parisian production of *Don Giovanni*, see Sabine Henze-Döhring, "E. T. A. Hoffmann-'Kult' und 'Don Giovanni'-Rezeption in Paris des 19. Jahrhunderts: Castil-Blazes 'Don Juan' im Théâtre de l'Académie Royale de Musique [*sic*] am 10 März 1834," in *Mozart-Jahrbuch 1984/85 des Zentralinstitutes für Mozartforschung der Internationalen Stiftung Mozarteum Salzburg* (Kassel: Bärenreiter, 1986), 39–51; Katharine Ellis, "Rewriting *Don Giovanni*, or 'The Thieving Magpies,'" *Journal of the Royal Musical Association* 119 (1994), 212–250.

[7] For the complete range of Parisian arrangements, for keyboard and other instrumental combinations, see Dideriksen and Everist, "Patterns of Mozart Reception."

will add to the ongoing discussion of Mozart reception by considering this medium as a whole, and in doing so will explore the arrangement of classical works for social dance—the polka, quadrille, and waltz—as well as the iconographical significance of the publication of these 1866 arrangements of *Don Giovanni*. In general, the aim is not to privilege either the musically sophisticated or the works of well-known composers but to reconstruct the context within which such a work as Liszt's *Réminiscences de Don Juan* may be understood. But the operatic and cultural environment needs to be explained before this repertory can be effectively approached, and the institutional, textual, and aesthetic background to *Don Giovanni* in Paris in 1866 will be established in the first part of the chapter.

Text and Performance

Critical to an understanding of the reception of any work is the form in which it takes at a particular time and place: what theorists like to call the nature of the *Wirkungsträger*.[8] This means that it is simply insufficient to talk of three competing productions of *Don Giovanni* in 1866 without taking account of the different states of the three productions—their musical, poetic, dramaturgical, and choreographic texts. Naturally, the status of each of the three texts that supported the reception of *Don Giovanni* in 1866 depends to a certain degree on the institution that promoted it, and this affected the discursive mode adopted for the kinetic sections of the opera, the number of acts, the presence or absence of dance, and the language of the libretto.

Don Giovanni had a remarkable status worldwide by 1866. Dubbed the "Oper aller Opern" by E. T. A. Hoffmann as long ago as 1813, it had rapidly taken on canonic status, and perhaps more than any other opera in the nineteenth century had gone beyond the canonic and assimilated much of the sacred.[9] In France, much of this was related to the ownership and treatment of the work's autograph (explained in detail in chapter 6). But although the autograph made its impact on the Francophone world in the late 1850s, and although critics made allusion to it in the context of the 1866 productions that are part of the subject of this chapter, the precise status of *Don Giovanni* can only be gauged from what critics of exactly this period—the middle of the 1860s—wrote.[10] Axiological trajectories changed, and nowhere more quickly than in the hothouse of Parisian musical and operatic culture.

Parisian critics were enthusiastic about demonstrating their historical acumen, and with each accumulating performance in 1866—the Théâtre Italien in March,

---

[8] For *Wirkungsträger*, see Karl Robert Mandelkow, "Probleme der Wirkungsgeschichte," *Jahrbuch für internationale Germanistik* 2 (1970), 71–84.

[9] Hoffmann's key essay, "Don Juan: Eine fabelhafte Begebenheit, die sich mit einem reisendem Enthusiasten zugetragen," *Allgemeine musikalische Zeitung*, 31 March 1813, reprinted in *Fantasie-Stücke in Callot's Manier mit einer Vorrede von Jean Paul*, 2 vols. (Bamberg: Kunz, 1814), and its reception are discussed in chapter 8.

[10] Reviews of all three productions are in Mark Everist, "Mozart, *Don Giovanni* (1866), Collection 14," *Francophone Music Criticism, 1789–1914*, http://music.sas.ac.uk/fmc/ (accessed 30 June 2012).

the Opéra in April, and the Théâtre-Lyrique in May—critics went to immense lengths to explain the history of *Don Giovanni* and the Opéra, the Théâtre Italien, and other European opera houses, as well as detailing the history of the Théâtre-Lyrique, and how it managed to put itself in a position to mount the production by 1866. The press is full of this information, summarized below, but by May, even some of the critics had had enough. The anonymous critic of the Parisian English-language newspaper *Galignani's Messenger* put it well: "THEATRE LYRIQUE, where *Don Juan* appears as the successful rival of his peers at the French and Italian Operas; our readers will be fortunate in now escaping the dreary display of musical lore inflicted on them when *Don Juan* was first brought out at the former. There is, therefore, no need, nor would there be any excuse, for again parading that tremendous array of sesquipedalian science which was then inflicted on them."[11]

It is not hard to share the mild exasperation of the *Galignani's Messenger's* critic, but his Francophone colleagues' interest in *Don Giovanni*'s history betrays much about their view of the work in the abstract, which in turn reveals a good deal about their attitude to the work's status in 1866. Even *Galignani's Messenger* placed it "high above all criticism,"[12] but Benédict Jouvin, two months later, collapsed into unrestrained panegyric that would have had left his Anglophone colleague speechless with frustration:

> What makes *Don Juan* a unique and exquisite work, alongside works that are more colossal and, in appearance, more grandiose, is the measure of its perfection. This measure is no less admirable in the use of modest artistic material than in the melodic sentiment and the ways in which the characters are drawn. The melody, harmony, scoring are balanced with marvelous ease which, constantly varying the ear's surprise, brings back musical pleasure to the unity of the work. Each voice on the stage has its interest, each instrument in the orchestra its role; the science that governs them makes itself invisible.... The variety of musical forms, the science of contrasts, the suppleness of style are here no less worthy of admiration than the way in which the characters are drawn. What a succession of *tableaux*, dark, laughing, striking, veiled![13]

---

[11] *Galignani's Messenger*, 19 May 1866.

[12] Ibid.

[13] "Ce qui fait de *Don Juan* une œuvre exquise et unique, à côté d'œuvres de proportions plus colossales et, en apparence, plus grandioses, c'est la mesure dans la perfection. Cette mesure n'est pas moins admirable dans l'emploi des moyens matériels de l'art que dans le sentiment mélodique et le dessin des caractères. Le chant, l'harmonie, l'instrumentation s'équilibrent avec une aisance merveilleuse, qui, en variant sans cesse la surprise de l'oreille, ramène le plaisir musical à l'unité de l'œuvre. Chaque voix sur la scène a son intérêt, chaque instrument dans l'orchestre a son rôle; la science qui les maîtrise se fait invisible. . . . La variété des formes musicales, la science des contrastes, la souplesse du style sont ici choses non moins dignes d'admiration que le dessin des caractères. Quelle succession de tableaux, sombres, riants, éclatants, voilés!" (*Le Figaro*, 5 April 1866). Jouvin's review dates from just after the opening of the production at the Opéra.

Jouvin's technique here is to outline the context in which a series of value judgments might be made, but never to substantiate them. So, in his claim that *Don Giovanni* is unique and exquisite alongside more grandiose operas (he is almost certainly speaking of Parisian *grand opéra,* which had reached its apogee with Meyerbeer's posthumous *L'africaine* of the previous year), he argues that it is the measure of perfection, which he then equates with the material resources of art, melodic sentiment, and the drawing of characters. This is then glossed by reference to the balance of vocal writing, harmony, and scoring that he argues helps align musical pleasure with the unity of the work. But after continuing to enumerate voices and instruments, he undercuts any expectation of an explanation for his initial claim by telling his readers that "the science that controls them all makes itself invisible"—in other words, he is absolving himself from any responsibility for explaining how any of this might actually be the case. His account continues much further and ends with unexplained exclamations.

Jouvin's commentary gives an explanatory veneer to simple claims to greatness pronounced by his colleagues. Achille Denis gave a clear verdict on the work:

No-one expects, certainly, an appreciation of this masterpiece consecrated by secular admiration. *Don Juan* has been, for a long time, an opera that one does not discuss. It is a musical monument before whose majesty one can only incline one's head.[14]

No longer a work that is discussed, then, but a musical monument that provokes secular consecration, a majesty before which one must bow: a blunter but no less clear account of the work than Jouvin's lengthy exegesis.

But although *Don Giovanni* as a work could brook no criticism, performances could certainly be dragged before the courts of midcentury Parisian aesthetics, and the three Parisian performances of 1866 elicited some of the most elaborate and far-reaching commentary on the opera anywhere in the world at midcentury. And the work's textuality was at the center of discussions, so when Achille de Lauzières-Thémines demanded "Give me back *Don Juan* as Mozart wrote it" and went on to declare "Mozart's work is beautiful in its own terms; it cannot be pared without damaging its eternal beauty," he clearly had a sense that exactly the work that Mozart had written—and in the form in which it had left the composer's pen—was recoverable.[15] Furthermore—and this is the key point—he thought that the work *tel que Mozart l'a écrit* was what he could hear at the Théâtre Italien, an idea that could have been very easily contradicted by placing the version at the

---

[14] "On ne s'attend pas, sans doute, à une appréciation de ce chef-d'œuvre consacré par une admiration séculaire. *Don Juan* n'est plus, depuis longtemps, un opéra que l'on discute. C'est un monument musical devant la majesté duquel on ne peut plus que s'incliner" (*Le messager des théâtres,* 3 April 1866).

[15] "Qu'on me rende le *Don Juan,* tel que Mozart l'a écrit.... L'œuvre de Mozart est belle par elle-même; on ne la pare pas sans nuire à sa beauté éternelle" (*La Patrie,* 10 April 1866).

Théâtre Italien alongside any version produced during Mozart's lifetime (the detail of the production is described below).

If the critic of *Galignani's Messenger* was irritated by his Parisian colleagues' displays of historical learning, his Parisian colleagues were equally irritated by arguments over which production (at the Opéra in April or at the Théâtre-Lyrique in May—the quality of the production at the Théâtre Italien had ruled it out of court) was better. Answers hinged on two questions: the size of the halls and the nature of the work; both reveal much about views of the opera in the 1860s, and it is remarkable—but perhaps not surprising, given the work—how little the quality of the singers mattered, especially given some of the names in play: Patti, Miolan-Carvalho, Faure, and Nilsson.[16] Some critics advanced the argument that because the opera house in Prague was small and intimate, the Théâtre-Lyrique, considered to be of similar dimensions, could claim the victor's laurels.[17] This was not a bad argument at all, but the one that seemed to occupy most critics was the one that pointed to the dual nature of *Don Giovanni*—the *semiseria* nature implied by its generic title, *dramma giocoso*, and the range of characters from the highborn Donne Anna and Elvira, Commendatore, Don Octavio, and Giovanni to the lowborn Leporello, Masetto, and Zerlina. For many critics this meant that both the Théâtre-Lyrique (which excelled at the comic parts of the opera featuring the lowborn characters) and the Opéra (which gave a better frame for the aristocrats and the tragic elements in the libretto). Edouard Monnais was typical:

> This work encompasses all genres, adopts all tones, and ... the mad gaiety of the *dramma giocoso* there allies itself without effort to the sublime terrors of death, to the redoubtable anger of the heavens, to the righteous punishments of hell, because an entire village world rubs shoulders with a world of aristocrats, and because never have comedy and tragedy been brought into a closer alignment. Well, this double nature, this double character of Da Ponte's play, transfigured by Mozart's genius, the Opéra and Théâtre-Lyrique compared themselves with their natural instinct, each of them insisting on the part that best suited its genre, its conventions. Here, we had a high-style *Don Juan*, the wonderful and pompous *Don Juan*, supported by choruses of which Mozart had never dreamed, decorated with dances for which he had not written the music; there, we were given a *Don Juan* less

---

[16] The legendary Adelina Patti was already an established figure by the age of twenty-three, when she took the role of Zerlina at the Théâtre Italien in 1866; she was perhaps the only artist there to win consistent approval. Marie-Caroline Mionan-Carvalho took the same role at the Théâtre-Lyrique, Jean-Baptiste Faure was the Opéra's title role, and Kristina Nilsson was the Théâtre-Lyrique's Donna Anna.

[17] Lauzières-Thémines wrote that "at the Lyrique, the masterpiece took back its character, its nature, and none of its thousand fine points are lost to the enthusiast" ("Au Lyrique, le chef-d'œuvre a repris son caractère, sa nature, et aucune de ses mille finesses n'est perdu pour l'amateur"; *La Patrie*, 15 May 1866).

proud, less splendid, less active; it was an attempt to reproduce the original *Don Juan* of the Prague theatre.[18]

Monnais then sums up large tracts of the Parisian press. The answer to the question "which of the two opera houses produced the best performance" was "neither, and both." Neither was a winner, and neither a loser: the victors, predictably, were *Don Giovanni* and Paris.

Don Giovanni had received its Paris premiere at the Théâtre Italien in 1811, and had appeared a handful of times each year there with important revivals in 1838 and 1847, when the numbers of performances moved into double figures.[19] The production in 1866 was the first for two years, and there had been forty performances only in the previous decade. The defining production at the Opéra was not the first, which dated from 1805,[20] but the one in which *Don Giovanni* was reinterpreted as a *grand opéra* in five acts with a ballet; this dated from 1834, and although it enjoyed an important revival in 1841, by 1866 it had not been heard at the Opéra for twenty-two years.[21]

Each of the three 1866 productions depended on different performance traditions: the Théâtre Italien's production differed little from what was understood in 1811 to be Mozart's original conception of the work, while the Opéra's depended directly on the 1834 version, significantly updated.[22] The Théâtre-Lyrique was in a position largely to invent its own tradition, and did so by creating a version out of the Frey published edition of 1820, with the French text in the edition almost completely retranslated by Henry Trianon. Each of the three traditions had a direct impact on the nature of the version presented at each opera house.

---

[18] "Cette œuvre embrassait tous les genres, prenait tous les tons, et . . . la folle gaieté du *dramma giocoso* s'y alliait sans effort aux sublimes terreurs de la mort, aux redoutables colères du ciel, aux justes châtiments de l'enfer, parce que tout un monde villageois y coudoyait tout un monde de grands seigneurs, et que jamais la comédie et la tragédie ne s'étaient embrassées plus étroitement. Eh bien, cette double nature, ce double caractère de la pièce de Da Ponte, transfigurée par le génie de Mozart, le Grand-Opéra et le Théâtre-Lyrique s'en sont comparés avec leur instinct naturel, chacun d'eux insistant de préférence sur la part qui convenait le plus à son genre, à ses habitudes. Ici, nous avons eu le *Don Juan* de haut style, le *Don Juan* [*Don Giovanni*] formidable et pompeux, soutenu par des chœurs auxquels n'avait jamais songé Mozart, orné de danses pour lesquelles il n'avait pas écrit de musique: là, on nous a donné un *Don Juan* moins fier, moins splendide, moins bruyant; on s'est efforcé de reproduire le *Don Juan* [*Don Giovanni*] original du théâtre de Prague"; *La revue contemporaine*, 31 May 1866 (signed Wilhelm).

[19] Albert Soubies, *Le Théâtre-Italien de 1801 à 1913* (Paris: Fischbacher, 1913), 47–54.

[20] For the 1805 *Don Juan* see Laurent Marty, *1805: La création de "Don Juan" à l'Opéra de Paris*, Univers musical (Paris: L'Harmattan, 2005).

[21] Albert Soubies, *Soixante-sept ans à l'Opéra en une page du "Siège de Corinthe" à "La Walkyrie" (1826–1893)* (Paris: Fischbacher, 1893).

[22] The only sources from which the 1811 version of *Don Giovanni* at the Théâtre Italien may be reconstructed is the libretto: IL DON GIOVANNI, / DRAMMA GIOCOSO IN DUE ATTI. / . . . / DON JUAN / OPERA-COMIQUE EN DEUX ACTES, / Représenté, pour la première fois, à Paris, sur le / Théâtre de l'IMPÉRATRICE, le [ ] Octobre 1811 / DE L'IMPRIMERIE DE HOCQUET ET Cie / RUE DU FAUBOURG MONTMARTRE, N°. 4 / PARIS / AU THÉÂTRE DE L'IMPÉRATRICE / — / 1811; sources abound for the 1834 version of the piece at the Opéra, and are discussed in the articles cited in note 6.

Recovering the 1866 text for each of the three versions is not without its difficulties. No libretto survives from the 1866 production at the Théâtre Italien, and understanding of this version depends on a libretto published in 1856 for the same theater.[23] If anything, the textual tradition of the Opéra version is even more complex: the published libretto is largely based on the 1841 text, which is in turn based on the 1834 version; there are, however, important changes introduced both in 1841 and in 1866.[24] The music of the Opéra version is all included in the so-called archive score, in which the Opéra kept the work up to date during the nineteenth century; rationalizing the musical sources with the printed libretto is the only way of reconstructing the musical text of this version, and that creates numerous difficulties.[25] Only the version of the Théâtre-Lyrique is straightforward: the original annotated Frey score survives,[26] and so do most of the performance material, the printed libretto, the censors' libretto, and the piano-vocal and piano solo scores that claim to be the "seule[s] édition[s] conforme[s] à l'interprétation du Théâtre Lyrique";[27] there are even traces of a campaign to publish a series of *morceaux*

[23] DON GIOVANNI / DRAMMA GIOCOSO IN DUE ATTI / MUSICA / DI W.-MOZART. / — / PARIGI / MICHEL LÉVY FRERES, ÉDITEURS / RUE VIVIENNE, 2 BIS / — / 1856 / DON JUAN / OPÉRA BOUFFON EN DEUX ACTES / MUSIQUE / DE W.-A. MOZART / — / PARIS / MICHEL LÉVY FRERES, ÉDITEURS / RUE VIVIENNE, 2 BIS / — / 1856.

[24] The two additional libretti are, for 1841, DON JUAN, / OPÉRA EN CINQ ACTES / DE MOZART, / TRADUCTION FRANCAISE / DE MM. ÉMILE DESCHAMPS ET HENRY BLAZE, / DIVERTISSEMENS DE M. CORALY.—DÉCORS DE MM. CICÉRI, FEUCHÈRE, / DESPLÉCHIN, LÉGER, FILASTRE ET CAMBON. / Représenté pour la première fois, à Paris, sur le théâtre de l'Académie / Royale de Musique, le 10 mars 1834, et repris sur le même théâtre, / le 26 mars 1841 / NOUVELLE ÉDITION, / Conforme à la Repésentation. / PARIS. / MICHEL FRÈRES, LIBRAIRES, / RUE ET TERRASSE VIVIENNE, 1, ET RUE MARIE-STUART, 6. / C. TRESSE, / LIBRAIRE AU PALAIS-ROYAL, / Mᵉ Vᵉ JONAS, / LIBRAIRE DE L'OPÉRA. / 1841; and, for 1866, MOZART / DON JUAN / OPÉRA EN CINQ ACTES / TRADUCTION FRANÇAISE DE MM. ÉMILE DESCHAMPS ET HENRI BLAZE / REPRÉSENTÉ POUR LA PREMIÈRE FOIS, A PARIS, SUR LE THÉÂTRE DE L'ACADÉMIE ROYALE DE MUSIQUE, / LE 10 MARS 1834, ET REPRIS SUR LE MÊME THÉATRE, L2 2 AVRIL 1866 / NOUVELLE ÉDITION / PARIS / MICHEL LÉVY FRÈRES, LIBRAIRES ÉDITEURS / RUE VIVIENNE, 2 BIS, ET BOULEVARD DES ITALIENS, 15 / A LA LIBRAIRIE NOUVELLE / — / 1866.

[25] Bibliothèque-Musée de l'Opéra, Bibliothèque nationale de France, Paris, *F-Po* A.400.c.I–VII.

[26] The Frey score that served as the basis for the Théâtre-Lyrique's production is DON GIOVANNI / *Dramma Giocoso* / in due Atti / *Messo in Musica dal Signor* / W. A. MOZART / *Edition Dédiée* / *Aux Souscripteurs* / PAR L'ÉDITEUR / No. 2 de la Collection des Opéra[s] de Mozart / *A PARIS* / *Au Mag*ⁱⁿ *de J. FREY, Artiste de l'Académie Royale, Editeur de Musique…* / Plce des Victoires No. 8 (hereafter "working score"). This, together with the manuscript performance material, is now at the Bibliothèque nationale de France, *F-Pn* MAT. TH. 416.

[27] The printed libretto is NOUVELLE BIBLIOTHÈQUE DRAMATIQUE / ÉDITION DU THÉÂTRE LYRIQUE / — / DON JUAN / OPÉRA / EN DEUX ACTES ET TREIZE TABLEAUX / MUSIQUE DE MOZART / (T. G. C.) / *Deuxième Édition* / — / PARIS / LIBRAIRIE INTERNATIONALE / 15, BOULEVARD MONTMARTRE / A. LACROIX, VERBROECKHOVEN & Cᵉ, ÉDITEURS / à *Bruxelles, à Leipzig et à Livourne*; two copies of the censors' libretto are in the Archives nationales Paris, *F-Pan* F¹⁸. 738; see Odile Krakovitch, *Censure des répertoires des grands théâtres parisiens (1835–1906): Inventaire des manuscrits des pièces (F¹⁸ 669à 1016) et des procès-verbaux des censeurs (F²¹ 966à 995)* (Paris: Centre Historique des Archives Nationales, 2003); 249; the piano-vocal score is SEULE ÉDITION / CONFORME à L'INTERPRÉTATION DU THÉÂTRE LYRIQUE / DON / JUAN / Opéra en 2 Actes et 12 Tableaux / MUSIQUE DE / MOZART / *Partition Chant & Piano* / A PARIS, CHOUDENS / EDITEUR, Rue Sᵗ Honoré, 265, Près de l'Assomption / *Propriété* / pʳ. tous Pays.

détachés (single extracts) of the work.[28] All the printed musical material appeared from the publisher Choudens.

Treatment of the kinetic sections of the opera differed at all three institutions. *Recitativo semplice* continued in productions at the Théâtre Italien, while accompanied recitative remained de rigueur at the Opéra, and the 1866 productions of *Don Giovanni* were no exception to this general rule. Only the Théâtre-Lyrique had any scope for artistic decision: it could equally well have chosen the same approach as the one to which the Opéra was bound—the use of accompanied recitative—or employed some sort of spoken dialogue or even *recitativo semplice*. The first two options figured in the repertory the Théâtre-Lyrique had cultivated since the beginning of the decade, so its choice to employ spoken dialogue was an unfettered artistic decision that simply made an appropriate compromise between what it understood as Mozart's original and what it thought it needed to satisfy its audiences.

Many aspects of the overall structure were conventional at each of the three opera houses. At the Théâtre Italien, the division into two acts with the larger finale at the end of the first act was paramount, and it was almost inconceivable that this would be altered. Equally inconceivable was to produce a version of *Don Giovanni* at the Opéra in anything other than five acts with a ballet, which had been the case since 1834; the ballet—although massively rewritten and rechoreographed for 1866—was located at the end of the second act of five. As before, the Théâtre-Lyrique could choose how to articulate the structure of the work: it presented the opera in two acts in all its printed material, but divided it into thirteen tableaux according to the libretto and twelve according (apparently) to the material produced by the more superstitious Choudens. But this gesture was undercut by the working score that the Théâtre-Lyrique used, which clearly broke the opera into *four* acts, simply eliding acts 3 and 4 of the Opéra version and calling act 5 at the Opéra act 4.[29] There were good reasons for this, however, since the final act at the Théâtre-Lyrique contained more music.

The immediate consequences of these decisions were more immediately felt at the Opéra and Théâtre-Lyrique. At both houses, the first act ended with the last note of "Or sai chi l'onore," and the following recitative was abandoned. Similarly, the recitative after the sextet (which ended its third act) was omitted at the Opéra, but because there was no act change at this point at the Théâtre-Lyrique, the recitative was recast, as was the case everywhere else in that version, in spoken dialogue. The Théâtre-Lyrique's possibly cynical attempt to revert to four acts created a large number of entr'actes between the twelve or thirteen tableaux, which were

---

[28] THÉÂTRE LYRIQUE IMPÉRIAL / DON JUAN / *OPÉRA EN DEUX ACTES* / *et douze Tableaux* / TRADUCTION française de H. TRIANON et *** / MOZART / *Catalogue des Morceaux de Chant séparés avec accompagn^t de Piano* / . . . / Paris rue St Honoré, 265 chez CHOUDENS, Éditeur, (près de l'Assomption) [single number ("Frappe, frappe") only].

[29] *F-Po* A.400.c.I–VII.

badly received by the press. The critic Marie Escudier simply could not understand what they were doing:

> But why cut *Don Juan* into twelve or thirteen *tableaux* and separate them by interminable entr'actes? It is to put the patience, or rather the nervous system, of the audience to a terrible test. The member of the audience who puts up with the three-quarters of an hour of entracte, is no longer in any state to judge well. He is irritated, annoyed, paralyzed.[30]

Escudier's colleague Armand de Pontmartin (who considered the production at the Opéra infinitely superior to the one at the Théâtre-Lyrique) turned the excessive entr'actes to good effect:

> The most important thing for the witty arrangers of this third *Don Juan* to do is to remove at least one of the entr'actes, not to make the masterpiece last two hours longer than at the Théâtre-Italien. Just imagine, if one of these evenings, some criminal in E♭ or a minor stopped the escapees from the Théâtre-Lyrique at one in the morning on the Boulevard de Sebastopol, and proved to them, watch in hand, that *Don Juan* is a marvelous opera, exquisite, suave, divine, ineffable, heavenly, ethereal, delicious, adorable, but... a little boring![31]

The textual histories of the Théâtre-Lyrique's entr'actes are difficult, however, to establish. Only fragments, possibly cues only, survive in the working score, and even then only at the beginnings of acts 2, 3 and 4; it would appear that they were copied elsewhere and this material was then lost. Public disapproval of the entr'actes and the consequent length of the Théâtre-Lyrique's performance was, however, ubiquitous.

Although the production at the Théâtre Italien remained in two acts, the aria "Ho capito" in act 1 was suppressed, and the aria "Mi tradi" was placed after "Là ci darem la mano" and replaced "Ah fuggi il traditor." The tradition of so placing "Mi tradi"—so far from its original location in the 1788 Vienna production for which it was written—was continued in both the Opéra and Théâtre-Lyrique versions, but at the 1866 Opéra production "Ah fuggi il traditor" was reinstated, as well as "Mi tradi." Although "Ho capito" had been excised from the 1834 and 1841 Opéra productions, it, too, was reinstated in both the Opéra and Théâtre-Lyrique versions of

---

[30] "Mais pourquoi découper *Don Juan* en douze ou treize tableaux et les séparer par d'interminables entr'actes ? C'est mettre la patience ou plutôt le système nerveux des auditeurs à une terrible épreuve. L'auditeur qui a supporté les trois quarts d'heure d'entracte, n'est plus en état de bien juger. Il est agacé, énervé, perclus" (*La France musicale*, 13 May 1866).

[31] "L'essentiel, pour les spirituels arrangeurs de ce troisième *Don Juan* [*Don Giovanni*], est de supprimer au moins un entracte . . . de ne pas faire durer le chef-d'œuvre deux heures de plus qu'au Théâtre-Italien. Songez donc . . . si, un de ces soirs, quelque malfaiteur en *mi bémol* ou en *la mineur* arrêtait à une heure du matin, sur le boulevard de Sébastopol, les échappés du Théâtre-Lyrique, et leur prouvait, montre en main, que *Don Juan* est un opéra merveilleux, exquis, suave, divin, ineffable, céleste, éthéré, délicieux, adorable, mais . . . un peu ennuyeux!" (*La gazette de France*, 13 May 1866).

1866 (although it did not figure in the libretto of the Opéra performance, since so much of that document was merely a reprint of the 1841 version).

Two numbers that were consistently excluded from all the productions in 1866 were from act 2. "Ah pietà" had been suppressed at the Théâtre Italien since 1811, as it had been in Vienna in 1788, and no one made any attempt to reinstate it. The same was true of "Metà di voi," except that a translation exists of the number in the Théâtre-Lyrique score, which suggests that it was at least considered for inclusion but eventually rejected. Johannès Weber knew *Don Giovanni* well and regretted this omission at the Opéra:

> Don Juan's aria, "Meta di voi," is a model of comic music; it is suppressed at
> the Opéra as well as at the Théâtre-Italien. Were one really to understand the
> character of the role, this vandalism would be avoided. At the Théâtre-Ital-
> ien, the piece is replaced by a few gestures; at the opera by a dialogue with
> music by Castil-Blaze.[32]

When the same excision was practiced at the Théâtre-Lyrique, Weber was even less pleased by the dialogue that replaced it.[33] Weber was an ambitious theoretician and writer on music, and in arguing for the retention of "Metà di voi" was setting the textual bar higher than all his other journalistic colleagues.

For any *grand opéra* premiere in Paris, the dance element and the choreography were a central point of interest, and nineteenth-century productions of *Don Giovanni* were no exception. By 1866—and this had been less the case in 1834—much of the dance in such a work was collected into a single elaborate *divertissement*.[34] In both the 1834 and 1866 productions, the location for the *divertissement* was irresistible: the original act 1 finale (the finale to act 2 in the 1834 and 1866 *Don Juan*). Insofar as it is possible to establish, the 1834 *divertissement* interrupted Mozart's original finale just afterward and introduced a range of music taken largely from *Le nozze di Figaro* and *Die Zauberflöte*. It may also have included the minuet from the Symphony no. 40 in g minor, K. 550 (not the trio nor the reprise of the minuet), since this was incorporated (the only part to be so) in the 1866 *divertissement*.

The makeup of the 1866 *divertissement* is shown in table 4.1. The choreography is difficult to recover from surviving sources, but according to Henri Heugel, Saint-Léon had been recalled from Saint Petersburg specifically to compose and direct this *divertissement*, one based largely on "a cloud of butterflies in watered silk swirling among the roses."[35] As far as can be established, the

---

[32] "L'air de Don Juan [Don Giovanni]: *Meta di voi*, est un modèle de musique comique; on le supprime à l'Opéra comme au Théâtre-Italien. Si l'on comprenait réellement le caractère du personnage, on se garderait bien de ce vandalisme. Au Théâtre-Italien, on remplace le morceau par quelques gestes; à l'Opéra, par un dialogue avec musique de Castil-Blaze" (*Le Temps*, 18 April 1866).

[33] Ibid., 16 May 1866.

[34] This is a tendency throughout the period from 1830 to 1860; see Mark Everist, "Grand Opéra—Petit Opéra: Parisian Opera and Ballet from the Restoration to the Second Empire," *19th-Century Music* 33 (2010), 199–200.

[35] "Une nuée de papillons moirés tourbillant parmi des roses" (*Le Ménestrel*, 1 April 1866).

TABLE 4.1: Structure of *Don Giovanni* act 2 *divertissement*, Paris Opéra, 1866

F-Po A.400.c.I-VII	Borrowed material reworked for dance context
IV:12–25	Minuet of Symphony in g minor K. 550 (the only remnant of the 1834 *divertissement*)
IV: 26–53	Trio and reprise of K. 550 minuet (Auber)
IV: 54–60	No. I. Theme and first variation of String Quartet in d minor K. 421 finale
IV: 61–66	No. II. D major variation and *più allegro* of String Quartet in d minor K. 421 finale.
IV: 67–71	No. III. Minuet of String Quartet in d minor K. 421
IV: 72–74	No. IV. Trio of String Quartet in d minor K. 421
IV: 75–83 and 84–99	No. V. Trio from String Quintet in E♭Major K. 614 (transposed to D major)
IV: 100–102	No. VI. Trio of String Quartet in d minor K. 421
IV: 103–107	No. VII. Minuet of String Quartet in d minor K. 421
IV: 108–169	No. VIII. Finale of Piano Sonata in A K. 311

selection of the music was made by the Opéra's conductor, Georges Hainl, and its *chef du chant*, François-Eugène Vauthrot, but the veteran Auber (aged eighty-four at this point) was responsible for the orchestration of the movement from the K. 311 piano sonata, and the "imperceptible joins" (*d'imperceptibles soudures*) between the movements.[36]

The critical view of the ballet was one of almost unbridled enthusiasm, tempered only occasionally with the tiniest points of criticism. Léon Kreutzer spoke for almost all of the press when he wrote:

> There is absolutely no point in praising the dance; dance makes our Académie Impériale de Musique truly the queen of the musical world. Nothing is more seductive than the ballet of love, butterflies and roses. Roses quivering, butterflies fluttering: it is really charming; all the more because the ballet is short.... The minuet in g minor is again introduced into it [which suggests that it did form a part of the 1834 ballet]; the minuet and sicilienne of the d minor quartet (by Mozart of course), since no-one (I presume, and am not entirely sure) would have dared touch the sacred work.[37]

Kreutzer's enthusiasm for the *divertissement* was shared by almost all his journalistic colleagues.

The question was asked on several occasions why Auber had been asked to reorchestrate the so-called Marche Turque when not only was there a perfectly serviceable orchestration by Prosper Pascal but also this arrangement had been

---

[36] Ibid.

[37] "Il est parfaitement inutile de louer les danses: c'est par la danse que notre Académie Impériale de musique est véritablement la reine du monde musical. Rien de plus séduisant que le ballet des amours, des papillons et des roses. Roses de s'effeuiller, papillons de papillonner: C'est un véritable charme; d'autant plus que le ballet est court.... On y a introduit encore le menuet en sol mineur; les menuet et Sicilienne du quatuor en ré mineur (de Mozart, bien entendu), car personne (je le suppose, et n'en suis pas absolument sûr), n'eût osé toucher à l'œuvre consacrée" (*L'union*, 10 April 1866).

used at the Théâtre-Lyrique's production of *Die Entführung aus dem Serail* as an entr'acte (this might explain some journallists' confusion between the orchestration in K. 311 and the Turkish choruses in *Die Entführung*). There was some discussion of the way the Opéra had simplified the enmeshing of the three orchestras in the act 2 (originally act 1) finale: the opera had simply moved all the music (in 2/4 and 3/8 and in 3/4) into 3/4, much to the disgust of Marie Escudier, who described it as a crime of *lèse-chef-d'œuvre*.[38] The only serious criticism was made by a correspondent signing himself "L. E." in *L'art musical* who suggested that the placement of the ballet (which he otherwise adored) cut into the action of the finale too much, a finale that he argued was "Mozart's most beautiful, dramatic and grandiose inspiration."[39]

Complexities surrounding the *divertissement* of the 1866 *Don Giovanni* are restricted to the production at the Opéra itself. Not so those surrounding the supper scene and the *scena ultima* at the end of the first act of the original (end of the fourth and fifth acts at the Théâtre-Lyrique and Opéra, respectively). Of direct relevance to the history of keyboard arrangements of *Don Giovanni* discussed below is the handling of the three operatic citations in the supper scene: Mingone's aria "Come un agnello" from Giuseppe Sarti's *Frà i due litiganti il terzo gode*, "Oh quanto un si bel giubilo" from Vincente Martin y Soler's *Una cosa rara,* and "Non più andrai" from Mozart's own *Le nozze di Figaro*. The way these three external citations are introduced untexted in the orchestra and the way Leporello identifies them is familiar to anyone who knows the opera. But in the Opéra version, Leporello identifies *Una cosa rara* by name, whereas *I due litiganti* is not mentioned at all; he identifies the source and the composer of "Non più andrai." Conversely, in the version at the Théâtre-Lyrique, *Una cosa rara* is only identified in the stage directions in the libretto, whereas Leporello pronounces the title *l due litiganti*; he translates Da Ponte's wit directly when he fails to cite the name of "Non più andrai" but simply says that it is a melody he knows too well. The result of this is the elision of the works by Sarti and Martini into the field of material that could be selected by keyboard arrangers as coming from *Don Giovanni* (this is to say nothing of "Non più andrai," which undergoes the same transformation).

The way *Don Giovanni* was made to end in the nineteenth century is contested territory, and to understand the position in Paris in 1866, reviewing the material is useful. As is well known, Donna Elvira leaves at the end of the act 2 finale, encountering the Commendatore as she exits, and knocking at the door is then heard. The Commendatore enters, accompanied by the music from the slow introduction to the overture, and after several exchanges Don Giovanni offers him his hand (più stretto: "Oimè!"), which triggers—over figures developed out of the music for the duel in the *Introduzione*—the demands and refusals for Don Giovanni to repent.

---

[38] *La France musicale*, 8 April 1866.
[39] "La plus belle inspiration dramatique et la plus grandiose de Mozart" (*L'art musical*, 5 April 1866).

The eponym is dragged down to Hell in a d minor chorus (Allegro) over which he and his servant are projected in perhaps predictable ways. As known in the contemporary world, *Don Giovanni* then concludes with a three-part *scena ultima* featuring the entire cast except Giovanni. In the first section (Allegro assai, G major), everyone not present at the end of the act 2 finale demands to know where Giovanni is and tries to extract an explanation from Leporello; in the second (Larghetto), each character outlines his or her plans for his or her future life, which leads into the final moralizing fugue (Presto, D major), *l'antichissima canzon*.

However the *scena ultima* was treated during the eighty years after its premiere (and there were many responses to this ending, the most common being simply to omit it), none of the conclusions to the 1866 *Don Giovanni* are unproblematic. The version from the Théâtre Italien seems to end without the *scena ultima* and ends with Don Giovanni's descent into Hell, according to the conventional accounts of nineteenth-century treatments of the opera. However, the 1856 Théâtre Italien libretto (and presumably the 1866 version) includes the text for Leporello "E sparito, andiamo via; / Ritorniano all'osteria / A cercar padron miglior," which has much in common with his lines "Ed io vado all'osteria / A trovar padron miglior"; but these lines are found not only in the *scena ultima* of which nothing else remains but in its middle section, the *Larghetto*. This leaves some considerable doubt as to exactly how this text was worked into a version that ostensibly ended with Giovanni's descent into Hell.[40]

From 1834 to 1844, performances of *Don Giovanni* at the Opéra had ended not with Don Giovanni's descent into Hell but with an extensive tableau at the end, based on "O voto tremendo" from *Idomeneo* and the Dies Irae from the *Requiem*, and set in the garden of Don Giovanni's villa. In advance of the 1866 Opéra performance, Heugel asked whether "the *Dies irae* and the chorus from *Idomeneo*, with which the final scene formerly ended, would this time be preserved; *Le Figaro*, in an article both literary and interesting and published this week, replied to the question: 'Mozart is retained, pure and simple; nothing more, nothing less.'"[41]

What is clear from this exchange is that Mozart, "pure and simple, nothing more, nothing less" meant ending *Don Giovanni* with the descent into Hell, and the complete suppression of the *scena ultima*, and this is what happened at the Opéra in 1866. The printed libretto, which exactly duplicates the layout of the 1841 version, differs only in the its very last page, where the 1841 version has the additional tableau

---

[40] The additional text is found in libretti from the Théâtre Italien from as early as 1820; see IL DON GIOVANNI / DRAMMA GIOCOSO IN DUE ATTI. / — / DON JUAN / OPERA BOUFFON EN DEXU ACTES, / Représenté, pour la première fois, à Paris, sur le / Théâtre royal Italien, Salle de Louvois, le 3 / Octobre 1820. / PARIS, / AU THÉÂTRE LOUVOIS / — / De l'Imprimerie de HOCQUET, rue du Faubourg Montmartre / — / 1820. Had the performance material survived, it would have revealed the way this part of the text was reworked into the finale before Giovanni's descent into Hell.

[41] "Le *Dies irae* et le chœur d'*Idoménée*, par lesquels jadis se terminait la scène finale, seraient cette fois maintenus; le *Figaro*, dans un article très-intéressant et très-littéraire, publié cette semaine, a répondu à la question: "On s'est tenu à la note de Mozart pure et simple: rien de plus, mais aussi rien de moins" (*Le Ménestrel*, 1 April 1866).

and the 1866 version ends before the *scena ultima*. Achille Denis was enthusiastic about the mise-en scène of the end of the act 2 finale:

> Don Giovanni falls exhausted at the feet of the vengeful statue, having again become silent and immobile. A curtain opens and reveals in the depths of the stage the phantoms of the dead seducer's victims. The effect is very fine, to repeat, and the impression of the audience was profound. It was difficult to conclude this enchanting evening in a more dramatic fashion.[42]

This enthusiasm was shared by most of his colleagues, although there were plenty of voices who lamented the *scena ultima*. Weber—and it is already clear that he knew the score well—could suggest that "it is normal to suppress the sextet that ought to end the opera, for the excellent reason that the devil has carried off Don Giovanni, the public declares itself satisfied and wants to hear nothing more. What does it matter what Donna Anna, Elvira, Zerlina, Don Ottavio, Masetto, Leporello and Mozart might have to say!"[43] And Léon Kreutzer politely inquired, "If we did not fear for showing ourselves a little too curious, we would ask why Mozart's real finale has been suppressed. It is a magnificent chorus, in which is found the moral of the work."[44]

The inclusion of the *scena ultima* was critical to the production at the Théâtre-Lyrique: the libretto and score include its first and third sections, and a certain amount of Leporello's dialogue is superimposed over the final bars of the act 2 finale that precedes it: "Oh mes gages, mes gages. Voilà par sa mort en chacun satisfait. Ciel offensé, lois violées, filles séduites, familles déshonorées, parents outragés, femmes mises à mal, maris poussés à bout, tout le monde est content, il n'y a que moi seul de malheureux, mes gages, mes gages, mes gages." But this must have been a very congested end to the act, since the Théâtre-Lyrique version also massively abbreviated the chorus (cutting bars 554–593 and reducing the section from forty-eight bars to nine), moving almost directly from the Commendatore's "Pour toi plus de merci" ("Ah tempo più non v'è" in Da Ponte and Mozart's original) to the end of the act. And although the libretto gave the entire passage in translation, the score is unequivocal in cutting most of it. The Théâtre-Lyrique also cut

---

[42] "Don Juan [Don Giovanni] tombe abattu aux pieds de la statue vengeresse, redevenue immobile et silencieuse. Un rideau s'ouvre et découvre dans le fond les fantômes des victimes du séducteur foudroyé. L'effet est très beau, répétons-le, et l'impression du public a été profonde. Il était difficile de terminer d'une façon plus dramatique cette soirée d'enchantements" (*Le messager des théâtres*, 3 April 1866).

[43] "Il est d'usage de supprimer tout le sextuor qui doit terminer l'opéra, suppression fondée sur l'excellente raison, que lorsque le diable a emporté Don Juan [Don Giovanni], le public se déclare satisfait et ne veut plus entendre rien. Que lui importe ce que Donna Anna, Elvire [Elvira], Zerline [Zerlina], Don Ottavio, Mazetto [Masetto], Leporello et Mozart peuvent avoir à lui dire!" (*Le Temps*, 18 April 1866).

[44] "Si nous ne craignions de nous montrer un peu trop curieux, nous demanderions pourquoi on a supprimé le véritable final composé pour Mozart. C'est pourtant un magnifique chœur, dans lequel se trouve la morale de la pièce" (*La France musicale*, 8 April 1866).

the central section of the *scena ultima*, transposing the end of the first to prepare for the fugue in D major rather than the middle section in G. In doing so, it certainly responded to some critics' observations that the moral of the piece was lost without the final fugue.

Shockingly for modern observers, and surprisingly for the Théâtre-Lyrique, the inclusion of the *scena ultima* was a move appreciated by none. Joseph d'Ortigue declared to his readers in the *Journal des Débats* that:

> performing these three pieces [that make up the *scena ultima*] was quickly abandoned and possibly during Mozart's lifetime. However fine they may indeed be, they can only weaken the effect of this scene that ends the action in a decisive and conclusive fashion. When Mozart wrote these pieces, he only heard, so to speak, his music through the libretto, and he was under the influence of Da Ponte's ideas. It could therefore be said that he did not yet know his own work, at least through the means of performance. The Théâtre-Lyrique had the good intentions to pay the most complete homage possible to Mozart; but it will be good to end the second act in accordance with usage almost everywhere else, and that in the interest of success, of the work and of the public.[45]

D'Ortigue's preference was clearly for ending the opera with Don Giovanni's descent into Hell, and his explanation attempts to save Mozart from himself—he only understood his own music from the libretto and was working under the influence (we may assume unfavorable) of Da Ponte. D'Ortigue has to rely on Mozart only being able to understand his own work at the moment of performance, and to make the assumption that Mozart would have changed the ending as soon as he heard it. Regardless of the absence of logic in this argument, what is important is that d'Ortigue is trying to defend what he and other critics simply called *usage*—conventional practice—by appeals to textual authority (however misguided that might have been). Escudier simply did not see this need: he recognized that the final fugue existed in the original manuscript but remarked that "it has never been performed in France, and that is right." De Pontmartin cited the *scena ultima* specifically when he complained about the length of the production. Edouard Monnais simply condemned the reinstatement of the scene: it was not the result of any conscientious purpose, and nobody wanted it.[46]

---

[45] "On a bien vite renoncé, et peut-être du vivant de Mozart, à exécuter ces trois morceaux. Si beaux qu'ils soient, en effet, ils ne peuvent qu'affaiblir l'impression de cette scène qui termine l'action d'une manière décisive et concluante. Lorsque Mozart écrivait ces morceaux, il n'entendait pour ainsi dire sa musique, qu'à travers le livret, et il était sous l'influence des idées de Da Ponte. On peut donc dire qu'il ne connaissait pas encore son propre ouvrage, du moins de cette connaissance que révèle la représentation. Le Théâtre-Lyrique a eu la bonne intention de rendre son hommage à Mozart le plus complet possible; mais il fera bien de terminer le second acte conformément à l'usage suivi partout ailleurs, et cela dans l'intérêt du succès, de l'œuvre et du public" (*Journal des Débats*, 19 May 1866).

[46] *La gazette de France*, 13 May 1866 (Armand de Pontmartin), and *La revue contemporaine*, 31 May 1866 (Edouard Monnais, writing as Wilhelm).

Having scorned the action of the *scena ultima*, Théophile Gautier, in a passage that deserves quotation for its beauty, went so far as to question its absolute value:

> Is it true that they are really that happy, his fine ladies still so enraged, this coquette Zerlina so naively seduced, and do they not regret a little this Don Giovanni, young, handsome, seductive, proud, bold, who never inspired fear in men, ghosts or creditors, and who climbed so lightly up silken ladders before sweet hands held out in the shadows, and who breathed better than anyone the Spanish serenade in front of windows and under balconies! It would not surprise us, and we think that this fugal curse is there only for the sake of morality. Libertines have always pleased women, and Don Ottavio, the good young man, seems like a poor man alongside Don Giovanni.[47]

Gautier's last line may contain echoes of the truth, but when he says that Giovanni never inspired fear in men, ghosts, or creditors, he seems to have forgotten about the murder of the Commendatore. But what is so interesting here is the defense of Don Giovanni that we will see taken up with such enthusiasm by Shaw twenty years later (see chapter 8), and despite Gautier's idiosyncratic—but prophetic—verdict on the eponym, like all his colleagues he was happier with his opera ending in the fires of Hell than with a moralizing fugue.[48]

Keyboard Arrangements: Ideology and Genre

Compositions for keyboard based on preexisting operatic music came in for much criticism in the second half of the nineteenth century, and because so much came from Austro-German musical traditions, large parts have adhered to musical discourses ever since. One of the difficulties with the blitzkrieg against an entire musical culture is that descriptions of that culture become badly impoverished. In the present case, criticisms of the "travelling virtuoso," operatic *potpourri*, transcription, "salon music," *paraphrase*, and *funtaisie* are elided and sacrificed on the altar of newly composed Austro-German instrumental music, the main competitor for the types of composition under discussion here. So genre, performing

---

[47] "Est-il vrai qu'elles s'en réjouissent autant que cela, ses belles dames si éprises encore dans leur colère, cette coquette Zerline si naïvement éblouie, et ne le regrettent-elles pas un peu ce Don Juan jeune, beau, séduisant, fier, hardi, que n'effrayaient ni les hommes, ni les spectres, ni les créanciers, qui montait si légèrement sur les échelles de soie au-devant des douces mains tendues dans l'ombre, et soupirait mieux que personne la sérénade espagnol devant les grilles et sous les miradors!—Cela ne nous surprendrait pas, et nous pensons que cette malédiction fuguée est là seulement pour la morale. Les libertins ont toujours plu aux femmes, et Don Ottavio, le bon jeune homme, paraît un pauvre sire près de Don Juan" (*Le moniteur universel*, 14 May 1866).

[48] Although paradoxically, Shaw seems to have based his commentary on a reading of *Don Giovanni* that most certainly did include the *scena ultima*.

space, performer, and musical style become confused in the rush to put as much intellectual and musical space between, for example, a piano sonata by Johannes Brahms and a *fantaisie* by Henri Herz.

Somewhere around four dozen arrangements based on music from *Don Giovanni* were published in Paris in 1866, including ones for solo bugle and brass ensemble, orchestra, flute and piano, piano and harmonium, organ and piano, piano four hands, flute and violin, and military band.[49] But by far the largest category was for solo piano: around thirty works were so composed. Generic problems abound in this repertory, however, and titles are a treacherous guide to how composers or consumers thought about or understood the music they were composing or buying. For the twenty-eight coherently titled compositions (excluding those that simply identify themselves as part of *Don Giovanni* (*Scène de bal, Sérénade*, and so on), there are no less than twenty different titles, including *Paraphrase, Fantaisie, Fantaisie brillante, Souvenirs, Souvenirs mélodiques, Mélange, Mosaïque, Illustration,* and *Bouquet* (this is a tiny cross-section of the range of titles). While it is true that works that include the word "Fantaisie" in their title tend to exhibit a wider range of material chosen from the opera and to exploit more obviously bravura styles, this is far from always the case.

Some sort of generic understanding of this *corpus* is always possible. Compositions that take numbers from *Don Giovanni* and recast them in the form of any of the three principal dance forms—polka, quadrille, or waltz—clearly separate themselves out from the rest of the repertory, as do works designed for children or with specific technical problems explicitly excluded.[50] Some works restrict themselves to simple transcription of the material they borrow, although as the next section and other studies show, transcription is a highly contested area, both musically and aesthetically. Perhaps the most familiar generic model found in these keyboard works based on *Don Giovanni* is that of the variation, although the technique is rarely used for more than a single variation, and sets of variations are unknown. But none of this helps account for the largest group of compositions, which are discussed here under the title *fantaisie,* in the knowledge that such a procedure encompasses many works that do not share the title and excludes some that do. But as a way of aligning discussions of a range of different musical processes, it is a satisfactory heuristic tool.

Matching repertory of this sort to performing spaces falls foul of inadequate sources: it is impossible to pin down exact performances of any of the works discussed here. However, differing types of space may be hypothesized for parts of the repertory. The simplest types of transcription and works for juveniles would not have migrated far beyond the domestic drawing room with a tiny

---

[49] See Dideriksen and Everist, "Patterns of Mozart Reception."

[50] The best introduction to social dance in this period is a text that would have been well known to most of its practitioners in the 1860s: Henri Cellarius, *Danses des salons* (Paris: author, 1847; reprint, with an introduction by Rémi Hess Grenoble, Millon, 1993).

number of participants in the event. At the other end of the scale, it is not impossible to imagine any of the larger-scale *fantaisies* appearing at concerts in any of the concert rooms of the capital. But even here, distinctions must be drawn between the Salle Herz, which seated nearly seven hundred, in fixed seating and the Salle Pleyel, which had more the feeling of a salon (albeit a large one) to it.[51] In between lay the salons themselves, which could easily accommodate anywhere up to a hundred listeners. Pauline Viardot's salon (see the description and illustration in chapter 6) is a good example of this sort of space, and it is possible that the dance music based on *Don Giovanni* could have been performed in environments as small as these.

Trying to gain some precision about the real performing spaces in which these keyboard works found a home is perhaps less fruitful than the analysis of the imaginary spaces created by the title pages of some of them. Many of the works have decorative title pages that simply figure generic images: Friedrich Burgmüller's *Valse de salon* is one of these.[52] But others take a single image from the drama. Figure 4.1 is the title page of Jean-Baptiste Duvernoy's *Don Juan fantaisie*, op. 284, which shows a decanter, a goblet, and a stemmed plate, a visual image of Don Giovanni's "Fin ch'han dal vino," a transcription of which closes the piece (fig. 4.1).[53]

Similarly, Pierre Croisez's *Petite fantaisie sur Don Juan* features a single image (fig. 4.2).[54] Here, a group of three specters represents an abstract view of the opera that is at odds with the music chosen for Croisez's *Petite fantaisie*. As its title implies, it is a modest work based on three of the sunniest pieces in the opera: Zerlina's mild reproach to Masetto "Batti, batti," "Là ci darem la mano," and the orchestral minuet from the act 1 finale. The title page therefore does important work as it helps maintain the balance in the piano work between the serious and comic elements (the latter embodied in the piano composition) in the opera.

The title page of Charles Magne's *Airs de ballets intercalés dans l'opéra de Don Juan* develops the registral oppositions still further (fig. 4.3).[55]

---

[51] Joël-Marie Fauqet and Laure Schnapper, "Salle de Concert," *Dictionnaire de la musique en France au xixe siècle*, ed. Joël-Marie Fauquet (Paris: Fayard, 2003), 1113–1114.

[52] A Mademoiselle / MARIE MONTFORT / DON JUAN / de MOZART / VALSE de SALON / POUR PIANO PAR / Fréd. BURGMÜLLER /.../ Paris, LÉON GRUS, Editeur, 31 Boulev.t Bonne Nouvelle. / *Londres et Mayence, Schott.*

[53] A Mademoiselle / *JOSÉPHINE CUVRU* / DON JUAN / DE MOZART / FANTAISIE pour PIANO / *J. B. DUVERNOY.* / *OP. 284* / PR 7f 50 / PARIS / G. BRANDUS ET S. DUFOUR Editeurs, 103 rue Richelieu.

[54] PETITE FANTAISIE / SUR / DON JUAN / de MOZART / Pour le Piano / PAR / A. [sic] CROISEZ / Paris, COLOMBIER, Editeur, 6, r. Vivienne, au coin de la Galerie Vivienne.

[55] AIRS DE BALLETS INTERCALÉS DANS L'OPÉRA / DE / DON JUAN / DE / W. MOZART / À / l'Académie Impériale de Musique / TRANSCRITS POUR LE PIANO PAR / CHARLES MAGNE / PARIS / MAISON ARTISTIQUE, 8 rue Ollivier en face N. D. de Lorette, rue Fléchier, 2, H. L. D'AUBEL EDITR.

FIGURE 4.1: *Title page of Jean-Baptiste Duvernoy,* Don Juan fantaisie, *op. 284 (Paris: Brandus et Dufour, 1866).*

Reproduced with permission, Bibliothèque nationale de France.

It does this by juxtaposing a stern Commendatore (on a plinth outside, so this must be "O statua gentilissima") with what—from an examination of the libretto—must be three of the dancers from the act 2 *divertissement*: two roses and a butterfly. The Commendatore leans back on his right leg, the better to examine the antics of the dancers. Only the dance music is present in the keyboard work, and the Commendatore figures not at all, so again the title-page graphic works toward rebalancing the equilibrium between the various elements in the opera. It also rebalances the authority of the composer, given that none of the music in Magne's collection is from *Don Giovanni* itself.[56] When the publisher, D'Aubel, reused the same title-page images for Carlo Micheli's *Polka sur les motifs de Don Juan* (which uses "Fin ch'han dal vino" and

---

[56] Discussed below.

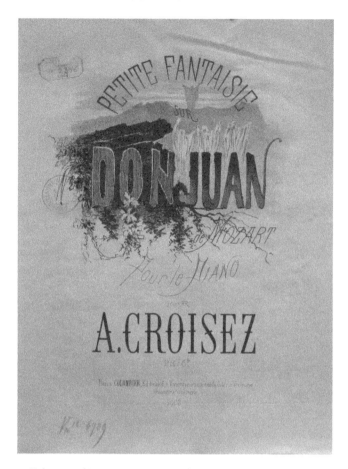

FIGURE 4.2: *Title page of Pierre Croisez,* Petite fantaisie sur Don Juan *(Paris: Colombier, 1866).*

Reproduced with permission, Bibliothèque nationale de France.

"Notte e giorno faticar"), any connection between image and musical content was severed.[57]

The most sophisticated treatment of the relationship between decorative title page and musical contents is found in Henri Marx's *Don Juan... Quadrille*.[58] The detail of its music will be discussed later, but it uses six musical borrowings from *Don Giovanni*: the chorus "Giovenette che fate"; "Batti batti"; "Là ci darem la mano"; "Fin ch'han dal vino"; and two citations from the act 2 finale: Martin y

---

[57] POLKA / *sur les motifs de* / DON JUAN / DE / W. MOZART / Pour LE PIANO PAR / CARLO MICHELI / PARIS / MAISON ARTISTIQUE, 8 rue Ollivier en face N. D. de Lorette, rue Fléchier, 2, H. L. D'AUBEL EDIT[R].

[58] *RÉPERTOIRE DU THÉÂTRE IMPÉRIAL DE L'OPÉRA à Monsieur EMILE PERRIN* / DON JUAN / DE MOZART / QUADRILLE / POUR PIANO / PAR / HENRI MARX / — / Paris: en dépot chez BBandus [*sic*] et Cie. 103 r. de Richelieu / *Propriété de l'Editeur.*

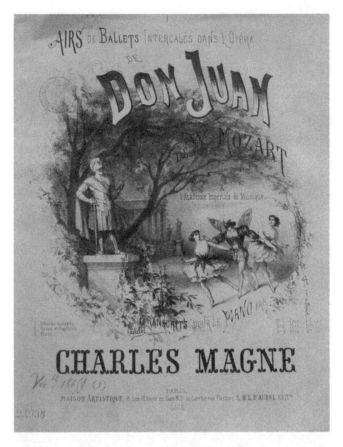

FIGURE 4.3: *Title page of Charles Magne,* Airs de ballets intercalés dans l'opéra de Don Juan *(Paris: Maison Artistique, 1866).*

Reproduced with permission, Bibliothèque nationale de France.

Soler's *Una cosa rara* and Mozart's own *Le nozze di Figaro*. Turning to the work's title page (fig. 4.4), none of these works are referenced.

In the same way that the various musical elements draw attention to, and make connections with, disparate sections of the narrative of *Don Giovanni*, the title page gives us two different views of the Commendatore: on a plinth, the victim of Giovanni's scorn in "O statua gentilissima," and with his hand on the protagonist's hand as he encourages repentance. But these are contrasted with the ball scene from act 1 of the opera, and Don Giovanni's sword, hat, and mandolin, which clearly invoke "Deh vieni alla finestra." None of this music is present in Marx's *Don Juan…Quadrille,* and the title page here both adds in numbers that it does not treat musically ("Deh vieni," "O statua gentilissima," for example) and again contributes to a registral imbalance by drawing attention to the final moments of the opera and the scene in the cemetery where they are set up.

To be sure, the exact selection of individual numbers was a matter for the individual composer of the work, and if there was any plan to it, as will be seen to

FIGURE 4.4: *Title page of Henri Marx,* Don Juan…Quadrille *(Paris: Brandus, 1866). Reproduced with permission, Bibliothèque nationale de France.*

often have been the case, this would also have affected choice. Nevertheless, the frequency of choice of particular numbers gives some indication of the color of this particular site of reception—not just the reception of *Don Giovanni* but the internal valuation of single numbers (table 4.2).

Table 4.2 gives all the numbers from *Don Giovanni* that play some role in the work's reception within the domain of keyboard compositions in 1866, the number of different works in which the number is found, and the number of sections in which it is found. "Là ci darem la mano," "Fin ch'han dal vino," "Batti, batti," and "Deh vieni" head the list, and none of this is particularly surprising. What is perhaps more striking is the importance composers in 1866 attached to the orchestral minuet from the act 1 finale. Of the other purely instrumental music, only the slow introduction to the overture and the reprise of the same music at the end of act 2 make any significant appearance.

Table 4.2 shows a preference largely for arias and duets, so the quartet "Non ti fidar" (no. 9), the trio "Ah taci" (no. 15), and the sextet "Sola sola" (no. 19) figure not at all. The reluctance to make use of ensembles may also explain the absence of "O statua gentilissima" (no. 22), which was considered, and titled, a trio in most nineteenth-century French scores because of the Commendatore's contribution—negligible in terms of number of notes, critical in terms of impact. Neither of the two arias prefaced with elaborate *scene*—"Or sai chi l'onore" (no. 10) or "Mi tradi" (no. 21b)—figures, and the absence of the aria "Ah fuggi il traditor" (no. 8) speaks

Table 4.2: Incidence of numbers from *Don Giovanni* in 1866 keyboard works

Number	Title	Works	Sections
	Overture introduction / Commendatore entrance	4	4
	Overture allegro	1	2
1	Notte e giorno	3	3
3	Ah chi mi dice mai	1	1
4	Madamina	1	1
5	Giovenette	2	2
7	Là ci darem la mano	19	29
10a	Dalla sua pace	1	1
11	Fin ch'han dal vino	13	17
12	Batti batti	13	16
13.1	Opening of act 1 ball scene	2	2
13.2	Tra quest'arbori	3	3
13.3	Act 1 finale gavotte	1	1
13.4	Bisogna aver corragio	1	1
13.5	Orchestral minuet act 1	10	16
13.6	Protegga il giusto cielo	1	1
13.7	Act 1 finale "Viva la libertà"	1	1
13.8.1	Divertissement Scherzo K. 550	1	1
13.8.2	Divertissement Minuet and finale K.421	1	1
13.8.3	Divertissement K. 331	1	1
16	Deh vieni	11	11
18	Vedrai carino	3	3
21	Il mio tesoro	7	7
23	Non mi dir	1	1
24.1	Act 2 finale opening	1	1
24.2	*Una cosa rara* (Martín y Soler)	1	1
24.3	Tra i due litiganti (Sarti)	2	2
24.4	Non più andrai	6	6
24.5	Final d minor chorus	1	1

volumes for the melodic criteria preferred by musicians in 1866—it is difficult to imagine how to extract a melody and accompaniment out of the complex three-part melodic texture, of which Donna Elvira's voice is but one (and in any case it figured only at the Opéra production). It is no surprise that "Metà di voi qua vadano" is ignored, given its omission from all staged productions, and "Ho capito" (no. 6), despite reinstatement at the Opéra, never appeared among keyboard reworkings.

Even outside dance compositions for piano, music from the ball scene was popular for piano treatments, especially if the numbers that immediately precede it ("Fin ch'han dal vino" and "Batti, batti") were taken into consideration. But the orchestral minuet from the act 1 finale, already noted, not only appears in ten separate works but is found sixteen times within those works. It will reappear in discussions in the rest of this chapter, especially as the recurrent epicenter of Wilhelm Krüger's *Scène du bal du Don Juan*.[59]

What is perhaps striking is the importance given to the citations from outside *Don Giovanni* in the act 2 finale, included in keyboard compositions alongside all

---

[59] À Mr Michel Bergson / *SCÈNE DU BAL* / DU / DON JUAN / DE / *MOZART* / MENUET / Trio des Masques / Air de Don Juan / Transcrits et variés / *PAR* / W. KRÜGER / *Op 140* / AU MÉNESTREL rue Vivienne 2bis, HEUGEL & Cie, / *Editeurs, Fournisseurs du Conservatoire* / *Londres et Mayence Schott.*

the other music genuinely part of the opera. The extracts from Martin y Soler's *Una cosa rara* and Sarti's *Fra i due litiganti* appear in three separate pieces, and Mozart's own "Non più andrai" from *Le nozze di Figaro* in no less than six. According to Weber, in the French version of *Don Giovanni* (he is reviewing the Opéra version when he says this) Leoporello's identifications were all suppressed.[60] However, as shown, most of these remain at least in the written records of the Opéra, so unless Weber is confused, he is reporting some sort of verbal, ad hoc, adjustment akin to Offenbach's *cascades*.[61]

Transcription

The fundamental basis for all types of keyboard arrangement—whether as complex and ambitious as the *fantaisie brillante* or as modest as the *Mosaïque enfantine*—is the transcription. Most of the compositions under consideration here at some point engage in simple transcription, as the basis for variation, as an alternation with something more complex or as the basis for the entire work. Sitting behind the transcriptions of individual numbers are three versions of the entire opera for piano solo (without voices): an anonymous transcription, published by Choudens, that claimed to match the text used at the Théâtre-Lyrique (and was a pair to Choudens similar piano-vocal score), a second, anonymous, transcription published by Escudier claiming fidelity *à l'original de Mozart*; and a third, published by Heugel and prepared by Georges Bizet *d'après l'édition originale*, which seems to suggest that Bizet had worked from or at least seen the autograph of the work.[62] While the purpose of the Escudier edition remains unclear, the Choudens score is clearly an attempt to record the production at the Théâtre-Lyrique. Bizet's score attempts something different, and is less attached to any of the three productions mounted in Paris in 1866. It prides itself on its being carefully (*soigneusement*) revised and fingered, and on including indications of orchestration and of voices.

A sense of the different ambitions of each of the three 1866 piano transcriptions may be gained from a comparison of the ways the three handle the opening of "La ci darem la mano," the duettino for Don Giovanni and Zerlina from act 1 of the opera (ex. 4.1).

---

[60] *Le Temps*, 18 April 1866.

[61] Discussed earlier.

[62] These three editions are SEULE ÉDITION. / CONFORME À L'INTEPRÉTATION DU THÉÂTRE LYRIQUE / DON / JUAN / Opéra en 2 Actes et 12 Tableaux / MUSIQUE DE / MOZART / PARTITION PIANO SOLO / A PARIS, CHOUDENS, EDITEUR, / Rue St Honoré, 265. (Près de l'Assomption) / *Propriété* / pr tous Pays.; DON JUAN / (DON GIOVANNI) / OPÉRA DE / MOZART / *Partition Piano seul complète.* / *PRIX NET: 5 FRANCS* / Paris, Editeur, LÉON ESCUDIER, 21, r. de Choiseul; PARTITION COMPLÈTE / DU / DON JUAN / DE / MOZART / D'APRÈS L'ÉDITION ORIGINALE / TRANSCRITE POUR / PIANO SOLO / PAR / GEORGES BIZET / — / PARTITION SOIGNEUSEMENT REVUE, DOIGTÉE / AVEC / LES INDICATIONS D'ORCHESTRE ET DE CHANT / Prix Net: 8 francs / — / PARIS, AU MÉNESTREL, 2 BIS, RUE VIVIENNE / HEUGEL & Cie / ÉDITEURS-FOURNISSEURS DU CONSERVATOIRE.

EXAMPLE 4.1A: *Opening of "La ci darem la mano," in piano transcription; Mozart,* Don Giovanni *(Paris: Choudens, 1866).*

EXAMPLE 4.1B: *Opening of "La ci darem la mano," in piano transcription; Mozart,* Don Giovanni *(Paris: Heugel, 1866).*

EXAMPLE 4.1C: *Opening of "La ci darem la mano," in piano transcription; Mozart,* Don Giovanni *(Paris: Escudier, 1866).*

The two anonymous transcriptions have much in common: both reduce the accompaniment to its lowest common denominator, although Escudier's attempts a certain amount of voicing of the inner parts by a more elaborate left hand; the Choudens transcription is the most simple imaginable. Both place Zerlina's reply to Don Giovanni up an octave, whether the roles are indicated in the score (Choudens) or not (Escudier). Bizet however attempts something much more elaborate, placing the melody lines in exactly the register in which they are found in the original and imitating the exact voicing and rhythm of the accompaniment. The result is much more complex than in the other two examples, a complexity that goes beyond the addition of names of roles and indications of instrumentation.

Discussion of "La ci darem la mano" leads directly into how chains of transcriptions could be assembled. One of the most problematic of these is the *Bouquet de melodies... Don Juan*, attributed to Cramer. "Cramer" may be a real name, or it may be a simple variant on the pseudonym "Cramer," which Fétis explained as a means Parisian music commerce used for the authorship of piano works taken from fashionable operas and of which "it is impossible to tell the real provenance."[63] Whoever put the work together, it consists of transcriptions of the "Viva la libertà" chorus from act 1, the orchestral minuet from act 2, "La ci darem la mano," "Deh

---

EXAMPLE 4.1D: *Opening of "La ci darem la mano," Mozart,* Don Giovanni *in full score.*

vieni all finestra," "Batti, batti," and "Fin ch'han dal vino."[64] Transcriptions follow
the lines of the Choudens transcription, as the beginning of "La ci darem la mano"
shows (ex. 4.2).

---

[64] *Bouquet de Mélodies / POUR / PIANO / PAR / CRAMER / 21. DON JUAN, opéra de Mozart /
Paris, rue St Honoré, chez CHOUDENS, Éditeur.*

EXAMPLE 4.2: *Opening of "La ci darem la mano," in "Cramer,"* Bouquet de mélodies…
Don Juan *(Paris: Choudens, 1866).*

The only exceptions to literal transcription concern the linking passages from one number to the next, where short passages, newly composed but based on the material of the preceding number, create the necessary modulatory link from, in the case of example 4.3, the end of "La ci darem la mano" (A major) to "Deh vieni alla finestra" (D major) (ex. 4.3).

The transcription continues faithfully up to the last two bars before the change to D major and 6/8 where Zerlina's final exclamation "Anima…" instead of ending on a V^6_5 to prepare for the second section of the duettino in A major is modified to the dominant of D major for the transcription of "Deh vieni alla finestra."

The *Mosaïque sur Don Juan* attributed to "E. Cramer" behaves similarly to the *Bouquet de melodies…Don Juan*, as do Magne's transcriptions of three of the dance numbers from the ballet and Maresse's *Transcriptions*, as their name implies. The Cramer *Mosaïque* consists of simple transcriptions of "Vedrai carino," "Fin ch'han dal vino," the numbers from *I due litiganti* and *Le nozze di Figaro* quoted in the act 2 finale, and the orchestral minuet from the act 1 finale.[65] Maresse's transcription is

---

[65] MOSAÏQUE / SUR / DON JUAN / DE / *MOZART* / POUR PIANO / *PAR* / E. CRAMER / *PARIS,* EUG. MATHEIU, *ÉDIT.* / 30 rue Bonaparte.

EXAMPLE 4.3: *Transition from "La ci darem la mano" to "Deh vieni alla finestra," in "Cramer,"* Bouquet de mélodies…Don Juan *(Paris: Choudens, 1866).*

much more modest, containing as it does a transcription of the same orchestral minuet from act 1, of "Deh vieni alla finestra," and of a reprise of the orchestral minuet.[66] Because Magne's transcriptions are of the dance music, none comes from what we know today as *Don Giovanni.* The first, called "Scherzo-Minuetto," is taken from the third movement of the g minor Symphony, K.550, and the finale from the A Major Piano Sonata, K. 331. Although the second transcription seems not to survive, it must—as it is called "Roses et Papillons"—have been taken from either the d minor string quartet K. 421 or the E-flat major string quintet K. 614, and like its fellows was probably a straightforward transcription for piano of what had become an orchestral transcription from chamber music for strings.

Maurice Lee reaches the furthest point in creating a sequence of transcriptions in his *Mélange sur Don Juan;* he runs no less than seven transcriptions back to back, almost leaning on his title in his refusal to engage in any further development of his material.[67] Even his introduction, the one place where transcribers did feel free to elaborate beyond the simple transcription, he presents the opening nine bars of "Notte e giorno fatigar" with the shortest possible transition to his next transcription, of "Il mio tesoro." The Cramer *Bouquet* and *Mosaïque,* as well as Lee's

---

[66] ECOLES FRANCAISE, ALLEMANDE, ITALIENNE. / CHEFS D'ŒUVRE / DES / GRANDS MAITRES / TRANSCRIPTIONS / POUR PIANO PAR / LEO MARESSE / Paris chez FÉLIX JANET, EDIT[R] Boulevart Poissonnière, 5.

[67] À Melle Marie Lemaire / DON JUAN / Opéra de Mozart / MÉLANGE / *des plus jolis motifs arrangés* / POUR / PIANO / *PAR* / MAURICE LEE / Prix: 6f / *Paris,* JULES HEINZ *éditeur* / *146 rue de Rivoli.*

Mélange, come close—in terms of their musical ambition (expressed in terms of the number of extracts they combine rather than techniques they employ)—to the scale of the more elaborate *fantaisie*.

Variation

Straightforward transcription is relatively easy to identify, and if it is reasonable to so categorize a work, the same is not true of variation. Sets of variations are unknown among the 1866 arrangements of *Don Giovanni*, and the presence of more than a single variation is relatively rare. René Favarger's *Don Juan Sérénade* offers a complex transcription of "Deh vieni alla finestra" that would have done justice to a Liszt or a Thalberg (ex. 4.4) in its use of the right hand to preserve the tenor register of the original melody and a cross-hands technique for Faverger's version of the accompaniment.[68]

Liszt would almost certainly have attempted to include the mandolin part in his transcription (Liszt did not include "Deh vieni alla finestra" in his *Réminiscences de Don Juan*), and Thalberg of course did just that.[69] But as can be seen from the example, Favarger simply repeats the melody before moving to the second strain, with a variational accompaniment. This is all before the variation that follows (ex. 4.5), which consistently exploits the melody in the upper register with an accompaniment in triplet sixteenth-notes *avec grâce*. The single variation is the only example in this composition, however.

The distinction between transcription and variation can be occasionally blurred: J. Charles Hess's version of "Vedrai carino" begins in a way that could at least be considered a transcription (there are important changes to harmony and voicing), but bars 23–33 of the aria are massively rewritten: the number of bars remains the same, the harmony remains mostly the same, but as the example shows, the melody is varied to such an extent that it is unrecognizable (ex. 4.6).[70]

The extract immediately yields to a simple transcribed reprise of the opening, which is again modified at the end to make a transition to the version of "Batti, batti"; this makes no claim whatsoever to any sort of transcription, varies mere fragments of the original material, constructs new transitions, and rapidly passes through similar treatments of "Fin ch'han dal vino," the orchestral minuet from the act 1 finale, and "Deh vieni alla finestra." We are here in the world of the *fantaisie*, as Hess's title suggests.

---

[68] ŒUVRES / DE / RÉNÉ FAVARGER / OP. B. Don Juan, 1re fantaisie / PARIS / ALFRED IKELMER ET Cie, EDITEURS-COMMISIONNAIRES / 4, BOULEVARD POSSONNIÈRE.

[69] Grande / *FANTAISIE* / POUR LE PIANO / *Sur* / La Sérénade et Le Menuet. / DE / DON JUAN / *Par* / S. THALBERG / *Paris chez E Troupenas & Cie Rue Nvev Vivienne, 40*, 8.

[70] À MADAME FÉLIX FAURE / DON JUAN / DE / MOZART / Fantaisie / *Pour le piano* / PAR / J. CH. HESS / Op: 101 / Prix: 6fr / *PARIS,* / *Chez GAUVIN, Editeur de Musique, Rue Montpensier, N° 1*, 2.

EXAMPLE 4.4: *Opening of transcription of "Deh vieni alla finestra" in René Favarger,* Don Juan Sérénade *(Paris: Ikelmer, 1866).*

EXAMPLE 4.5: *Variation of "Deh vieni alla finestra" in René Favarger,* Don Juan Sérénade *(Paris: Ikelmer, 1866).*

Dance

François Rysler's *Don Juan Mosaïque*, in the context of this discussion, begins relatively straightforwardly.[71] It consists largely of transcriptions of the minuet (F major) from the act 1 finale, "La ci darem la mano" (B-flat major but in 4/4 with note-values doubled) and "Batti, batti" (in E-flat again with note values doubled). There are eight modulatory bars between the minuet and "La ci darem la mano," and after an elaborate cadenza, its final strain is lightly varied; a similar process is applied to "Batti, batti." The last extract, "Deh vieni alla finestra," is treated differently. First of all, the mandolin obbligato that opens the aria is given as a modulatory bridge from E-flat major to A-flat major that accelerates, as the citation breaks down, toward an A-flat major presentation of the melody of "Deh vieni alla finestra" in a *tempo di valza*. Presumably faster than Mozart's *allegretto* tempo mark-

---

[71] DON JUAN / Opéra de / Mozart / *MOSAÏQUE*, / Pour / Le PIANO *par* / FR. RYSLER / . . . / *Paris, LÉON GRUS, Editeur, 31, Boulevart Bonne-Nouvelle.*

EXAMPLE 4.6: *Variation of "Vedrai carino" in J. Charles Hess,* Don Juan de Mozart: Fantaisie *(Paris: Gauvin, 1866).*

ing, the translation into waltz style is made smoother by Mozart's original scoring, which places first violin chords on offbeats (in Rysler's waltz, note values are again doubled to turn Mozart's 6/8 into a 3/4 waltz). The first two dozen bars are thus given in transcription, at which point Rysler begins to extemporize, in fantasia style, to set up a dominant preparation of F major, at which point the waltz recommences in that key. With a return to the key in which he started, Rysler looks like he is going to end with the waltz version of "Deh vieni alla finestra"; however, he closes with a fleeting reference to "La ci darem la mano," also in waltz rhythm (ex. 4.7).

Although recomposing "Deh vieni" as a waltz involves shifts of tempo, the rhythmic and phraseological structure of the music remains largely unaltered. The changes to "La ci darem la mano" are more far-reaching: pitch remains unchanged, but durations are modified to fit the 3/4 meter, and the accompaniment (logical at least for "Deh vieni") remains that of Rysler's waltz, therefore changing Mozart's original textures out of all recognition.

Changing the rhythmic and metrical structure—even just for a couple of bars— of "La ci darem la mano" to accommodate a waltz gives a context to such a work as Burgmüller's *Valse de salon*. The core of the piece consists of two statements of the second (6/8) section of "Batti, batti" reworked as a waltz in 3/4. This is introduced

EXAMPLE 4.7: *Ending of François Rysler,* Don Juan Mosaïque *(Paris: Grus, 1866).*

by the first section of "Batti, batti," simply transcribed for its first eight bars, followed by short link into the first of the waltzes (ex. 4.8).

Before the final statement of the waltz "Batti, batti," and similar to the Rysler, there is a waltz version of "Deh vieni alla finestra," but between it and the first statement of the "Batti, batti" waltz is the most striking section of the piece: a reworking in triple time—and as a waltz—of "Il mio tesoro" (ex. 4.9).

EXAMPLE 4.8: *Transcription of "Batti, batti" in Friedrich Burgmüller's* Valse de salon *(Paris: Grus, 1866).*

This marks a different approach to reworking, abandoning the original 4/4 context in favor of a 3/4 waltz, completely replacing the accompaniment, changing the harmony, and to a large extent changing the tone of the aria—Mozart's *con sordino* string accompaniment is far removed from the admittedly more subtle treatment of the waltz accompaniment than in the "Deh vieni" sections. It sets up the possibility that in dance music, almost any melody of Mozart could be reworked in almost any meter, style, or dance genre.

EXAMPLE 4.8: *Continued*

EXAMPLE 4.9: *Reworking of "Il mio tesoro," in triple time from Friedrich Burgmüller's* Valse de salon *(Paris: Grus, 1866).*

The two 1866 polkas demonstrate the degree to which extracts from *Don Giovanni* could be used in a dance context. Both make use of straightforward transcriptions of pitch and rhythm, and Micheli's *Polka sur les motifs de Don Juan* takes "Fin ch'han dal vino" and "Notte e giorno faticar" as the basis for a polka and trio. All piano-vocal scores and transcriptions of the entire opera that date from 1866 and that give metronome indications offer half note = 104 for "Notte e giorno fatigar," exactly the speed Maxime Alkan gave Cellerier for the polka.[72] The same sources offer half note = 116 for "Fin ch'han dal vino," so Micheli's polka requires only a slightly more deliberate pace than conventionally accepted for the piece in 1866. Micheli notates both in halved values (so quarter note=104, exactly as spelt out by Alkan), and uses "Fin ch'han dal vino" as the polka and "Notte e giorno fatigar" as the trio with a coda also based on "Fin ch'han dal vino."

Although Micheli's *Polka sur les motifs de Don Juan* does relatively little violence to the pitch and rhythm of the extracts it selects, Wolframm Caron's *Polka espagnole* takes "La ci darem la mano" and pushes its tempo from an 1866 quarter note=44 to more than double that to Cellarius's polka tempo of quarter note = 104.[73] Caron takes the first section of "Batti, batti" for his trio, given an identical tempo indication to "La ci darem la mano" (quarter note = 44), and again moves it up to polka speed.[74] There is no *da capo* of the polka here, as there was in Micheli, and the composition ends with a coda based again on "La ci darem la mano."

By the mid-1860s, the quadrille had taken on a form it had possessed for at least a quarter of a century. Cellarius's definition responds well to the two quadrilles based on *Don Giovanni*.[75] It is based on five movements, each of which has a different set of steps, as follows:

1. *Pantalon*
2. *L'été*
3. *Poule*
4. *Pastourelle*
5. *Finale*

In both quadrilles, by Marx and Strauss, at least one different extract from *Don Giovanni* figures in each of the five movements. There are obvious points of overlap, but neither uses the same music in the same context except once, so while Marx uses "Giovenette che fate" as the first movement (*Pantalon*), Strauss uses it as his *Pastourelle*.[76] Marx's *Pastourelle* is "La ci darem la mano," while the same number occurs as the middle section of Strauss's finale. Both begin their finales with "Fin ch'han dal vino," but Marx

---

[72] Cellarius, *Danses des salons*, 61, note.

[73] À Melle Isabelle VINCHON / Souvenir / de Mozart / . . . / N°. 2 / DON-JUAN / POLKA ESPAGNOLE / 2 / Polkas Brillantes / POUR LE PIANO / PAR / G. WOLFRAMM CARON / . . . / Paris, JOLY, Editeur / Imp^r. de Musique / *rue Bonaparte, No. 3*, 1–2.

[74] Ibid., 2.

[75] Cellarius, *Danses des salons*, 53–57.

[76] Marx, *Don Juan . . . Quadrille*, 1; DON JUAN / DE / MOZART / QUADRILLE des Bals de la Cour et de L'OPÉRA / PAR / STRAUSS / . . . / Paris, AU MÉNESTREL, 2bis. rue Vivienne HEUGEL & Cie / *Editeurs-Libraires pour la France et l'Étranger*, 4.

EXAMPLE 4.10: *Reworking of "Fin ch'han dal vino", "Non più andrai," and "Là ci darem la mano," in Henri Marx,* Don Juan . . . Quadrille *(Paris: Brandus, 1866).*

shifts the metrical emphasis by half a bar, presumably to enable the dovetailing with his middle sections based on "Non più andrai" and "Là ci darem la mano" (ex. 4.10).

The two versions of "Giovenette che fate" also treat their metrical structure differently. Here, Mozart's 3 + 3 = 6 phrasing cannot possibly serve for a quadrille, and both Marx and Strauss find different solutions to the same problem, Strauss by adding two bars creating a 3 + 3 + 2 = 8 structure and Marx by creating two four-bar phrases (ex. 4.11).

EXAMPLE 4.11A: *Reworking of "Giovenette che fate," in Henri Marx,* Don Juan...
Quadrille *(Paris: Brandus, 1866).*

It is difficult to know what relationship exists between the two 1866 *Don Gio-vanni* quadrilles. Both use "Fin ch'han dal vino" as the basis for their finales but for the rest studiously avoid duplication—to the point of selecting different foreign material from the act 2 finale: the extract from Martin y Soler's *Una cosa rara* in the case of Marx and Mozart's own "Non più andrai" in Strauss's case. Given that Strauss's *Don Juan Quadrille* was published as much as ten weeks earlier than Marx's, it is entirely possible that Marx was aware of the Strauss work and could adjust his choice of pieces accordingly.[77]

---

[77] Strauss, *Don Juan de Mozart: Quadrille* was released for sale on 16 June 1866 and Marx's *Don Juan de Mozart: Quadrille* on 25 August. See *Journal général de l'imprimerie et de la librairie* for the two respective dates.

EXAMPLE 4.11B: *Reworking of "Giovenette che fate," in Strauss,* Don Juan de Mozart: Qua-drille *(Paris: Au Ménestrel, 1866).*

Fantaisie

What marks out the *fantaisie* from other arrangements in which *Don Giovanni* is embedded is its use, in the same work, of transcription, possibly variation, and elaborated transition, all of which have been seen in the transcriptions and dances already analyzed. But in addition, the *fantaisie* is characterized by a level of invention not found in either the transcription or the dance; such invention consists of both fragmentation and development, and since these works play off transcription and variation alongside newly invented material, it is hardly surprising that much of the innovative material finds its way into transitions.

The *fantaisie* not only allows the coexistence of transcription and variation but also allows the seamless merging from one to the other in a way that neither transcriptions or variations permit. After an astonishing introduction that manages to mix the slow introduction to the opera with fragments of "Là ci darem la mano," the part of Adolphe Bouleau-Neldy's *Souvenirs mélodiques de Don Juan* dedicated to "Là ci darem la mano" begins with a very simple transcription for the first few phrases, nicely distinguishing between Don Giovanni and Zerlina in terms of range (ex. 4.12).[78]

But, seemingly out of nowhere, the following phrases are varied in a blizzard of thirty-second notes. When the main theme returns after this section, it returns in a straightforward transcription, but only for three bars, at which point Zerlina and Don Giovanni are again whirled off into a bravura labyrinth, this time not to escape until Bouleau-Neldy turns his attention to Zerlina alone and "Batti, batti."

G. Redler's *Don Juan Fantaisie* immediately shows how treacherous terminology can be.[79] It is no more ambitious than any of the sets of transcriptions and signficantly more modest than the Cramer *Mosaïque* and *Bouquet* and Lee's *Mélange*. But other works that do not flaunt the title *fantaisie*, such as Duvernoy's first *Pensée dramatique*, can offer a transcription of "Deh vieni alla finestra," a good half of which represents fragmentation and development (ex. 4.13).[80]

The straightforward transcription of "Deh vieni alla finestra" in F major is immediately visible, but the material is fragmented at the *Poco animato* on the fifth system and is then treated to four bars of highly varied transcription in A-flat major, which in turn is followed by sequential development and a ritenuto into the transcription of "Là ci darem la mano."

Similarly, Joseph Rummel's *Fantaisie brillante* derives its name from its use of bravura writing, and Rummel follows twenty-six bars of variation of "Là ci darem la mano" with no less than twenty bars of highly developed working of the same material—as ever, as a form of transition to the next item (ex. 4.14).[81]

Variation of the last strain of the *brillante* variation of "Là ci darem la mano" yields to a *moderato* section that fragments elements of the theme and leads it flatward from B-flat major to D-flat major and then back to F major for the orchestral minuet from act 1 of *Don Giovanni*. Rummel's introduction to his *fantaisie* is completely newly composed and makes no reference to the work on which it is based.

If one were to judge the success or even the value of such works discussed in this chapter according to the amount of entirely newly composed material, the

[78] A Mlle CAROLINE LÉVY / DON JUAN / DE / MOZART / Souvenirs Mélodiques / POUR LE PIANO / PAR / A. BOULEAU-NELDY / OP: 43 PR: 7^f 50 / *Paris, au Magasin de Musique du Bazar de l'Industrie française* / O. LEGOUIX, Edit^r, Boulev^d Poissonnière, 27, 2–3 for the slow introduction, 4–6 for "Là ci darem la mano."

[79] DON JUAN / Fantaisie / pour Piano / PAR / G. REDLER / Op. 110 / *À PARIS CHEZ EMILE CHATOT ÉDITEUR DE MUSIQUE, / 2 rue de la Feuillade Place des Victoires.*

[80] PENSÉES DRAMATIQUES / SIX FANTAISIES TRANSCRIPTIONS / POUR LE / PIANO / . . . / PAR / J. B. DUVERNOY / OP. 294 / 3 Don Juan . . . MOZART / . . . / Paris, LÉON GRUS Editeur, 31, Boulev^t Bonne Nouvelle, 4–5.

[81] À Mademoiselle / Mathilde Sautter / Don Juan / Opéra de MOZART / *FANTAISIE BRILLANTE* / pour / LE PIANO PAR / J. RUMMEL / *Paris, LÉON GRUS, Editeur, 31, Boulevart Bonne-Nouvelle,* 6–7.

EXAMPLE 4.12: *"La ci darem la mano," in Adolphe Bouleau-Neldy,* Souvenirs mélodiques de Don Juan *(Paris: au Magasin de Musique du Bazar de l'Industrie française, 1866).*

Don Juan Fantaisie Brillante by Ignacio Leÿbach would certainly stand head and shoulders above the others.[82] The overall pattern of this work is as follows (table 4.3):

But such a schema fails to do justice to the levels of new composition involved in every movement of the work. The transitions from "Là ci darem la mano" to "Batti, batti" are not only of enormous proportions but also have little or no relationship either to the music just varied or that just about to be, as is usually the case. Leÿbach makes no attempts to make any kind of bridge between "Batti, batti" and "Deh vieni

[82] A MADEMOISELLE ELISABETH de PRADES / DON JUAN / de / W. MOZART / FANTAISIE BRILLANTE / POUR LE PIANO / PAR / J. LEŸBACH / Paris, COLOMBIER, Editeur, 6, r. Vivienne, au coin de la Galerie Vivienne.

EXAMPLE 4.13: *"Deh vieni alla finestra" in Jean-Baptiste Duvernoy,* Pensées dramatiques: Six fantaisies transcriptions...op. 294—Don Juan de Mozart *(Paris: Grus, 1866).*

EXAMPLE 4.13: *continued*

TABLE 4.3: Ignacio Leÿbach, *Don Juan Fantaisie Brillante*: structure

Section	Bars	Material employed
1	1	Freely composed introduction based on minuet (finale 1, bars 220–223), C major
2	2–3	"Tra quest'arbori" (finale 1, bars 92–121), F major, transcribed and developed
3	4–6	Minuet, 1st section transcribed, 2nd section varied and closes with cadenza
4	7–8	Trio des Masques "Protegga il giusto cielo," B♭ major transcription (finale 1, bar 251)
5	8	Freely composed bravura interlude based on minuet, B♭ to V of d minor
6	9–10	"Bisogna aver corragio" (bar 172), complex transcription mixes melody and accompaniment, d minor
7	10–11	Freely composed interlude based on "Fin ch'han dal vino," V of F major
8	11–12	"Fin ch'han dal vino," B♭ major
9	13	Highly varied minuet, E♭ major
10	13–14	"Fin ch'han dal vino," B♭ major

alla finestra," interrupts the end of the former enharmonically, and includes a newly composed interlude. He does the same in the middle of what is otherwise little more than a simple transcription of "Deh vieni alla finestra," where the four extracts from "Deh vieni" (three of the accompaniment figure and one of the melody) are interrupted by music that is not only newly composed but also much more elaborate (pianistically much more sophisticated) than the transcriptions of Mozart.

It is rare to find any attempt among any of the 1866 compositions based on *Don Giovanni* to generate any type of narrative; an exception is Wilhelm Krüger's *Scène*

EXAMPLE 4.14: *"La ci darem la mano" in Joseph Rummel,* Don Juan de Mozart: Fantaisie brillante *(Paris: Grus, 1866).*

EXAMPLE 4.14: *continued*

du bal du Don Juan. Here, Krüger restricts his choice of material to the ball scene in the act 1 finale of *Don Giovanni,* to which he adds Don Giovanni's closely related "Fin ch'han dal vino."[83] In doing this, Krüger creates a narrative that subtly changes that of Mozart's original. The *Scène du bal* falls into ten sections (table 4.4):

TABLE 4.4: Wilhelm Krüger, *Scène du bal du Don Juan:* structure

1	Freely composed introduction based on Minuet (Finale 1, 220–223) C major
2–3	"Tra quest'arbori" (Finale 1, 92–121) F major transcribed and developed
4–6	Minuet, first section transcribed, second section varied and closes with cadenza
7–8	*Trio des Masques "Protegga il giusto cielo"* B♭ transcription (finale 1 bar 251
8	Freely composed bravura interlude based on Minuet B♭ to V of d minor
9–10	"Bisogna aver corraggio" (bar 172) complex transcription mixes melody and accompaniment d minor
10–11	Freely composed interlude based on "Fin ch'han dal vino" V of F major
11–12	"Fin ch'han dal vino" B♭ major
13	Highly varied minuet E♭ major
13–14	"Fin ch'han dal vino" B♭ major

The act 1 orchestral minuet plays a key role in structuring the entire work: the basis of the introduction, the interlude in section 5, and itself the subject of transcription and variation in sections 3 and 9, it takes on the role of an element of consistent scene-setting throughout the composition. The last occurrence separates out the two statements of "Fin ch'han dal vino." Strictly speaking, this number is not from the ball scene, but its depiction of the protagonist's attitude to such events and its relative proximity to the scene make it a logical conclusion. Krüger takes three sections of the act 1 finale (sections 2, 4, and 6 of the *Scène du bal du Don Juan*) and

---

[83] The extensive use of the act 1 minuet has already been discussed.

resequences them. "Tra quest'arbori" is the first extract from the finale, transcribed and developed by Krüger, and comes right after the freely composed introduction. Krüger inverts the two sections of the *Trio des masques*, placing "Protegga il giusto cielo" before "Bisogna aver corragio"; although this of course does away the Mozart's undercutting of the maskers' anger by interrupting them with a couple of bars of the onstage minuet, it does allow an emphatic cadence at the end of Krüger's sixth section, as a point of articulation before the move to "Fin ch'han dal vino." Placing "Fin ch'han dal vino" after the transcriptions of the music from the act 1 finale rather than before them again resequences Mozart's original, this time in order to generate a presto finale to the composition itself.

Extended transitions between transcriptions and/or variations of known material permitted composers on at least two occasions to bring similar elements of different numbers into a close relationship. At one level, this might be judged to be little more than smoothing over a join between two transcriptions or variations; at another, it could be viewed as having a pedagogical purpose: demonstrating points of musical similarity. After an elaborate transcription of "Tra quest'arbori" (from the act 1 finale of *Don Giovanni*), Eugène Ketterer's *Souvenirs mélodiques de Don Juan* introduces a fragment from the overture—the unison figure that descends five steps and its quaver complement—and uses it as a link to a transcription of "Batti, batti" (ex. 4.15).[84]

Now, the melody of "Batti, batti," of course, descends five steps in the same way and in almost the same rhythm. Ketterer also places the two fragments in the same tempo. It is impossible to prove that Ketterer was making a largely uncontentious but perhaps inconsequential musical point about the relationship between the two parts of the work. The lack of consequence is perhaps vitiated by the means Ketterer uses to make it.

A similar observation may well be being made in Duvernoy's *Don Juan fantaisie,* where at the end of his treatment of "Là ci darem la mano," he puts the opening bar of the *duettino* into a *poco più animato* tempo, into which he can also put the opening of "Fin ch'han dal vino" (ex. 4.16).[85]

The melodic point to be made here is no more subtle than the one Ketterer may have been making: that the rhythmic and melodic skeleton of the first bar of "Là ci darem la mano" and the first two bars of "Fin ch'han dal vino" may be shown to have points of similarity (ex. 4.17)

Putting the two fragments into close juxtaposition, and particularly in the same tempo—which is the main reason for thinking that Duvernoy has some higher purpose here—points up a very simple musical truth, and one that can be illustrated neatly by comparing his versions of the two numbers concerned.

---

[84] Hommage à Madame Tarpet-Leclercq / *Professeur au Conservatoire* / DON JUAN / *Opéra de Mozart* / *Souvenirs Mélodiques* / POUR LE PIANO / *PAR* / E. KETTERER / *A PARIS,* / E & A. GIROD *EDITEURS.*

[85] Duvernoy, DON JUAN / DE MOZART / FANTAISIE pour PIANO, 9.

EXAMPLE 4.15: *Transition to "Batti, batti," in Eugène Ketterer,* Souvenirs mélodiques de Don Juan *(Paris: Girod, 1866).*

Some of the procedures involved in reworking the opera for dance may be seen in the same two works just discussed: Ketterer's *Souvenirs mélodiques de Don Juan* and Duvernoy's op. 284 *fantaisie.* Both works end with up-tempo reworkings of slow movements from the opera in the same way as was seen in Rysler's *Mosaïque,* for example. At the end of the Duvernoy is a treatment of "O mio tesoro" at the same *allegro vivace* speed used for "fin ch'han dal vino";[86] similarly, Ketterer ends his *Souvenirs mélodiques* with "Là ci darem la mano" in double octaves, *fortissimo,* at a tempo that he marks *brioso.*[87] Whether Koch's 1802 description of this term (*männlich*) has any relevance to Ketterer's view of

---

[86] Ibid., 12–13.
[87] Ketterer, DON JUAN / *Opéra de Mozart* / *Souvenirs Mélodiques,* 12.

EXAMPLE 4.16: *Elision of "Là ci darem la mano" with "Fin ch'han dal vino," in Jean-Baptiste Duvernoy,* Don Juan fantaisie *op. 284 (Paris: Brandus et Dufour, 1866).*

EXAMPLE 4.17: *Jean-Baptiste Duvernoy, putative analysis of melodic similarities between openings of "Là ci darem la mano" and "Fin ch'han dal vino."*

the outcome of the narrative underpinning "Là ci darem la mano" is a suitably open question with which to close this discussion.

PART II

Holy Spirits

{5}

"Mozart's" "Twelfth Mass"

CASE CLOSED?

One of the dubious pleasures of the early twenty-first century is the convenience of regional airports with flights to other cities in the United Kingdom, Europe, and the Channel Islands. And one of the Channel Islands, the Bailiwick of Guernsey, celebrated the opening of a new airport terminal as recently as March 2004 with publicity photographs replete with a completely deserted building, architectural flagpoles, and a flaming sunset (fig. 5.1).[1]

FIGURE 5.1: *Opening of Guernsey Airport, publicity photograph, March 2004 Chris George–Coast Media.*

---

[1] The event was described in *Guernsey Weekly Press*, 26 March 2004. The image was mounted on a related website, http://www.thisisguernsey.com, which has since been taken down.

FIGURE 5.2: *De Havilland Nimrod MR2 Derek Bower.*

The celebrations centered on two events. The first was a low-level fly-past by a De Havilland Nimrod MR2 from the Royal Air Force's 201 Squadron, conventional almost to the point of obligatory on such occasions (fig. 5.2).

More relevant to current concerns, the opening of Guernsey Airport was also celebrated with a blessing by the dean of Guernsey, in the presence of the bailiff and lieutenant-governor of the island. There was, at the end of the formal ceremony and just before the fly-past, an event that can be considered almost equally conventional: a performance of the "Gloria" from "Mozart's" "Twelfth Mass."[2]

The opening of Guernsey's airport terminal may be compared with a second vignette that moves geographically north and chronologically back to the Yorkshire village of Loftus in 1859, to a brass band competition between five local ensembles. The event was reported by John Hollingshead in the journal *All the Year Round*, then in the capable editorial hands of one Charles Dickens.[3] Each competitor was required to play the test piece, James Sidney Jones, *Grand Parade March on English National Melodies,* and a work of its own choice: selections from *La sonnambula, Lucrezia Borgia,* and *Il trovatore* competed with the "Hallelujah Chorus" and

---

[2] The literature on Mozart's "Twelfth Mass" is almost nonexistent. None of the essays in Sabine Coelsch-Foisner, Dorothea Flothow, and Wolfgang Görtschacher, eds., *Mozart in Anglophone Cultures,* Salzburg Studies in English Literature and Culture 4 (Frankfurt-am-Main: Lang, 2009), mentions the work, let alone the signficance for nineteenth- and twentieth-century culture discussed in this chapter.

[3] "A Musical Prize-Fight," *All the Year Round,* 12 November 1859. The competition had taken place on 30 September 1859. For the attribution to Hollingshead, see Ella Ann Oppenlander, *Dickens' "All the Year Round": Descriptive Index and Contributor List* (Troy, N.Y.: Whitston, 1984), 73 and 276.

extracts from Mozart's "Twelfth Mass."[4] Loftus, on the coast midway between Whitby and Redcar, hosted ensembles from Aislaby (Bellini), Farndale (Donizetti), Guisborough (Verdi), its own sax-horn band (Handel), and Bilsdale, whose brass band had chosen Mozart.[5] Much to the disgust of many participants, the home team won, and Bilsdale's performance of Mozart's "Twelfth Mass" came second to last. The resulting disturbance made the organizers grateful that they had recruited police officers from every village within twenty miles to ensure good order at the competition.[6]

These two examples are typical of the simply colossal number of instances from the early nineteenth century to the present when Mozart's "Twelfth Mass" has stood—and continues to stand in certain circles—not only as an important feature on the landscape of nineteenth- and twentieth-century music but also as an emblem of the composer's emerging stature. In the world of oratorio, of the drawing room, in both Anglican and Catholic rites, and even in the theatre, Mozart's "Twelfth Mass" was an important vehicle of effect that established and promoted Mozart's music in general throughout nineteenth- and twentieth-century Britain and America. This is all the more remarkable since the "Twelfth Mass" is clearly not by Mozart; it is now thought to be by Wenzel Müller, the pupil of Dittersdorf and composer of *Kaspar der Fagottist* and *Die Schwestern von Prag*. Müller did not begin his composing career until after Mozart's death, died himself in 1835, and must have written the work we know as the "Twelfth Mass" before its appearance in a library catalogue in 1803.[7]

The dissemination and influence of the "Twelfth Mass" is critical to an understanding of the ways it has been responsible for supporting the reputation of a composer who did not write it. The power of this work, whose attribution has been dismissed in conventional musicological circles but whose reputation as a work by

---

[4] The only surviving copy of the test piece is a piano arrangement: MUSICAL BOUQUET / GRAND PARADE MARCH / ON ENGLISH NATIONAL MELODIES. / HEARTS OF OAK, RULE BRITANNIA / GOD SAVE THE QUEEN / Arranged for the Piano-Forte / BY / J. SIDNEY JONES /.../ LONDON: / MUSICAL BOUQUET OFFICE, 192 HIGH HOLBORN; / & J. ALLEN, 20, WARWICK LANE, PATERNOSTER ROW. A note on the title page records that "this beautiful March may be had arranged by J. S. Jones for a Brass Band for 16 Instruments."

[5] The competitors from Aislaby, Bilsdale, and Farndale were what were called "moor-bands," with members living up to twenty miles from each other, while the Guisborough ensemble came "from a town that boasts a railway terminus." The only genuinely village band was the one from Lofthouse ("A Musical Prize-Fight").

[6] "The excitement when the prizes were declared . . . was sufficient to show that the cudgels and the wrestling ring had not altogether been exchanged for the harp; and the cheers and groans were sufficiently loud and antagonistic to warrant the presence of the police officers, who had come from every village within twenty miles" (ibid.).

[7] The attribution to Wenzel Müller was established in 1966 by Karl Pfannhauser, ("Epilogomena Mozartiana," *Mozart-Jahrbuch 1971–72 des Zentralinstitutes für Mozartforschung der Internationalen Stiftung Mozarteum Salzburg* [Kassel: Bärenreiter, 1973], 268–312) on the basis of an attributed score in Vienna, and Wolfgang Plath found a reference to the work dated 1803 in a catalog in Litomyšl; Plath, "Kleine Mozartiana," in *Festschrift Rudolf Elvers zum 60. Geburtstag*, ed. Ernst Herttrich and Hans Wolfgang Schneider (Tützing: Schneider, 1985), 397–406.

Mozart remains immense, is easy to underestimate. The difference between the musicological status of Mozart's "Twelfth Mass" and its standing in the musical world at large, however uncomfortable, requires acknowledgement. And the musicological status of Mozart's "Twelfth Mass" could today not be clearer. A German-speaking tradition of doubting its authenticity goes back to the 1820s, shortly after its publication by Simrock around 1821.[8] Commentaries on the work in German have permanently refused it a place in the Mozart canon. The earliest edition of Köchel explicitly denies its attribution, and this has continued in all its subsequent editions;[9] it is known as Köchel Appendix 232/C1.04 today. Otto Jahn excluded the work from the first edition of his life and works of Mozart in the 1850s, there is no place for the "Twelfth Mass" in the *Neue Mozart Ausgabe*, and no professional ensemble has attempted to record it for at least thirty years.[10] For the musicological Mozart industry in Germany, it has always been a closed case.[11]

As the first of the two examples that open this chapter show, however, this was not the case in Anglophone circles: in Great Britain, its colonies, and the United States, the work took on a significance for Mozart reception out of all proportion to the position it ought to have held in the Mozart canon.[12] The second example shows how, despite the recent conversion of Anglophone musical scholarship to the view that the "Twelfth Mass" is not by Mozart, the attribution to him has a magnetic quality that continues well into the twenty-first century. There is no convert like a recent convert, and the tardy recognition by the Anglophone musicological establishment that Mozart was not the composer of the "Twelfth Mass" made for some harsh words in the third quarter of the twentieth century. Robin

---

[8] *Messe / à 4 Voix /* avec accompagnement de / *2 Violons, 2 Altos, Violoncelle et Basse /* 2 Hautbois, 2 Cors, 2 Trompettes, Timballes / et Orgue / Composée par / W. A. MOZART / *Partition /* Prix 20 Fr⁵. N⁰. VII / BONN et cologne chez N. SIMROCK. / Propriété de l'éditeur. / 1815. Simrock responded to Seyfried in November 1826; "Erklärung der Verlagshandlung von N. Simrock betreffend *die Echtheit der Mozartischen Messe Nr. 7,*" *Caecilia: Ein Zeitschrft für die musikalische Welt, herausgegeben von einem Vereine von Gelehrten, Kunstverständigen und Künstler* 6 (vol. 21) (1827), 129–131, naming Carl Zulehner as the source for his edition.

[9] Ludwig Ritter von Köchel, *Chronologisch-thematisches Verzeichnis sämtlicher Tonwerke Wolfgang Amadé Mozarts* (Leipzig: Breitkopf und Härtel, 1862), 521. The entry in the eighth edition, ed. Franz Giegling, Alexander Weinmann, and Gerd Sievers (Wiesbaden: Breitkopf und Härtel, 1983), 812, hardly changes a word of Köchel's original text.

[10] Otto Jahn, *W. A. Mozart,* 4 vols. (Leipzig: Breitkopf und Härtel, 1856–59), 1:672.

[11] This view is also repeated in modern dictionaries and encyclopedias of music (themselves a not-unimportant site of reception). See, for example, H. C. Robbins Landon, *The Mozart Compendium: A Guide to Mozart's Life and Music* (London: Thames and Hudson, 1990), 352. The comment that "the editor has discovered the name of the real composer [of the "Twelfth Mass"]" is incomprehensible.

[12] An early scholarly view from the British Isles that challenged the authenticity of the "Twelfth Mass" was in Cecil Oldman, "Mozart and Modern Research," *Proceedings of the Musical Association* 58 (1931–32), 58. Oldman's view, that "other… [spurious works] might well have continued to pass as Mozart's work if their real authors had not been discovered—and as a matter of fact, some of them still do. It would be interesting to try to isolate the particular elements in them that made their claims so long seem plausible. I suggest the so-called 'Twelfth Mass' as a suitable work on which to start," is an early identification of a key element in the work's reception diagnosed in this chapter: that despite scholarly attribution to Wenzel Müller, the more general attribution to Mozart remains indelible.

Langley, for example, in the context of an article on Weber, hoped that it could be "relegated to oblivion."[13] Such severe commentary merely served to demonstrate the deep-seated renown the work enjoyed in English musical circles by the 1950s, and how as late as 1976 critics still felt the need to decry it.

It hardly needs to be said that the work cannot be relegated to oblivion, or at least, it can only be set aside if histories of music are deemed to concern works and composers alone and to ignore the sorts of musical culture that was recorded in Loftus in 1859, for example, or indeed in Guernsey in 2004. The proposal simply to "relegate [the "Twelfth Mass"] to oblivion" may be countered with an investigation of its reception that simultaneously acknowledges both its probable attribution to Wenzel Müller—hence not to Mozart—and its importance for Mozart reception in the last two hundred years. Two tasks will accomplish this: to outline the impact of the work, especially in the English-speaking world in the two centuries after its first appearance, and then to examine in some detail a particularly influential text by Mozart's first English biographer, Edward Holmes, that set the aesthetic and axiological agenda for discourses that supported the work for the next 150 years.

The publication of the piano-vocal score by Vincent Novello in 1819 gave the work its name.[14] Twelfth in a series of eighteen masses attributed to Mozart published between 1819 and 1824, it rapidly assumed a significance in performance, publication, and aesthetic reputation that by the end of the century had outstripped most of Mozart's other works, and much other contemporary sacred music besides. Novello's edition of the "Twelfth Mass" reappeared separately in 1850, and was included—along with Haydn's *Nelson Mass* and Beethoven's *Mass in C* as a set known as the *Three Favourite Masses* published again by Novello in 1850; this inclusion cemented its attribution as the representative sacred work by the third member of the Viennese classics, alongside two works whose attribution has never been in doubt.[15] Its status as one of these three selected works remained even when

---

[13] Robin Langley, "Weber in England," *Musical Times* 117 (1976), 479.

[14] *MOZART'S MASSES /WITH /an Accompaniment for /THE /Organ, /arranged from the Full Score /BY / VINCENT NOVELLO / Organist to the Portuguese Embassy in London. / No. [1–18] / London. Published b W. Gallaway at his Music and Musical Instrument Warehouse / No.21 Wigmore Street. Cavendish Square.* The prefatory notice to no. 6, which covered masses 8–12 and was dated November 1819, stated that it came "from a Manuscript Score in the possession of Mr Edmund Harris, Bath." Novello recognized that the "grand scale upon which all the movements are constructed, was evidently intended by its' Author for the very highest Festivals of the Year: but it will probably be found too long for the usual duration of the Service on Sundays in general, unless it be considerably curtailed."

[15] THE THREE / FAVORITE MASSES, / COMPOSED BY / MOZART, HAYDN, / AND / BEETHOVEN, / IN VOCAL SCORE, / WITH AN ACCOMPANIMENT FOR THE ORGAN OR PIANO FORTE, / BY / VINCENT NOVELLO. / — / MOZART'S TWELFTH MASS [HAYDN'S THIRD (OR IMPERIAL) MASS; BEETHOVEN'S MASS, IN C]. / — / In addition to the original Latin Words, an adaptation to English Words has been added by R. G. Lorraine, Esq. / — / LONDON SACRED MUSIC WAREHOUSE: / J. ALFRED NOVELLO, MUSIC SELLER (BY APPOINTMENT) TO HER MAJESTY, / 69, DEAN STREET, SOHO, AND 24, POULTRY; / SIMPKIN, MARSHALL, & Co., STATIONERS' HALL COURT.

it was then published separately: for example, when Novello's edition was reissued in 1865 bound together with an essay by Edward Holmes (discussed later in this chapter), it was specifically identified as one of the *Three Favourite Masses*.[16]

By the mid-1860s, publication of the "Twelfth Mass" in its original form for SATB soloists and chorus had already spawned versions in English that moved the work from a Catholic ecclesiastical context into an Anglican one, a move that was enhanced by a further range of retexting of individual movements that then became freestanding anthems: the earliest surviving example is the retexting of the "Et incarnatus" as "I will cry unto God with my voice" by Charles Ashton.[17] Similar reworkings of the "Qui tollis," "Kyrie," "Dona nobis pacem," and "Gloria" followed in the next twenty years.[18] Presumably for use within a sacred or paraliturgical environment were the large numbers of arrangements of individual movements for organ and harmonium. And as the century progressed, the work appeared in various vocal arrangements: equal voices, women's voices, men's voices, both in conventional notation and—in the 1880s and 1890s—in tonic sol-fa.[19]

Well before the "Twelfth Mass" had achieved the illustrious status of one of the *Three Favourite Masses*, it had begun to enter the world of the drawing room. Remarkably, no other sacred work could match the number and range of publications of the "Twelfth Mass" destined for domestic consumption. It far exceeds any of the masses correctly attributed to Mozart, including the *Requiem*, both the other "Favourite Masses" and such a popular work as Mendelssohn's *St. Paul*. Even

---

[16] THE THREE / FAVORITE MASSES, / COMPOSED BY / MOZART, HAYDN, / AND / BEETHOVEN, / IN VOCAL SCORE, / WITH AN ACCOMPANIMENT FOR THE ORGAN OR PIANO FORTE, / BY VINCENT NOVELLO. / — / MOZART'S TWELFTH MASS. / — / In addition to the original Latin Words, an adaptation to English Words has been added by R. G. Lorraine, Esq. / To this Edition is added Mr E. HOLMES' Critical Essay, extracted from the "Musical Times." / — / LONDON SACRED MUSIC WAREHOUSE: / NOVELLO & CO., MUSIC SELLERS (BY APPOINTMENT) TO HER MAJESTY, 69, DEAN STREET, SOHO, / AND 35, POULTRY; ALSO IN NEW YORK, AT 1, CLINTON HALL, ASTOR PLACE.

[17] Anthem / "I WILL CRY UNTO GOD WITH MY VOICE," / (MOZART.) / *Adapted expressly for the* / Choir of Durham Cathedral, / (BY A FORMER MEMBER.) / *from the* / "ET INCARNATUS', & 'ET RESURREXIT," MASS Nº 12. / *revised, edited, & respectfully dedicated by permission to* / The Honourable George Wingfield Bourke, / PRESIDENT, / *AND THE GENTLEMEN OF THE CHORAL SOCIETY OF UNIVERISTY COLLEGE DURHAM,* / BY / CHARLES ASHTON, / OF THE CATHEDRAL CHOIR. / . . . / LONDON / *Published for the Editor, by* / JOSEPH WILLIAMS, 123, CHEAPSIDE. / J SMITH, & T. KAYE, MUSIC SELLERS, DURHAM.

[18] The "Dona nobis pacem" appeared in 1874 as "Hear us when we call, O Lord" in The Musical Bouquet 4161; Hear us when we call, O Lord / ("DONA NOBIS PACEM.") / Written and Arranged by / J. A. WADE, / from the / 12TH MASS / composed by / Mozart. / LONDON: PUBLISHED BY C. SHEARD, MUSICAL BOUQUET OFFICE; 129 HIGH HOLBORN.

[19] Wilberforce George Owst arranged the Gloria of the "Twelfth Mass" translated into English as "Glorious is thy name, Almighty Lord" for three-part women's chorus in 1927: G. Schirmer's Octavo Church Music / General / Anthems / No. 7212 / Gloria in Excelsis / From / W. A Mozart's Twelfth Mass / Arranged / For Three-Part Chorus / Of Women's Voices / By / W. G. Owst / G Schirmer Inc., New York). Curwen published nine sections of the "Twelfth Mass" as "Choruses" in 1895; the first is MOZART'S TWELFTH MASS "CHORUSES."—NO. 1. / Kyrie Eleison. / J. CURWEN & SONS LTD., 24 BERNERS STREET, W. Price 1d.

Mendelssohn's *Elijah* cannot match it.[20] No fewer than three arrangements of the "Gloria"—by Herrmann Paer, Henry Farmer, and Henry George Nixon—were made for piano solo before 1850, and this triggered large numbers of similar arrangements in the second half of the century.[21] One of the great William Crotch's retirement projects was to arrange four of the subjects from the "Twelfth Mass" for piano duet in a way that was more familiar from his treatments of Handel. Together with this assimilation of Mozart's sacred music with the drawing room went the arrangements of the entire work for larger instrumental ensemble: for piano duet; flute, violin, and cello; violin and piano; and six hands at one piano.[22] Moving outside the drawing room, there were arrangements for brass band, string ensemble, full orchestra, and fife and drum band.[23]

Beyond publication, the "Twelfth Mass" took on a key role in the emergent British world of the oratorio and harmonic society, in its full form for soloists, chorus, and orchestra. Early in the history of the Sacred Harmonic Society (the Exeter Hall Society, founded in 1832), the "Twelfth Mass" broke through the Handelian stranglehold of the organization and was programed alongside the *Dettingen Te Deum* in 1837.[24] Early performances are recorded by the Eastern Harmonic Society in 1848 (in Poplar), the Settle Choral Society in 1850, and the Limehouse

---

[20] A useful comparison may be made between the number of surviving arrangements of the "Twelfth Mass" studied for this chapter and perhaps the best known authentic work by Mozart, the Coronation Mass, K. 317: the "Twelfth Mass" enjoyed around 120 publications of arrangements; K. 317 less than twenty. The arrangements from *Elijah* number similarly.

[21] GLORIA IN EXCELSIS DEO / *FROM* / *Mozart's 12th Mass* / ARRANGED FOR THE / Pianoforte / *and Dedicated to* / The Misses Musters, / *(of Colwick, near Nottingham[)]* / BY / HENRY FARMER / LONDON / JOSEPH WILLIAMS, 123, CHEAPSIDE; MOZART'S / GLORIA IN EXCELSIS / *from his 12th Mass,* / Arranged expressly / FOR THE / Piano Forte / BY / H. G. NIXON / *LONDON* / HARRY MAY, / MUSIC PUBLISHER AND PIANO FORTE MANUFACTURER, 11 HOLBORN BARS.

[22] THREE MOVEMENTS / from / MOZART'S MASS, Nº 12, / VIZ. / GLORIA IN EXCELSIS DEO / BENEDICTUS QUI VENIT, / CUM SANCTO SPIRITU, / *Arranged for the Two Performers* / on the / Piano Forte, / WITH ACCOMPANIMENTS (AB LIBITUM) FOR / FLUTE, VIOLIN & VIOLON-CELLO / *By* / W. WATTS. / LONDON, / C. LONSDALE, 26, OLD BOND STREET. KYRIE ELEISON / FROM / MOZART'S 12TH MASS / *Arranged as a* / PIANOFORTE TRIO / BY / GEORGE FREDER-ICK WEST / PR: 5 / — / LONDON: ROBERT COCKS & Cº / NEW BURLINGTON ST, REGENT ST W. A similar undertaking is IN THREE BOOKS / Mozart's Service / Nº 12. / ARRANGED EXPRESSLY FOR / TWO PERFORMERS / ON THE / PIANO FORTE / *With ad lib. Accompᵗˢ for Flute, Violin, & Violoncelli* / BY / WILLIAM HUTCHINS CALLICOTT. / *London, Published by LEADER & COCK, 63, New Bond Street.* Nos. 1, 3, 4, and 5 of the "Sacred Series" were arrangements for violin and piano with a second violin or cello ad libitum of the Gloria, Dona nobis pacem, Quoniam, and Benedictus of the Twelfth Mass by Benjamin Barrow, the first of which was Sacred Series / Nº 1 / Gloria in Excelsis / FROM / MOZART'S 12TH MASS / FOR / Violin and Pianoforte / *with Second Violin & Violoncello, (ad. lib.)* / BY / BENJAMIN BARROW / London, / S. WHITE, 37, BOOKSELLERS ROW, STRAND, W.C.

[23] For the brass band version see AGNUS DEI / 12TH MASS / MOZART / Arrᵈ by E. C. F. HARE / At LAFLEUR and SON, Music Publishers, 15 Green Street, Leicester Sq: London W.C [1873]. For the arrangement for fife and drum band, see J. R. LAFLEUR & SON'S FIFE & DRUM JOURNAL. / SACRED MARCH / GLORIA / From Mozart's 12th Mass. / EDWIN HARE.

[24] *Musical World* 7 (1837), 156–157.

Choral Society in 1852.[25] Reports of an 1852 performance, again by the Sacred Harmonic Society, were reported as far away as New York,[26] and from the early 1850s, performances were mounted at most major festivals and by most major societies: Manchester, Liverpool, Newcastle, Hereford, York, Bristol, and Birmingham.[27] Whether the tailing-off in interest after the mid-1860s is a result of the challenges to the work's authenticity (discussed below) is difficult to say. The work was paired with Mendelssohn's works for soloists, chorus, and orchestra—*Elijah*, *St. Paul*, *Lobgesang*, Haydn's *Creation*, and Handel's *Judas Maccabeus*, as well as Beethoven's *Christus am Ölberge*.

Music and Words

Contexts for the public cultivation of this intriguing piece ranged from the most modest to the most elaborate, from the local brass band competition to the openings of new technological achievements. Further afield, but rather more prestigious than most, was the dedication of the organ of St. Patrick's cathedral in Melbourne in 1880. Here, the "Twelfth Mass" was presented in its entirety with interpolated additional numbers from Rossini's *Stabat mater* in the context of one of the decade's most important musical events in the city.[28]

Two events on the other side of the Atlantic may serve as a reminder that the "Twelfth Mass" was a talisman for Mozart's reputation throughout the entire English-speaking world. In his *Chronicles of Baltimore*, Thomas Scharf drew attention to what he called "one of the finest civic displays ever witnessed in this country... the laying of the corner-stone of the new Masonic Temple for the members of the Masonic fraternity in Maryland" on 20 November 1866.[29] The musical events were again dominated by the "Twelfth Mass," whose "Gloria," after a performance of some choruses from Haydn's *Creation*, closed the proceedings.

Even more high-profile was the role the work played in one of the most important transport undertakings of the nineteenth century: the completion of the transcontinental railroad in 1869. This technological achievement was mirrored by the telegraphic technology used to relay the information from the point at which the Central and Union Pacific Railroads joined—Promontory, Utah—to New York and other major U.S. cities. As a feat of technology, it was mirrored by the photographic forms used to record it. There were several attempts to photo-

---

[25] *Musical Times* 3 (1848), 21; 4 (1850), 72; 4 (1851), 241.

[26] *New York Musical World* 4 (1852), 21.

[27] Performances are recorded in large quantities in the *Musical Times*.

[28] "The New Organ at St. Patrick's (R.C.) Cathedral, and the Opening Ceremony," *Australasian Sketcher*, 27 March 1880.

[29] Thomas Scharf, *The Chronicles of Baltimore; Being a Complete History of "Baltimore Town" and Baltimore City from the Earliest Period to the Present Time* (Baltimore: Turnbull, 1874; reprint, Middle Atlantic States Historical Publications 15, Port Washington and London: Kennikat, 1972), 666–667.

graph the event, and many prints survive. Those of Andrew J. Russell are probably the best known and most often reproduced.

The joining of the rails was celebrated with a religious ceremony at Trinity Church in New York, which culminated in a performance of the "Gloria" from the "Twelfth Mass." The *New York Times* cited the words of Alexander Hamilton Vinton as he wrapped up his address and cued the music: "So this Pacific Railway is a means, under Divine Providence, for propagating the Church and the Gospel from this, the youngest Christian nation, to the oldest land in the Orient, now sunk in Paganism and idolatry, and so will revive the worship of the Triune God—the God of our salvation—in the farther East, the birthplace of Christianity. For this we celebrate this great event. Join with me, therefore, in singing an anthem of praise to God, "'Glory to God in the highest; on earth peace, good will to men.'" The *New York Times* then ended: "The choir then pealed forth the Gloria in MOZART'S immortal Twelfth Mass, the rendering throughout being superbly grand."[30] The "Twelfth Mass" also probably featured in Patrick Gilmore's second monster concert in Boston in 1869 (fifty thousand in the audience, eleven thousand on stage), and had concluded the collaborative "grand centennial celebration of the birth of Mozart" in Philadelphia in 1856, after the seemingly obligatory ode, an address titled "The Life and the Genius of Mozart," and the crowning of a bust of the composer.[31]

Words and Music

The density and distribution of performances and publication of the "Twelfth Mass" were more than enough to establish it—in one form or another, and however erroneously—as one of the central works in the Mozart canon during the nineteenth century and well into the twentieth. But the words used to describe the work went beyond such conventional descriptors as "favorite," "celebrated," and so on; as we have seen, when the work ended the service in Trinity Church in New York in 1869, it was described as "immortal." But if immortality could characterize Mozart's "Twelfth Mass" in 1869, thirty years earlier its reputation had already become even more remarkable: it was now part of a vision of Heaven. Here is an extract from an early nineteenth-century account of the architecture of the city of York. We have just entered the Minster via the South transept:

> Straight before you, at the extremity of the opposite or northern transept, your eyes sparkle with delight on a view of the stained-glass lancet windows.

---

[30] *New York Times*, 11 May 1869.

[31] For the former, see Michael Broyles, "Art Music from 1860 to 1920," in *The Cambridge History of American Music*, ed. David Nicholls (Cambridge: Cambridge University Press, 1998), 233. The "selections from a Mozart mass" could be from none other than the "Twelfth Mass"; for the latter, see Dorothy Turner Potter, "The Cultural Influences of W. A. Mozart's Music in Philadelphia, 1786–1861" (Ph.D. diss., University of Virginia, 2000), 184–186 and 335.

How delicate—how rich—how chaste—how unrivalled! All the colours
seem to be intertwined, in delicate fibres, like Mechlin lace. There is no glare:
but the tone of the whole is perfectly bewitching. You move on. A light
streams from above. It is from the Lantern, or interior summit of the Great
Tower, upon which you are gazing. Your soul is lifted up with your eyes: and
if the diapason harmonies of the organ are let loose, and the sweet and soft
voices of the choristers unite in the Twelfth Mass of Mozart—you instinctively clasp your hands together and exclaim, "This must be Heaven!"[32]

This text moves from sensory pleasure—"your eyes sparkle with delight"; "delicate
fibres, like Mechlin lace"—to progressively more sacred images: the light streaming
from above redolent of the Annunciation, the Light of the World, or any number
of biblical references, leads to the lifting up of the eyes in a reference to Psalm 121
and finally to a celestial vision. But the penultimate milestone on this architectural
and heavenly journey is a performance, by clearly worldly choristers and organ, of
the "Twelfth Mass."

The contexts presented so far demonstrate the very wide dissemination the
"Twelfth Mass" received in print, and the wide range of uses to which it was put,
ranging from social diversion to sacred fetish. The previous, essentially literary,
example points to a further way the work takes on a particular resonance: its
almost incidental mention in works of imaginative fiction. Incidental these occurrences might be, but their apparently casual appearance is testimony to the degree
of purchase the "Twelfth Mass" had on literary culture by the end of the nineteenth
century. Two examples, one from each side of the Atlantic, make the point. Here is
an extract from chapter 25 of Jack London's 1910 novel *Burning Daylight*, which
begins in the Klondike of 1893, just before the 1898 Gold Rush. The climax of the
book comes after the Yukon visionary turned California plutocrat Elam Harnish—
known as Burning Daylight—has renounced his wealth to live off the land with
Dede Mason. With the trope of fire and burning running throughout the novel,
the completion of the fireplace in their resurrected home is an important climactic
point in the work. The two have invited their neighbor Ferguson to witness their
first fire:

Ferguson shook Daylight's hand ecstatically, and Daylight shook his with
equal fervour, and, bending, kissed Dede on the lips. They were as exultant
over the success of their simple handiwork as any great captain at astonishing victory. In Ferguson's eyes was actually a suspicious moisture while
the woman pressed even more closely against the man whose achievement it
was. He caught her up suddenly in his arms and whirled her away to the
piano, crying out: "Come on, Dede! The Gloria! The Gloria!"

[32] Thomas Frognall Dibdin, *A Bibliographical, Antiquarian and Picturesque Tour in the Northern
Counties of England and in Scotland,* 3 vols. (London: author, 1838), 1:174–175.

And while the flames in the fireplace worked, the triumphant strains of the Twelfth Mass rolled forth.[33]

It is completely logical that the first work London reached for to cap off this particular scene is a piece that both commands appropriate authority and is sufficiently commonplace to guarantee recognition. London also uses the "Twelfth Mass" to similar effect in a scene in his 1914 novel *Mutiny on the Elsinore*.

A second example comes from a literary text written just over a decade after *Burning Daylight*, but from one where the logical is supplanted by the surreal, domestic achievement replaced by something very different:

> So they passed on to chatting about music, a form of art for which Bloom, as a pure amateur, possessed the greatest love, as they made tracks arm-in-arm across Beresford place. Wagnerian music, though confessedly grand in its way, was a bit too heavy for Bloom and hard to follow at the first go-off but the music of Mercadante's *Huguenots,* Meyerbeer's *Seven Last Words on the Cross,* and Mozart's *Twelfth Mass,* he simply revelled in, the *Gloria* in that being to his mind the acme of first class music as such, literally knocking everything else into a cocked hat.[34]

There is much in this extract from chapter 16 of James Joyce's *Ulysses*. Joyce is successfully attempting to attribute to Bloom a middlebrow appreciation of music by choosing what for the second decade of the twentieth century were uncontentious and well-known works: Mercadante's *Le sette ultime parole* of 1841, the most frequently performed opera of the previous century, Meyerbeer's *Les Huguenots* of 1836, and one of the best known works by one of the best known composers: the "Twelfth Mass." Bloom's tenuous grasp of the subject is revealed by his reversal of composer and work in the cases of Mercadante and Meyerbeer, and it is just possible that Joyce was at least aware of the issues surrounding the attribution of the "Twelfth Mass," although he would have had to have been very well informed indeed to have worked this implication into the text. It would, however, have added to the image of Bloom punching above his musical weight. But, as in the case of *Burning Daylight*, the almost casual inclusion of the "Twelfth Mass"—unintroduced and unexplained— bears witness to the work's status in the literary imagination of the early twentieth century.[35]

How could this curious state of affairs have arisen? How could a misattributed work—and an attribution that had been under serious challenge throughout the

---

[33] Jack London, *Burning Daylight* (New York: Macmillan, 1910; reprint, 1961), 244.

[34] James Joyce, *Ulysses: A Critical and Synoptic Edition*, ed. Hans Walter Gabler, Wolfhard Steppe, and Claus Melchior, 3 vols. (New York and London: Garland, 1984), 3:1443.

[35] Very little of this figures in the literature on *Ulysses*. The transposition of composer and work is noted in Don Gifford and Robert J. Seidman, *"Ulysses" Annotated: Notes for James Joyce's "Ulysses,"* 2nd ed. (Berkeley: University of California Press, 1988), 560, but the account of the "Twelfth Mass" is badly garbled (96).

nineteenth century, albeit in almost exclusively German-speaking circles—come to have assumed such a revered, if not hallowed, status a century after its first publication? This returns the discussion to the central question of this book: if this chapter took as its subject either of the two other "favorite masses," this chapter's work would consist of tracing performances and perhaps musicological status of Haydn's *Nelson Mass* and Beethoven's *Mass in C*. It would be a straightforward matter of tracing the fortunes of a part of the canon—a part whose attribution is uncontentious—of two well-known figures. The "Twelfth Mass," however, acts as a *Wirkungsträger* under what might be considered false pretences—a work considered to be by Mozart but whose attribution to another composer is now clear—but has an immense significance for Mozart's reception and renown. The question—how this could have happened—is worth repetition.

The question was asked and answered with some ferocity in 1936—a key period for the reception of the "Twelfth Mass," as the tide turned against the rejection of German views on its authenticity—in the article "Question and Answer Box," published in *Caecilia: Monthly Magazine of Catholic Church and School Music*, in which Dom Gregory Hügle, prior of the Conception Abbey in Conception, Minnesota, undertook to answer questions ranging from "How can I overcome my aversion to singing in unison?" to "Is it permissible to chant or recite any stanzas of the Dies irae at will, without regard for special verses? Does this privilege apply also to other parts of the Mass?" One question was bluntly put:

Can it be proved that the so-called Twelfth Mass of Mozart is the work of a swindler?

To which Hügle responded with an account of the German tradition from Seyfried onward, which triggered the same question posed here: "How was it possible for this Mass to become so immensely popular when it is known not to be by Mozart?" Hügle enumerated five reasons:

1. The uncritical, credulous age.
2. Mozart's great name. Enthusiastic music lovers in England and America did much towards the spread of this Mass.
3. Love of spectacular music for state occasions, along the popular axiom: ["]the more noise the better." In point of bombastic display this composition has no equal.
4. Low standards of musical education; depraved taste; pioneer conditions; the Mass was easy and effective.
5. The spirit of liberalism and secularism; the make-believe that the musical heroes of Vienna: Haydn, Mozart, Beethoven, were infallible leaders and interpreters of church music.[36]

---

[36] *Caecilia: Monthly Magazine of Catholic Church and School Music* 63 (1936), 521.

It is difficult to account for laying the blame on the "uncritical, credulous age," "depraved taste," or the "spirit of liberalism and secularism," except in the context of Hügle's view that probably the only music tolerable in the church was plainsong. However, when he points to "enthusiastic music lovers in England and America," this is part of a tradition that this chapter has been careful to describe, and "the make-believe that the musical heroes...were infallible leaders" aligns itself well with the subject matter of this entire book. When he points to the "easiness" and "effectiveness" of the "Twelfth Mass," though, he is indicating quite bluntly the work's difference from most other sacred works not only by Mozart but by his contemporaries as well: it lacks particularly the challenge of elaborate vocal solos and of orchestral writing that places undue demands on individual players or ensemble skill.

Hügle indicates a performance quality that accords well with the evidence that has been presented throughout this chapter. Whether, in his unequivocal invocation of "pioneer conditions," he was alluding to the possibility of enhancing liturgical celebrations with music by a known master such as the one in Little Rock, Arkansas, described by the local newspaper as follows, depends much on definitions of "pioneer": "The leader of the Choir of St. Andrew's Cathedral, (Roman Catholic), is Professor E. Wiedemann, who is a fine organist. On Sunday last, the splendid twelfth mass of the immortal Mozart was rendered in a manner worthy of the great Master. Prof. W. showed a pure appreciation of this gem of music. Several solos were [finely] executed and it is seldom that sacred music has been so finely, and purely rendered in our city."[37]

Hügle's answers to his interlocutor's questions are colored by an extreme view of the propriety of sacred music. A broader answer that is likely to be hard to accept at the beginning of the twenty-first century is that musicians, audiences, and congregations 150 years ago found pleasures in the "Twelfth Mass" that more recent critics have struggled to identify. Such pleasures may well be related to the ambivalent position of Mozart's music in the context of early nineteenth-century Anglican worship, as filtered though Attwood and Spohr. Mozart's sacred music was frequently problematic because of its operatic nature and its perceived difficulty for audiences, and it may well have been thought that the Mozart canon could only have been enriched by a work, apparently untainted by the theater, that was perhaps more acceptable as sacred music than the rest of the composer's known output. But there are some more direct answers: the extensive publication of the work and extracts from it was not merely a consequence of the work's success but largely generated it, as Hügle's answer suggested. Large tracts of the early publication history of the "Twelfth Mass"—in all its versions—were the result of the publishing industry of Vincent Novello, the individual originally responsible for presenting the English-speaking world with the work in the first place: he not only published the work in the format that gave it his name but also set it alongside

---

[37] *National Democrat*, 31 December 1864.

Haydn and Beethoven as one of the *Three Favourite Masses*, and published *The Musical Times and Singing Class Circular*, in which one of the most influential texts on the "Twelfth Mass" was published.

A further question that demands an answer is how Anglophone musicians responded when confronted with the German view that the "Twelfth Mass" was not by Mozart. Having spent two significant periods in Europe, Alexander Wheelock Thayer—midcentury doyen of Beethoven studies in the United States—was well placed to raise this issue. In *Dwight's Journal of Music*, he discussed the Mass VII published by Simrock, the doubts about its authenticity in the *Leipziger musikalische Zeitung*, Seyfried's doubts in *Caecilia*, Simrock's reply, and the note in Jahn's *Life of Mozart*, and went on to ask: "But why have I spent so much time upon this matter? Because this "Mass for four voices, No. VII.," of which I have a copy in Simrock's edition, is, note for note, that which in our country is so popular under the title of *Mozart's Twelfth Mass*!"[38] Published in 1856, the article remained without comment until six years later, when Dwight serialized an article from the Viennese *Deutsche Musik-Zeitung*; in the first issue of the serialization, the editorial commentary reported the challenge to Mozart's authorship, and the comments in Jahn and the work's absence from Köchel: "Many lovers of Mozart's Mass music will be surprised not to find their favorite 'Twelfth Mass' (in G) even alluded to in this review; in spite of its beauties and strong Mozartean [*sic*] features, we believe it is now generally conceded among the learned ones in Germany, that Mozart never wrote it."[39] Shortly afterward, however, an author of an article titled "Florentine Epistles," who identified himself merely as "F. B.," asked:

> Will you, Mr Editor, oblige a constant reader by publishing this fact so that it will be known and acknowledged, and that there shall be no excuse hereafter for ignorance. Let this be the last we hear of "Mozart's Twelfth Mass." Let not the soul of the gifted composer be disturbed by such Masses as this. Nail the counterfeit to the counter, and let us hear on this side of the Atlantic, too, the blows of the hammer, which none can wield better than yourself?[40]

---

[38] *Dwight's Journal of Music: A Paper of Art and Literature*, 6 December 1856.

[39] Ibid., 4 October 1862. Dwight had previously written an essay on the "Twelfth Mass," an astonishing encomium of the work that simply translated notes into words: "Mozart's Twelfth Mass," *Graham's Magazine* 38 (1851), 1–5. Most of the essay is a blow-by-blow translation of the music into prose: "A single firm bass voice commences the *Kyrie eleison*, and prononunces these words twice in a grave and slowly measured tone of supplication" (3); "The commencement of the *Credo* is a quick movement in C major, full of spirit and decision, and of an upsoaring faith. The voices climg above their respective natural limits, semitone by semitone, lesiurely exulting upon each new height won; and it seems as if the whole tone-structure would grow up into the sky" (4); "And then that most exquisite introductory symphony—almost overture—to the *Benedictus qui venit* (Blessed is he who cometh) with its innocent, blithe pastoral warble of reed instruments, is played in the key of F, which is always like a soothing walk with nature" (5).

[40] *Dwight's Journal of Music: A Paper of Art and Literature*, 24 January 1863.

"F. B." reminded readers of Thayer's 1856 article. Dwight's reply picked up on words in his earlier article as a prelude to a riposte that is important for its clever temporizing:

> *In spite of all its beauties and strong Mozartean features*, we still say. No one denies that it has beauties, or very much that is suggestive of Mozart. Few will doubt that the *Gloria*, the fugue: *Cum sancto spriritu*, &c., are fine, and in point of essential inspiration, if not in all technical respects, not unworthy of Mozart—at least of his other masses, mostly written in his youth....Now, for our own part, undoubtedly we have lost much of the enthusiasm with which we could speak about this Mass, at a time when it was one of the very few Masses which we knew at all. But we are far from discarding it as worthless, or as so much inferior to some of the others by Mozart. Seyfried's internal objections, as summed up by "A. W. T." in the article referred to...are mostly technical and special, while to the general character of the work he only objects that it is not sufficiently church-like.
>
> But we feel no call nor inclination to go into more discussion of it. We trust that "T. B." [*sic*] is now satisfied, and that *he* too will "let this be the last we hear of Mozart's Twelfth Mass."[41]

Dwight carefully shifts the nature of the claim away from direct issues of attribution and toward its "beauties" and features that are "suggestive of Mozart" or (double negative) "not unworthy" of the composer. He then goes on to dismiss Seyfried's "internal" objections cited by Thayer as "mostly technical and special" and to set aside his comments on the "general character" of the work. But in calling for an end to discussion, Dwight seemingly deliberately misreads his correspondent—who is surely calling for an end not only to performances of the work but also to the types of discourses outlined in this chapter—and assumes that he wants to close the correspondence. Dwight, clearly anxious to protect the work from the predations of "F. B." and Thayer, is only too happy to oblige.

On the other side of the Atlantic, not only was the fallout from Jahn and Köchel similar but so, too, were the responses. A correspondent in the *Musical World* posed the question in the same terms as had Thayer: Jahn's view was that the "Twelfth Mass" was not by Mozart, so: "Might I ask if this opinion be held in England? If so, it should be distinctly notified to the Sacred Harmonic Society, and other similar societies who persist in giving periodical performances of this Mass as Mozart's."[42] Like Thayer's, this inquiry went without response. But two years later, a staff reporter on the *Manchester Guardian* reviewed a performance at the Birmingham Festival that included, alongside Beethoven's *Christus am Ölberge*, op. 85, selections from Handel's *Solomon*, Mendelssohn's *Elijah*, and Guglielmi's "Gratias agimus," "Mozart's" "Twelfth Mass." Having praised the performance, the

---

[41] Ibid.
[42] *Musical World*, 25 October 1862.

anonymous reviewer issues an unremitting challenge to the authenticity of the work. Pointing out that "Of the so-called Twelfth Mass I would rather not speak, but I may as well chronicle my conviction...that Mozart had nothing at all to do with it, that the *real* Twelfth Mass, which is very well known in Germany, is of a much higher character, and that this spurious thing, which I suspect to have been the result of a publisher's trick, has been put together by some mediocre musician, who knew Mozart's style, and who may possibly have had access to the numerous scraps of melody which he left behind him. I confess I do not understand how Mr Costa can shut his eyes to the palpable weakness and incorrectness of the thing, for Mozart was never either weak or incorrect."[43] Had the author not chosen the words "the result of a publisher's trick," the article would probably have remained unknown outside that part of the readership of the *Manchester Guardian* interested in musical affairs in Birmingham. However, it could only be expected that a gauntlet thrown down to the publisher of the "Twelfth Mass"—Vincent Novello (who had only died three years previously—could only be picked up by with alacrity by the *Musical Times and Singing-Class Circular*. For his skill in turning an ill-judged criticism of a publisher into a site of reception that reinscribes the value of the "Twelfth Mass" so successfully, Henry Charles Lunn's article in the *Musical Times* deserves quotation. After citing some phrases verbatim from the *Manchester Guardian* article, Lunn continues:

> Now of course we can have no desire to question the opinion—even when it amounts to a "conviction"—of any individual who is desirous of perpetuating his name by disagreeing with the popular voice; but that he should bring a wholesale and entirely unsupported charge against respectable publishers, and especially that the *Manchester Guardian* should give publicity to it, we sincerely regret. We should have imagined that the name of Vincent Novello (than whom no more conscientious musician ever lived), under whose direction the Mass was first printed in England, would have been a sufficient guarantee against the possibility of his being party to a "publisher's trick"; and amongst those with whom this work has so long been a favourite we could mention a host of eminent professors, including the most earnest disciple of Mozart, the late Mr Edward Holmes, who had studied the works all his life, and who wrote an elaborate analysis of this very Mass. That a "Twelfth Mass" exists in Germany, and of a "higher character," is no proof that the work so numbered in England is a "spurious thing." In the edition of the Full Score published by Messrs Simrock, of Bonn, it is marked "No. 7," and this, for aught we know, may be correct; the work, and not the number, being the important matter. The critic in the *Manchester Guardian* has a perfect reliance upon the soundness of his own opinion; for he accuses Mr Costa of "shutting his eyes to the palpable weakness and incorrectness" of the

---

[43] *Manchester Guardian*, 10 September 1864.

work. Yet, as he states that he believes "Mozart had nothing to do with it," and afterwards admits that the "mediocre musician" who put it together may have had access to the composer's "scraps of melody," we do recognize one twinge of conscience which, whilst it does credit to his judgment, somewhat weakens the effect of his previously expressed "conviction."[44]

The aim is clear: to defend the "Twelfth Mass" as vigorously as Dwight. The strategy is well defined: to undermine the author by exploiting any evenhanded qualification and by accusing him of maligning an individual. So the possibility that the composer of the "Twelfth Mass" might have had access to "scraps of melody which he [Mozart] left behind him" is turned around into a "twinge of conscience," and the largest part of the article does not address the substance of the issue but merely condemns the critic for daring to impugn the name of Vincent Novello. The critic wrote back, citing such authors as Oulibicheff, Jahn, Köchel, and even Hallé, and absolutely savaging Holmes, whom the *Musical Times* had held up as its star witness. Observing that he had not known that Novello had been the first to publish the work in England, the critic concluded:

> you will perhaps allow me to inform you, that throughout the many years during which I have been connected with the Manchester press, I have never at any time been "desirous of perpetuating my name by disagreeing with the popular voice." I have lived long enough to estimate at its true value the popular voice, and I am neither inclined blindly to bow to it, nor to any other authority, so long as there is any chance of arriving at truth by an honest, but free exercise of my *own* faculties.[45]

The testy exchange did not stop there, since the *Musical Times* glossed the letter, and Lunn claimed that the "present communication throws no new light upon what is already known respecting this work" (patently untrue) and simply argued that Mozart's authorship had to be accepted unless "very substantial and conclusive proofs can be furnished to the contrary."[46]

Twenty years later, the *Musical Times* returned to the fray, citing an article in "a Scotch paper" (which has resisted identification) that said "On the whole, the Mass, which is certainly not Mozart's, though the name is too important, for publishing reasons evidently, to be taken away from it, is hardly worth the study of any Society of intelligence and taste." Here, the reaction of the *Musical Times* comes close to ridicule; failing to adduce any evidence (except to criticize the original for lack of evidence): "We should be sorry to believe that this critic could make such an assertion without being in the possession of facts hitherto unknown to prove it. But apart from this, it does appear strange that, presuming the Mass not to be by

---

[44] *Musical Times and Singing-Class Circular*, 1 October 1864.
[45] Ibid.
[46] Ibid.

Mozart, it should suddenly be discovered that it is "hardly worth the study of any Society of intelligence and taste." For our part—knowing the work tolerably well from years of study—we cannot but think it a great pity that, if Mozart were not the composer of it, the real author did not write another."[47] Snide, certainly, but the effect was to ride out yet another challenge to the authenticity of the "Twelfth Mass," as the certainties of German scholarship fell to the onslaught of the Novello steamroller.

Clear from much of the foregoing is the degree to which Edward Holmes's essays on Mozart's masses, and on the "Twelfth Mass" in particular, are a constant point of reference in the debates about the authenticity of the work in the 1860s. And Holmes's "Twelfth Mass" essay was an important site of reception for the work, and itself a *Wirkungsträger*, authored as it was by a member of the Novello circle, indeed Novello's apprentice, and arguably one of the finest writers in English on music in the second quarter of the nineteenth century. Holmes is perhaps best known for his 1845 *Life of Mozart*, a work much praised by Jahn in his own biography a decade later, but he was also a prolific and wide-ranging music critic.[48] Between 1852 and 1855, Holmes published a series of nearly two dozen articles on Mozart's masses in the fifth and sixth volumes of Novello's *Musical Times*.[49] The series of articles dedicated to Mozart's "Twelfth Mass" was the second longest in the series.[50] Hardly surprisingly, given its highly contested status by the mid-1850s, the *Requiem* was the subject of the longest essay, but the one on the "Twelfth Mass" was more than four times as long as that devoted to any other work.[51]

Holmes begins by telling us what we already know from the evidence revealed in this chapter; that the "Twelfth Mass" enjoyed a reputation second to none in English musical culture: "its history in England is peculiar—for never has any work of this kind been so popular, its melodies almost rivalling in that respect those of the *Zauberflöte* or *Don Giovanni*."[52] He goes on to draw attention to the

---

[47] Ibid., 1 June 1882.

[48] Edward Holmes, *The Life of Mozart* (London: Chapman and Hall, 1845). It was reissued, edited by Ebenezer Prout, in 1878 (London: Novello, Ewer & Co., 1878), and again, edited by Ernest Newman, in 1912 in the Everyman's Library series. For Jahn's comments, see his *Life of Mozart*, trans. by Pauline D. Townsend from the German, 3 vols. (London: Novello, Ewer, 1882), 1:ix–x.

[49] The series of twenty-one articles began on 1 October 1852 and concluded on 15 April 1855. In order, the works discussed were K. 317; K. 257; K. 192; K. 258; K. 220; K. 194.; K. Anh. 233 (C1.07); K. Anh. 234 (C1.08); K. Anh. (C1.09); K. 275; K. 259; K. Anh. 232 (C1.04) (the "Twelfth Mass"); K. 626 (the *Requiem*); and K. 337. Apart from the "Twelfth Mass" and the *Requiem*, no work was allotted more than a single article, and each ran from between one and a half columns (K. 233) to five and a half columns (K. 257).

[50] The series was in three parts: 1 March 1854; 15 April 1854; and 1 June 1854 (a total of twenty-three and a half columns).

[51] The *Requiem* was in six instalments: 1 August 1854; 1 October 1854; 1 December 1854; 15 January 1855; 15 February 1855; 15 March 1855; and 15 April 1855. It ran to forty-two columns of text.

[52] [Edward Holmes], *A Critical Notice of Mozart's Twelfth Mass, Extracted from the Papers on Mozart's Masses in the "Musical Times"* (London: Novello, s.d.), ii/2 (all references to Holmes's text are from this edition, with the page number preceding the column number).

various contexts in which the "Twelfth Mass" was enjoyed: the Catholic church, the Anglican cathedral, and the drawing room.[53] He also adds a fourth—one that serves to establish his long engagement with the subject: the theater. The example he cites is the use of the "Gloria" for the representation of the cathedral at Reims for the coronation of Charles X at a production at Covent Garden during Charles Kemble's tenure, a set of circumstances that places the event between 1825 and 1832.[54] He also alludes, in his recollection of the end of the "Gloria," to the quality of performance by the South Street Choir—in the chapel of the Portuguese Embassy, where Vincent Novello was organist for the entire first quarter of the century and where the "Twelfth Mass" was performed for the first time in England.[55]

Holmes sets his comments in the well-known context of Mozart's music as a type that requires multiple hearings in order to yield up its secrets; here he spins that particular trope in terms of a desire to have all Mozart's music available in full score. Until the time, he writes, when we "are able both to read and hear [the scores], it is impossible to appreciate fully the services he rendered to music."[56] A further context for Holmes's comments is the image of Mozart the synthesist: a composer with the ability to take music of diverse styles and impart greater value to the product. Within the framework of a set of observations on the presence of what he calls the "Italian style" in the "Twelfth Mass," Holmes suggests: "Whatever of foreign style passed through the mind of this composer, whether majestic, elegant, or fanciful, came out in the imitation heightened and embellished. He seized upon what was excellent in the minds of others as well as in his own; the same power which gave him the perfect control of his own ideas, made him equally master of those of others."[57]

Holmes's account of the work describes a seriatim commentary on each of the movements and within each movement a sequential reading of each subsection. The section of the work to which he devotes most words and greatest intellectual energy is the first section of the "Gloria" (ex. 5.1).

The points Holmes ostensibly makes concern the scoring of the opening passage, the typically Mozartian treatment of the text "Pax hominibus," the crescendo on the words "Bonae voluntatis," and the modulatory scheme that precedes the return of the opening material at the words "Domine deus." But in his commentary on these passages, he invokes and reinforces a number of tropes that have had an immense impact on the musicography on Mozart in the following 150 years.

---

[53] Ibid.
[54] Ibid., iv/1.
[55] Ibid., viii/2.
[56] Ibid., i/1.
[57] Ibid., ii/1.

EXAMPLE 5.1: *"Mozart": "Twelfth Mass," Gloria, opening.*

The treatment by the composer of the section "Bonae voluntatis" called forth from Holmes a remarkable explanation of the history and significance of the orchestral crescendo. For Holmes, this must have been something of a rarity for Mozart, not found apparently in any opera or mass known to him. But this passage prompted in Holmes a reflection on how it established in instrumental music a domain of its

own, and imparted to inarticulate sounds a vivacity and force of description by turns beautiful or sublime. Through the art of musical painting, exemplified in contrasts of light and shade, and the varied tones and *timbre* of instruments, composers have become among all the brotherhood of poetry, the artists most powerful in their impressions on the sensibility of mankind. They place us, at will in

Arcadian scenes of soft repose and luxurious enjoyment, or amid the direst con-
vulsions and heroes of nature, in which they "ride the whirlwind and direct the
storm."[58]

---

[58] Ibid., iv/2. The quotation at the end of this passage is from Joseph Addison's poem celebrating the
allied victory over the French and Bavarians at the Battle of Blenheim (1704). The poem (1705), entitled

Holmes proposes the crescendo as a piece of evidence to demonstrate the poetic qualities of music, whether that be in the description of Arcady or the field of Blenheim, and to consider Mozart as perhaps the most poetic of composers—al-

---

"The Campaign," includes the lines "And, pleased th' Almighty's orders to perform, / Rides in the whirl-wind, and directs the storm."

though, as Holmes admits, "to say that Mozart first invented the crescendo would be to assume too much."[59] And the trope of "Mozart the Poet" is one to which Holmes returns in his explanation of the power of the simple harmonic repetitions that characterize the setting of the words "Laudamus, benedicimus, adoramus."

---

[59] Holmes, *Critical Notice*, iv/2.

Mozart "saw, *like a poet,* beauties in familiar things, which were overlooked by others, because of their familiarity."[60]

Holmes summons initiates into a closed world of understanding Mozart. In the little fragment setting the words "Pax hominibus," Holmes draws attention to "this

---

[60] Ibid., v/2.

uncommonly elegant and characteristic phrase, in which the real author will be instantly recognised," but Mozart introduces this phrase—according to Holmes— "for better hearers," for the cognoscenti, for those who have put in the time for multiple hearings of the work and who perhaps own the full score to which he alludes at the beginning of the article.[61] But the point of Holmes's commentary on this passage is that this is the moment that Mozart chooses to introduce *tenuto* chords in the woodwind, and that in finding and exploiting such opportunities Mozart's "work is to him manifest enjoyment."[62] Here is another well-known Mozartian trope: the idea of the act of composition as pleasure, and it is one that Holmes deploys again in the account of the modulatory scheme preceding the return of the opening of the movement on the words "Domine deus." The modulations encompass e minor, d minor, C major, c minor, A-flat major, and return via a German sixth to the dominant of C. Holmes invites us to admire not only these modulations but all the other traits that "distinguish[ed the composer's] voluptuous ear and the spirit of enjoyment which possessed him."[63] We have here examples of claims that endeavors in instrumentation and harmony were both compositional activities that brought pleasure to Mozart and that make that pleasure manifest to his listeners.

Holmes offers a frame to his comments on this part of the "Gloria" that evokes two more general Mozartian tropes: "Mozart the dramatist" and "Mozart as the embodiment of music." He was clearly concerned about possible charges of vulgarity being leveled at the opening of the movement, with its heavily scored subject derived from the tonic arpeggio perhaps not quite matching what he had hoped for from Mozart. For Holmes, the explanation is that "Mozart did not wish miscellaneous hearers to hesitate in their impressions of this part of the work, but that it should strike at once: hence its fitness *for dramatic purpose*," and he here introduces the recollection of the Covent Garden performance from the 1820s already mentioned. And in noting that the trumpets are silent in the opening bars, Holmes observes that "the passage is saved from a certain vulgarity which would have ensued, had too much been done; and the effect . . . is enhanced."[64] Even in the most unlikely place, in the context of a sacred work, the composer of *Don Giovanni* and *Die Zauberflöte* cannot escape praise as a dramatic composer.

The account of this section of the "Gloria" concludes with some comments on the composer's use of accompaniment in the "Gratias agimus," and gives Holmes the chance to contrast the complexity of modern composition with what he calls the "clear thoughts, rapidly committed to paper, and easily expressed" that mark out Mozart's music. His modern competitors are Mendelssohn, Meyerbeer, and Berlioz—to the last of whom Holmes was a recent convert. He points to the scale on

---

[61] Ibid., iv/1–2.
[62] Ibid., iv/2.
[63] Ibid., v/2.
[64] Ibid., iv/1.

which this music is written, concluding: "we cannot take [the music of Meyerbeer or Berlioz] home with us and enjoy it at the pianoforte like that of Mozart," a tidy way of reminding his readers of the place of the "Twelfth Mass" in the drawing room that he has already stressed. But his final comments come close to the idea that Mozart *embodies* music: not only will his compositions "be always better liked" but this will be because they are "more in the nature of music itself."[65] Whereas the works of Holmes's contemporaries and immediate predecessors—Mendelssohn, Meyerbeer, and Berlioz—are "coldly and deliberately planned, however effective under circumstances," Mozart's works—including the "Twelfth Mass"—align themselves more clearly with an abstract sense of musical perfection.

The "Twelfth Mass" wrongly attributed to Mozart has been an important marker for the status of Mozart's work in the Anglophone world for at least 150 years. It has undertaken cultural work on Mozart's behalf that—certainly in the nineteenth century and well into the twentieth—has been as important as that developed by *Don Giovanni* or *Die Zauberflöte*. The aspects of the work's history outlined here go some way toward explaining its extraordinary success: its publication, its performance, its flexibility both in terms of medium and of performance context, and the wide range of textual reference from the purely imaginative to the more clearly technical. But these explanations cannot by themselves account for the affection in which the work has been held in the hearts of musicians on both sides of the Atlantic. We cannot escape the fact that a work probably by Wenzel Müller was viewed in purely aesthetic terms as (1) of sufficient worth to be accepted as a work by Mozart, despite its clear exclusion from the Mozart canon by every writer in German on the subject, and (2) as of such exceptional worth that it could take on the iconic status outlined in this chapter.

It is difficult to escape the conclusion, then, that the history of the "Twelfth Mass" provides evidence that the reputation of one of the central supports for the contemporary category of "classical music" is more contentious than Mozart's current reputation might allow. Whatever contribution the "Twelfth Mass" made to the musical culture of the nineteenth and twentieth centuries—and the tiny fragment of the evidence presented in this chapter suggests that it was vast—its contribution to the status Mozart holds in our affections today is worthy of serious attention. Careful reading of the score of the "Twelfth Mass" reveals a work that—in 1819—could quite reasonably have been considered a work composed before 1791, and by no means presents a musical persona that dresses up Victorian or romantic mutton as late eighteenth-century Viennese lamb. The work sits plausibly alongside the other two "favorite masses" composed in 1798 and 1807, respectively, and these would not have been unreasonable dates (so a view from 1819 would have had it) for Wenzel Müller to have composed it.

[65] Ibid., vi/1.

The "Twelfth Mass"—still as a work attributed to Mozart, and still enjoying such descriptors as "immortal," "unforgettable," and so on—is today performed from San Antonio to Exeter and from Vancouver to Hong Kong. Its piano-vocal score is still in print, and the performance materials may be hired from Chester-Novello without the slightest hint that it is not by Mozart.[66] And a website dedicated to the digital encoding of "illustrious but unknown compositions" berates visitors to the site for the absence of any complete modern recording of the "Twelfth Mass," still with its apparently cast-iron attribution to Mozart.[67]

It's clear that for many in the musicological world today, the case of the "Twelfth Mass" is definitively closed. For the Salzburg-orientated world of the *Mozart-Jahrbuch*, the "Twelfth Mass" is off the radar, and has been for some time. But for those who might be interested in the musical cultures of the nineteenth and twentieth centuries that are still so influential on our own, the case of "Mozart's" "Twelfth Mass" remains wide open.

[66] www.chesternovello.com/default.aspx?TabId=2432&State_3041=2&WorkId_3041=10783 (accessed 30 June 2012).

[67] At http://peyot.com/page2.html (accessed 20 March 2006; since taken down).

{ 6 }

Enshrining Mozart

DON GIOVANNI AND THE VIARDOT CIRCLE

In a memoir published posthumously, the singer and pedagogue Pauline Viardot described attending a performance of *Don Giovanni*.[1] Her abiding memory was of being scared to death, as she wandered backstage, by bumping into the Commendatore, who had yet to change out of his costume for the act 2 finale. Viardot—or Pauline Garcia, as she was then—was four years old, and the date was 1825.[2] It was a striking first encounter with a work that was to figure prominently throughout her life. Just as striking was the performance itself. The principal roles were taken by two of Europe's most renowned soloists both of whom were also members of

---

[1] The standard texts on the life of Pauline Viardot are April Fitzlyon, *The Price of Genius: A Life of Pauline Viardot* (London: Calder, 1964), and Aleksandr Semoenovitch Rozanov, *Polina Viardo Garsia* (Leningrad: Editio Muzika, 1969). They should be read alongside the much fuller study by Yvette Sieffert Rigaud, "Pauline Viardot: Mythe et Réalité" (Thèse d'État, Université de Rouen, 1991). Despite the large number of studies of Viardot and her family (cited in Rigaud's bibliography), none add a great deal to those of Fitzlyon, Rozanov, and Rigaud.

[2] "In New York, still, *Maman* had allowed me to be taken to a performance of *Don Giovanni*, in which the principal roles were taken by my father, my brother Manuel and my sister Maria. I remember that I enjoyed myself enormously…up to the moment when I wanted to go and kiss my father. I was so well behaved that I was taken backstage. There, again, a fantastic apparition arose in front of me. It was a tall man all in white, a white face with a great white helmet and white shoes. What did he want? He looked at me in a way that was not reassuring at all. At least, that was what I imagined. He also leant towards me, perhaps to kiss me….I started to cry harder than ever and….you know the rest. This man, all in white, I don't need to tell you, was none other than the artist charged with the role of the statue of the *Commendatore*." "A New York, toujours, maman avait permis qu'on me conduisit à une représentation de *Don Juan*, dont les rôles principaux étaient tenus par mon père, mon frère Manuel et ma sœur Maria. Je me rappelle que je me suis énormément amusée…jusqu'au moment où je voulus aller embrasser mon père. Je fis si bien qu'on me mena dans les coulisses. Là, encore [the anecdote follows a similar one set in London in 1824], une apparition fantastique surgit devant moi. C'était un grand homme tout blanc, le visage blanc, avec un grand casque blanc et les souliers blancs. Que me veut-il? Il me regarde d'un air qui n'a rien de rassurant. Du moins, je me l'imagine. Il se penche aussi vers moi, pour m'embrasser peut-être….Je me mets à crier plus fort que jamais et…vous savez le reste. Cet homme, tout de blanc costumé, je n'ai pas besoin de vous le dire, n'était autre que l'artiste chargé de représenter la statue du Commandeur." Pauline Viardot, "Mes Premiers Souvenirs," *Les Annales politiques et littéraires*, 29 May 1910, 524; summarily cited in Rigaud, "Pauline Viardot," 57–58.

Pauline's family: her father, Manuel Garcia, and her sister, Maria Malibran.[3] It was the first time *Don Giovanni* had been heard in the United States, and if he is to be believed, Mozart's librettist Lorenzo Da Ponte took charge of many of the details of the performance.[4] For Viardot, it was the beginning of an engagement with a work almost unique in the history of music. Having met the work's librettist, she performed two of the principal roles in the opera for nearly twenty years. Equally important, she owned the autograph of *Don Giovanni* for half a century, and—together with a group of associates—succeeded in establishing a shrine to the document, the work it embodied, and its composer, and in surrounding it with ritual discourses that can with reason be considered a cult.

Although Pauline Viardot is today most clearly associated with the creation in 1849 of the role of Fidès in Meyerbeer's *Le Prophète* and ten years later of the title role in the revival of Gluck's *Orphée*, she was remembered toward the end of her own lifetime for two roles that were not written especially for her: Valentine in Meyerbeer's *Les Huguenots* and Donna Anna in *Don Giovanni*.[5] Unlike her sister, who had specialized in the role of Zerlina, Pauline alternated the roles of Donna Anna and Zerlina in different productions. There is even a believable report that she also sang Donna Elvira.[6] She was singing both Zerlina and Donna Anna in productions from the early 1840s, and continued in both roles for nearly twenty years. Her legendary wide range made the two roles physically possible, but her idiosyncratic interpretation of the role of Zerlina, which she set down in writing in 1859, enabled her to countenance both.[7] She explained to the conductor and scholar Julius Rietz that Zerlina was "not at all a doll dressed up as shepherdess, a soubrette who pretends to be naïve, a flirt who leads Don Giovanni on while all the time simpering her innocence." Zerlina was by contrast a "boldly naïve...child...of the south" who "involuntarily comes under the influence of D[o]n G[iovanni]'s demonical nature, she is fascinated by him like a bird by a snake." To do this, Don Giovanni had to "acquire some resemblance to the serpent" and to "get into its skin for a few minutes." According to Viardot, Don Giovanni's "demonic power...is admirably reflected in the music. Mozart understood and portrayed it, in spite of

---

[3] The background to the Italian opera seasons in New York is given in Karen Ethel Ahlquist, "Opera, Theatre and Audience in Antebellum New York" (Ph.D. diss., University of Michigan, 1991), published as *Democracy at the Opera: Music, Theater, and Culture in New York City, 1815–60*, Music in American Life (Urbana: University of Illinois Press, 1997); see also Molly Nelson, "The First Italian Opera Season in New York City: 1825–1826" (Ph.D. diss., University of North Carolina at Chapel Hill, 1976), and James Radomski, *Manuel García (1775–1832): Chronicle of the Life of a Bel Canto Tenor at the Dawn of Romanticism* (Oxford: Oxford University Press, 2000), 184–210.

[4] Lorenzo Da Ponte, *Mémoires (1749–1838) suivies de lettres inédites de Lorenzo Da Ponte à Jacques Casanova*, ed. Raoul Vèze, Jadis et Naguère (Paris: Jonquières, 1931), 264.

[5] Camille Saint-Saëns, *École Buissonnière: Notes et souvenirs* (Paris: Lafitte, 1913), 223.

[6] The reference is in an aside by Glinka described in Fitzlyon, *The Price of Genius*, 153. See Mikhail Ivanovich Glinka, *Literaturnoe nasledie*, 2 vols., ed. Valerian Mikhailovich Bogdanov-Berezovskogo (Leningrad and Moscow: Gos. muzykalnoe izd-vo, 1952–53), 1:233.

[7] Pauline Viardot-Garcia to Julius Rietz, 8 May 1859, New York Public Library, JOE 82-1. See Theodore Baker, trans., "Pauline Viardot-Garcia to Julius Rietz (Letters of Friendship)," *Musical Quarterly* 1 (1915), 556–557.

the words, which are certainly the most shocking in the world."[8] Whether taking a *soubrette* role and attempting to turn it into a part more akin to the other two female roles was an attempt to compete with the *prime donne* or simply overinterpreting the role that she was given, the effect was to bring the character of Zerlina more into line with that of Donna Anna.

Viardot's interpretation of Donna Anna was renowned across Europe. Henry Morley praised her highly in London in 1854,[9] and Julius Stockhausen, after hearing her sing one of Donna Anna's arias in 1849, wrote to his father that he "marvelled both with my eyes and with my ears at the expression of the great singer."[10] George Sand—who was a close friend and could criticize without damage—had mixed feelings, however, about Viardot taking the role. She asked in the summer of 1849, "When will it be that I hear you in *Don Giovanni*? For the moment, I would return to Paris to hear you, since certainly it is *Don Giovanni*, always *Don Giovanni* that I take up as the image of perfection. Is the role of Donna Anna in your voice? Yes, but all your voice is not developed for it. It is for you only half a role, it seems to me. But how beautiful that role is, and how beautiful you will be in it."[11] Sand, paradoxically, was able to

---

[8] "You ask me for a physical and moral description of my *Zerlina*, but that is very difficult! Zerline, according to me, is not merely a doll attired as a shepherdess, a maid who acts naïve, a flirt, who appals Don Giovanni while simpering her innocence. She is boldly naïve, very childish, but a child of the south, flesh and bone—she submits involuntarily to the influence of Don Giovanni's demonic nature—she is fascinated by him, like a bird by a snake. I make Don Giovanni play the role differently during their duo differently to normal. If Don Giovanni takes the attitude of an ordinary seducer, this scene becomes disgusting. But if the man can infuse himself with some resemblance to the serpent (the one of the Garden of Good and Evil especially), if he can put himself in its skin for a few minutes, then the demonic power (with which one has always gratified Don Giovanni is no longer an invention of Hoffmann and before him the Spaniards), this power—I repeat—is found admirably in the music. Mozart understood and depicted it, in spite of the words which are the most shocking in the world." "Vous me demandez une description physique et morale de ma *Zerline*, mais c'est très difficile cela! Zerline, d'après moi, n'est nulle-ment une poupée *attifée* en bergère, une soubrette qui fait la naïve, une coquette, qui agace Dⁿ Giovanni tout en minaudant l'innocence. Elle est hardiment naïve, très enfant, mais enfant du midi, en chair et en os—elle subit involontairement l'influence de la naturedémoniaque de Dⁿ G.—elle est fascinée par lui, comme un oiseau par un serpent. Je fais jouer Dⁿ G. pendant leur duo autrement que d'habitude. Si Dⁿ G. prend l'attitude d'un séducteur ordinaire, cette scène devient écœurante. Mais si l'homme peut se donner quelque ressemblance avec le serpent (celui du Paradis terrestre surtout), s'il peut se mettre dans sa peau pendᵗ. quelques minutes, alors la puissance démoniaque (dont on a voulu toujours gratifier Dⁿ G. n'est plus une invention de Hoffmann et avant lui des Espagnols) cette puissance, dis-je, se retrouve admirablement dans la musique. Mozart l'a comprise et rendue, en dépit des paroles qui sont bien les plus choquantes du monde" (ibid.). That Viardot's prose description of the role of Zerlina had much in common with her portrayal on the stage is confirmed by a review of her performance of the role in Manchester in October 1860: "Zerlina is not the most important female role in the work however, she became so, the other night, in the hands of Mme Viardot. The country girl, pretty and with a certain spirit, moderately susceptible to flattery, hates vice with all her heart, and distances herself from its masked face," *Manchester Guardian*, 8 October 1860, cited in Rigaud, "Pauline Viardot," 253.

[9] Henry Morley, *The Journal of a London Playgoer* (London: Routledge, 1866), 90.

[10] "Mit den Augen sowohl wie mit den Ohren den Ausdruck der großen Sängerin bewunderte"; in Julia Wirth, ed., *Julius Stockhausen: Der Sänger des deutschen Liedes nach Dokumenten seiner Zeit* (Frankfurt am Main: Englert und Schlosser, 1927), 106.

[11] "Quand est-ce que je vous entendrai dans *Don Juan*? Ah pour le coup, je retournerais à Paris pour vous entendre, car décidément c'est *Don Juan*, toujours *Don Juan* que je reprends comme le type de

realize that however much Viardot might be able to adjust the character of Zerlina to her own preferences, she could never change the music of the role of Donna Anna. Given that her real strengths lay in an extended mezzo-soprano range (as in the roles of Fidès and Orphée that were written or adapted for her), her musical grip on the role of Donna Anna would never be as strong as her control over the part of Zerlina.

During the years Pauline Viardot was singing the roles of Zerlina and Donna Anna on stages from London to Prague, the autograph of *Don Giovanni* was simultaneously crisscrossing Europe. The manuscript had been sold by Constanze Mozart to Johann Anton André in 1800, at whose death in 1842 it had passed to his daughter, Augustina, who was married to Johann Baptist Streicher; it was then offered for sale to the Imperial Library in Vienna, the Royal Library in Berlin, and the British Museum in London, and all three invitations to purchase were declined.[12] While the manuscript was in London in 1855, Pauline Viardot acquired it for 180 pounds. To many, she was an obvious person into whose hands the autograph of *Don Giovanni* could be entrusted, and this was stressed by an anonymous London correspondent to the *Revue et gazette musicale de Paris*: "The noble [Mme Viardot] has gladly sacrificed something like Ff5000 of her diamonds in order to acquire this manuscript beyond price. Could this treasure have fallen into more worthy hands? Who, more than the great artist, the daughter of Garcia, the Don Giovanni of whom Mozart must have dreamed, merits being the guardian of this precious relic?"[13] This apparently innocuous text is packed with heavily loaded terms that would recur throughout the next half century of the manuscript's history. The author invokes the idea of sacrifice as the price of acquisition, and describes the autograph as treasure; despite giving the purchase price of the document, he then goes on to describe it as "beyond price" (*inappréciable*). The status of the object purchased is therefore of no comparison with the objects exchanged for it (Viardot's diamonds). The final words of this text set up a frame for the future of the autograph of *Don Giovanni*. Viardot is no longer simply the owner of the manuscript; she is its "guardian." The document is no longer merely the autograph

---

perfection. Le rôle de Donna Anna est-il dans votre voix? Oui, mais toute votre voix n'y serait pas développé. Ce n'est pour vous que la moitié d'un rôle, il me semble. Mais qu'il est beau, ce rôle, et comme vous y seriez belle!" (George Sand to Pauline Viardot, 18 June 1849; George Sand, *Correspondance (janvier 1849–décembre 1850)*, ed. Georges Lubin, George Sand Correspondance, 9 (Paris: Garnier, 1972), 196–197.

[12] The best summary of the history of the autograph of *Don Giovanni* before 1855 is François Lesure, "Le Manuscrit de *Don Giovanni*," in *Edition Princeps: W. A. Mozart, Don Giovanni, opéra en deux actes: Fac-similé in extenso du manuscrit autographe conservé à la Bibliothèque Nationale*, ed. François Lesure, René Dumesnil, and Jacques Duron (Paris: La Revue Musicale; Maisonneuve, n.d.), [1]–[2], which depends to a large extent on Julien Tiersot, "Étude sur *Don Juan*," *Le Ménestrel*, 21 March 1897, 89–90, reprinted in his *Don Juan de Mozart: Étude historique et critique, analyse musicale*, Les chefs d'œuvre de la musique expliqués (Paris: Mellottée, [1930]), 135–140. Given that the British Museum approached the monarch for financial support for the purchase of the manuscript (which was not forthcoming), it is likely that the Vienna and Berlin libraries turned down the offer to purchase because the price was too high.

[13] "La noble artiste a sacrifié avec joie quelque chose comme Ff5000.00 de ses diamants pour posséder en échange cet inappréciable manuscrit. Ce trésor aurait-il pu tomber dans les plus dignes mains? Qui, plus que la grande artiste, que la fille de Garcia, le Don Juan tel que Mozart a dû le rêver, méritait d'être gardienne de cette précieuse relique?" *Revue et gazette musicale de Paris*, 5 August 1855, 246.

of *Don Giovanni*; it is now a "precious relic." During the next forty years, it was transformed from cultural artifact into object of veneration, and Pauline Viardot emerged from operatic fame as the priestess of a *Don Giovanni* cult.

Cults frequently center on the veneration of relics, which are both guarded by priests and priestesses and protected by reliquaries. From the very earliest Christian period, relics of the saints had been protected in a variety of objects. The oldest type of reliquary was a simple casket; more ornate types were in the shape of crosses and rings, tables and—perhaps best known from the late Middle Ages and Renaissance—models of buildings. The most elaborate reliquaries were those that mirrored the shape of the relic itself—arm or foot, for example; these were known as "speaking reliquaries."[14] From the thirteenth century onward, reliquaries began to include translucent material that allowed the relic to be viewed without removal; these were called monstrances.[15]

The autograph of *Don Giovanni* was protected by an object commissioned by Pauline Viardot shortly after the purchase of the manuscript. Certainly, it could have been expected that such a document would be protected by luxury binding, or possibly a case, since it consisted of unbound fascicles. The object in which the autograph was in fact preserved is nothing short of a reliquary (fig. 6.1).[16]

FIGURE 6.1: *Mozart, autograph score of* Don Giovanni. *General view of case.* F-Pn *MS 1548. Reproduced with permission, Bibliothèque nationale de France.*

---

[14] Joseph Braun, *Die Reliquiare des christlichen Kultes und ihre Entwicklung* (Freiburg im Breisgau: Herder, 1971), 146–162; see also *The New Catholic Encyclopedia*, 17 vols. (New York: McGraw-Hill, 1967–79), s.v. "Relic" and "Reliquary," 12:234–239 and 335–336.

[15] Jacques Dubois and Jean-Loup Lemaitre, *Sources et méthodes de l'hagiographie médiévale* (Paris: Cerf, 1993), 296.

[16] Mozart, *Don Giovanni*, autograph score, Bibliothèque nationale de France, Paris, MS 1548 (1–8). There is a poorly reproduced image in Jean Mongrédien, "A propos du manuscrit autographe de *Don Giovanni*," *Cahiers Ivan Tourguéniev, Pauline Viardot, Maria Malibran* 2 (1978), 45, and (in color, but now almost unobtainable); Catherine Massip, *Le Chant d'Euterpe* (Paris: Hervas, 1991), 172.

FIGURE 6.2: *Mozart, autograph score of* Don Giovanni. *Detail of top of case.* F-Pn *MS 1548. Reproduced with permission, Bibliothèque nationale de France.*

In this way and within a very few years, a document that had been shunned by three of the most important libraries in Europe was elevated to the position of a relic surrounded by a reliquary that befitted its newly acquired status. The box is made out of thuya wood finished in brass, with an escutcheon in the shape of an *M* and on the lid an inscription (fig. 6.2).

The text gives the name of the work, and around it in a pseudo-gothic script in Latin are the dates of Mozart's birth and death; the text reads "J. C. W. A. Mozart. / Natus: Jan: 27. 1756. / Obiit : Dec : 5. 1791," and its style and language evoke the veneration of medieval sacred artifacts. A student of material culture would have little hesitation in identifying this object as a neo-gothic "casket reliquary," which could be compared with thousands of similar objects produced from the twelfth to the nineteenth centuries. Relics preserved in a reliquary traditionally rested on purple velvet, and similarly the fascicles of the *Don Giovanni* autograph were encased in purple leather as they rested inside the box. Pauline Viardot's reliquary adapted the idea of the monstrance to the very particular circumstances of the relic of which she was the guardian. Embedded in the inside of the lid is a small glass panel (fig. 6.3) that can be dropped down so that the manuscript can be viewed through glass, protected from the touch of the uninitiated, in the same way that a medieval relic could be protected from overenthusiastic devotees.

An immediate context for the *Don Giovanni* reliquary, a similarly personal and intimate means of preserving documents of great value, was the reliquary commissioned in 1871 by Queen Victoria to contain various pieces of memorabilia

FIGURE 6.3: *Mozart, autograph score of* Don Giovanni. *Detail of interior of case.* F-Pn *MS 1548. Reproduced with permission, Bibliothèque nationale de France.*

connected with the Prince Consort, who had died ten years earlier. This object was designed to hold Albert's season ticket to the Great Exhibition of 1851 (with which he had been closely associated) and volumes of his life and speeches; it was built in ebony with silver gilt mouldings.[17] In contrast to the *Don Giovanni* reliquary, the sides of the casket were of glass to allow direct sight of the objects, but the purpose was the same, and both objects' background in the tradition of the medieval monstrance unequivocal.

Relics were surrounded by, or placed in, a shrine or temple, either freestanding or in a side-chapel of a larger ecclesiastical building. Similarly, the autograph of *Don Giovanni* was assigned a place of honor where its location could be identified permanently and venerated by initiates. Pauline Viardot, in a letter to Rietz written at the end of 1858, described the layout of her rooms in her house on the rue de Douai and obligingly drew a plan of the most important parts (fig. 6.4).[18]

Viardot's two rooms are in the center of the diagram. At the top is the picture gallery where her husband, Louis Viardot, displayed his collection of paintings

---

[17] The object is now in the Victoria and Albert Museum, London, catalog no. 319–1872.
[18] Pauline Viardot to Julius Rietz, 30 December 1858, New York Public Library, JOE 82-1. The letter, but without the illustration, is edited and translated in Baker, "Pauline Viardot-Garcia to Julius Rietz (Letters of Friendship)," 366–369. The Viardots lived in the house on the rue de Douai from 1848 until 1863, when they moved to Baden-Baden; they returned to the rue de Douai in 1871 after a short sojourn in London and remained there until Louis' death in 1883; Pauline then moved to the Boulevard St. Germain. At the same time, they maintained a country residence at Courtavenel from 1843 to 1863 and at Bougival from 1875 to 1883.

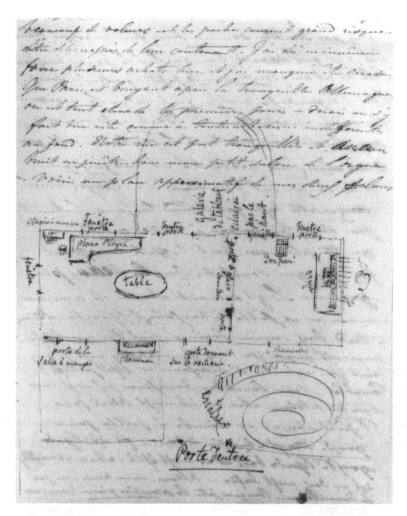

FIGURE 6.4: *Autograph sketch of the ground floor of Pauline Viardot's house, rue de Douai. Pauline Viardot to Julius Rietz, 30 December 1858. New York Public Library, JOE 82-1. Reproduced with permission, New York Public Library.*

and at the bottom the dining room. Pauline's rooms are of different sizes: the room on the left is dominated by the table and the piano, is reached directly from the hall, and gives onto both the gallery and dining room. The much smaller room ("my little organ room") on the right can only be reached from the larger room, and contains Viardot's two greatest treasures: her Cavaillé-Coll organ and the shrine to *Don Giovanni*, indicated with an exclamation mark in her diagram. The surface separating the two rooms consists of two large doors between which is plate glass. With the doors closed, the room has exactly the same characteristics of the reliquary in which the autograph of *Don Giovanni* itself was housed: it could be seen through glass, but only initiates could to approach the shrine, by invitation. Viardot had configured two rooms, one as a public space where she could receive guests, where she could play through works for four hands at one piano, and where scores could be read and discussed, and the other as a much more private space dominated physically by the organ but intellectually by the shrine to *Don Giovanni*.[19]

This shrine has its origins in, but is distinct from, more public memorials to Haydn, Mozart, and Beethoven raised in the first half of the nineteenth century. Such institutional displays of veneration as the monument to Mozart in Salzburg or that to Beethoven in Bonn (1842 and 1845, respectively) were well known; Pauline Viardot must have been aware of these initiatives.[20] Haydn is a curious case in this regard, since he was the subject of several personal monuments, many of which were put up before his death. Count Karl Leonhard von Harrach's monument (built in 1793) admittedly celebrated the fact that Haydn had been born in Rohrau, but was built in the grounds of Harrach's own castle on an artificial island in the River Leita, which ran through the count's grounds.[21] Although the existence of the memorial was broadcast by Johann Friedrich Rochlitz in 1800,[22] its intimate

---

[19] Viardot's "little organ-room" had not always looked like it did in the plan she drew for Rietz in 1859. The space occupied by the organ had originally been a greenhouse on the side of the building, but had been added into its fabric in 1851 to house the new organ; Louis Viardot to Ivan Turgenev, 12 August 1850, F-Pn n.a.f. 16275, fols. 326v–327r, cited in Carolyn Schuster-Fournier, *Les Orgues de salon d'Aristide Cavaillé-Coll*, special issue of *L'Orgue: Cahiers et Mémoires* 57–58 (1997), 27. An engraving dating from 1853, after the installation of the organ but before the acquisition of the autograph of *Don Giovanni*, shows that the separation of the single large room into two perhaps still was to be accomplished, and the audience—at least fifty are visible in this picture—seems to spill over the point at which the division was to take place; Augustin-Joseph du Pays, "Pauline Viardot," *L'Illustration* 10 (525), 19 March 1853, 185; reproduced in Schuster-Fournier, *Les Orgues*, 29. This was exactly the configuration described later by Saint-Saëns: "from the salons dedicated to secular instrumental and vocal music, where could be seen the famous portrait by Ary Scheffer, you went down a couple of steps to a gallery of valuable paintings that ended in an exquisite organ, a masterpiece by Cavaillé-Coll; there was the temple of sacred music" (Des salons, où se voyait le fameux portrait d'Ary Scheffer, consacrés à la musique profane instrumentale et vocale, on descendait par quelques marches à une galerie de précieux tableaux aboutissant à un orgue exquis, chef-d'œuvre de Cavaillé-Coll; la était le temple de la musique sacrée; Saint-Saëns, *École Buissonnière*, 220). The 1853 engraving also permits a glimpse at the place where the shrine to *Don Giovanni* would be located two years later; there is a nondescript neoclassical urn on a plinth in the place where the *Don Giovanni* autograph would be positioned. In 1853, the organ room was a place where recitals could be given in front of such a large audience. After the establishment of the *Don Giovanni* shrine, audiences heard the music from the picture gallery that was reached from the main room. The room that housed the autograph was reserved for Viardot and her performers (Schuster-Fournier, *Les Orgues*, 36–37).

[20] See Rudolph Angermüller, *Das Salzburg Mozart-Denkmal: eine Dokumentation (bis 1845) zur 150–Jahre-Enthüllungsfeier* (Salzburg: Internationale Stiftung Mozarteum, 1992); Ingrid Bosch and Horst Hallensleben, eds., *Monument für Beethoven: zur Geschichte des Beethoven-Denkmals (1845) und der frühen Beethoven-Rezeption in Bonn* [Catalog of an exhibition at the Ernst-Moritz-Arndt-Haus, Bonn, 1995] (Bonn: Stadtmuseum, 1995); Alessandra Comini, *The Changing Image of Beethoven: A Study of Mythmaking* (New York: Rizzoli, 1987).

[21] See Matthew Head, "Music with 'No Past'? Archeologies of Joseph Haydn and *The Creation*," *19th-Century Music* 23 (2000), 191–192.

[22] "Monumente deutscher Tonkünstler," *Allgemeine musikalische Zeitung*, 12 March 1800, 420, cited in ibid., 192, note 8.

location is far removed from, for example, Julius Hähnel's monument to Beethoven on the Münsterplatz in Bonn, and von Harrach's more private shrine to Haydn thus has much more in common with Viardot's shrine to *Don Giovanni*. All these monuments are to composers rather than to works, and it is not until the preparation of the silk-bound manuscript of *Parsifal* that Wagner gave to Cosima that a treatment analogous to that of the autograph to *Don Giovanni* is found.[23] However, the most striking parallel to the *Don Giovanni* shrine (a document of essentially German art in a Parisian setting) was the library built by Princess Scay-Monbéliard to house a further manuscript of *Parsifal* between 1889 and 1892; like Pauline Viardot, she commissioned an artifact to protect her relic, in this case a ceramic door to the library decorated with images from *Parsifal* by the Parisian ceramist Jean Carriès. The fact that Scay-Monbéliard began planning this shrine to Wagner in the same year that Pauline Viardot announced her intention to bequeath the autograph of *Don Giovanni* to the French state is not unremarkable, and Scay-Monbéliard might well have been influenced in her actions by those of Viardot.[24]

According to the most influential medieval authorities, a relic was deemed by the faithful to provide a vision of the saint: viewing the remains of the arm of St. Thomas was tantamount to an encounter with St. Thomas himself.[25] Rituals therefore became associated with viewing a relic. The rare exposure of the autograph of *Don Giovanni* was an important part of its veneration, and the assimilation of the autograph to the work itself, and then to its composer, followed logically. The ritual associated with the shrine differed for various groups of initiates, and followed perhaps predictable paths. Various members of the Viardot entourage were invited to inspect the shrine and its enclosed relic, and reports of encounters with the cult were to become an important part of its dissemination.

---

[23] Egon Voss and Martin Geck, *Richard Wagner: Parsifal*, 3 vols., Sämtliche Werke 14 (Mainz: Schott, 1972–73), 3:157; John Deathridge, Martin Geck, and Egon Voss, *Wagner Werk-Verzeichnis (WWV): Verzeichnis der musikalischen Werke Richard Wagners und ihrer Quellen* (Mainz: Schott, 1986), 545. The binding illustrates a Madonna and Child in a manner that evokes a range of sacred iconologies from trecento sacred art to the painted icons of the Orthodox Church. A color facsimile of the binding is given on page 104 of Oswald Panagl, "Direct and Indirect Routes to the Sketch of a Music Drama: *The Victors* and *Parsifal*," in *Bayreuther Festspiele 1994* ([Bayreuth]: n.p., 1994), 97–104.

[24] See Matthias Waschek, "Zum Wagnérisme in den bildenden Künsten," in *Von Wagner zum Wagnérisme: Musik, Literatur, Kunst, Politik*, ed. Annegret Fauser and Manuela Schwartz, Deutsch-Französische Kulturbibliothek 12 (Leipzig: Universitätsverlag, 1999), 542. The standard life and works of Carriès is Arsène-Pierre-Urbain Alexandre, *Jean Carriès, imagier et potier: Etude d'une œuvre et d'une vie* (Paris: Librairies-imprimeries réunies, 1895); for a reproduction of the model of the door, see *Marianne et Germania (1789–1889), un siècle de passions franco-allemandes, Musée du Petit Palais, 8 novembre 1997–15 février 1998* (exhibition catalog) (Paris: Paris Musées, [1997]), 283. The claim that Carriès had gone as far as having "a huge ceramic tabernacle built in an extravagant Ludwig II style to house a Wagner manuscript, recently acquired by Winaretta [the Princesse Scay-Monbéliard was born Winaretta Singer, and subsequently became the Princesse Edmond de Polignac] and revered as though it were a sacred relic," Michael de Cossart, *The Food of Love: Princesse Edmond de Polignac (1865–1943) and Her Salon* (London: Hamish Hamilton, 1978), 26, is not based on any surviving evidence.

[25] *The New Catholic Encyclopedia*, s.v. "Relic," 12:234.

The core of the Viardot circle consisted for nearly forty years of Pauline, her husband, and Ivan Turgenev.[26] Although Turgenev was not a permanent part of the household, he spent substantial amounts of time lodging with the couple, and was in more or less constant correspondence with both when they were apart. Commentary on this ménage à trois has followed the rather predictable paths of salacious bourgeois comedy, and has focused on the potentially adulterous relationship between Pauline and Turgenev.[27] Ménages à trois were not, however, at all uncommon among nineteenth-century working-class families, and were not always adulterous, although by the time they reached the attention of adherents to middle-class family values, such arrangements had acquired an adulterous and often criminal reputation. The advantages to a single working man, as to the host couple, were mainly financial, and such arrangements could and did work extremely efficiently.[28]

The Viardot family were far from working-class. Nor were they obvious members of the bourgeoisie. In Baden-Baden, they entertained the King of Prussia and other heads of state, and it was probably this status that allowed the three to weather any criticism leveled at them; it mostly took the form of censuring Pauline's treatment of Turgenev.[29] There is no doubt about Turgenev's passion for Pauline, but the voyeuristic quality of a good deal of the writing about the Viardot circle has obscured the intellectual dynamics among the three. Louis Viardot comes off particularly badly at the hands of his wife's biographer, April Fitzlyon, where he is portrayed as an amiable, simple-minded cuckold.[30] The Turgenev scholar Patrick Waddington rightly describes this as "a quite fantastic distortion of the truth," but even Waddington's defense of Louis scarcely does justice to his achievements, or to the intellectual contribution he made at the core of the Viardot circle.[31] As a journalist with strongly republican sympathies, he collaborated on *Le Globe* alongside George Sand, on *Le National,* and on *La Revue Républicaine,* and

---

[26] Still the best biographical outline of Louis Viardot is in Pierre Larousse, *Grand dictionnaire universel du xix* siècle*, 15 vols. with multiple supps. (Paris: Administration du Grand DictionnaireUniversel, 1866–76), 15:978. For a still useful introduction to the Viardot circle, see Thérèse Marix-Spire, "Gounod and His First Interpreter," *Musical Quarterly* 31 (1945), 193–211 and 299–317.

[27] Such commentaries range from Fitzlyon, *The Price of Genius*, where the focus on the relationship between the three is embedded throughout, to the fictionalized romance in Olga Rachmanova, *L'Amour d'une vie: Ivan Tourgueniev–Pauline Viardot Garcia*, trans. Pierette Viardot (Paris: author, [1996]), which was completed in 1952.

[28] See Joëlle Guillais, *La Chair de l'autre* (Paris: Olivier Orban, 1986), trans. Jane Dunnett as *Crimes of Passion: Dramas of Private Life in Nineteenth-Century France* (Cambridge: Polity, 1990), 149–150 (p. nos. refer to English trans.).

[29] Patrick Waddington, "Turgenev and Pauline Viardot: An Unofficial Marriage," *Canadian Slavonic Papers* 26 (1984), 55.

[30] The nadir of Fitzlyon's commentary on Louis Viardot is reached when she states: "For a woman the presence of the man whom she does not love is often more intolerable than the absence of the man she loves. Louis Viardot's very unhappiness was a reproach to her, and his love must have been unbearable" (*The Price of Genius*, 199).

[31] Waddington, "Turgenev and Pauline Viardot," 50.

was one of the founders of the *Revue Indépendente*. He was a prolific writer on artistic matters, and was the owner of a significant art collection which included Rembrandt's painting *The Butcher's Stall*, now in the Louvre. But as the discussion of Pushkin's play *The Stone Guest* will make clear, his greatest contribution to letters was as a translator, latterly—and often in collaboration with Turgenev—from Russian, but particularly from Spanish.

It will never be known whether Turgenev's passion for Pauline Viardot was ever physically reciprocated (nor can the paternity of her four children be definitively settled); if it was, this would not necessarily have been cause for the breaking of the other bonds that tied the ménage à trois together. The marital ties that connected Pauline and Louis were probably more cerebral than physical, and Pauline was more than willing to accept the great intellectual debt she owed her husband.[32] Turgenev benefited from Pauline's views on his poetry, and it seems that in later years he wrote little that did not receive her imprimatur. He sympathized with Louis' republican views, as well as with his love of hunting; their literary collaborations are evident from published work. It is far from clear what intellectual benefit Pauline received from Turgenev, who seemed anxious to defer to her on most things. He certainly encouraged her to read Goethe while preparing Gluck's *Iphigénie en Tauride* and Shakespeare before Verdi's *Macbeth*, and he was clearly a stimulating reading partner, but this seems relatively little in comparison with the intellectual benefits Turgenev apparently claimed in return.[33]

In the convoluted correspondence between Pauline and Turgenev, which reflected the even more confused relationship between the two, music in general and Mozart in particular played a crucial part. In a written form, it could take on the role of a language encoded between the two protagonists that enabled Turgenev in particular to exclude others—especially Louis. In February 1853, Turgenev wrote to Pauline: "I beg you to get hold of a copy of the *Fantasia in c minor* by Mozart...and to tell me what you think of it. The third movement, which I am talking about, has the effect on me of expressing precisely the current state of my soul; I cannot listen to it without finding myself upset, emotional, troubled. In a word, it is adorable and poignant; genius flows there in great quantities."[34] Turge-

---

[32] Ibid., 51.

[33] Ibid., 56, and 62–64.

[34] "Je vous conjure de vous procurer la fantaisie de Mozart (voici son titre: Grande fantaisie en ut mineur arrangée pour l'orchestre par [Ignaz Xaver von] Seyfried [1776–1841], sans titre d'œuvre) et de me dire ce que vous en pensez. Le troisième mouvement dont je vous parle (il n'y a que trois) me fait l'effet d'exprimer précisément l'état actuel de mon âme—je n'ai pu l'entendre sans me sentir tout bouleversé, ému, troublé, en un mot, c'est adorable et c'est poignant—le génie y coule à pleins bords." Turgenev, in Spasskoïé, 16–18 February 1853, to Viardot, in Ivan Turgenev, *Lettres inédites à Pauline Viardot et à sa famille*, ed. Henri Granjard and Alexandre Zviguilsky, Collection slavica (Lausanne: L'Âge de l'Homme, 1972), 65. The work is an orchestration of Mozart's *Fantasie* K. 457 and Sonata K. 475. [Ignaz Xaver von] Seyfried, *Grande fantaisie en ut mineur arrangée pour l'orchestre*, autograph manuscript, A-Wn, Mus. Hs. 3291/1, published Leipzig: Breitkopf und Härtel, 1812, pl. 1689. See Ludwig Ritter

nev was not prepared in this or any other letter to detail the state of his soul but was content to allow the meaning, and the effect it might have on his correspondent, to remain as elusive as such musical reference might be.

The core of the Viardot circle was surrounded by a group of individuals whose lives crossed regularly and frequently with those of the Viardot household: George Sand, Rossini, Berlioz, and Ary Scheffer. Although physically close to Pauline only during the years they lived in Baden-Baden together, Clara Schumann was a life-long friend; the two corresponded frequently and met regularly all over Europe. Chopin was a member of the circle, and Gounod replaced him after 1849. Others who conducted correspondence with the Viardots but met them less frequently included Dickens, the reclusive Flaubert, Musset, and Julius Rietz. Meyerbeer's relationship with the Viardots is still far from clear beyond the obvious work on *Le Prophète*. As time went on, the Viardots' sphere of influence broadened to encompass a network of acquaintances right across Europe. On their return to Paris from Baden-Baden, these included Saint-Saëns, Tchaikovsky, Fauré, Massenet, and Ambroise Thomas.

The most striking responses to the enshrining of *Don Giovanni* came from composers, particularly those with a documented predilection for Mozart, and performers. Gabriel Fauré was allowed to see the autograph of *Don Giovanni* in the early summer of 1877 at the Viardots' house in Paris. He wrote: "On Thursday evening, we looked, with all the admiration that it inspires, at the manuscript score of *Don Giovanni*."[35] This brief mention, in a letter to Camille Clerc, invokes admiration and inspiration, terms that themselves invoke none of the tropes of the sacred that the shrine to *Don Giovanni* was inviting him to adopt. Although Fauré's less than obvious devotion to the relic and its cult might be explained by his imminent engagement to Viardot's daughter, Marianne, the scope of his account reduces further interpretation to speculation.

Descriptions are preserved of two further composers, both with a great enthusiasm for Mozart, worshipping at the *Don Giovanni* shrine. Both are equivocal and demonstrate, in the case of Tchaikovsky, a friction between public and private veneration of the relic, and in the case of Rossini, the use to which a possibly equivocal encounter could be put by members of the Viardot family. When Tchaikovsky was in Paris in 1886, he was admitted into the circle of those who participated in the ritual of unveiling the autograph of *Don Giovanni*. He described his first visit to Pauline Viardot on 31 May 1886 in a letter to Nadezhda von Meck: "Have I told you my dear friend that I spent two hours chez Viardot in leafing

von Köchel, *Chronologisch-thematisches Verzeichnis sämtlicher Tonwerke Wolfgang Amadé Mozarts*, 8th ed., ed. Franz Giegling, Alexander Weinmann, and Gerd Sievers (Wiesbaden: Breitkopf und Härtel, 1983), 788–789.
[35] "Jeudi soir [31 May 1877] nous avons regardé, avec toute l'admiration qu'elle inspire, la partition manuscrite de *Don Juan!*" Gabriel Fauré, *Correspondance*, ed. Jean-Michel Nectoux, Harmoniques (Paris: Flammarion, 1980), 51.

through an *authentic score* of Mozart (*Don Giovanni*), which about thirty years ago Viardot's husband had *acquired* by accident and very cheaply. I cannot express the feeling that overcame me when I was looking at this *holy* musical *object*! [It was] as if I had shaken the hand of Mozart himself and conversed with him."[36] In this description, the word *Svyatïnya* has the sense, certainly, of a holy or sacred object—a relic—but it also has the broader sense of a holy place, temple, or shrine. Tchaikovsky's use of the word resonates broadly with the physical discourses with which Pauline Viardot adorned the autograph of *Don Giovanni*, locates his experience clearly within the domain of ritual, and provides a verbal account that elides the document both with the work itself and with its composer. In line with the traditional veneration of relics, Pauline Viardot's shrine to the autograph of *Don Giovanni* had already become a shrine to the work, and in Tchaikovsky's letter, a shrine to the composer.[37] Tchaikovsky gave a more neutral account of the encounter in his diary for 31 May 1886: "We went to Viardot. Thunderstorm. We were soaked to the bone. What a first acquaintance! However, we were not allowed to go home. This occurrence made acquaintance easier. Lunch. The old Mme Viardot enchanted me. Her sycophant. In the drawing room. Her pupil, a Russian lady, sang an aria from *Lakmé*. SAW THE ORCHESTRA SCORE OF MOZART'S *DON JUAN* WRITTEN IN HIS OWN HAND! Went home."[38] The difference in lexical choice between the letter to von Meck and his diary entry could merely be explained by differences in genre—the one a communication, the other a record—but the contrast between the two might also be the result of Tchaikovsky's using the cultic experience at the Viardots' to attempt to convince a sceptical von Meck of Mozart's value while he himself was more suspicious of the cult than his letter suggests. Alternatively, the diary entry might have represented an immediate aide-mémoire (devoid of any imaginative use of language) whereas the letter, written at leisure and with hindsight, could have arisen out of a greater degree of reflection on the composer's encounter with the autograph of the work that had been central to his musical existence.

---

[36] "Pisal li ya Vam, milïy drug, chto ya provyol dva chasa u Viardo v perelistïvanii *podlinnoy partiturï* Motsarta ('*Don-Zhuan*'), kotoruyu yeshcho let tridtsat' tomu nazad muzh *Viardo* sluchayno i ochen' dyoshevo *priobryol*? Ne mogu vïrazit'chuvstva, kotoroye okhvatilo menya pri prosmotre etoy muzïkal'noy *svyatïni*! Tochno budto ya pozhal ruku samogo Motsarta i besedoval s nim." Pyotr Il'yich Tchaikovsky, *Perepiska s N.F. fon-Mekk*, 3 vols., ed. V. A. Zhdanov and I. T. Zhegin (Moscow and Leningrad: Academia, 1934–36), 3:426. In strictly legal terms, Tchaikovsky was correct in his identification of the ownership of the document. During the Third Republic, "the husband was the head of the family, had sole paternal authority, and managed the property of…his wife without, however, being able to appropriate or mortgage it without her approval." Anne-Marie Sohn, "The Golden Age of Male Adultery: The Third Republic," *Journal of Social History* 28 (1995), 469.

[37] Tchaikovsky must have participated in this ritual in Viardot's apartment on the Boulevard Saint-Germain, where she had moved after the death of her husband and Turgenev both in 1883.

[38] *The Diaries of Tchaikovsky*, trans. Wladimir Lakond (New York: Norton, 1945; reprint, Westport, Conn.: Greenwood, 1973), 82.

Tchaikovsky's enthusiasm for Mozart, and especially for *Don Giovanni*, is evident from his own writings, from those of his contemporaries, and from his own output.[39] His participation in the *Don Giovanni* cult is one of the contexts for his work on the Suite No. 4 "Mozartiana," op. 61, which was orchestrated and performed in 1887, the centenary of *Don Giovanni*'s Prague premiere. It seems likely that Tchaikovsky considered the work his personal celebration of this event. He had the idea for the suite in May 1884,[40] but by February 1886 was still trying to decide what music to include.[41] Between these two dates, he wrote to Sergei Ivanovich Taneyev to remind him that "we shall have to celebrate the centenary of *Don Giovanni* on 27 October 1887," suggesting that he associated the suite with this commitment to celebrate the work's centenary.[42]

If Pauline Viardot was the priestess of the temple to *Don Giovanni*, and Tchaikovsky one of probably many initiates, Rossini appeared to be the prophet who identified divinity in the relic that was so carefully protected; in the same way as Tchaikovsky's, his position was similarly equivocal. Louis Viardot wrote an important article on the autograph of *Don Giovanni* in which he described Rossini's encounter with the cult in late 1855:

> The illustrious emulator of Mozart had come to visit the daughter of the dearest of his old friends, of the artist for whom he wrote the most important roles in his repertoire. He listened to her, at the piano and organ, with a paternal generosity, with that tender emotion that illness appeared to have added, like a new quality of the heart, to all the qualities of the spirit. Then he asked to see the manuscript of his favourite opera. "I am going," he said "to genuflect in front of this holy relic." Then, having leafed through a few pages in a religious contemplation: "My friend," he said to me, stretching out his hand on Mozart's writing, "he is the greatest, he is the master of all, only he had as much science as genius and as much genius as science." I have gathered these words of Rossini piously.[43]

---

[39] Tchaikovsky's attempts to convince Nadehza von Meck of Mozart's value are described in Alexandra Orlova, *Tchaikovsky: A Self-Portrait* (Oxford: Oxford University Press, 1990), 117–118. In an interview conducted as late as 12 November 1892, he related how he had heard *Don Giovanni* at age sixteen, and how this early experience had colored his later views of the work and its composer. Alexander Poznansky, *Tchaikovsky through Others' Eyes* (Bloomington and Indianapolis: Indiana University Press, 1999), 203.

[40] *Diaries*, 36 (17 May 1884).

[41] Ibid., 48 (8 February 1886).

[42] "27 oktyabrya 1887 g. nuzhno prazdnovat' stoletiye 'Don Zhuana.'" P. I. Tchaikovsky, S. I. Taneyev, *Pis'ma*, ed. V. A. Zhdanov (Moscow: Gosudarstvennïy Literaturnïy Muzey, 1951), 137. Before beginning the arrangement, Tchaikovsky recorded in his diary that he had read everything in Jahns's biography of Mozart that related to *Don Giovanni*. *Diaries*, 120 (19 September 1886); and the sequence of work on the suite is clear from 183–196.

[43] "L'illustre émule de Mozart était venu visiter la fille du plus cher de ses anciens amis, l'artiste éminent pour lequel il écrivit les plus grands rôles de son répertoire. Il l'avait entendue, au piano et à l'orgue, avec une bonté toute paternelle, avec cette émotion attendrie que la maladie semble avoir ajoutée, comme une nouvelle qualité de cœur, à toutes les qualités de l'esprit. Alors il demanda à voir le

Rossini's actions, according to Viardot, developed many characteristics of ritual. He was accompanied by members of the family only. He genuflected in front of the relic, and touched it "in religious contemplation," an action that both hints at the ceremonial laying on of hands and, in Viardot's implicit permission for Rossini to bypass the careful construction of the reliquary that was designed to protect the document from handling, points to Rossini's particular status in this ritual. This may be read as an intensification of Tchaikovsky's less extravagant respect for the object of their veneration and his more human handshaking with Mozart, but when Rossini claimed "He is the greatest, he is the master of all," he was moving the ritual from simple veneration of a relic in the direction of divine revelation. The move from veneration to divinity was one of the most important pieces of cultural work undertaken on the autograph's behalf in the second half of the nineteenth century. Louis Viardot's tiny codicil "I have gathered these words of Rossini piously" read very much like the colophon to a medieval *acta sanctorum*, where the scribe, in an attempt to lend authority to his text, claimed to have witnessed a miracle with his own eyes. But Viardot's closing words may perhaps betray an excess of enthusiasm for Rossini's participation in the cult, an eagerness that could conceal an irony in Rossini's original words. It is not hard to envisage an alternative reading of this encounter in which Rossini's "I am going to genuflect in front of this holy relic" could be underpinned by a satirical veneration of the relic that might in turn validate Rossini's own participation in the ritual. His turn to entirely nonritual language at the end of the quotation ("only he had as much science as genius and as much genius as science") would support such a view.

This event was also related by Louise Viardot, Pauline and Louis' other daughter, and published in 1922.[44] This is unlikely to have been an independent account, since it was written over half a century after the fact by someone who had been fourteen years old at the time; it is more likely an embellishment of her father's text. Mythologies develop, however, and in this account, Rossini does not lay his hands on the document but kisses it, and his words concerning genius and science are translated into a single utterance: "It is God himself."[45] Whichever version of

---

manuscrit de son opéra de prédilection: 'Je vais, dit-il, m'agenouiller devant cette sainte relique.' Puis, après avoir parcouru quelques feuillets dans un recueillement religieux: 'Mon ami, me dit-il, en étendant sa main sur l'écrit de Mozart, c'est le plus grand, c'est le maître de tous, c'est le seul qui ait eu autant de science que de génie, et autant de génie que de science.' J'ai recueilli pieusement cette parole de Rossini." Louis Viardot, "Manuscrit autographe du *Don Giovanni* de Mozart," *L'Illustration* 27 (1856), 10–11 (reprinted in smaller format, Paris: *L'Illustration*, 1856); also in *Revue et gazette musicale de Paris* 23 (1856), 12–13 and 27–29; partially reedited in *Espagne et Beaux Arts: Mélanges* (Paris: Hachette, 1866) 426–438, and in *Cahiers Ivan Tourguéniev, Pauline Viardot, Maria Malibran* 2 (1978) 49–63, 11 (p. nos. refer to original 1856 publication in *L'Illustration*).

[44] Louise Héritte de la Tour, *Une grande famille de musiciens: Notes et souvenirs anecdotiques sur Garcia, Pauline Viardot, La Malibran, Louise Héritte Viardot et leur entourage* (Paris: Stock, 1922), 103.

[45] "As soon as he had turned the first page of the score, he genuflected, kissed the leaf fervently and cried 'It is God himself!'. And, indeed, in this exclamation, there was no affectation: it was simply a cry torn from his admiration." "Dès qu'il eut tourné la première page de la partition, il s'agenouilla, baisa

this story we choose to believe, and however we chose to interpret Rossini's partic-ipation in this ritual, both—by the fact that this particularly private action was so fully documented twice by two members of the same family—contribute to the hagiography engendered by the relic, the cult surrounding it, and its accompa-nying discourses. The fact that the two authors were the husband and daughter of the cult's priestess simply develops the hermetic nature of the devotion within a closed world open only to initiates.

Rossini's behavior before the autograph of *Don Giovanni* would have been entirely consistent with two other anecdotes that connect Rossini with Mozart and his opera. The first involves a gathering at which Rossini was asked to identify the best loved of his operas. Some prompted him with *Il barbiere di Siviglia* or *Otello*, others with *La gazza ladra, Semiramide,* or *Guillaume Tell.* Rossini thought briefly and said "You wish to know…which of my works I love the best; very well, it is *Don Giovanni.*"[46] The second, not directly related to *Don Giovanni* itself, starts from a similar point of departure at which Rossini was asked about whether he had known Beethoven when he was in Vienna. "No, replied Rossini; he was a very bad character, he refused to receive me, he detested my music. Which does not, he added with a smile, prevent him from being the greatest composer in the world." Rossini's interlocutor then quizzed him about Mozart, to which Rossini apparently replied: "Oh, him, he is the only one."[47]

All three composers' responses to the Viardot's *Don Giovanni* cult represent some sort of negotiation or compromise. It was left to a German art historian to describe the cult of *Don Giovanni* in the Viardot circle in the most explicit terms. Ludwig Pietsch published a report in the *Vossische Zeitung* in 1864 on the paintings in the newly assembled Villa Viar-

---

avec ferveur le feuillet et s'écria: 'C'est Dieu lui-même!' Et, certes, dans cette exclamation, il n'y avait pas d'affectation: c'était simplement un cri arraché à son admiration" (ibid., 103–104).

[46] "Vous voulez connaître…celui de mes ouvrages que j'aime le mieux; eh bien, c'est *Don Giovanni*" (Viardot, "Manuscrit Autographe," 11).

[47] "Non, répliqua Rossini, c'était un fort mauvais caractère, il ne voulut pas me recevoir; il détestait ma musique. Ce qui n'empêche pas, ajouta-t-il avec un sourire, que ce gaillard-là est le premier com-positeur du monde. Peste, comme vous y allez, fit M. Lavoix, le premier compositeur du monde! Et Mozart qu'en faites-vous, cher maître? Oh, riposta Rossini, celui-là, C'EST LE SEUL!" Victor Wilder, *Mozart, l'homme et l' artiste: Histoire de sa vie d'après les documents authentiques et les travaux les plus récents* (Paris: Le Ménestrel, 1880), 259. The story, according to Wilder, was related to Michel-Henri Lavoix, the father of the music critic Henri Lavoix (see *Grand dictionnaire universel du xixe siècle,* 10:274, s.v. "Lavoix, Michel-Henri"), and shares much of its vocabulary with an account of Franz Liszt's contest with Sigismund Thalberg in the spring of 1837. Most biographies of Liszt repeat the supposed words of the Princess Cristina Belgiojoso-Trivulzio, "Thalberg is the first pianist in the world—Liszt is the only one." Alan Walker, *Franz Liszt: The Virtuoso Years, 1811–1847* (New York: Knopf, 1983), 240. However, Belgiojoso's most recent biographer suggests that this might be a misquotation: "What Cris-tina said was 'There is only one Thalberg in Paris, but there is only one Liszt in the world.' The oft-re-peated version has her saying: 'Thalberg is the best pianist in the world and Liszt the only one.'" Beth Archer Brombert, *Cristina: Portraits of a Princess* (New York: Knopf, 1977; reprint, Chicago: University of Chicago Press, 1983), 340. The source Walker cites for Brombert's "oft-repeated version" is substan-tially later than the one that records Rossini's use of the formulation to compare Mozart and Beethoven: Ida Marie Lipsius [La Mara], *Liszt und die Frauen,* Breitkopf und Härtels Musikbücher (Leipzig: Breit-kopf und Härtel, 1911), 240.

dot in Baden-Baden. He noted the presence of works from the Spanish and Netherlands school, and commented on the exquisite taste of the owners, their profound knowledge of the history of art, and their critical sense. He went on to observe that conversations were held in all European languages, including Russian, and that there was a common appreciation for each national school of art and for their masters. He continued: "however the flame on the high altar to the highest God burns with the German spirit. Like a reliquary [*heilige Lade*], the manuscript of the score of Mozart's *Don Giovanni* is preserved in a precious shrine."[48] In two lines, Pietsch makes explicit the status of the autograph as relic through the use of the same vocabulary as Viardot, Rossini, and Tchaikovsky, and goes further by associating them with the flame on the high altar.[49] In the same way as that of the other worshippers, Pietsch's view represented a particular negotiation, between French- and German-speaking culture, that will be further discussed below.

Pauline Viardot herself contributed to this verbal discourse, if not on the autograph of *Don Giovanni*, then certainly on the work itself and the status it held for her and

---

[48] "Aber dem deutschen Genius flammt hier doch der Hauptaltar als dem obersten Gott. Wie eine heilige Lade steht dort der kostbare Schrein, der Mozarts Handschrift der Don Juan-Partitur umschließt." Max Kalbeck, *Johannes Brahms*, 4 vols. (Berlin: Deutsche Brahms-Gesellschaft, 1921; reprint, Tützing: Schneider, 1976), 2:88.

[49] Clara Schumann, who owned property close to Viardot in Baden-Baden, must have been admitted to the circle of initiates, although there is no record of this. See Beatrix Borchard, "'Ma chère petite Clara—Pauline de mon cœur': Clara Schumann et Pauline Viardot, une amitié d'artistes franco-allemande," *Cahiers Ivan Tourguéniev, Pauline Viardot, Maria Malibran* 20 (1996), 127–143, and "Zwei Musikerinnen—zwei Kulturen: Unveröffentlichte Briefe von Clara Schumann und Pauline Viardot-Garcia," in *Pauline Viardot in Baden-Baden und Karlsruhe*, ed. Ute Lange-Brachmann and Joachim Draheim, Baden-Badener Beiträge zur Musikgeschichte 4 (Baden-Baden: Nomos, 1999), 71–80. So, too, must Brahms, who was a visitor and admirer of Viardot. She premiered the *Alto Rhapsody* op. 53 and fitted words to two of his Hungarian Dances, and he apparently wrote a *Morgenständchen* for her forty-fourth birthday; he left no record, however, of ever having seen the autograph of *Don Giovanni* (Kalbeck, *Johannes Brahms*, 2:169). It is, however, difficult to imagine that he would have spent time at the Villa Viardot without being invited to view the relic; his interest in the opera is evident from the fact that he had been the recipient of a gift from Ferdinand David in 1856 of an early score of the work. *Clara Schumann–Johannes Brahms: Briefe aus dem Jahren 1853–1896*, ed. Berthold Litzmann, 2 vols. (Leipzig: Breitkopf und Härtel, 1927; reprint, Hildesheim: Olms, 1970), 1:168; see, for a general account of Brahms's engagement with Mozart, Imogen Fellerer, "Brahms's View of Mozart," in *Brahms: Biographical, Documentary and Analytical Studies*, ed. Robert Pascall (Cambridge: Cambridge University Press, 1983), 41–57. Likewise, it is impossible to accept that Gounod or Berlioz were refused glimpses of the autograph, and perhaps the strangest thing is that, among Berlioz's extensive writings, there is no record of his encounter with the document. This may be the result of intemperate outbursts on the composer's part in the early days of 1856. Eugène Delacroix described the event well: "17 January [1856]—Mme Viardot, Bertin, Moreau. At Mme Viardot's residence, she again sang the aria from *Armide*, 'Sauvez moi de l'amour'. Berlioz impossible, complaining endlessly about what he considered barbarity and the most detestable taste, trills and other ornaments in Italian music. He did not even recognise their worth in such ancient composers as Handel; he condemned the *fioriture* in Dona Anna's great aria." "17 janvier [1856]—Mme Viardot, Bertin, Moreau.—Chez Mme Viardot: elle a chanté de nouveau l'air d'*Armide…Sauvez-moi de l'amour!* Berlioz insupportable; se récriant sans cesse sur ce qui lui semble la barbarie et le goût les plus détestables, les trilles et autres ornements particuliers dans la musique italienne. Il ne leur fait même pas grâce dans les anciens auteurs, comme Hændel; il se déchaine contre les fioritures du grand air de D. Anna." André Joubin, ed., *Journal de Delacroix*, 3 vols. (Paris: Plon, 1932), 2:423. The date 17 January 1857, given in Hugh MacDonald and François Lesure, eds., *Hector Berlioz: Correspondence Générale V: 1855–1859*, Nouvelle Bibliothèque Romantique (Paris: Flammarion, 1989), 418–419, note 2, is wrong.

members of her circle. In Stuttgart in 1869, she pronounced on the opera in terms that found their mark with Stockhausen, who quoted her comments in a letter to Brahms as follows: "But *Don Giovanni*, my friend, one can no longer listen to it these days, we know it by heart! Without a perfect performance, one can no longer listen to *Don Giovanni*."[50] Her claims that the opera had, by the late 1860s, transcended performance— or at least unattainable perfection in performance—complement the sacralizing vocabularies of Rossini and Tchaikovsky, and the physical discourses with which she surrounded the autograph of the work. In her words to Stockhausen, she enhances the veneration of *Don Giovanni* by attempting to remove the opera from the stage, and to place the work outside the grasp of those yet to be initiated into its secrets.

At midcentury, such attempts at inscribing *Don Giovanni* within the discourse of art-religion coexisted happily with an emerging scholarship that was underwritten by very different aesthetic paradigms. Scholars and editors who viewed the manuscript, especially during the 1860s, by which time it had been transferred to the Villa Viardot in Baden-Baden, left little trace of their reactions, and were perhaps more impervious than others to what they might have thought of as threats to their essentially positivist endeavors. John Ella, who visited in 1866 on a secret mission to attempt purchase of the manuscript, simply noted Viardot's generosity in allowing him to look at the document,[51] and Franz Gugler, the editor of the 1868 Leuckhart score of the work, prefaced his edition with prosaic thanks to the owner of the manuscript, who provided him with a room at the Villa Viardot during his visits there.[52] Köchel also visited during the 1860s without leaving any written record of his impressions.[53]

Louis Viardot's account of Rossini's veneration of the autograph of *Don Giovanni* was but a small part of his contribution to the cult of the work and its composer. As the director of the Théâtre Royal Italien from November 1838 to February 1840, he had been the eventual beneficiary of the fire at the Salle Favart that had begun after—but not as a result of—a performance of *Don Giovanni*; the conflagration had killed his predecessor.[54]

---

[50] "Mais *Don Juan*, mon ami, on ne peut plus l'entendre aujourd'hui, nous le savons par coeur! à moins d'une exécution parfaite on ne peut plus entendre *Don Juan!*" Wirth, *Julius Stockhausen: Der Sänger des deutschen Liedes*, 326.

[51] *Musical Sketches, Abroad and at Home with Original Music by Mozart, Czerny, Graun etc....* (London: Ridgway, 1869), 169.

[52] Bernhard Gugler, ed., *Mozart's Don Giovanni: Partitur erstmals nach dem Autograph herausgegeben unter Beifügung einer neuen Textverdeutschung* (Breslau: Leuckart, [1868]), v. The edition was dedicated to Pauline Viardot. When Octave Fouque reviewed the work, he reported that he, too, had consulted the manuscript; Octave Fouque, "Une Nouvelle Édition de Don Juan," *Revue et gazette musicale de Paris* 41 (1874), 35.

[53] *Revue et gazette musicale de Paris*, 29 January 1865, 35–36. There are no noticeable differences in Köchel's treatment of the autograph between the first (1862) and second (1905) editions of Ludwig Ritter von Köchel, *Chronologisch-thematisches Verzeichnis sämmtlicher Tonwerke Wolfgang Amadeus Mozart's nebst Angabe der verloren gegangenen, unvollendeten, übertragenen, zweifelhaften und unterschobenen Compositionen desselben* (Leipzig: Breitkopf und Härtel, 1862; 2nd ed. rev. and enl. by Paul Graf von Waldersee, 1905).

[54] Nicole Wild, *Dictionnaire des théâtres parisiens au xixᵉ siècle: Les théâtres et la musique* (Paris: Amateurs des Livres, 1989), 199.

While his wife was assembling the details of the reliquary and shrine in their house in the rue de Douai, Louis was at work with his pen. He published an article in *L'Illustration* in January 1856, in which he described Rossini's encounter with the shrine to *Don Giovanni*, that was ostensibly a report on the autograph itself. However, the result was a contribution of a literary text to the hagiography of *Don Giovanni*; in the Middle Ages, this would have been as much a *vita sanctorum* or an *acta sanctorum* as his account of Rossini's veneration of the shrine to the opera. Like medieval lives or acts of the saints, Louis' article was a far from original document but rather took up a number of themes in the mythology of *Don Giovanni* and in the life of Mozart, reshaping them for the mid-1850s, and provided a context that could take account of the work's autograph and its rapidly developing cult. Viardot subjected the autograph to careful scrutiny and brought forward several important observations on, for example, the melodic changes in the vocal line of "Or sai chi l'onore," the lack of authenticity of various added chorus parts common in the middle of the nineteenth century, the absence of the recitative at the beginning of the Cemetery scene, and the indications of mise en scène in the autograph.[55]

Viardot could speak with some authority on—or at least contribute something original to—the mythology of Mozart's death, since he had visited the place where Mozart had written *Die Zauberflöte*. His short commentary on the end of Mozart's career, however, digests received wisdom from many preexistent sources. In the context of current veneration for the composer, Viardot was interested in his neglect in 1791 when, "worn out by nights of incessant labour, Mozart at thirty-six, younger than Raphael, died in misery, abandoned, in the pain of having obtained too late an insignificant post of *maître de chapelle* that would have enabled him to live, his mortal remains were taken to a solitary place where vainly, since then, one has searched for the place where they were buried."[56] Apart from drawing a further analogy with Cervantes, which Viardot was well placed to make, he could describe in some detail the state of the room inhabited by the composer who was "already ill, already condemned to an early death.... It is an attic under the eaves furnished with a folding bed, a straw chair and a pine table; it is a servant's room."[57] Viardot's text reinscribes many of the mythologies surrounding Mozart's last days: condemnation to an early death, the comparison with Raphael, destitution, burial in a pauper's grave, and the treatment of genius as servant. A clear example of Viardot's contribution to the mythic status of Mozart biography is his version of the history of the composition of the overture to *Don Giovanni*. A dissipated Mozart wrote the overture the night before the premiere, the score was taken to the copyist with the

---

[55] Viardot, "Manuscrit Autographe," 10.

[56] "Usé par les veilles et l'incessant labeur, Mozart, à trente-six ans, plus jeune que Raphaël, s'éteignait dans la misère, dans l'abandon, dans la douleur d'obtenir trop tard une petite place de maître de chapelle qui l'eût fait vivre, ses dépouilles mortelles furent emportées au milieu d'une telle solitude, que vainement, depuis lors, on a cherché la place où elle furent inhumées" (ibid.).

[57] "Déjà malade, déjà condamné à une mort précoce.... C'est une mansarde sous les toits, garnie d'un lit de camp, d'une chaise en paille et d'une table en sapin; c'est une chambre de domestique" (ibid.).

ink still wet, the orchestra successfully sight-read the overture, and Mozart good-naturedly observed that several notes dropped under the music stands. The mythic track of this narrative runs from Niemetschek (1798), through Johann Friedrich Rochlitz (in a series of articles from the same year until 1801), Arnold's *Mozarts Geist* of 1803, and Nissen's 1828 biography. The myth would not end there; it was picked up by, among others, Genast in 1862, Wilder in 1880, and then endlessly—as befits a myth—thereafter.[58] Viardot's contribution lies right in the middle of the myth's development, and he has a particular slant—a particular element to contribute—to the myth: firsthand experience of the autograph. After taking the story up to the night before the premiere, Viardot continues: "But soon, when the Muse moved him, he dismissed his wife, put down his glass, lit his pipe, and all in one go, all in one breath, without hesitation, without corrections, without retouching, he wrote the overture from the beginning to the end. It is easy to see on the manuscript, which is in a single ink, with a single pen, in a single script, with what incredible rapidity he conceived and threw down on the paper this powerful overture [*symphonie*]";[59] the account then concludes with the parts being copied during the day and the orchestra sight-reading the overture. Viardot's aim was to use the apparent clarity evident in the autograph to support an argument that the movement was written at speed and that it was written in accordance with the prevailing mythology of Mozart's effortless fluency. Even by the paleographical standards of 1856, Viardot was making a bold claim when he suggested that the textual efficiency of the autograph revealed the fluency with which it was conceived. All that the autograph could have revealed was how the work was written out. But Viardot's confrontation with the autograph of *Don Giovanni* gave him the imaginative space to contribute to the hagiography of the composer. Under the guise of a scholarly account of the autograph of *Don Giovanni*, he contributed to, and attempted to validate, a process of mythmaking that was already over fifty years old.

The ultimate paradox in Viardot's article is that although he recognized the *scena ultima* of *Don Giovanni* as part of the autograph and not—as was the norm in nineteenth-century performances—separate so that the work ended with Don Giovanni's descent into Hell, Viardot could not accept this conclusion to the opera on aesthetic grounds. His apologia for contemporary practice, and his ultimate acceptance of the primacy of tradition over textual authority, reads as follows:

---

[58] See William Stafford, *The Mozart Myths: A Critical Reassessment* (Stanford: Stanford University Press, 1991), 20 and 106–107.

[59] "Mais bientôt, la Muse venant à souffler, il congédia sa femme, déposa son verre, éteignit sa pipe, et tout d'un trait, tout d'une haleine, sans hésitation, sans corrections, sans retouches, il écrivit l'ouverture du commencement à la fin. On voit aisément sur le manuscrit, qui est d'une seule encre, d'une seule plume, d'une seule écriture, hâtive et comme emportée, avec quelle rapidité incroyable il conçut et jeta sur le papier cette puissante symphonie" (Viardot, "Manuscrit Autographe," 10).

If the [dramatic] situation and the poetry of this finale are not very strong, it has to be admitted that the composer nevertheless very much *warmed them up with his music*. After the astonishing scene that begins with the entrance of the Commendatore and finishes with the swallowing-up of his murderer hardened by his crime, Mozart himself could go no higher; he had reached the extreme summit of dramatic grandeur, and any piece following it, however worthy it might be of a place in another work, or in another place in the same work, ought necessarily to appear feeble and cold. The latter is also the only one that Mozart had written, materially, with confusion, in disorder, where work took the place of inspiration. It is quite right, it appears to me, to suppress it in the theatre and to relegate it from now on to engraved scores.[60]

Even when the mythology involved traditions pointing to the suppression of parts of the work that Viardot knew, from the document in front of him, to be authentic, and despite his efforts elsewhere in the same text to dispel such textual anachronisms, he preferred the mythology of the nineteenth century to the imperatives of firsthand documentary evidence. This tension reappeared a decade later when the Théâtre-Lyrique produced a version of the work that reinstated the *scena ultima* (discussed in chapter 4).

When Viardot republished his essay on the *Don Giovanni* autograph in 1866, he wrote a new companion piece: "Un souvenir du *Don Juan* de Mozart: Juin 1861."[61] This is an entirely fictional piece of work fused with some self-congratulatory autobiography. Viardot addresses his story to an anonymous eighteen-year-old who is dissatisfied with his prospects; the narrator relates how, when he was the same age, he was taken to a performance of *Don Giovanni* by his mother; as a result he spent a lot of time at the Théâtre Italien, and he remembers how one of his neighbors brought a score of the work with him. In conclusion, Viardot reveals to his interlocutor that, one day, the penniless student—and it is now clear that it is Viardot himself—was to become the director of the opera house, was to marry the prima donna, and was to own Mozart's original manuscript of the opera. The moral that could be drawn was that however grim things might look for a young

---

[60] "Si la situation et si la poésie de ce final ne sont pas très fortes, il faut avouer que le compositeur ne les avait pas non plus très-*réchauffées des sons de sa musique* [emphasis original]. Après la scène prodigieuse qui commence à l'entrée du commandeur et finit à l'engloutissement de son meurtrier endurci dans le crime, Mozart lui-même ne pouvait s'élever plus haut; il avait atteint l'extrême sommet de la grandeur dramatique, et tout morceau venant à la suite, fût-il très digne de prendre place dans un autre ouvrage, ou dans un autre endroit de cet ouvrage même, devait nécessairement paraître faible et froid. Celui-là est le seul aussi que Mozart ait écrit, matériellement, avec confusion, avec désordre, où le travail se sente au lieu de l'inspiration. L'on a donc bien fait, il me semble, de le supprimer au théâtre, et de le reléguer désormais dans les partitions gravés" (ibid., 11).

[61] Louis Viardot, "Un souvenir du *don juan* de Mozart," in *Espagne et Beaux Arts: Mélanges* (Paris: Hachette, 1866), 439–446; reprinted in *Le Ménestrel* 46 (1879–80), 65–67, and in *Cahiers Ivan Tourguéniev, Pauline Viardot, Maria Malibran* 2 (1978), 64–71.

republican without prospects in Paris in the middle of the Second Empire (and the Viardots were to remain in Paris for less than two years before leaving the country), hope could always triumph over adverse experience.

Two of the scenes that had attracted Louis Viardot's attention in his 1856 article were those involving the statue of the Commendatore. These are also the two scenes around which Aleksandr Pushkin built his *Kamennïy gost* (The stone guest). Completed in 1830 but published posthumously in 1839, Pushkin's verse drama embeds the narrative from the cemetery and supper scenes from *Don Giovanni* in a drama that betrays traces of Hoffmann and Byron, and has served as an important mediating text between Mozart's opera and posterity.[62] *The Stone Guest* was known to the rest of Europe via its translation into French published in 1862. Six years after Louis Viardot's text on *Don Giovanni*, he and Ivan Turgenev translated both Pushkin's drama and its companion text, *Mozart and Salieri*, into French.[63] The literary tradition that supported the reception of *Don Giovanni* before 1860 includes more or less well-known texts by E. T. A. Hoffmann, Grabbe, Kahlert, Gautier, Sand, Musset, and Mörike, as well as by Pushkin. When Turgenev and Viardot translated Pushkin's *Stone Guest*, they associated a well-established literary tradition of *Don Giovanni* reception with the particular cult surrounding *Don Giovanni* and its autograph promulgated by the Viardot circle.[64]

Pauline Viardot's position as the guardian of the shrine to *Don Giovanni* is entirely compatible with the more general image of her as a priestess of music and the arts. Although this image of self-sacrifice in pursuit of artistic ideals was largely promoted by others, she never made any public attempt to neutralize it, and such actions as her elevation of the shrine to *Don Giovanni* contributed to the same

---

[62] Aleksandr Pushkin, "Kamennïy gost" [The stone guest], *Sto rousskikh literatorov* [A hundred Russian authors], ed. Aleksandr Filippovich Smirdin, 3 vols. (Saint Petersburg: Smirdin, 1839–45), 1:49–85. Evidence that Pushkin knew Hoffmann's essay on *Don Giovanni* is slight; the essay was translated into French in 1829 and into Russian in 1833; see Wladimir Troubetzkoy, "Pouchkine, Alexandre (1799–1837)," in *Dictionnaire de Don Juan*, ed. Pierre Bunel, Bouquins 752 (Paris: Laffont, 1999).

[63] Louis Viardot and Ivan Turgenev, trans., "L'Invité de Pierre," in *Poèmes dramatiques d'Alexandre Pouchkine* (Paris: Hachette, 1862), 237–279.

[64] Louis Viardot's literary interest in Russia was sparked by the three annual visits he made with his wife between 1844 and 1846. The eight published articles included a number of topological, political, and anthropological studies and an account "De quelques instituts de musique en Russie," published in the *Revue et gazette musicale de Paris*. These were followed by several studies of European museums in which Russian institutions figured largely. Viardot published French versions of two Russian texts as early as 1846; although the translations of Pushkin's *La Fille du capitaine* and Lermontov's *Un Héro de notre temps* bear Viardot's name, his introductions hint at his collaborators—the young Turgenev and Stephan Gedeonov (the son of the director of the St. Petersburg theatre)—and make clear his own limited comprehension of Russian. See Michel Cadot, "Turgenev und Louis Viardot als Mittler russischer Literatur in Frankreich," *Zeitschrift für Slavistik* 32 (1987), 442–444. In a letter to the publisher Hetzel in 1859, Viardot spelt out exactly how he produced translations from Russian in collaboration with Turgenev: "A friend dictates a verbal translation to me and I write the French; that is all. This friend [is] Ivan Turgenev" (cited in ibid., 447). This symbiotic relationship between Turgenev, Viardot, and their Russian texts in French translation outlines well the third limb of the relationship between Pauline Viardot and the two men.

image. Liszt, for example, claimed in his 1859 essay on Pauline Viardot that "she gave herself with sacred dedication to her calling, she consistently seriously focused on the ideal of art, and devoted herself to the cult of beauty with the enthusiasm of an adolescent, which prompted her best friend to write one of her finest masterpieces, *Consuelo*."[65] George Sand, that best friend, had already written in 1842 to Pauline as she was writing *Consuelo* (whose protagonist is a fictionalized portrayal of Pauline) and had declared more bluntly to her: "You are the priestess of the ideal in music, and your mission is to proselytise, to make it understood and to lead recalcitrants to an instinct for, and a revelation of, the truth and the beautiful."[66] Both Liszt's essay and Sand's letter are emblematic of a range of texts that develop the general view of Pauline Viardot as a priestess of art and music. Viardot's correspondence with Rietz makes it clear that she was content with this image. In Christian iconography, models for a priestess (or patron saint) of music are easily found, and when Ary Scheffer supplied the medallion that adorned Viardot's Cavaillé-Coll organ, he painted "musical inspiration in the indistinct traits of a young woman: Saint Cecilia or Pauline Viardot";[67] in doing so, Scheffer twisted the traditional relationship between saint and attribute in a truly spectacular way: Saint Cecilia (or Pauline Viardot) is embedded in a tiny medallion in the casework of the organ, as opposed to the traditional presentation of Saint Cecilia seated at a small portative organ.[68] *Don Giovanni* provided a specific focus for the generalized association of Viardot with a priestess or patron saint of music, and the verbal and physical discourses that surrounded her relationship with the autograph of the work promoted, in microcosm, the image of a priestess of music that was so admired generally.

The Second Empire was exactly the context into which the role of priestess of art and of the shrine to *Don Giovanni* could readily be introduced. Following the wave of anticlericalism that accompanied the revolutions of 1848, the Papacy countered with a series of measures designed to promote the veneration of the Blessed Virgin Mary at exactly the same time Pauline Viardot was developing the *Don Giovanni* cult. The government of the Second Empire was simultaneously restoring all the images of the Virgin that had been damaged or removed in the 1848

---

[65] "Mit Weihe ihrem Beruf hingegeben, ernsten Blickes am Ideal der Kunst hängend, von der Andacht für das Schöne mit einer jugendlichen Begeisterung erfüllt—einer Begeisterung, welche ihre große Freundin zu einer ihrer schönsten Schöpfungen, der *Consuelo*, hinriß." Franz Liszt, "Pauline Viardot-Garcia 1859," *Neue Zeitschrift für Musik*, 28 January 1859, reprinted in Franz Liszt, *Dramaturgische Blätter: Essays über musikalische Bühnenwerke und Bühnenfragen, Komponisten und Darsteller*, Gesammelte Schriften von Franz Liszt 3/1 (Leipzig: Breitkopf und Härtel, 1881) 123.

[66] "Vous êtes la prêtresse de l'idéal en musique, et vous avez pour mission de le répandre, de le faire comprendre et d'amener les récalcitrants à un instinct et à une révélation du vrai et du beau." Georges Sand to Viardot, 25 and 28 June 1842 (Sand, *Correspondance*, 5:705).

[67] "L'inspiration musicale sous les traits indécis d'une jeune femme: Sainte Cécile ou Pauline Garcia" (du Pays, "Pauline Viardot," 185, cited in Schuster-Fournier, *Les Orgues*, 31).

[68] The standard text on Saint Cecilia and her iconography is Thomas Connolly, *Mourning into Joy: Music, Raphael and Saint Cecilia* (New Haven and London: Yale University Press, 1994).

revolution.[69] In 1854, a year before the *Don Giovanni* cult was established, Pius IX proclaimed the Immaculate Conception of the Blessed Virgin,[70] and the resulting growth in Marian worship threatened both to eclipse and to merge into the reverence for the female revolutionary image of French liberty, Marianne.[71] This growth was given a massive impetus only two years later by the vision of Bernadette of Lourdes, who claimed to have been addressed by the Virgin; this manifestation was particularly important because the Virgin was reported to have confirmed herself the truth of the Immaculate Conception. Although Bernadette was not canonized until 1933, the authenticity of her vision was confirmed as early as 1862,[72] and during the last decade of his reign, Napoleon III enthusiastically supported Pius IX by encouraging pilgrimages to Lourdes.[73] The competition between Marianne, the female allegorical figure of the state, and the Blessed Virgin Mary, the female embodiment of the Church for the 1850s and 1860s, left open large amounts of cultural space for such individuals as Pauline Viardot to be described as, and act in accordance with an image of, priestesses of art and music.

Such cultural spaces were essential to Viardot's accomplishments and presented the possibility of an alternative to the "domestic and reproductive space that men had marked out" for women of her position.[74] In confrontation with the two choices for a woman's life in the mid-nineteenth-century—conventional marriage or transgressive eroticism[75]—she engaged both alternatives rather than adopting, for example, situations that had worked for her friend George Sand: she married strategically—with Sand's help—but at the same time conducted a relationship with Turgenev that was tinged with elements of the transgressive and erotic. The question mark over the nature of her relationship with Turgenev identified her as a member of that group of "strong women of exceptional accomplishment [who]...have a frustrated love affair somewhere in their pasts."[76] Family precedents for successful women's biographies were rare: her sister Maria had attempted a marriage with Eugène Malibran that had promptly failed, and then embarked on a transgressive relationship with Charles de Bériot in 1830 that was not legalized until her first marriage was annulled just before her death in 1836; her subsequent

---

[69] Nicholas Perry and Loreto Echeverría, *Under the Heel of Mary* (London: Routledge, 1988), 109.

[70] Ibid., 118.

[71] For the points of difference and overlap between the Virgin Mary and Marianne, see Stéphane Michaud, *Muse et madone: Visages de la femme de la révolution française aux apparitions de Lourdes* (Paris: Seuil, 1985); the best introduction to the iconography of Marianne is Maurice Agulhon, *Marianne au combat: L'imagerie et la symbolique républicaines de 1789 à 1880*, Bibliothèque d'ethnologie historique (Paris: Flammarion, 1979).

[72] Lisa Lieberman, "Crimes of Reason, Crimes of Passion: Suicide and the Adulterous Woman in Nineteenth-Century France," *Journal of Family History* 24 (1999), 131.

[73] Perry and Echeverría, *Under the Heel of Mary*, 120.

[74] Christine Battersby, *Gender and Genius: Towards a Feminist Aesthetics* (London: Women's Press, 1989), 22.

[75] For a discussion of these two alternative narratives, see Carolyn G. Heilbrun, *Writing a Woman's Life* (New York: Ballantine, 1988), 48.

[76] Ruth Solie, "Changing the Subject," *Current Musicology* 53 (1993), 55.

demise in Manchester, after a fall from a horse in London, reinforced the image of retribution fueled by transgression.[77] Explanations for Viardot's life after her retirement in 1863 depend as much on her image as a priestess of music—or of the cult of *Don Giovanni*—as they do on the other discourses that circumscribed the second half of her life: composition, pedagogy, correspondence, writing about music, and support to composers, young and old.[78]

In this context, the appropriation of *Don Giovanni* as a subject for treatment as a relic at the center of a cult dedicated to its composer evokes Parisian resonances of the gendered status of music in the decade before the purchase of the manuscript. For the 1840s, music before Beethoven, which formed such an important part of the repertory of the "reign of women pianists" in Paris, was gendered female.[79] A woman's appropriation of *Don Giovanni* would have seemed more in keeping with decorum and less transgressive than, say, her erecting a shrine to Beethoven. The matter is complicated further by the clearly gendered elements of the libretto of *Don Giovanni* itself, and by the paradoxical placing at the centre of an artistic cult of a work that appeared to the nineteenth century as the embodiment of punished immorality. This paradox suggests that by the middle of the century, the status of *Don Giovanni* as a work—rather than as a performance or spectacle (and this is fully congruent with Viardot's own pronouncements on the subject)—had effaced the content of its libretto.

Tensions concerning the French ownership of what was rapidly emerging as a monument to German art were clear from claims made in both languages concerning the *Don Giovanni* cult promoted by the Viardot circle. Louis Viardot's 1856 text on the autograph opens with a lengthy commentary on how badly German-speaking musicians had been treated in their own lands, and how many had found a home in France.[80] Cut from the 1866 edition of the text (Viardot was then, after all, living in Baden-Baden), the opening paragraphs of the article contain a long list of German musicians who failed to receive the esteem in their country that was their due: Handel had to leave for Italy and England, both Gluck and Meyerbeer had to find their fortunes in France and French opera, Beethoven's distress was only assuaged by a Russian prince, Weber died penniless in London, and

---

[77] April Fitzlyon's biography of Maria Malibran is still the most reliable: *Maria Malibran: Diva of the Romantic Age* (London: Souvenir, 1987).

[78] In a rather different context, Elizabeth Wood has explored how such a multiplicity of discourses can combine "contrapuntally" in the music, autobiography, and correspondence of Ethel Smyth; see her "Lesbian Fugue: Ethel Smyth's Contrapuntal Arts," in *Musicology and Difference: Gender and Sexuality in Music Scholarship*, ed. Ruth A. Solie ((Berkeley: University of California Press, 1993), 164–183. This paragraph has benefited greatly from a consideration of the issues raised, and sources cited, in Jeanice Brooks, "*Noble et grande servante de la musique*: Telling the Story of Nadia Boulanger's Conducting Career," *Journal of Musicology* 14 (1996), 92–116, especially 94–97.

[79] See the careful diagnosis of gender and repertory in Katharine Ellis, "Female Pianists and Their Male Critics in Nineteenth-Century Paris," *Journal of the American Musicological Society* 50 (1997), 353–385.

[80] Viardot, "Manuscrit Autographe," 10.

Mendelssohn escaped misery solely because of his inheritance. While establishing the background to Viardot's description of Mozart's domicile in 1791, this litany also set up an antagonism between German-speaking composers and their homeland, and between those lands and France. There was a certain triumph in Viardot's account of how his wife refused to allow the autograph of *Don Giovanni* to join so many others at the Imperial Library in Vienna for the centennial celebrations in 1856. Viardot's text implicitly explored the link between German-speaking states' poor treatment of their artists and an appropriate home for the autograph in France.

From the other side of the Rhine, Ludwig Pietsch's account of music at the Villa Viardot, with the shrine to *Don Giovanni* at its center, concluded with a fantastic account of the musical atmosphere of the room in which the autograph was preserved: "and when the shadows of the night or the fantastic shimmer of moonlight envelop the forests and mountains, the ethereal sounds of the powerful and perpetual rhythms of Sebastian Bach, the majestic lament of Gluck, the magical music of Beethoven with its sweet and grandiose melancholy and its triumphal splendour, or the mysterious and miraculous sounds of the romantic Robert Schumann, mingle frequently in the light evening breeze that plays gently with the luxuriant vines at the open windows of that room."[81] Pietsch's invocation of Bach, Gluck, Beethoven, and Schumann translated the pantheon of German music history to the music-making at the Villa Viardot without mention of the "French" Chopin, Meyerbeer, Berlioz, Liszt, or Gounod—or Mozart, for that matter. The nationality of the autograph of *Don Giovanni* and its composer would remain a feature of the landscape of Franco-German music history for the next half century.

The last quarter of the nineteenth century saw the enshrined autograph of *Don Giovanni* appropriated as a French national monument, and witnessed a mingling of the discourses of the Viardot circle with patriotic imperatives. Napoleon III's surrender on the battlefield at Sedan was mirrored by the Viardots' retreat from Baden-Baden; their exile in England ended only with the establishment of the Third Republic.[82] With them came the shrine to *Don Giovanni,* which would be appropriated for celebrations of French musical culture at the Exposition Universelle of 1878, and the centenary celebrations of the premiere of *Don Giovanni* in 1887; it would be donated to the French state in 1892.

---

[81] "Und wenn das nächtliche Dunkel oder der phantastische Schimmer des Mondlichts auf Wald und Gebirge ringsum liegt, mischt sich in das weiche Säußeln des Abendwindes, der leise mit dem vollen Rebenlaub um die offenen Fenster dieses Saales spielt, am häufigsten der eherne Klang der machtvollen, ewigen Rhythmen Sebastian Bachs, die erhabene Klage Glucks, der Zaubergesang Beethovens mit seiner süssen, überwältigenden Schwermut und seiner triumphierenden Pracht, oder die geheimnisvollen Wundertöne Robert Schumannscher Romantik" (Kalbeck, *Johannes Brahms,* 2:88).

[82] For the Viardots' exile in England, see Fitzlyon, *The Price of Genius,* 407–415.

The 1878 Exposition Universelle was the first occasion when the autograph of *Don Giovanni* was exposed to public view. The tenth section of the Musée Rétrospectif at the Trocadéro was devoted to music, mostly organology. Two displays contained manuscript documents outlining the history of music; the most recent example was that of an aria by Berton to be inserted into Salieri's *Les Danaïdes.*[83] Visitors to the exhibition would have learned a history of mostly eighteenth-century music through a series of autographs of works that included Haydn (the "Paris" Symphony no. 91 and the "London" Symphony dedicated to Cherubini, no. 103), Cherubini's *Les Deux Journées,* works by Lully, Rameau, Gluck, Gossec, Grétry, and Berton, Sacchini's *Dardanus,* and Salieri's *Tarare.* Much of the French music that was exhibited was by naturalized foreigners (Lully, Cherubini) or musicians writing according to the conventions of French operatic institutions (Gluck, Sacchini, Salieri); even Grétry had been born in Liège when it was a prince-bishopric and part of the Empire. The only work without an obvious French pedigree was a Bach autograph, but that had been lent by Pauline Viardot; in the light of the main attraction in the exhibition, there was a logic to this choice.[84] At the center of this part of the exhibition was the autograph of *Don Giovanni.* Whereas each of the other composers was represented by a single document, often merely a fragment, all seven parts of the *Don Giovanni* autograph—the act 1 finale, the tenor aria "Dalla sua pace" added for Vienna, for example—were exhibited separately.[85] When Pauline Viardot had declined to send the autograph of *Don Giovanni* to Vienna in 1856, she had already implicitly thrown into question the nationality of the document, the work, and its composer. Its appearance in the Exposition Universelle placed it centrally in a tradition of French composition and cultivation of music in the previous century, and the opera was put to an essentially political use: seven years after the Franco-Prussian War, when Paris displayed its musical past to the world, it could include a work to which the newly emergent and empire-hungry Germany might with some justification have felt that it had some claim.

Less than a decade later, Viardot's prized possession was again on public view. The most generous description of the 1887 centenary celebrations of *Don Giovanni* in Paris is that they were well intentioned. They took the form of a revival of the work at the Palais Garnier, a celebratory poem declaimed at the performance, and an exhibition. Various small-scale commemorations took place. *Le Carillon Théâtral,*

---

[83] Em[ile] Mathieu de Monter, "Exposition Universelle de 1878...Le Musée Rétrospectif," *Revue et gazette musicale de Paris* 45 (1878), 226–229 [21 July 1878].

[84] The work was the Cantata for the twentieth Sunday after Trinity, *Schmücke dich, o liebe Seele,* BWV 180. Viardot's interest in Bach is confirmed by the fact that she was one of the first three French subscribers to the Bach-Gesellschaft edition of his works; the other two were Alkan and Jean-Joseph Bonaventure Laurens. See Joël-Marie Fauquet and Antoine Hennion, *La Grandeur de Bach: L'amour de la musique en France au xixe siècle,* Les Chemins de la Musique (Paris: Fayard, 2000), 80.

[85] A lock of Mozart's hair (and a copy of the printed libretto to *Don Giovanni*) accompanied the autograph. The presence of an object so much more obviously associated with the traditional veneration of relics in this context is congruent with the presentation of the *Don Giovanni* autograph by Pauline Viardot and her circle.

for example, extracted short commentaries from modern composers on Mozart and *Don Giovanni*; these ranged from Gounod's "Mozart! The most perfect of all musicians! Music itself!" through an anecdote told by Saint-Saëns, a preposterously overlong text by Gervais-Bernard Salvayre, and Massenet's droll "I agree absolutely with my illustrious colleagues."[86]

The 1887 revival of the work was less than successful. The curtain rose on a bust of Mozart, and Jean Lassalle, who took the title role, declaimed a celebratory poem by Henri Bornier that at best could be called academic.[87] The performance was, according to all accounts, weak. Despite a strong showing from Lassalle, unfavorable comparisons were made with Jean-Baptiste Faure, who had taken the role in the influential and successful 1866 revival, and the rest of the cast—which nevertheless included the De Reske brothers as Leporello and Ottavio—were not at all favorably received.[88] Other critics exhibited a lack of sympathy with the style of the work.[89] But it was not merely a poor performance that marked down the revival. The same week saw the 500th performance of Gounod's *Faust*, and this prompted a number of comparisons between the status of the two works, one a hundred years, one twenty-eight years (but five hundred performances) old.[90] Camille Bellaigue's thoughtful review in the *Revue des deux mondes* came close to Pauline Viardot's 1869 comments to Stockhausen about how impossible it was to listen to *Don Giovanni*, and for only slightly different reasons. He suggested that audiences had grown tired of *Don Giovanni* in a way they had not of *Faust*.[91] By 1887, the explicit rhetoric of divinity that so characterized the Viardots' veneration for the autograph of the work could be projected into the public domain. Bellaigue was unlikely to be contradicted when he claimed that Mozart "is the only composer; he is the God," and pointed to the "sacred and divine"[92] place the composer held "in the admiration, in the adoration of humanity. We still love it, *Don Juan*, the masterpiece of masterpieces, beautiful with a unique beauty, almost supernatural, around which has formed over the last century an aura of glory."[93] Bellaigue's way out of the difficulty of a near-sacred work that was no longer popular was to adopt

---

[86] "Mozart! Le plus parfait de tous les musiciens! La musique même" [Gounod]; "Je suis absolument de l'avis de mes illustres confrères" [Massenet] (*Le Carillon Théâtral* 3, 1 November 1887, 34 and 36).

[87] Henri de Bornier, *Poésies Complètes (1850–1893)* (Paris: Dentu, 1894), 221–224.

[88] See, for example, "Semaine Théâtrale: Le Centenaire de *Don Juan*," *Le Ménestrel*, 30 October 1887, 347–348.

[89] *Le Carillon Théâtral* 3, 1 November 1887, 41–6, reprinted a wide range of views pro and contra the performance.

[90] Ibid., 36–40.

[91] Camille Bellaigue, "Revue Musicale: Théâtre de l'Opéra—Le centenaire de *Don Juan*, la cinq-centième représentation de *Faust*," *Revue des deux mondes*, 15 November 1887, 443.

[92] "Une place sacrée et comme divine" (ibid., 444).

[93] "Dans l'adoration de l'humanité. Nous l'aimons toujours, *Don Juan*, le chef d'œuvre des chefs d'œuvre, beau d'un beauté unique, presque surnaturelle, autour de laquelle s'est formée depuis un siècle une auréole de gloire" (ibid.). The idea of the masterpiece of masterpieces is presumably a parody of Hoffmann's description of *Don Giovanni* as "die Oper aller Opern."

the mythology that "Mozart had written *Don Giovanni*, he said, for himself and for a few friends. It must be heard among friends, and in circumstances where all the details are evident, where not a smile, not a tear of this exquisite music is lost."[94] As for Pauline Viardot, so for Bellaigue—the only satisfactory performance of *Don Giovanni* was a perfect, and therefore unattainable, one.

It was appropriate, then, that the audiences at the 1887 revival of this "masterpiece of masterpieces" could while away the interval looking at an exhibition of Mozart memorabilia: various autographs (the piano and wind quintet, the Andante for flute and orchestra), medals, and letters. Pride of place, however, went to the autograph of *Don Giovanni*.[95] Exactly how successful this exhibition was is difficult to judge. It was only briefly mentioned, and then slightingly, in a report in the *Journal des Débats*: "To celebrate the glorious centenary of Mozart's masterpiece, a brilliant revival, supported by a genuinely remarkable performance, would perhaps have sufficed. The directors of the Opéra preferred to give more and less. To get over a revival whose performance was hardly transcendent—they would have needed more—they added a little ceremony, a little poem and a little exhibition."[96] It is more than possible that Pauline Viardot saw the public face of *Don Giovanni*— allied to an unexceptional performance, and almost ignored by the press—being defamed by the sort of overexposure that fell far short of her sacralized ideals of the work.

Two years later, when Pauline Viardot announced her intention to bequeath the autograph of the opera to the nation, she simultaneously managed to develop the idea of *Don Giovanni* as a piece of specifically French cultural history while restoring something of the mystique her cult had erected around her shrine to the work and its composer. She announced her bequest in October 1889, and in February 1892 chose to hand over the document before her death (she did not die until 1910). The exchanges between Viardot and the state concerning the bequest of the autograph are loaded with the ritualistic vocabulary that had already characterized so much of the cult. She wrote to the director of the Conservatoire, Ambroise Thomas, in by now familiar terms: "I want you to be the first to learn that, according to a clause in my will, I am leaving my most precious jewel, the original score of *Don Giovanni*, to the library of the Conservatoire. I do not know of any place where this inestimable autograph could be better placed than in the institution of

---

[94] "Mozart avait écrit *Don Juan*, disait-il, pour lui même et pour quelques amis. C'est entre amis qu'il faudrait l'entendre, et dans un cadre moyen où tous les détails porteraient, où ne se perdrait pas un sourire, pas une larme de cette exquise musique" (ibid., 448).

[95] The contents of the exhibition were described in "Le Centenaire de *Don Juan*," *Le Ménestrel*, 30 October 1887, 350.

[96] "Pour célébrer le glorieux centenaire du chef-d'œuvre de Mozart, une brillante reprise, soutenue par une interprétation vraiment remarquable, eût peut-être suffi. Les directeurs de l'Opéra ont préféré donner plus et moins. Pour faire passer une reprise dont l'interprétation n'a rien de bien transcendant,— il s'en faut même de beaucoup,—ils ont ajouté une petite cérémonie, un petit à-propos poétique et une petite exposition" (cited in *Le Carillon Théâtral*, 39).

which you are the illustrious and beloved director. The most important of our artistic institutions will be its guardian for ever."[97] Thomas's response describes the act in terms that complement Viardot's words with explicitly patriotic ones: "In bequeathing to our library a masterpiece unique in the world, you are performing *an act of patriotism* that will be applauded by all those who subscribe to the religion of art [emphasis original]."[98]

When Viardot decided in February 1892 that she wanted to hand over ("translate" would be a not inappropriate term here) the autograph directly to Thomas, it was clear that it was he, in particular, who had been singled out as her successor as guardian of the shrine. She wrote: "I would be honoured to see [the autograph] enter *your* hands, because it is to *you* that I wish to give it, then finally in its resting place in our handsome library. As long as I have had the honour to possess the divine manuscript, I have never agreed to lend it to any of the numerous foreign exhibitions who have asked me. At the library, it will be *at home, but on the formal condition that it will never leave it* [emphasis original]."[99] In accordance with Viardot's wishes, a formal transfer of the relic from its old to its new guardian took place on 6 July 1892: "M. Ambroise Thomas presented himself [at Viardot's house], and she placed into his hands the precious manuscript. The director of the Conservatoire thanked Mme Pauline Viardot for this gift, and that very evening, the score of the immortal masterpiece, completely written in Mozart's hand, was deposited in the library of our school of music."[100] Right up to the end of her guardianship of the document, Viardot carefully controlled the verbal and ritual discourses surrounding the relic, and by the terms of her will, continued to control them after her death.

From the mid-1850s, the autograph of *Don Giovanni* held a particular place within the Viardot circle. Pauline Viardot preserved the document in an artifact that was as close in construction to a reliquary as its nature would allow, and treated it as a

---

[97] "Je veux que [vous] soyez le premier à apprendre que, par une clause de mon testament, je lègue mon bijou le plus précieux, la partition originale de *Don Giovanni* à la Bibliothèque du Conservatoire. Je ne sache pas d'endroit où cet inestimable autographe puisse être mieux placé que dans la maison dont vous êtes l'illustre et bien aimé directeur. La plus importante de nos institutions artistiques en sera à jamais la gardienne" (*F-Pn* L.A.S. 109, fol. 223r).

[98] "En dotant notre Bibliothèque d'un chef-d'œuvre unique au monde, vous faites *un acte de patriotisme* auquel applaudiront tous ceux qui ont le culte de l'Art [emphasis original]" (Mongrédien, "A propos du manuscrit manuscrit autographe," 40).

[99] "Je serai honorée de le voir entrer *vos* mains, car c'est à *vous* que je veux le remettre, puis enfin à sa place définitive, dans notre belle bibliothèque. Tant que j'ai eu l'honneur de posséder chez moi le divin manuscrit, je n'ai jamais consenti à le prêter à aucune des nombreuses expositions étrangères qui me l'ont demandé. A la bibliothèque, il sera *chez lui, mais à la condition formelle qu'il n'en sortira jamais*" [emphasis original] (*F-Pn* L.A.S. 109, fols. 224r–224v).

[100] "M. Ambroise Thomas s'est rendu chez elle, et elle a remis entre ses mains le précieux manuscrit. Le directeur du Conservatoire a remercié Mme Pauline Viardot de ce don et, le soir même, la partition de l'immortel chef-d'œuvre, écrite tout entière de la main de Mozart, a été déposée dans la bibliothèque de notre École de musique" (*Le Ménestrel*, 10 July 1892, 3–4).

shrine. Visitors to her homes in Paris and Baden-Baden behaved exactly as if they were in the presence of a relic. The autograph was elevated to the status of a national monument when it was displayed at the Exposition Universelle of 1878, and at the anniversary exhibition of the premiere of *Don Giovanni* in 1887. When it was donated to the library of the Conservatoire in 1892, its sacred and national characteristics were elided. Positioning such a work as *Don Giovanni* within the context of the religion of art, promoted for the nineteenth century by Wackenroder, Tieck, and Herder, and culminating in Hoffmann, is hardly rare.[101] The circumstances of the inclusion of *Don Giovanni* within this context are marked by the dense intersection of several subtropes of the religion of art. The cult of the composer, taking genius as axiomatic, the association of the sacred and profane, the aesthetic of the autonomous and textual mythologies are all tinged by the voice of the diva, and are all in play in the history of the *Don Giovanni* autograph in the second half of the nineteenth century. Pauline Viardot's treatment of a physical document, and her manipulation of the material discourses with which it was surrounded, were a considerable force in the ongoing project of enshrining Mozart.

---

[101] See, for a recent account of a subject with a burgeoning bibliography, Wilhelm Seidel, "Absolute Musik und Kunstreligion um 1800," in *Musik und Religion*, ed. Helga de La Motte-Haber (Laaber: Laaber, 1995), 89–114.

PART III

Specters at the Feast

7

Mozart in Two Worlds

THE WRITINGS ON MUSIC OF BLAZE DE BURY

Of all the sites of reception that populate the afterlife of a composer's works, and that are discussed in this book, the press ought to be one of the easiest with which to come to terms. By the time of Mozart's death, the daily press had developed a publication framework that remained largely unchanged until the end of the twentieth century, and within a couple of decades a music press had been established in several languages.[1] And in comparison with the analysis of performances—especially once one goes beyond the well-documented performances of stage music, the history of publication and a composer's status in the history of ideas, especially within the domain of imaginative literature, control over the subject is patchy to the point of caprice. So it is very odd to find that, with respect to the reception of Mozart during the nineteenth and twentieth centuries, very little of the press has been systematically analyzed. True, the Francophone, Germanophone, and Anglophone press has been plundered for information about performances and reviews, but a consideration of individual critics' views of Mozart have been rare. Only relatively recently have we been able to read a coherent account of, say Friedrich Rochlitz or Ludwig Borne's views of Mozart,[2] or even—to bring things closer to the subject of this chapter—Berlioz's admittedly slender view of the subject.[3] There is no shortage of general accounts, but much is based on biographical texts rather

---

[1] The beginning of a sustained publication of the music press begins with the *Allgemeine musikalische Zeitung* in 1798, followed by the *Quarterly Musical Magazine and Review* in 1818 and the *Revue musicale* in 1827. See Imogen Fellinger et al., "Periodicals," in *Grove Music Online-Oxford Music Online*, www.oxfordmusiconline.com/subscriber/article/grove/music/21338 (accessed 10 July 2012).

[2] See Ulrich Konrad, "Friedrich Rochlitz und die Entstehung des Mozart-Bildes um 1800," in *Mozart: Aspekte des 19. Jahrhunderts*, ed. Hermann Jung and Imogen Fellerer, Mannheimer Hochschulschriften 1 (Mannheim: Palatium, 1995), 1–22; Elmar Werner, "Der 'gottliche' Mozart: Die Mozart-Kritiken Ludwig Bornes," *Acta Mozartiana* 32 (1985), 13–17.

[3] Hugh Macdonald, "Mozart?," in *The Cambridge Companion to Berlioz*, ed. Peter Bloom (Cambridge: Cambridge University Press, 2000), 211–222.

than on the press itself, and where the press is considered, Germanophone-centered accounts focus, perhaps predictably, on Rochlitz.[4]

These studies represent very little in comparison with the gallons of ink spilt on other sorts of texts about Mozart discussed in this book and elsewhere: biographical texts, the more imaginative work of Mörike, Musset, Pushkin, or Kierkegaard, and, as we move into the twentieth century, texts ranging from Shaw to Schaffer. In the context of a systematic consideration of the relationship between words and notes, then, an attempt to redress this balance could do much worse than trying to analyze the views of a single critic on the single phenomenon we know—and this critic knew—as Mozart.

Ange-Henri Blaze was known to the nineteenth-century musical and literary community as Blaze de Bury. His most extensive body of writing was his music journalism in the *Revue des deux mondes* from 1833 to 1884.[5] With a musico-literary career spanning over half a century, and one almost completely restricted to a single journal, he is a more important figure in the history of nineteenth-century music than his inexplicable exclusion from the *Revised New Grove Dictionary of Music and Musicians* might suggest. His editorial loyalty to the *Revue des deux mondes*, from a methodological point of view, enables the tracking of a single journalistic career, in a single publication that was edited—at least until 1869—by a single person, François Buloz;[6] it is a more manageable possibility than handling more normal careers, which jump from journal to journal, often of a very different political and aesthetic stripe.[7]

Blaze de Bury was born on 19 May 1813 in Avignon, the son of the music critic at the *Journal des Débats*, François-Henri-Joseph Blaze (known as Castil-Blaze). His early career was as both a diplomat and a writer, and he served in Weimar from 1839.[8] There, he made a translation of *Faust,* for which he received the title of baron from the duke of Saxe-Weimar, at which point he added his mother's name (Bury) to his own.[9] He married the Scottish journalist and political fixer Rose Stuart in 1844 (she was described as a plenipotentiary to several European politicians in the 1850s and 1860s). Both were vigorous opponents of the regime of

---

[4] Belinda Cannone, *La Réception des opéras de Mozart dans la presse parisienne (1793–1829)* (Paris: Klincksieck, 1991); William Robinson, "Conceptions of Mozart in German Criticism and Biography 1791–1828: Changing Images of a Musical Genius" (Ph.D. diss., Yale University, 1974).

[5] Fully edited in Mark Everist, "Blaze de Bury: Writings on Music," *Francophone Music Criticism, 1789–1914*, Collection 1, www.music.sas.ac.uk/fmc (accessed 10 July 2012).

[6] See Marie-Louise Pailleron, *Les derniers romantiques*, François Buloz et ses amis [3] (Paris: Perrin, 1923).

[7] For the history of the *Revue des deux mondes*, see Nelly Furman, *La Revue des deux mondes et le romantisme (1831–1848)*, Histoire des idées et critique littéraire 149 (Geneva: Droz, 1975); Gabriel de Broglie, *Histoire politique de la Revue des deux mondes de 1829 à 1979* ([Paris]: Perrin, 1979); Thomas Loué, "L'inévidence de la distinction: *La Revue des Deux Mondes* face à la presse à la fin du XIXe siècle," *Romantisme* 33 (2003), 41–48.

[8] Michel Prévost, "Blaze de Bury (Ange-Henri)," in *Dictionnaire de biographie française*, ed. Michel-Prévost and Jean-Charles Roman d'Amat (Paris: Letouzey et Ané, 1933–), 6:659–660.

[9] Marie-Louise Pailleron, "Les Blaze de Bury et l'Autriche," *Revue de Paris*, 1 July 1922, 126–148.

Napoleon III and spent much of the period between 1851 and 1864 outside France, a fact that had a significant influence on Blaze de Bury's output for the *Revue des deux mondes,* since it meant that his routine reviewing activity was curtailed and that he continued to write longer reflective articles from a distance. The situation did, however, place him exactly among the group of individuals—Frenchmen living outside France—that François Buloz, the editor of the *Revue des deux mondes*, had identified as his key authorial base in 1829.

Blaze de Bury's family background was congenial to music journalism: by the time he starting writing in 1833, his father, Castil-Blaze, had been the music critic at the *Journal des Débats* for a decade and was then at *Le constitutionnel*.[10] Blaze de Bury was therefore the son of the inventor of modern music criticism (pace Fétis and Berlioz, who owed much to Castil-Blaze) and brother-in-law as well to the editor of the *Revue des deux mondes*, François Buloz, who had married Castil-Blaze's daughter, Christine.[11] But although Blaze de Bury's music journalism is central to his literary legacy, it would be wrong to prize this more highly than some of his other literary endeavors. Alongside his essays on music, his art criticism—also mostly published in the *Revue des deux mondes*—figures importantly. Also published in the same journal were a handful of novels, some poetry, and a closet drama entitled *Le souper chez le commandeur*, which dramatized fictional events from after the end of *Don Giovanni* and is an important way station on the route between E. T. A. Hoffmann's and George Bernard Shaw's essays on *Don Giovanni* (discussed in chapter 8).[12] Blaze de Bury's 1840 translation of Goethe's *Faust*—which claimed to have the advantage over the one by Gérard de Nerval by virtue of its completeness—ran to a new edition a year until 1847,[13] and his *Ecrivains et poètes d'Allemagne* was judged a classic by Pierre Larousse.[14] But the two pieces of imaginative literature that are likely to be best known to the musical world are his play *La jeunesse de Goethe,* for which Meyerbeer wrote incidental music in the early 1860s,[15] and—together with Émile Deschamps—the libretto of the epoch-

---

[10] Castil-Blaze has had, until recently, a bad press in scholarly circles, especially from those who read the character assassination in Berlioz's *Mémoires* at face value. For a more considered opinion of his music journalism, see Donald Garth Gislason, "Castil-Blaze, *De l'Opéra in France* and the Feuilletons of the *Journal des Débats* (1820–1832)" (Ph.D. diss., University of British Columbia, 1992), and for an account of his first engagement with Berlioz see Mark Everist, "Gluck, Berlioz and Castil-Blaze," in *Reading Critics Reading: French Music Criticism, 1789–1848*, ed. Mary Ann Smart and Roger Parker (Oxford: Oxford University Press, 2001) 86–108.

[11] John Singer Sargent's portrait of the widowed Christine Buloz, dating from 1879, two years after her husband's death, is now in the Los Angeles County Museum of Art. See Ilene Fort and Susan and Michael Quick, *American Art: A Catalogue of the Los Angeles County Museum of Art Collection* (Los Angeles: Museum Associates, 1991), 163–164 (with a reproduction on p. 163).

[12] Blaze de Bury, "Le souper chez le commandeur," *Revue des deux mondes,* 1 June 1834, 497–558.

[13] Blaze de Bury, *Le Faust de Goethe, traduction complète précédée d'un essai sur Goethe, accompagnée de notes et de commentaires et suivie d'une étude sur la mystique du poème* (Paris: Charpentier, 1840).

[14] Blaze de Bury, *Écrivains et poètes de l'Allemagne* (Paris: Lévy, 1846).

[15] Blaze de Bury, *La jeunesse de Goethe* (Paris: Revue des deux mondes, 1857).

making 1834 production at the Paris Opéra of *Don Giovanni*, a musical and literary text that remained in use until 1896.[16]

The *Revue des deux mondes* was first published in 1829 with the intention of creating intellectual links between France and the rest of the world, or as Buloz put it in his 1829 manifesto, "to see the same principles differently understood, and applied in France and England, in Brazil and Germany, on the banks of the Delaware to the coasts of the Southern Ocean."[17] The review's focus was wide: literature and science were preferred over immediate responses to politics and current affairs, as befitted a journal published only twice a month. Blaze de Bury contributed two types of article: the larger group of around 144 reviews were of either premieres or new productions of stage music, and 43 much longer essays were opportunities to reflect on questions of music history, aesthetics, reviews of books, or more wide-ranging polemics. Although it was impossible for him to continue writing reviews of live events while he was away from Paris or under threat of immediate deportation in the period 1851–64, he published at least one essay each year in the *Revue des deux mondes,* including a series of three long essays on Rossini's life and works and a sustained article on Meyerbeer. Since the *Revue des deux mondes* was published only twice a month, Blaze de Bury was not under the same sort of pressure to produce reviews within hours of the event, and even his reviews of premieres are significantly longer than those published elsewhere.

As was the case with many successful journalists, Blaze de Bury collected his writing in two volumes: *Musiciens contemporains* was published in 1856 and *Musiciens du passé, du présent, et de l'avenir*—with a title that betrayed his interest in Wagner—in 1880.[18] And as with so many of these collections, not only does the ordering of the contents distort the original context, but the texts themselves are sometimes sanitized to bring them into line with changing fashions and fortunes. Such republication also formally revealed the authorship of the texts for the first time: Blaze de Bury had written almost exclusively under a pseudonym throughout his period at the *Revue des deux mondes,* first as Hans Werner and then as F. de Lagenevais. Whether such a revelation was of any real significance is doubtful, since the identity of the two pseudonymous authors was probably as much an

[16] See Sabine Henze-Döhring, "E. T. A. Hoffmann-'Kult' und 'Don Giovanni'—Rezeption im Paris des 19. Jahrhunderts: Castil-Blazes 'Don Juan' im Théâtre de l'Académie Royale de Musique [*sic*] am 10 März 1834," *Mozart-Jahrbuch 1984/5 des Zentralinstitutes für Mozartforschung der Internationalen Stiftung Mozarteum Salzburg* (Kassel: Bärenreiter, 1986) 39–51, and Katharine Ellis, "Rewriting *Don Giovanni*, or 'The Thieving Magpies,'" *Journal of the Royal Musical Association* 119 (1994), 212–250. The consequences of this production are discussed in chapter 4.

[17] "De voir les mêmes principes diversement compris, et appliqués en France et en Angleterre, au Brésil et en Allemagne, sur les bords de la Delaware et sur les rivages de la mer du sud" (François Buloz, "Avertissment," *Revue des deux mondes*, 1 July 1829, iii).

[18] Blaze de Bury, *Musiciens contemporains*, Collection Michel Lévy (Paris: Lévy, 1856); Blaze de Bury, *Musiciens du passé, du présent et de l'avenir*, Bibliothèque contemporaine (Paris: Calmann-Lévy, 1880).

open secret as the identity of the journalist identified as XXX: Blaze de Bury's father, François-Henri-Joseph Blaze, the redoubtable Castil-Blaze.

Mozart resides at the center of Blaze de Bury's pantheon, as a constant point of reference for his critique of contemporary instrumental and sacred works, and of music for the stage. While this was a common position to adopt in the 1830s, it was progressively more difficult to sustain after midcentury, especially when Mozart's unquestioned position was coming under greater challenge from those interested in supporting Beethoven, and—closely bound up with this question—the shifting balance in French musical circles between instrumental music and opera.

In his reception of Mozart, Blaze de Bury sits at a key point. By the time he started writing, not only were many of the key tropes in the texts surrounding the composer well established, but those that had originated in German-speaking traditions had found their way into Francophone consciousness. The issues surrounding the authorship of the *Requiem*, the contrapuntal challenges of the *Dissonance Quartet,* and the question of Mozart's supposed poisoning were already well known in French musical circles, for example, and a further one—the parallel between Mozart and Raphael—emerged during Blaze de Bury's own career.[19] In other words, Blaze de Bury's Mozart reception is shot through with the tropes that had characterized the subject for the previous forty years. So it is not surprising to find various retellings of legends associated with biographical and axiological approaches to Mozart, and in themselves their repetitions are not of importance. What is critical to an understanding of Blaze de Bury's view of Mozart, and how it contributes to the ongoing process of establishing renown, is what material he selects, how he then uses it, and the friction between claims and the evidence brought forth to support them.

Influences on Blaze de Bury's journalism are varied and complex. As Castil-Blaze's son, he defined himself almost by opposition to his father's critical positions. In all his journalism, most evidently in the *Journal des Débats* and *Le constitutionnel,* Castil-Blaze promoted a practically based, technically informed journalism the like of which had never been seen before. In doing so, he was treading the path Berlioz would follow a decade later, and from this may come some of Berlioz's particular animosity toward Castil-Blaze; when the two went head-to-head over Gluck in the late 1820s, it was in a language that only the most musically literate could understand.[20] By contrast, Blaze de Bury—clearly able as he was to write with the same level of technical control as his father—recognized that the

---

[19] For the *Requiem*, see Christoph Wolff, *Mozarts Requiem: Geschichte, Musik, Dokumente, Partitur des Fragments* (Munich: Deutscher Taschenbuch Verlag; Kassel: Bärenreiter, 1991), trans. as *Mozart's Requiem: Historical and Analytical Studies, Documents, Score* (Oxford: Clarendon, 1994); for the "Dissonance Quartet," see Julie-Anne Vertrees, "Mozart's String Quartet K. 465: The History of a Controversy," *Current Musicology* 17 (1974), 96–114.

[20] Everist, "Gluck, Berlioz and Castil-Blaze."

readership of the *Revue des deux mondes* would respond badly to the degree of technical display exhibited by his father and his adversary.

And of course, Blaze de Bury was just the writer to respond well to the eclectic readership of the *Revue des deux mondes*. Equally at home in art and literary criticism, he could call on a wide range of reference, modern, classical, and antique. Even in his commentaries on Mozart, he spoke as freely about Virgil as about Plato, about Goethe as about Beethoven, and about Racine as about Raphael. Blaze de Bury's early diplomatic career in Weimar clearly had an impact on his view of Goethe—an interest that would last most of his life—but it also sensitized him to German romanticism in general. And notwithstanding his preference for Mozart (whose national status was—as will be seen—a contentious issue for Blaze de Bury) over the more obviously German Beethoven, his appreciation of German culture was marked, most particularly by his indebtedness to E. T. A. Hoffman. This is visible in the text of his earliest essay and in publications throughout his career.[21] It remained an important part of his critical outlook, one that encouraged its 1866 description by Larousse as "imprinted with a sort of softened Germanicism."[22]

Although Blaze de Bury's reviews were significantly shorter than his essays, they by no means conformed to the usual pattern found in the daily, theatrical, or even music press, where much of the text is taken up with a serial account of the libretto, followed by a view on the music and then a commentary on the performers. Whether he is reviewing the premieres of Donizetti's *Marino Faliero* in 1835 or Bizet's *Carmen* in 1875, Blaze de Bury avoids such blow-by-blow accounts and replaces them with synoptic commentaries on the characters, the forms—duos, arias, and so on—or other routes through the work.[23] Longer essays naturally took on an even more fluid aspect, especially when they were historical—"Jean Sébastien l'organiste" (1836)—or more discursive— "La musique française: Un mot sur son avenir et son présent" (1872).[24] But occasionally, Blaze de Bury took the view that a particular premiere or revival was either so important that it warranted a full essay or that such a performance could serve as a peg on which to hang something he was likely to write anyway. His essay on the premiere of Meyerbeer's *L'africaine* is an example of the former, and an essay that dates also from

---

[21] Hans Werner [Ange-Henri Blaze], "Histoire et philosophie de l'art," *Revue des deux mondes*, 1 May 1833, 241.

[22] Pierre Larousse, "Blaze de Bury," in *Grand Dictionnaire universel du xixe siècle français, historique, géographique, biographique, mythologique, bibliographique, littéraire, artistique, scientifique, etc.*, 17 vols. (Paris: Grand Dictionnaire Universel, 1866) 2:813.

[23] Hans Werner [Ange-Henri Blaze], "Revue musicale," *Revue des deux mondes*, 15 March 1835, 724–729; F. de L[agenevais] [Ange-Henri Blaze], "*Carmen* à l'Opéra-Comique," *Revue des deux mondes*, 15 March 1875, 475–480.

[24] [Ange-]Henri Blaze, "Jean-Sébastien l'organiste," *Revue des deux mondes*, 15 September 1836, 712–754; F. de Lagenevais [Ange-Henri Blaze], "La musique française: Un mot sur son avenir et son présent," *Revue des deux mondes*, 15 February 1872, 843–849.

1865 based on an important revival of *Die Zauberflöte* at the Théâtre-Lyrique an example of the latter.[25] It is therefore the essays that—in terms of Mozart at least—embed large amounts of documentary and biographical material, and it is also here where we can see the clearest development and reinscription of preexisting tropes of Mozart reception.

Blaze de Bury's reception of Mozart circles around four nodes: (1) a set of critical positions centered on the opposition between instrumental and vocal music; (2) the appropriation of Mozart for other critical ends; (3) Mozart, improvisation, and the fantastic; and (4) the critical and axiological placement of the composer. Each will be considered in turn.

Instrumental and Vocal Music

Blaze de Bury approaches the question of the relationship between instrumental and vocal music in a variety of different ways. As early as his well-known essay on Berlioz in 1838, Blaze de Bury was drawing a distinction between contemporary *musique pittoresque* and Mozart and Cimarosa, who "addressed themselves exclusively to the human soul."[26] Mozart plays a key role in the relationship between contemporary instrumental music and opera of the previous century; at one level he is made the standard-bearer of vocal music in opposition to Beethoven. This is a simple position to defend as far as Beethoven is concerned: *Fidelio* and the large-scale sacred music can all be argued away as symphonic music, with the sorts of consequences for Blaze de Bury's later Wagner criticism that may be imagined.[27] For Mozart, it is much more problematic: in a review of an 1882 revival of *Le nozze di Figaro,* he attempts to elide the opera with the piano sonatas. Having made the point that the opera downplays much of Beaumarchais's politics—he calls it "a court comedy"—he then invokes the piano:

> Remember the world of the sonatas, it is the same thing [a court comedy] that unfolds before your eyes during the performance; fine gentlemen in silk stockings; lofty and unconstrained movement, smiling, young despite the powder and pomade which give them an old-fashioned look, noble ladies who disguise themselves as shepherdesses, pages cooing romances at the feet of their lady while the lord hunts and exercises his falcons in the *Pays de*

---

[25] F. de Lagenevais [Ange-Henri Blaze], *"L'Africaine* de Meyerbeer à l'Opéra," *Revue des mondes,* 15 May 1865, 424–446; Henri Blaze de Bury [Ange-Henri Blaze], "Mozart et *La flûte enchantée*: Souvenirs d'Allemagne," *Revue des deux mondes,* 15 March 1865, 412–445.

[26] "Ne s'adressaient jadis qu'à l'ame humaine"; [Ange-] Henri Blaze, "Musiciens français II: De l'école fantastique de M. Berlioz," *Revue des deux mondes,* 1 October 1838, 102.

[27] See Blaze de Bury's earliest view of *Fidelio* in Hans Werner [Ange-Henri Blaze], "Histoire et philosophie de l'art: I.—Beethoven," *Revue des deux mondes,* 1 May 1833, 233–257. His final commentary was in "Une nouvelle philosophie de l'opéra," *Revue des deux mondes,* 1 October 1884, 665–680.

Tendre; a ceremonial world, adorned with silver lace, flourishing with distinction, supreme and however capable of love, jealousy, even capable of naivety in its imprescriptible affection for etiquette.[28]

So, for Mozart, instrumental music and opera can inhabit exactly the same imaginary world. And nearly fifty years earlier, Blaze de Bury was already praising the composer for his melodic writing in his symphonies.[29] And, at root, Blaze de Bury's concern was essentially with the melodic as opposed to the unmelodic, and in this regard Mozart—whether in the opera house, the recital room, or the salon—could never fail.

Appropriating Mozart

No critic could pass up the opportunity to make use of a work or a composer that he relentlessly praised in order to praise or condemn another, and Blaze de Bury is no exception. Shortly after Meyerbeer's death, Blaze de Bury has Mozart give a review of a performance of *Le prophète* from the other world; the cast is stellar—in every sense.[30] Fidès is sung by Maria Malibran (died 1836), Berthe by Faustina Bordoni (one of Handel's preferred sopranos, who died in 1781), and Jean de Leyde by no less than Alessandro Stradella (who had been dead for 180 years); Mozart's own first Idomeneo—Anton Raff—is given a walk-on role (he died in 1797). And the orchestra is conducted by Gluck. It is easy for Mozart to write his review; he ends "the performance confirms the great glory of the composer, whose name was triumphantly acclaimed." As an aside, Blaze de Bury wittily apologizes to *le conteur berlinois* before launching into this piece of froth, a rare instance of Blaze de Bury trying to outdo E. T. A. Hoffmann.[31]

Less amusingly, Mozart could be used as a tool of censure, as in the case of Blaze de Bury's review of Niedermeyer's opera *Stradella*, premiered in 1837. The luxury of the costumes and of the mise-en scène of the production had been the subject of endless discussions well before the premiere, and the critic spent no small amount of time reflecting on the relationship between musical quality and the wealth of

---

[28] "Souvenez-vous du monde des *Sonates,* c'est le même qui défile devant vos yeux pendant la représentation; de beaux messieurs en bas de soie; le geste haut et familier, sourians, jeunes malgré la poudre et le fard qui leur donnent un petit air vieillot, de nobles dames qui se déguisent en bergères, des pages roucoulant la romance aux pieds de leur châtelaine, tandis que le seigneur est à la chasse et braconne au pays de Tendre; un monde cérémonieux, galonné, fleuri de distinction, suprême et pourtant capable d'amour, de jalousie, capable même de naïveté dans son imprescriptible attachement à l'étiquette" (F. de Lagenevais [Ange-Henri Blaze], "L'Opéra-Comique: *Les noces de Figaro*; Un mot sur Méhul à propos de la reprise de Joseph," *Revue des deux mondes*, 15 July 1882, 455).

[29] [Blaze d Bury], "Musiciens français II," 115.

[30] F. de Lagenevais [Ange-Henri Blaze], "Revue musicale: La reprise du *Prophète* de Meyerbeer," *Revue des deux mondes*, 1 July 1869, 250.

[31] Ibid.

the nonmusical components. He concluded that "it is from now on, between music and the mise-en-scène, a struggle to the death." Now, this was a simple—perhaps simplistic—conclusion concerning an issue that was discussed endlessly during the late 1830s. Blaze de Bury posed two hypothetical questions about Niedermeyer's music: "in what system is M. Niedermeyer's music written" and "if this time an overture would be heard"; to both, Blaze de Bury claimed that the only responses were to entirely other questions, and expressed in terms of mise-en-scène. Thus, to the question of musical system, the answer was simply "there was a Triumph at the Capitol of which marvelous things were expected," and to that of the presence of an overture, "in the fifth act the Doge was married to the Adriatic Sea." This was an ideal solution, according to Blaze de Bury, for "an ingenious and facile musician" whose attention was drawn by so many objects of so many colors, objects that ended up always by bringing delight. But for Blaze de Bury, for such a task only Mozart would be successful.[32]

But Mozart could also bring succor to contemporary composers. In an account of Donizetti's *Linda di Chamonix*, whose libretto Blaze de Bury thought had a monotonous character, or perhaps no character at all, he was quick to defend the composer, who had not quite succeeded in overcoming the weaknesses of the libretto and had failed to make sufficient use of the situations given him by the librettist. Blaze de Bury brought Mozart and *Le nozze di Figaro* to Donizetti's aid. "Mozart himself would not have acted differently," wrote Blaze de Bury. Thus, "when he found those nuances that music can not render, he idealizes, and the comic characters grow to heroic proportions.... Without being Mozart, M. Donizetti used the procedures of the master, and if we have a single complaint to make to him it is not to have used

---

[32] "Well before the performance, word was only of the unheard-of splendour of the mise-en-scène and of the variety of the costumes. If you tried to find out in what system M. Niedermeyer's music was written, you would be told that in the fourth act there was a Triumph at the Capitol of which marvellous things were expected; and if, little satisfied, you hazarded another question, asking if the master had gone against current habit at the Opéra and if this time one was to hear an overture, you would have received the response that in truth there was no overture in M. Niedermeyer's score, but that in the fifth act could be seen the marriage of the Doge with the Adriatic.... The means, in effect, when one is only an ingenious and facile musician, to attract the attention that so many objects of so many colors compete for your attention and always end up by delighting you. For such a task, you need Mozart. At the point we have reached with this insatiable visual pleasure, it is henceforth a struggle to the death between music and the mise-en-scène. Recently, music has emerged victorious, thanks to M. Meyerbeer, but also this time, it has to be said, it has failed." Bien avant la représentation, on ne parlait que du faste inouï déployé dans la mise en scène et de la variété des costumes. Si vous cherchiez à savoir dans quel système la musique de M. Niedermeyer était écrite, on vous disait qu'il y avait au quatrième acte un triomphe au Capitole dont on attendait merveille; et si, peu satisfait, vous risquiez une nouvelle question, demandant si le maître avait dérogé à la coutume usitée aujourd'hui à l'Opéra, et si l'on entendrait cette fois une ouverture, on vous répondait qu'à la vérité il n'y avait pas d'ouverture à la partition de M. Niedermeyer, mais qu'on voyait au cinquième acte le doge se marier avec l'Adriatique....Le moyen en effet, lorsque l'on n'est qu'un musicien ingénieux et facile, d'attirer sur soi l'attention que tant d'objets de toutes les couleurs vous disputent et finissent toujours par vous ravir. Pour une pareille tâche

them enough."[33] Using Mozart's practices, if not even being equal in stature to the composer, was enough here to absolve Donizetti of perceived weakness.

Wagner did not fare so well as Blaze de Bury continued to ventriloquize Mozart. In an 1875 article that reviewed books on Mozart by Francis Hueffer and Wilhelm August Ambros, Blaze de Bury took such "reformers" as Wagner to task; even Gluck did not escape opprobrium here. "Gluckisme" is portrayed as a sort of tempest that it took Mozart, "the pacifying angel," to quiet, and Mozart was able to drag from the chaos "all sorts of precious elements that Gluck in his reforming fury had thrown overboard, perhaps to the great advantage of lyric drama, but certainly to the great detriment of music."[34] Wagnerian attempts to promote Gluck's achievements, wrote Blaze de Bury, at best failed to take account of Mozart, and at worst reversed history. Mozart had "reconciled melody and drama" and had deployed the orchestra as imaginatively as Gluck, "but with what a growth of riches and what superiority of color!"[35] And as Blaze de Bury developed his view that "reformers write prefaces and large books, but it is through masterpieces that true reform is effected,"[36] he was able to declare that "all romantic opera proceeds from *Don Giovanni*" and that "*Lohengrin* is nothing other than a systematic *rifacimento* of Weber."[37]

Mozart, Improvisation, and the Fantastic

Mozart's improvisation and his relationship to the fantastic overlaps with the relationship between instrumental and vocal music, insofar as much of the discussion of

---

il faudrait Mozart. Au point où l'on en est venu avec cet insatiable plaisir des yeux, c'est désormais entre la musique et la mise en scène une lutte à mort. Dernièrement la musique en est sortie victorieuse, grace à Meyerbeer, mais aussi cette fois, il faut le dire, elle a échoué" (H[ans] W[erner] [Ange-Henri Blaze], "Revue musicale," *Revue des deux mondes*, 15 March 1837, 761–762).

[33] "Lorsqu'il se trouve de ces nuances que la musique ne peut rendre, il idéalise, et les personnages de comédie grandissent à des dimensions héroïques....Sans être Mozart, M. Donizetti a usé du procédé du maître, et, si nous avons un reproche à lui adresser, c'est d'en avoir usé trop peu" (Hans Werner [Ange-Henri Blaze], "Revue musicale," *Revue des deux mondes*, 1 December 1842, 855).

[34] "After the violent storms of *Gluckisme*, Mozart came right to the point. His face appeared as that of a pacifying angel, he quietened the storm, watched over the rescue, and pulled out of the squall all sorts of precious elements that Gluck, in his reforming fury had thrown overboard, perhaps to the great advantage of lyric drama but certainly to the great detriment of music." "Au lendemain des violens orages du *gluckisme*, Mozart arrive bien à point. Sa figure nous apparaît comme celle de l'ange pacificateur, il endort la tempête, veille au sauvetage et ravit à la bourrasque toute sorte d'élémens précieux que Gluck dans sa furie de rénovateur avait jetés par-dessus bord, peut-être au plus grand avantage du drame lyrique, mais certes au grand détriment de la musique" ([Blaze de Bury], "La musique et ses destinées," *Revue des deux mondes*, 15 October 1875, 819).

[35] "Il réconcilie la mélodie avec le drame, emploie comme Gluck l'orchestré au développement de l'expression scénique, mais avec quel accroissement de richesses et quelle supériorité de couleurs!" (ibid.).

[36] "Les réformateurs écrivent des préfaces et de gros livres, mais c'est par des chefs-d'œuvre que s'opèrent les vraies réformes" (ibid.).

[37] "De *Don Juan* [*Don Giovanni*] procède l'opéra romantique entier...*Lohengrin* n'est autre qu'un *rifacimento* systématique de la conception de Weber" (ibid.).

improvisation and the fantastic centers on the keyboard. In this respect, Blaze de Bury's commentaries on improvisation vary from three other types: vocal improvisation of cadenzas as structural points in opera, improvisation at the organ often for liturgical purposes, and the types of preludial, linking improvisation or improvisation on a given theme that characterized so much public solo piano performance in the nineteenth century. In the essay on Bach and the organ, Blaze de Bury writes as follows: "The piano exploits light and capricious melodies, stirring motifs and rapid notes; it is the instrument of fantasy, sometimes also of inspiration."[38] In another essay, one ostensibly on German artistry, he goes further and suggests that all of Mozart—including the stage music—could be revealed at the keyboard, whereas modern operatic composers (and he cites Meyerbeer) depend much more on theatrical contexts. He makes an explicit association of the keyboard with improvisation, nature, and the private:

> The other evening, I was in the country, in my room; the evening breeze began to fall, the sky to glitter with all the lustre of its stars; the tall limes in the park threw into the air a sweet and warm odor; the sounds of the day had stopped, those of the night already arose on all sides; the chattering birds were finally asleep; the little glow worms lit themselves up in the grass; from all the ponds arose, like a sonorous vapor, the monotonous song of the frogs whose plaintive and groaning voices increase the melancholy of the fine nights of summer. It is among those moments when the soul feels the need to align itself with nature and to share its joy and sadness; in these moments, the musician seats himself at the keyboard, since music has, like Solomon's key, the power to open the spirit world, and I do not know of a more certain means of penetrating the heart of nature than to abandon oneself to the adventurous wing of the senses. At this moment, if I had been Mozart, I would have improvised, and I do not doubt that the music would have soon made the tears that nature's sadness had stirred in their source run over the ivory of the keyboard. But who down here could think themselves Mozart, even in a moment of ecstasy or inspiration?[39]

---

[38] "Le piano a des chants légers et capricieux, des motifs entraînans, des notes rapides; c'est l'instrument de la fantaisie, quelquefois aussi de l'inspiration" ([Blaze de Bury], "Jean-Sébastien l'organiste," 712).

[39] "L'autre soir j'étais à la campagne, dans ma chambre; la fraîcheur commençait à tomber, le firmament à resplendir de tout l'éclat de ses lumières; les grands tilleuls du parc secouaient dans l'air une odeur douce et tiède; les bruits du jour avaient cessé, ceux de la nuit s'élevaient déjà de tous côtés; les oiseaux jaseurs s'étaient enfin endormis; les petits vers luisans s'allumaient dans l'herbe; de tous les bassins montait, comme une vapeur sonore, le chant monotone des grenouilles dont la voix plaintive et gémissante augmente encore la mélancolie des belles nuits d'été. Il est des momens où l'âme sent le besoin de se mettre en rapport avec la nature et d'en partager la joie ou la tristesse; dans ces momens, le musicien s'assied à son clavier, car la musique a, comme la clé de Salomon, le pouvoir d'ouvrir le monde des esprits, et je ne sais pas de plus sûr moyen pour pénétrer au cœur de la nature, que de s'abandonner à l'aile aventureuse des sens. A cette heure, si j'eusse été Mozart, j'aurais improvisé, et je ne doute pas que la musique n'eût bientôt fait ruisseler sur l'ivoire du clavier ces pleurs que la tristesse de la nature avait remués dans leur source; mais qui peut ici-bas se croire Mozart, même dans un moment d'extase et d'inspiration?" ([Ange-] Henri Blaze, "Poètes et musiciens d'Allemagne: Uhland et M. Dessauer," *Revue des deux mondes*, 15 October 1835, 131–132).

Blaze de Bury then goes off at a tangent onto one of his favorite themes—the unique character of *Don Giovanni* and its unassailable place at the pinnacle of operatic achievement. But in the context of his comments on the relationship between the soul and nature, he manages to create a sonorous dimension for the "melancholy of fine summer nights." Music is immediately given its esoteric power by means of an allusion to the Key of Solomon, and then Mozart is invoked, and specifically the Mozart of the keyboard, and in the context of improvisation, with the resulting music making "the tears that nature's sadness had stirred in their source run over the ivory of the keyboard." The link between Mozart's improvisation, the piano, and nature is made explicit before Blaze de Bury takes us off back into the mundane with "But who could think themselves Mozart?"

Although Blaze begins this account of Mozart's keyboard music with a *Lied* by Dessauer, it is not quite clear what genre is in play as he moves on to this remarkable account of Mozartian improvisation at the keyboard. If there is a possible comparison with any notated music, the d minor Fantasia, K. 397, is a plausible candidate (ex. 7.1).

So in a work that could well have been composed as a prelude, we have a range of improvisatory topics run together, sometimes with the crudest of breaks between them, cadenzas breaking out of apparently nowhere, all pointing toward the sort of improvisation Blaze de Bury may have had in mind.[40]

Mozart: Critical and Axiological Positioning

Placing Mozart was absolutely key to Blaze de Bury's view of him, and the place changed according to context and date. Blaze de Bury began his career as a music critic at the *Revue des deux mondes* when Italian opera in Paris was negotiating the arrival of new works by Bellini and Donizetti and the teams of artists that supported them: Grisi, Rubini, Tamburini, and so on. Two of his earliest reviews were of the competing works from Bellini and Donizetti from 1835 *I Puritani* and *Marino Faliero*.[41] But Blaze de Bury was just as interested in the traditional repertory of the Théâtre Italien, and it is here that he places Mozart clearly among the Italian classics. Halfway through the 1836 season, he pauses to praise the Italian Opera in Paris:

> Italian opera is successful; indeed, would you want it any other way? There is
> Mozart, Cimarosa, and Rossini for the important days, and in the intervals Bellini

---

[40] For the view of the d minor Fantasia, K. 397, as a prelude to a larger work, see Kenneth Hamilton, *After the Golden Age: Romantic Pianism and Modern Performance* (New York: Oxford University Press, 2008), 106.

[41] For *I Puritani*, see Hans Werner [Ange-Henri Blaze], "Revue musicale," *Revue des deux mondes*, 1 February 1835, 341–346; for *Marino Faliero*, see [Hans] W[erner] [Ange-Henri Blaze], "Revue musicale," 15 March 1835, 724–729.

EXAMPLE 7.1: *Mozart, Fantasia in* d minor, *K. 397, opening.*

and Donizetti, with their marvelous performers. On the one hand, it is the spirit
of the work that interests us, on the other it is the spirit of the performance.[42]

Mozart, Cimarosa, and Rossini are Blaze de Bury's classics, then, where the work
is central, and Bellini and Donizetti are reduced to the sidelines—their success
entirely contingent on the spirit of performance. And given that Mozart and Cimarosa were both dead (1791 and 1801, respectively), it is hardly surprising that
Rossini is occasionally dismissed from this triumvirate: "Mozart, Cimarosa, and
Rossini; they are the eternal guests of the Salle Favart. The compositions of these
great masters, of the first two especially, are still full of youth and future,"[43] and in
the rest of this 1834 article dedicated to the Parisian premiere of Donizetti's *Anna
Bolena*, his point of reference excludes Rossini to the profit of Cimarosa and
Mozart.

In opposition to this positioning of Mozart as an Italianate classic, Blaze de
Bury also sets Mozart up among the Germans:

> There is a striking alliance between poetry, music, and painting which it is
> impossible not to perceive, except by closing one's eyes or by being blind.
> I could cite in support of what I propose ten victorious and generous exam-
> ples from the names of Beethoven, Mozart, and Weber.[44]

The trilogy of these three composers was a consistent point of reference as Blaze
de Bury developed his critical stance during the 1830s and 40s, but Mozart was
always slightly difficult to absorb into this discourse. In an account of German
vocal music, Blaze de Bury observes how German composers "disdain the human
voice like a useless and parasitical instrument" and then goes on to say "I don't
know, but it seems to me that Mozart did not act this way."[45] And in a retrospective view of the previous fifty years published in 1838, Blaze de Bury sets up a
clear and unambiguous opposition between German and Italian music:

---

[42] "L'opéra italien réussit; en vérité, comme voulez-vous qu'il en soit autrement? Il y a là Mozart,
Cimarosa et Rossini pour les grands jours, et dans les intervalles Bellini et Donizetti, avec leurs inter-
prètes merveilleux. Ici, c'est le génie de l'œuvre qui nous attache; là, c'est le génie de l'exécution" (H[ans]
W[erner] [Ange-Henri Blaze], 'Revue musicale,' *Revue des deux mondes*, 1 January 1837, 110). The
position of Rossini in 1837 is a problematic one for Paris. Eight years after his last operatic success in the
capital, he had recently returned to Bologna, thus sparking a series of discourses around his creative
death. See Mark Everist, "'Il n'y a qu'un Paris au monde, et j'y reviendrai planter mon drapeau!' Rossini's
Second *Grand Opéra*," *Music & Letters* 90 (2009), 636–672.

[43] "Mozart, Cimarosa et Rossini, voilà les hôtes éternels de la salle Favart. Les compositions de ces
grands maîtres, des deux premiers surtout, sont encore pleines de jeunesse et d'avenir" (H[ans]
W[erner] [Ange-Henri Blaze], "Revue musicale," *Revue des deux mondes*, 15 December 1834, 770).

[44] "Il y a entre la poésie, la musique et la peinture, une alliance éclatante qu'il est impossible de ne
pas apercevoir, à moins de fermer les yeux ou d'être aveugle. Je pourrais citer à l'appui de ce que j'avance
dix exemples victorieux et forts des noms de Beethoven, de Mozart ou de Weber" ([Blaze de Bury],
"Poètes et musiciens d'Allemagne," 155).

[45] "Ils dédaignent la voix humaine comme un instrument inutile et parasite....Je ne sais, mais il me
semble que Mozart n'agissait pas ainsi" ([Blaze de Bury], "Uhland et M. Dessauer," *Revue des deux
mondes*, 15 October 1835, 152.

What a magnificent sight during the last fifty years! What an admirable succession of geniuses and masterpieces! On the one hand it is Mozart, Cimarosa, Rossini on the other, Mozart again, Beethoven and Weber; here *Il matrimonio segreto, Le nozze di Figaro, Otello, Semiramide*; there *Don Giovanni, Fidelio, Euryanthe, Der Freischütz,* and [Beethoven's] symphonies. Two majestic and sonorous rivers, that flow across the earth's beautiful landscapes, and go to the ocean without mixing their waters.[46]

Here Mozart is completely divided between the two traditions: *Le nozze di Figaro* on the one hand, *Don Giovanni* on the other. For Blaze de Bury, these are representatives of "majestic rivers that flow to the ocean without mixing their waters." He embeds these works in the opposition set up between Cimarosa and Rossini on the one side, Beethoven and Weber on the other, with Mozart perfectly poised between the two.

Such a positioning between German and Italian musical traditions is conditioned by an overriding sense of the absolute status of Mozart. Although this often has to be inferred from his writing, when Blaze de Bury is confronted with a composer who seeks to place another above Mozart, he makes his position clear. In the context of an essay on Berlioz—whose public view was that Beethoven should occupy the summit of musical achievement—Blaze de Bury felt the need to make his view of Mozart explicit:

Up till now, Mozart occupied a distinctive throne in the heavens of music, that no one had yet dared contest; below him, far away from the ethereal spheres where they had been blown by the winds of his melodies, floated the terrestrial clouds of other immortals.[47]

It is easy to imagine how Blaze de Bury would go on to develop this particular set of images in his defense of Mozart against the claims of Berlioz and Beethoven.

It was impossible for an author with such a wide frame of literary reference as Blaze de Bury to avoid other sorts of parallels—Mozart and Homer, Mozart and Boccaccio, and so on. But when he set up Mozart among other composers, it was always to give him an absolute and uncontested status at the same time as placing

---

[46] "Quel spectacle magnifique pendant les cinquante années qui viennent de s'écouler! quelle admirable succession de génies et de chefs-d'œuvre! D'un côté, c'est Mozart, Cimarosa, Rossini; de l'autre, encore Mozart, Beethoven et Weber; ici *le Mariage secret, les Noces de Figaro, Otello, Sémiramis*; là *Don Juan, Fidelio, Eurianthe, Freyschütz, les Symphonies.* On dirait deux grands fleuves majestueux et sonores, qui s'épanchent à travers les belles campagnes de la terre, et vont à l'océan sans confondre leurs eaux" ([Blaze de Bury], "Musiciens français II," 97–98).

[47] "Jusqu'ici Mozart occupait dans le ciel de la musique un trône à part, que nul n'avait encore osé lui contester; au-dessous de lui, bien loin des sphères éthérées ou l'avait poussé le vent formé de ses mélodies, flottaient les nuages terrestres des autres immortels" ([Blaze de Bury], "Musiciens français II," 99).

him either among the Italians, Rossini and Cimarosa, or among the Germans, Beethoven and Weber, or among both.

Later in his career, Blaze de Bury cast his net more widely for contexts in which Mozart could be placed and praised. Two are important: dramatists and the proverbial. In speaking of drama, Mozart could be aligned with Goethe and Shakespeare—both of whom had been absent from earlier, purely musical, contexts for Mozart—with specific works as emblematic: *Hamlet, Faust,* and *Don Giovanni.* Here, the national completely gave way to a pan-European context driven only by the idea of the dramatic. Similarly, Blaze de Bury made claims for Mozart that he had become proverbial: "you have [the melodies of *Don Giovanni*] so much," he wrote, "in your soul and in your spirit like certain lines of Virgil or Racine."[48] This was in the context of the multiple existences of *Don Giovanni* on multiple stages and in multiple versions, and again the placement of Mozart transcends the national, as found in Blaze de Bury's early writing, and achieves the status of the modern alongside the classical and the antique.

But one unchanging trope in Blaze de Bury's writing on Mozart was the parallel with Raphael. Such a comparison goes back at least to 1798 and Franz Xaver Niemetschek's biography of Mozart, and was formalized in Friedrich Rochlitz's article in the *Allgemeine musikalische Zeitung* of June 1800, and thereafter into the works of E. T. A. Hoffmann and Goethe, among others.[49] It is not at all clear that Blaze de Bury was familiar with this tradition; his *point d'appui* seems to have been a reference in Da Ponte's *Memorie*:

> "Raphael," said Da Ponte, "the angel Raphael, dead at thirty-seven years, lives again among us, and is called Mozart."[50]

One of Blaze de Bury's first attempts to spin this particular thread had Mozart and Raphael exchanging arts:

> Let Mozart contemplate the colors of beautiful nature; let Raphael listen to voices sing; let these two glorious angels change worlds so that they may return carrying on their wings a luminous and sonorous dust.[51]

---

[48] "vous les avez dans l'âme et dans l'esprit, comme certains vers de Virgile ou de Racine" (F. de Lagenevais [Ange-Henri Blaze], "Revue musicale; Le grand opéra à la salle Ventadour," *Revue des mondes,* 1 February 1874, 713).

[49] Franz Xaver Niemetschek, *Leben des K. K. Kapellmeisters Wolfgang Gottlieb Mozart, nach Originalquellen beschrieben* (Prague: Herrlisch 1798). For the trope in Rochlitz, see Konrad, "Friedrich Rochlitz und die Entstehung des Mozart-Bildes um 1800."

[50] "Raphaël, disait l'abbé Da Ponte, l'ange Raphaël, mort jadis à trente-sept ans, revit aujourd'hui parmi nous, et s'appelle Mozart" ([Blaze de Bury], "Mozart et *La flûte enchantée*: Souvenirs d'Allemagne," 420).

[51] "Que Mozart regarde les couleurs de la belle nature, que Raphaël écoute les voix chanter, que ces deux anges glorieux changent de monde, pour s'en revenir emportant sur leurs ailes une poussière lumineuse et sonore" ([Blaze de Bury], "Jean-Sébastien l'organiste," 732).

And as late as 1878, Blaze de Bury was still pairing Mozart with Raphael in an impassioned plea for the primacy of what he called "pure art": "A profession implies a people; art implies a people, even more a man. But I speak there of pure art, the art of Raphael... of Mozart."[52] The comparison between Mozart and Raphael was an important one for Blaze de Bury, and one he was committed to exploiting further in his criticism. In an essay from 1865, he brings both artists into alignment as a critical tool in an account of *Die Zauberflöte*.

Mozart, Raphael, and *Die Zauberflöte*

The manner in which Blaze de Bury develops the trope of "Mozart and Raphael" illustrates well the way this critic takes a particular idea, assimilates it to his own critical praxis, and goes on to make it undertake cultural work of a very distinct sort. His essay from 1865 on *Die Zauberflöte* gives the parallelism between Mozart and Raphael a concrete and specific form. This is combined with a diagnosis of two pairs of registers in play in the opera: the low-born Papageno and Papagena and the high-born Tamino and Pamina on the one hand and on the other the mortal, represented by those four characters, and the eternal—Sarastro, Die Königin des Nacht, the Drei Knaben, and other denizens of the world of what we today know as act 2.

So Blaze de Bury is taking what is by 1865 a well-worn trope—Mozart and Raphael—and trying to make it do highly focused and precise work in a critical context. But as will be seen, Blaze loses contact with the logic of reality, fails to establish any real link between the components of his argument, and—this is the important part—uses his critical skills simply to shower a lexicon of metaphysical praise on the work, exerting a crude but powerful canonic pressure.

This is a big essay running to just under fifteen thousand words, in which Blaze de Bury mingles a critique of the work with a good deal of biographical and historical material, which in turn provides the trigger for various unrelated anecdotes, a clever synopsis not of the opera but of Wieland's *Dschinnistan*, on which Blaze de Bury thought the libretto was exclusively based, all of which frames the central concern of the registral placement of the cast, the action, and the music. He begins with a lengthy account of the circumstances of composition of the work, stressing Mozart's sojourn in Schikaneder's summer house, and how Schikaneder set up a series of alternations of composition and pleasure. Blaze de Bury points out the similarity of these Viennese amusements to the naïve innocence of Papageno and Papagena, and goes further: "Tamino, Pamina, Sarastro, all the priests of Isis and Osiris... are they not also Vien-

---

[52] "Le métier suppose un peuple, l'art suppose un peuple, plus un homme. Mais je parle là de l'art pur, de l'art des Raphaël, des Mozart" (F. de Lagenevais [Ange-Henri Blaze], "Le budget des beaux-arts et la question musicale," *Revue des deux mondes*, 1 April 1878, 706).

nese?"[53] Neither the truth nor the precision of this claim is at issue here; its implausibility has to be taken as a critical ploy as Blaze de Bury attempts to link the Viennese bourgeois preparations for the opera into the plot of the opera itself.

Developing the idea of the pleasures with which Mozart alternated work on *Die Zauberflöte*, Blaze de Bury launches into an account of Mozart's affections for the two Weber sisters, Aloysia and Constanze, coupled to an account of what he sees as Mozart's libertine behavior and its relationship to creativity. Mozart ends up married to Constanze, but has little to offer that he does not put into his music, and at the same time pursues a life of debauchery. This puts the author in a position where he can move straight into a parallel with Raphael. The two artists, then—and Raphael's libertine existence, coupled to his aristocratic professional life, is well documented from Vasari onward—combine creative professional lives with debauched private ones.[54] They both have idealized females in their lives: for Mozart it is his wife's sister Aloysia Weber and for Raphael it is of course La Fornarina. And while Mozart's creative response to his muse finds its way into seven arias and a role in *Der Schauspieldirektor*, Raphael's is manifest in the painting *La Fornarina*. This elision of Mozart and Raphael is Blaze de Bury's prompt to take us into the Raphael canon as part of his explication of *Die Zauberflöte* (fig. 7.1)":[55]

> Who does not have the portrait of *La Fornarina* before their eyes, a splendid and fatal image of a model equally marked by the double sign of beauty and mortality? Rarely has something equally marvelous been painted as this arm gently rounded on the chest, and those eyes, is there anything more voluptuously shaded, sweeter, more carnally diabolical? A siren, woman, nymph, one gets the sense of perdition.[56]

Blaze de Bury here signs up unreservedly to the idea, widespread in the nineteenth century, that in *La Fornarina* Raphael lightly concealed a cancerous condition in a conventional artistic presentation of love. Blaze de Bury then sets up an opposition between *La Fornarina* with another of Raphael's best known canvases: the *Self-Portrait* (fig. 7.2).[57]

---

[53] "Tamino, Pamina, Sarastro, tous ces prêtres d'Isis et d'Osiris...ne sont-ils pas aussi des Viennois?" ([Blaze de Bury], "Mozart et *La flûte enchantée*," 419).

[54] Giorgio Vasari, *Le Vite de' piu eccellenti pittori, scultori, e architettori...di nuouo...riuiste et ampliate con i ritratti loro et con l'aggiunta delle Vite de' viui, & de' morti dall'anno 1550 insino al 1567...Con le tauole in ciascun volume, delle cose piu notabili, de' ritratti, delle vite degli artefici, et dei luoghi doue sono l'opere loro*, 3 vols. (Florence: Giunti, 1568), trans. by George Bull as *Lives of the Artists* (London: Penguin, 1987; reprint, With '2003), 197–199, (p. nos. refer to 1987 trans.).

[55] *La Fornarina*, probably painted between 1518 and 1520, is now in the Galleria Nazionale d'Arte Antica in the Palazzo Barberini, Rome.

[56] "Qui n'a présent devant les yeux le portrait de la Fornarina, image splendide et fatale d'un modèle également marqué du double signe de la beauté et de la fatalité? Rarement on a peint quelque chose d'aussi merveilleux que ce bras mollement arrondi sur la poitrine, et ces yeux, vit-on jamais rien de plus voluptueusement ombré, de plus doux, de plus charnellement diabolique? Sirène, femme, ondine, on sent que c'est la perdition" ([Blaze de Bury], "Mozart et *La flûte enchantée*," 422).

[57] Probably from c. 1506, the self-portrait is now in the Galleria degli Uffizi, Florence.

FIGURE 7.1: *Raphael,* La Fornarina

FIGURE 7.2: *Raphael,* Self Portrait

Now from this *Fornarina* approach in your mind's eye that portrait in the Borghese Gallery where the young Raphael represented himself, his glance burning with a dark flame, his lip moist, moved, as if to call out for pleasure. Poor child, you will cry out, who as long as he enlightens the world, consumes himself! She [*La Fornarina*] however bursts out with health, well-being; he is nothing but pallor, desire, suffering: you would say an ethereal substance, a soul reproduced by the magic of the finest, the most delicate, paintbrush. For her, it is the body, the form, in its triumphant harmony, the superb *contadina*, impassive, fatal, who allows herself to be loved in the same way as she allows herself to be painted, because she is beautiful.[58]

And the connection with Mozart is now made explicit via reference again to the Viennese maelstrom in which he found himself:

Thus I present again the melancholy, the ardent and mystic Mozart thrown by his libertinage as prey to all these sirens, half German and half Slav, of the Viennese whirlpool. Mystical and libertine, a believing soul, a spirit of scepticism and twisted senses, the example is too often seen for one to wonder at it![59]

So Blaze de Bury has set up a parallel between Mozart and Raphael, largely in biographical terms, with a focus on love and death. As he admits that the mysticism in *Die Zauberflöte* may challenge the intellectual endurance of audiences, he ironically acknowledges that there might be paintings and literary works more "amusing" than Raphael's *Transfiguration* and Plato's dialogues; this does not mean, he adds, that the *Phaedrus* does not have some value nor that the *Transfiguration* is not worth consideration. These are central works for Blaze de Bury's reading of *Die Zauberflöte*.

Raphael's *Transfiguration* (fig. 7.3)[60] should be read alongside Blaze de Bury's commentary:

---

[58] "Maintenant de cette Fornarina rapprochez par la pensée ce portrait de la galerie Borghèse où le jeune Raphaël s'est représenté lui-même, le regard embrasé de flamme sombre, la lèvre humide, émue, comme pour appeler la jouissance. Pauvre enfant, vous écrierez-vous, qui, tandis qu'il éclaire le monde, va soi-même se consumant! Elle cependant éclate de santé, d'embonpoint; lui n'est que pâleur, désir, souffrance: vous diriez une substance éthérée, une âme reproduite par la magie du pinceau le plus fin, le plus délicat. Elle, c'est le corps, c'est la forme, dans sa triomphante harmonie, la contadine superbe, impassible, fatale, qui se laisse aimer comme elle se laisse peindre, parce qu'elle est belle" ([Blaze de Bury, "Mozart et *La flûte enchantée*," 422–423).

[59] "Ainsi je me représente le mélancolique, l'ardent et mystique Mozart jeté par son libertinage en proie à toutes ces sirènes, moitié allemandes et moitié slaves, du gouffre viennois. Mystique et libertin, âme croyante, esprit sceptique et sens débauchés, l'exemple s'est vu trop souvent pour qu'on s'en émerveille!" ([Blaze de Bury], "Mozart et *La flûte enchantée*," 423).

[60] The *Transfiguration* was incomplete at Raphael's death in 1520, and may have been completed by Giulio Romano. It is now housed in the Pinacoteca Vaticana, Vatican City.

Impossible, on the other hand, to listen to this ideal score by Mozart ... without being struck, as in the Raphael painting, by this opposition between the terrestrial group, agitated in the lower part of the image, and the transfigured group that dominates the upper part in pure light. After this first act, that takes place on the real earth, where, with ravishing grace, distinction, enjoyment, the music seems not to breathe, to distribute around it nothing but exaltation, songs of life, here suddenly with the entry of the three spirits, the accents of a superior world.[61]

FIGURE 7.3: *Raphael,* Transfiguration

---

[61] "Impossible par contre d'écouter cette idéale partition de Mozart ... sans être frappé, comme dans le tableau de Raphaël, de cette opposition du groupe terrestre qui s'agite en bas et du groupe transfiguré

Exactly how this transposition of registers from opera to canvas should function is open to discussion: presumably Christ, Moses, and Elijah represent Sarastro and supernatural beings "in pure light," as Blaze de Bury puts it, and Papageno and Papagena form part of the terrestrial group, largely oblivious to events beyond their own current preoccupations. It could be argued that Pamina and Tamino should be there as well, but a group of intermediary figures in the middle of the canvas are clearly more engaged with the transfigured, and Blaze de Bury might have been happy to identify these with Tamino and Pamina: mortals with a more enlightened appreciation for the divine than the terrestrial bird catcher and his mate. His comparison of the canvas and the dramatis personae does not however extend this far.

Blaze de Bury's reference to the three spirits takes him directly to his parallel between Mozart and Raphael, the relationship between the metaphysical and the real, and the music of *Die Zauberflöte*. In particular, he uses these observations both to embed the parallels between Mozart and Raphael in a single work and to attempt an elision between the two artists' biographies and specific musical techniques.

For Blaze, the appearance of the three spirits at the beginning of Mozart's act 1 finale marks the change from terrestrial to celestial: from the bottom half of Raphael's transfiguration to the top. Blaze de Bury's three spirits are Mozart's Drei Knaben—roles that were given to women's voices in the 1865 production of *Die Zauberflöte* at the Théâtre-Lyrique that was Blaze de Bury's prompt for the essay.[62] The Drei Knaben make three further appearances in the opera—in the act 2 trio and twice in the act 2 finale:

1. Act 1 finale (no. 8): "Zum Ziele führt dich diese Bahn" [lead Tamino into the Temple, and offer words of advice]
2. Act 2 terzetto (no. 16): "Seid uns zum zweitenmal wilkommen" [return flute to Tamino and bells to Papageno]
3. Act 2 finale (no. 21): "Bald prangt, den Morgen zu verkünden" [dissuade Tamina from suicide and introduce her to Tamino]
4. Act 2 finale (no. 21): "Halt ein, halt ein! O Papageno" [dissuade Papageno from suicide and introduce him to Papagena]

---

qui plane en haut dans la pure lumière. Après ce premier acte, qui marche sur le sol réel, où, ravissante de grâce, de distinction, d'enjouement, la musique semble ne respirer, ne répandre autour d'elle que les ivresses, les chansons de la vie, voici tout à coup, avec l'entrée des trois génies, des accens d'un monde supérieur" ([Blaze de Bury], "Mozart et *La flûte enchantée*," 432).

[62] The production was premiered on 23 February 1865 in a translation by Nuitter and Beaumont, and in which not only were the *drei Knaben* sung by women (Mlles Daram, Willème, and Peyret) but three female artists also sang the roles of the *drei Damen* (Mlles Albrecht, Fonti, and Estagel). See THÉ-ATRE-LYRIQUE IMPÉRIAL / LA FLÛTE ENCHANTÉE / DE / MOZART / OPÉRA EN QUATRE ACTES / REPRÉSENTÉ AU THÉATRE-LYRIQUE IMPÉRIAL LE 23 FÉVRIER 1865 / TRADUCTION FRANÇAISE / DE / MM. NUITTER & BEAUMONT / ... / PARIS / Au MÉNESTREL, 2 bis, rue Vivienne / HEUGEL ET Cie, iii.

His account of the music for the three soprano voices goes back to eighteenth-century *opera seria,* a genre that, he observes, was written for sopranos and tenors—high voices, "as if high pitch could alone suit the expression of the musical sublime." He continues:

> In multiplying in his work the soprano parts to the point of rendering its execution so difficult, has Mozart only obeyed this law, or rather has his own perspicacity not shown him, that no voice more than the soprano is better at rendering these ideas of purity, of elevation of style, of eternal truth, which form the psychological theme which he has extracted from the sort of chaotic rhapsody offered his imagination?[63]

He sets up his discussion with the qualities he associates exclusively with the soprano voice: purity, elevated style, eternal truth. Although purity and eternal truth may have enough behind them to keep one guessing about Blaze de Bury's meaning for some time, "élévation"—though translated here as "elevated style"—has at least as much the meaning of a moral or spiritual elevation and possibly a elevation toward God as well.

Blaze de Bury then walks his readers through the second and third appearances of the three spirits: the terzetto in act 2 and the introduction of the act 2 finale. Again, for Blaze de Bury, the terzetto exhibits a supernatural and seraphic quality "admirably expressed by these violin figures with such a suavity that you would say it was the beating of wings on the strings" (ex. 7.2).[64]

But as soon as Blaze de Bury turns to a concrete example, his evidence for "this supernatural, seraphic character" is not the quality of the concerted soprano voices but the scoring, specifically the violin phrases. Nevertheless, he reserves his greatest praise for the opening of the act 2 finale: "It is especially in the introduction to the second finale that this divine splendor explodes and radiates out" (ex. 7.3).[65]

He goes on in the same vein, mixing analogies to Dante and to Fénelon: "the soul drowned in a sweet, kindly light…the idea of a vision of Paradise."[66] And he brings us back to Raphael, and the conjunction of the metaphysical and the real: "What ought only to be allegory becomes the most charming reality, and these adorable spirits, like Raphael's angels, only touch the supernatural with their

---

[63] "En multipliant dans son ouvrage les parties de soprano à ce point d'en rendre l'exécution si diffi-cile, Mozart n'a-t-il fait qu'obéir à cette loi, ou plutôt sa propre clairvoyance ne lui a-t-elle pas démontré que nulle voix plus que le soprano n'était de nature à rendre ces idées de pureté, d'élévation, de vérité éternelle, qui forment le thème psychologique dégagé par lui de l'espèce de chaotique rapsodie offerte à son imagination?" ([Blaze de Bury], "Mozart et *La flûte enchantée*," 432).

[64] "Admirablement exprimé par ces traits de violon d'une suavité telle qu'on dirait des battemens d'ailes sur les cordes" (ibid., 434).

[65] "Mais c'est surtout dans l'introduction du second finale qu'éclate et rayonne en sa plénitude cette splendeur du divin" (ibid.).

[66] "L'âme inondée d'une lumière douce, bienfaisante…l'idée d'une vision du paradis dantesque traversant l'âme d'un Fénelon!" (ibid.).

EXAMPLE 7.2: *Mozart,* Die Zauberflöte, *act 2 terzetto, opening.*

haloes, since, for the heart, they are human, but of a purified and sublimated humanity."[67] But again, he directs his readers' attention not to the soprano voices, which was his starting point; rather, he looks at the scoring for woodwinds. He writes: "The instrumentation of this trio plunges you into a state of ravishment."[68]

---

[67] "Ce qui semblait devoir n'être qu'allégorie devient la réalité la plus charmante, et ces adorables génies, comme les anges de Raphaël, ne touchent au surnaturel que par leurs nimbes, car, pour le coeur, ils sont humains, mais d'une humanité épurée, sublimée" (ibid.).

[68] "L'instrumentation de ce trio vous plonge dans le ravissement" (ibid.).

EXAMPLE 7.3: *Mozart, Die Zauberflöte, act 3 finale, opening.*

There is a serious disconnect in Blaze de Bury's account of the music for the Drei Knaben: the inventory of the attributes of this music is impressive:

- Purity
- Elevation of style
- Eternal truth
- The supernatural
- Seraphic
- The splendor of the divine

- The soul drowned in a sweet and kindly light
- A vision of paradise
- A purified and sublimated humanity

But his evidence at the beginning of the account, where he can speak in the abstract about the qualities of this music, centers on the soprano voice; where he tries to turn to the specific, to bring musical material into the argument, he shifts focus and moves to a discussion of instrumentation, which in turn leaves him free to return to the argument—made as ever by nothing more than assertion—of Mozart's equivalence to Raphael.

Blaze de Bury brings his essay on *Die Zauberflöte* to a close as follows:

> From now on divine beauty and human beauty will be one only; no more antagonism between the two principles, no more struggle as in the Middle Ages: the ideal in the sensual, the infinite in the finite, music that, if something could equal it, would find its point of comparison only in the sculpture of the Greeks or in the painting of Raphael.[69]

Having begun this paragraph with Beethoven's well-known view of *Die Zauberflöte*—that it was the first time that Mozart showed himself as a German composer, and that

---

[69] "Désormais le beau divin et le beau humain ne font qu'un; plus d'antagonisme des deux principes, de lutte comme au moyen âge: l'idéal dans le sensuel, l'infini dans le fini, une musique qui, si quelque chose pouvait l'égaler, ne trouverait son terme de comparaison que dans la plastique des Grecs ou la peinture de Raphaël" (ibid., 445).

it was his greatest masterpiece—Blaze de Bury recapitulates many of the themes developed in the previous fifteen thousand words. He goes back to the tendentious claims of the equivalences between Mozart, his characters, and the late eighteenth-century Viennese bourgeoisie by aligning divine and human beauty, but his closing shot could not be clearer. Any comparison with Mozart would have to involve Raphaël.

Blaze de Bury is a key player in the history of nineteenth-century French music criticism. In his unswerving enthusiasm for Mozart, which shifted over the course of fifty years from the conventional in the 1830s to perhaps the eccentric in the 1880s, he is an important figure in the reception of Mozart, not just in France but across Europe and beyond—the second of the two worlds in the title of the journal for which he wrote. He engages with Mozart at a number of levels, and puts him to a number of different uses, all of which constitute both sites of reception and pressures on the canon.

If there remains any doubt that the currency in which Blaze de Bury traded is still legal tender, two quotations are apposite:

> In short, [Mozart's] place in the artistic pantheon is as secure as those of Shakespeare, Raphael and Goethe.

> There was scarcely any conversation about Shakespeare that did not lead to Raphael and Michelangelo and then to Mozart.

The first is from the 2003 introduction to *The Cambridge Companion to Mozart*, the second from an 1875 essay by Blaze de Bury.[70] One could be forgiven for viewing them as more or less interchangeable. And while one is tempted to quote the words of the 1840s editor of *Le Figaro*, Jean-Baptiste Alphonse Karr—"Plus ça change, plus c'est la même chose"—the parallel points clearly to one of the recurrent themes in this book: the degree to which axiological and critical judgments on Mozart that have been made in the last two hundred–odd years still find a place in the critical language and aesthetics of the present.

---

[70] Simon Keefe, introduction to *The Cambridge Companion to Mozart* (Cambridge: Cambridge University Press, 2003), 2. "Il n'y avait guère de conversation sur Shakspeare [Shakespeare] qui ne vous conduisît à Raphaël et à Michel-Ange pour se terminer par Mozart" ([Blaze de Bury], "Revue musicale: Le nouveau théâtre lyrique, l'administration de l'Opéra," *Revue des deux mondes*, 1 August 1875, 718).

8

Speaking with the Supernatural

E. T. A. HOFFMANN, GEORGE BERNARD SHAW, AND *DIE OPER ALLER OPERN*

Chapter 2 of *Mozart's Ghosts* has already shown how Mozart could be embodied in literature, and how that embodiment could, as the literary work is transformed into other media, be weakened or strengthened. And in such literary traditions of embodying Mozart that have already been outlined in this book, no opera figures more widely than *Don Giovanni*.[1] The roll call of authors who have written imaginative fiction, of whatever genre, that touches on Mozart's and Da Ponte's opera reads like a *livre d'or* of nineteenth- and twentieth-century literature.[2] Such texts could be, and have been, interpreted according to a model of reception in which a work serves as a subject for the imaginative production of composers, writers on music, and literary figures who translate the work into other genres. The weakness of this model, derived from literary criticism of the 1960s and widely employed in contemporary musicological writing,[3] is that it too often fails to take account of

---

[1] General studies of the *Don Giovanni* legend abound. See Georges Gendarme de Bévotte, *La Légende de Don Juan*, 2 vols. (Paris: Hachette, 1911); Oscar Mandel, *The Theatre of Don Juan: A Collection of Plays and Views, 1630–1963* (Lincoln: University of Nebraska Press, 1963); Jean Rousset, *Le Myth de Don Juan* (Paris: Armand Colin, 1976; reprint, Prismes Littéraires 1994); John William Smeed, *Don Juan: Variations on a Theme* (London: Routledge, 1990); Jean Massin, *Don Juan: Myth littéraire et musical* (Paris: Éditions Complexe, 1993). For studies of *Don Giovanni* in the field of literature, see Erdmann Werner Böhme, "Mozart in der schönen Literatur (Drama, Roman, Novelle, Lyrik)," in *Bericht über die musikwissenschaftlicheTagung der Internationalen Stiftung Mozarteum in Salzburg vom 2. bis 5. August 1931* (Leipzig: Breitkopf und Härtel, 1931), 179–297; Böhme, "Mozart in der schönen Literatur: Ergänzungen und Fortsetzung," *Mozart-Jahrbuch 1959 des Zentralinstitutes für Mozartforschung der Internationalen Stiftung Mozarteum Salzburg* (1959), 165–187.

[2] See above, 11–12.

[3] The most accessible (but also one of the most contentious) statements about the study of reception in music history is Carl Dahlhaus, *Grundlagen der Musikgeschichte*, Musiktaschenbücher: Theoretica 13 (Cologne: Hans Gerig, 1977), trans. by J. R. Robinson as *Foundations of Music History* (Cambridge: Cambridge University Press, 1983), 150–165 (p. nos. refer to English trans.). For the most recent review of the question of reception studies in music history see Mark Everist, "Reception Theories, Canonic Discourses and Musical Value," in *Rethinking Music*, ed. Nicholas Cook and Mark Everist (Oxford: Oxford University Press, 1999), 378–402, and the sources cited there.

the changes to the work at its sites of reception; this is especially manifest, for example, in a reluctance to accept the event-based nature of opera and in the resulting instability of the operatic text. Were such an approach coupled to questions of the status of the musical work, such a methodology would be fruitful and rewarding. In the case of *Don Giovanni*, this would reflect a sensitivity to not only the so-called Prague and Vienna versions of the work, but also the various transformations it underwent throughout the nineteenth and twentieth centuries.[4] Too often, accounts of a work's reception focus on a trial of the text against a putative "original" version, whose nature is never made explicit. This model of reception cannot, however, take account of all the ways such a work as *Don Giovanni* interacts with nineteenth-century culture. A single case study, where the patterns of reception are more complex, shows that the model of Mozart's opera reappearing in the literary or musical work of another—or indeed the concept of "Mozart reception"—is simply insufficient to explain fully how Mozart's opera was received in the nineteenth century; it provides a valuable counterweight to the prevailing trajectories of *Don Giovanni* reception. The case study—of a short story by George Bernard Shaw and its origins—will show that although the author was ostensibly claiming to do one thing, writing a story about *Don Giovanni*, he was in fact undertaking very different cultural work, and reflecting on E. T. A. Hoffmann's better known story based on the opera.

The two texts that constitute this case study in the literary reception of *Don Giovanni* are E. T. A. Hoffmann's "Don Juan: Eine fabelhafte Begebenheit, die sich mit einem reisendem Enthusiasten zugetragen" (Don Juan: A fabulous incident which befell a travelling enthusiast") and George Bernard Shaw's "Don Giovanni Explains." The former was originally published in the *Allgemeine musikalische Zeitung* on 31 March 1813 and almost immediately reprinted in Hoffmann's collection *Fantasiestücke in Callots Manier;*[5] the latter was written in 1887 but remained in

---

[4] A good example of such a methodology would be, for example, a consideration of Berlioz's approach to *Don Giovanni,* which distinguished between the versions revived in Italian at the theatre of that name in Paris and those at the Académie Royale de Musique. For Berlioz's review of the 1834 Théâtre Italien production (with Tamburini, Rubini, Grisi, and Ungher) see *Le Rénovateur,* 5 January 1834, and for reviews of the 1834 production at the Académie Royale de Musique, see ibid., 16 and 23 March 1834. Modern editions of all texts are in *Hector Berlioz: La Critique Musicale, 1823–1863,* 10 vols. [only vols. 1–6 have appeared]' ed. H. Robert Cohen and Yves Gérard (Paris: Buchet/Castel, 1996), 129–131 and 196–202.

[5] Ernst Theodor Amadeus Hoffmann, "Don Juan: Eine fabelhafte Begebenheit, die sich mit einem reisendem Enthusiasten zugetragen," *Allgemeine musikalische Zeitung,* 31 March 1813; reprinted in *Fantasie-Stücke in Callot's Manier mit einer Vorrede von Jean Paul,* 2 vols. (Bamberg: Kunz, 1814); modern edition in *E. T. A. Hoffmann: Fantasie- und Nachtstücke: Fantasie-Stücke in Callots Manier, Nachtstücke, Seltsame Leiden eines Theater-Direktors,* ed. Georg von Maassen und Georg Ellinger, 6th ed. (Düsseldorf and Zurich: Artemis-Winkler, 1996), 67–78 (to which reference is made hereafter). The text is well known in English; see *Pleasures of Music,* ed. Jacques Barzun (London: Michael Joseph, 1952), 29–40; R. Murray Schafer, *E. T. A. Hoffmann and Music* (Toronto and Buffalo: University of Toronto Press, 1975), 63–73; the letter scene is translated in Julian Rushton, *W. A. Mozart: "Don Giovanni,"* Cambridge Opera Handbooks (Cambridge: Cambridge University Press, 1981; reprint, 1994), 127–131.

manuscript until 1932.[6] Hoffmann's "Don Juan" has been at the center of many discussions, not just of *Don Giovanni* but of German romantic writing about music in general;[7] the Shaw essay, by contrast, has not really been given its due; some recent work has pointed to connections between "Don Giovanni Explains" and Shaw's play *Man and Superman*, and no one should be surprised to find such correspondences, but the story figures hardly at all in the literature on Mozart's *Don Giovanni*.[8] It is possible to read these two stories against each other, to juxtapose particular features and characteristics, and to argue that Shaw's story is not so much reception of Mozart as a direct response to Hoffmann's tale.

---

[6] George Bernard Shaw, *Short Stories, Scraps and Shavings*, Works of Bernard Shaw 6 (London: Constable, 1932), 95–116. The text bears the date 1 August 1887 (116). The story is reprinted in Esther Menascé, *Minor Don Juans in British Literature*, Testi e studi de letterature moderne 2 (Milan: Cisalpino-Goliardica, 1986), 117–132 (p. nos. hereafter refer to 1932 original ed.).

[7] Various studies are mentioned as appropriate in the following notes. Other important contributions are Jean Margotton, "*Don Juan* ou Mozart vu par Hoffmann," in *Mozart: Origines et transformations d'une mythe: Actes du colloque international organisé dans le cadre du bicentaire de la mort de Mozart, Clemont-Ferrand, décembre 1991*, ed. Jean-Louis Jam (Berne: Lang, 1994), 171–83; Jean Giraud, "E. T. A. Hoffmann (1776–1822) ou Est-ce Mozart qu'on mythifie?," in Jam, *Mozart: Origines et transformations d'une mythe*, 185–205; Walter Moser, "Writing (about) Music: The Case of E. T. A. Hoffmann," in *The Romantic Tradition: German Literature and Music in the Nineteenth Century*, ed. Gerald Chapple, Frederick Hall, and Hans Schulte, McMaster Colloquium on German Studies 4 (Lanham, Md.: University Press of America, 1992), 209–226; Margarita Pustovalova, "Mocart I Gofman," *Sovetskaja muzyka* 12 (1991), 81–84. The standard bibliography on Hoffmann is Jürgen Voerster, 160 *Jahre E. T. A. Hoffmann-Forschung, 1805–1965: Eine Bibliographie mit Inhaltserfassung und Erläuterungen*, Bibliographien des Antiquariats Fritz Eggert 3 (Stuttgart: Eggert, 1967).

[8] Most commentators on *Man and Superman* find space to mention "Don Giovanni Explains": Carl H. Mills, "*Man and Superman* and the Don Juan Legend," *Comparative Literature* 19 (1967), 216–225; Robert L. Blanch, "The Myth of Don Juan in *Man and Superman*," *Revue des langues vivantes* 33 (1967), 158–163; Jean-Claude Amalric, "Shaw: *Man and Superman*," *Cahiers Victoriennes et Edouardiennes* 24 (1986), 153–160; Amalric, "Shaw's *Man and Superman* and the Myth of Don Juan: Intertextuality and Irony," *Cahiers Victoriennes et Edouardiennes* 33 (1991), 103–114; Carlyle A. McFarland, "*Man and Superman*: Shaw's Statement on Creative Evolution—A Modern Analysis," *Panjab-University Research Bulletin* 18 (1987), 75–80; Paulina Salz Pollak, "Master to the Masters: Mozart's Influence on Bernard Shaw's *Don Juan in Hell*," *Shaw: The Annual Review of Shaw Studies* 8 (1988), 39–68. For a more sustained critique, see Esther Menascé, *Il labirinto delle ombre: L'immagine di Don Giovanni nella letteratura britannica* (Florence: La Nuova Italia, 1986), 123–126, and Stanley Weintraub, "Genesis of a Play: Two Early Approaches to *Man and Superman*," in *Shaw: Seven Critical Essays*, ed. Norman Rosenblood (Toronto: Toronto University Press, 1971), 25–35, especially 25–31. Despite its promising title, Ruth Plant Weinreb, "In Defense of Don Juan: Deceit and Hypocrisy in Tirso de Molina, Molière and G. B. Shaw," *Romantic Review* 74 (1983), 425–440, makes no reference to "Don Giovanni Explains"; neither does Rama Kundu, "Sequel and Inversion: 'Don Juan in Hell': Shaw's Intertextual Sequel to Mozart's 'Opera of Operas,'" in *Mozart in Anglophone Cultures*, ed. Sabine Coelsch-Foisner, Dorothea Flothow, and Wolfgang Görtschacher, Salzburg Studies in English Literature and Culture 4 (Frankfurt-am-Main: Lang, 2009), 97–112. For an account of Shaw's attitude to Mozart in general, see Linda-Payne Osborne, "Shaw and Mozart: Dramaturgy and the Life Force," *Journal of Irish Literature* 11 (1982), 96–110. See also Stanley Weintraub's valuable summary of the scholarship on *Man and Superman* and allied texts in his *Bernard Shaw: A Guide to Research* (University Park: Pennsylvania University Press, 1992), 74–77.

In Hoffmann's story, the narrator puts up at a hotel and unexpectedly finds that his room is connected directly to a private box in the opera house just as a performance of *Don Giovanni* is beginning. The narrator describes the whole of act 1 and the finale of act 2 of the opera. During the course of act 1, another person—whom the narrator initially ignores—enters the box; at the interval he is surprised to find that it is Donna Anna, who has been with him since just after "Ah chi mi dice mai." They converse during the interval, and Donna Anna returns to the stage for the second act. At the end of the performance the narrator goes down to dinner, where he is disgusted by the indifferent reactions of his companions to a performance that he has found exhilarating. He returns to the box in the now deserted theater and writes a letter addressed to his friend Theodor (one of Hoffmann's original middle names), in which he sets out a paradigm of German romantic writing about opera.

Shaw's plot begins when the narrator, a young woman, is unexpectedly invited to a performance of *Don Giovanni* in the nearest big town. She describes an entirely wretched performance; on her way home, she takes a cab to the railway station and settles in a first-class compartment by herself. The ghost of Don Giovanni appears. After steadying the narrator's nerves, he explains who he is and how he came to be suspended in limbo. His explanation encompasses almost exactly the same parts of the opera as in Hoffmann's story. Although Shaw adds an account of the Cemetery Scene, and reduces to a single paragraph the section that Hoffmann omits completely (scenes 1–10 of act 2), Hoffmann and Shaw restrict their accounts of the work to the same parts of Mozart and Da Ponte's opera: the whole of the act 1 and the act 2 finale.

The purpose of Shaw's story is to exonerate Don Giovanni entirely with the defense that he was an attractive man and, far from seducing a fictitiously large number of women, was the passive object of their attentions and desires. The story derives much of its humor from the sustained development of the initial premise of Don Giovanni's innocence. When asked by the narrator why he is in Hell, for example, Giovanni explains that it was a misunderstanding, and that both Satan and the Commendatore believe he should be elsewhere. After death, according to Don Giovanni's explanation, he gets on rather well with the Commendatore: "[Having] made a determined attempt to murder me… [the Commendatore] has since confessed that he was in the wrong; and we are now very good friends; especially as I have never set up any claim to superiority as a swordsman on the strength of our encounter, but have admitted freely that I made a mere lucky thrust in the dark."[9] In response to further questioning, Giovanni describes the subsequent fate

---

[9] Shaw, "Don Giovanni Explains," 105. Shaw's orthography and approach to punctuation are idiosyncratic and much discussed. Here, all quotations are given as they are found in the 1932 collected works. For a collection of Shaw's texts on language, see Abraham Tauber, ed., *George Bernard Shaw on Language* (London: Peter Owen, 1965). For a rare mention of "Don Giovanni Explains" in the musicological literature, see Rushton, *Don Giovanni*, 58.

of three of the characters: Ottavio, Donna Anna, and Zerlina. The conversation over, Don Giovanni bids the narrator farewell and walks out through the closed door of the moving train.

Hoffmann's "Don Juan" and Shaw's "Don Giovanni Explains" share remarkable features in the scenarios set up by the two authors. The action in both is predicated on solitary travel that is interrupted by the unexpected appearance of a character from the opera: Don Giovanni in Shaw, Donna Anna in Hoffmann. The travel is of a superior quality in both cases: Shaw's narrator travels first class,[10] and Hoffmann's traveler is allowed to use the private box because it is reserved for refined gentlemen only. Performances are the context for both stories; key parts of the action in both (the writing of the letter in Hoffmann) take place after the performance; the time Shaw's young woman got home is not known exactly but was clearly late, and Hoffmann's narrator begins writing his letter to Theodor after dinner and finishes at exactly two o'clock in the morning. Don Giovanni's dress is sufficiently similar in both cases. Hoffmann describes the attire of the performers more or less in passing: "Don Juan unwraps his cloak and now stands splendidly in a red suit of slashed velvet with silver embroidery."[11] Shaw's description is similar but rather more fully developed: "There, seated right opposite me, was a gentlemen, wrapped in a cloak of some exquisitely fine fabric in an 'art shade' of Indian red, that draped perfectly, and would, I could see, wear a whole lifetime and look as nice as new at the end,"[12] and takes Hoffmann's simple red and elaborately plays with it at greater length.

Both texts take a fictitious performance of *Don Giovanni* as a pretext for a reading of the opera's libretto and music. For Hoffmann, the performance could not have been better. "The opening chords of the overture convinced me that, even if the singers were merely adequate, an excellent orchestra would afford me the most glorious enjoyment of the masterpiece."[13] At the beginning of the *introduzione*, he realizes that the work is to be sung in Italian: "In Italian then? Italian, here in this German town? *"A che piacere!"* I shall hear all the recitatives, everything just as the great master conceived and felt it!"[14] Shaw's performance is exactly the reverse—as bad as Hoffmann's performance was good:

The opera was *Don Giovanni*; and of course the performance was a wretched sell. The Don was a conceited Frenchman, with a toneless, dark, nasal voice.

---

[10] "I was in no very high spirits when the guard locked me into a first-class compartment by myself" (Shaw, "Don Giovanni Explains," 97).

[11] "Don Juan wickelt sich aus dem Mantel, und steht da in rotem, gerissenen Sammet mit silberner Stickerei, prächtig gekleidet" (Hoffmann, *Fantasie- und Nachtstücke*, 68).

[12] Shaw, "Don Giovanni Explains," 99.

[13] Die ersten Akkorde der Ouvertüre überzeugten mich, daß ein ganz vortreffliches Orchester, sollten die Sänger auch nur im mindesten etwas leisten, mir den herrlichsten Genuß des Meisterwerks verschaffen würde (Hoffmann, *Fantasie- und Nachtstücke*, 67).

[14] Also italienisch?—Hier am deutschen Orte italienische? Ah che piacere! ich werde alle Rezitative, alles so hören, wie es der große Meister in seinem Gemüt empfing und dachte! (ibid., 68).

Leporello was a podgy, vulgar Italian buffo, who quacked instead of singing. The tenor, a reedy creature, left out "Dall sua pace" [*sic*] because he couldn't trust himself to get through it.... Donna Anna was fat and fifty; Elvira was a tearing, gasping, "dramatic" soprano, whose voice I expected to hear break every time she went higher than f sharp; and Zerlina, a beginner on her trial trip, who finished "Batti, batti" and "Vedrai carino" with cadenzas out of the mad scene in Lucia, was encored for both in consequence. The orchestra was reinforced by local amateurs, the brass parts being played on things from the band of the 10th Hussars.[15]

Hoffmann's reading of the opera takes place in real time; his narrator works through the first act, pauses for his conversation in the interval with Donna Anna, and continues after the interval by moving directly to the act 2 finale. Although not the accompaniment to a performance, Shaw's presentation of Don Giovanni's narration is also embedded in the opera, and presents a scene-by-scene account of the plot.

Contrasting the two treatments of a single scene illustrates the working of specific detail. At the end of the act 2 finale, the statue of the Commendatore arrives to accept Don Giovanni's invitation to dinner, and as the Commendatore grasps Don Giovanni's hand, he makes physical contact with him for the first time since the Don Giovanni's fatal sword-thrust in the *introduzione*. For Hoffmann, the scene is impressive:

Elvira and the girls flee. The marble colossus enters, accompanied by the terrible chords of the spirit world, and towers over the pygmy form of Don Juan. The ground shakes under the thundering strides of the giant. Through the storm, through the thunder, through the howling of the demons, Don Juan shouts his terrifying "No!" The hour of damnation has come. The statue vanishes. The room is filled with thick smoke, out of which hideous spectres emerge. Don Juan writhes in the torments of hell; from time to time one catches sight of him among the demons. An explosion, as if a thousand thunder bolts were striking. Don Juan and the demons have vanished, one knows not how! Leporello lies unconscious in a corner of the room.[16]

---

[15] Shaw, "Don Giovanni Explains," 96–97.

[16] Elvira, die Mädchen entfliehen, und unter den ensetzlichen Akkorden der unterirdischen Geisterwelt, tritt der gewaltige Marmorkoloß, gegen den Don Juan pygmäisch dasteht, ein. Der Boden erbebt unter des Riesen donnerndem Fußtritt.—Don Juan ruft durch den Sturm, durch den Donner, durch das Geheul der Dämonen, sein fürchterliches: 'No!' die Stunde des Untergangs ist da. Die Statue verschwindet, dicker Qualm erfühlt das Zimmer, aus ihm entwickeln sich fürchterliche Larven. In Qualen der Hölle windet sich Don Juan, den man dann und wann unter den Dämonen erblickt. Eine Explosion, wie wenn tausend Blitze einschlügen—: Don Juan, die Dämonen, sind verschwunden, man weiß nicht wie! Leporello liegt ohnmächtig in der Ecke des Zimmers (Hoffmann, *Fantasie- und Nachtstücke*, 72–73).

Shaw selects many of the same features from this scene for his depiction: the size and mass of the statue, its footfall, and the verbal exchanges (Pentiti!—No!; Pentiti!—No!), but for the most serious scene in the opera Shaw puts as much distance as possible between the gravity of the events and the levity with which he treats them. The resulting burlesque contrasts radically with, but is clearly based on, Hoffmann's account of the same scene:

> I opened the door, and found the statue standing on the mat. At this my nerves gave way: I recoiled speechless. It followed me a pace or two into the room. Its walk was a little bandy, from the length of time it had been seated on horseback; and its tread shook the house so that at every step I expected the floor to give way and land it in the basement—and indeed I should not have been sorry to get it out of my sight even at the cost of a heavy bill for repairs....I had invited it to supper, it said; and there it was. It then said it would not trouble us, but would entertain me at supper if I had the courage to come with it. Had I not been frightened, I should have politely declined. As it was, I defiantly declared that I was ready for anything and to go anywhere....The thing then asked for my hand, which I gave, still affecting to bear myself like a hero. As its stone hand grasped mine, I was seized with severe headache, with pain in the back, giddiness, and extreme weakness....I was conscious of fearful sights and sounds. The statue seemed to me to be shouting "Aye, aye" in an absurd manner; and I, equally absurdly, shouted "No, no" with all my might, deliriously fancying that we were in the English house of Parliament, which I had visited once in my travels. Suddenly the statue stepped on a weak plank; and the floor gave way at last....I gave a terrible gasp as it went, and then found myself dead, and in hell.[17]

These extracts from the two descriptions of the end of the supper scene well illustrate how a single, perhaps insignificant, feature in Hoffmann—the weight of the Commendatore's step, for example—can be developed and amplified in a burlesque mode, symptomatic of the different styles and ambitions of the two stories.

The central focus of both texts is the supernatural. Shaw's presentation of a ghost story could not be clearer. When Don Giovanni introduces himself to the narrator, he speaks as follows: "'Pray be quiet,' he said in a calm, fine voice, that suited his face exactly; and speaking—I noticed even then—with no more sense of my attractiveness than if I had been a naughty little girl of ten or twelve. 'You are alone. I am only what you call a ghost, and have not the slightest interest in meddling with you.'"[18] Shaw's ghost story includes all those features one might expect: Don Giovanni asks the narrator to pass her fan through his arm, which of course she does,[19] and his point of exit is through the closed door of the moving

[17] Shaw, "Don Giovanni Explains," 111–112.
[18] Ibid., 99.
[19] Ibid., 100.

train.[20] More important, the entire narrative that occupies the second half of the story is given by a ghost.

Hoffmann's development of the supernatural in his story is similar to Shaw's, in that the supernatural is juxtaposed with the mundane; it is more elusive, however, and depends on a wider range of reference. There are two points at which Donna Anna's corporeal existence is in question. First of all, she appears in the narrator's box during the first act and apparently remains there while she is singing the act 1 quartet "Or sai chi l'onore" and the act 1 finale.[21] The narrator, when he turns round after the act 1 curtain to see who is sharing his box, admits: "it was Donna Anna, without a doubt. It did not occur to me to wonder just how she could possibly be on stage and in my box at the same time."[22] Furthermore, in the epilogue to the story, one of the narrator's despised companions states that Donna Anna was apparently in her dressing room—as well as in the narrator's box—during the interval.[23]

The second element of the supernatural concerns the timing of the end of the narrator's letter and of Donna Anna's death. As the narrator finishes his letter, he appears to encounter the olefactory and sonic qualities of Donna Anna once again:

> The clock strikes two. A warm, electrifying breath glides over me. I recognise the faint fragrance of the Italian perfume that yesterday first informed me of my neighbour's presence. I am seized by a blissful feeling that I believe I could only express in music. The air stirs more violently through the house; the strings of the grand piano in the orchestra vibrate. Heavens! As if from a great distance, borne by the floating tones of an ethereal orchestra, I think I hear Anna's voice: "Non mi dir bell'idol mio!"[24]

The timing of this description exactly matches that of Donna Anna's death in the final exchange of the epilogue, when one of the narrator's companions explains that the singer taking the role of Donna Anna died at exactly two o' clock in the morning.[25] The two points in Hoffmann's story in which the supernatural appears differ only slightly. In the first, Hoffmann is drawing on a variation of the concept of the *Doppelgänger*;[26]

---

[20] Ibid., 116.

[21] Hoffmann, *Fantasie- und Nachtstucke*, 70–72.

[22] "Die Möglichkeit abzuwägen, wie sie auf dem Theater und in meiner Loge habe zugleich sein können, fiel mir nicht ein" (ibid., 71).

[23] Ibid., 73.

[24] Es schlägt zwei Uhr!—Ein warmer elektrischer Hauch gleitet über mich her—ich empfinde den leisen Geruch feinen italienischen Parfüms, der gestern zuerst mir die Nachbarin vermuten ließ; mich unfängt ein seliges Gefühl, das ich nur in Tönen aussprechen zu können glaube. Die Luft streicht heftiger durch das Haus—die Saiten des Flügels im Orchester rauschen—Himmel! wie aus weiter Ferne, auf den Fittigen schwellender Töne eines luftigen Orchesters getragen, glaube ich Annas Stimme zu hören: "Non mi dir bell'idol mio!" (ibid., 78).

[25] Ibid.

[26] This is one of several examples in Hoffmann's output; the better known examples are *Das steinerne Herz* and *Der Sandmann*; see Andrew J. Webber, *The Doppelgänger: Double Visions in German Literature* (Oxford: Clarendon, 1996), 113–194 (the chapter is entitled "Hoffmann's Chronic Dualisms"), especially 182, on *Don Juan*. The slight slippage here is that Hoffmann is splitting a character

whereas in the second, it is the coincidence of the narrator's illusion of the figure and her simultaneous death that elicits the invocation of the supernatural.

Both stories develop an image of a single character from the cast of *Don Giovanni*: Donna Anna in Hoffmann, the eponym in Shaw.[27] Equally important is the relationship between the narrator and the chosen character. Both texts exploit this relationship in similar ways. It is perhaps hardly surprising that the future author of *The Intelligent Woman's Guide to Socialism and Capitalism* should seek to reverse gender relationships in his story.[28] Whereas in Hoffmann, the male narrator is overwhelmed by the vocal and psychosexual power of Donna Anna, Shaw ironically constructs his story so that his female narrator capitulates to Don Giovanni's (admittedly passive) charms.

The importance of the narrator in Shaw's "Don Giovanni Explains" is made explicit from the very first words: "That you may catch the full flavor of my little story I must tell you to begin with that I am a very pretty woman. If you think there is any impropriety in my saying so, then you can turn over to some of the other stories by people whose notions of womanly modesty are the same as your own."[29] The narrator's persona is developed at some length, for example in her view of her male contemporaries: "If it were not for the foolish boys, who dont gloat, but really worship me, poor fellows! and for a few thoroughgoing prigs who are always ready to botanize and to play the bass in pianoforte duet arrangements of Haydn's symphonies, I should count the hours I spend in male society the weariest of my life."[30] Her engagement with the protagonist develops step by step during the story and reaches a climax when, toward the end of the conversation, she says "If you were real, I would walk twenty miles to get a glimpse of you; and I would *make* you love me in spite of your coldness."[31] She acts, as Don Giovanni has made clear throughout the encounter, in exactly the same way as did all the other women in his account,

---

who is *not* the narrator (as is the case in traditional instances of the *Doppelgänger*). See also Otto Rank, *Der Doppelgänger: A Psychological Study*, trans. and ed. Harry Tucker Jr. (Chapel Hill: University of North Carolina Press, 1971), and Arnold Stocker, *La Double: L'homme à la rencontre de soi-même* (Geneva: Éditions de Rhône, 1946). For more on Hoffmann's approach to the subject, see Sandro M. Moraldo, *Wandlungen des Doppelgängers: Shakespeare, E. T. A. Hoffmann, Pirandello* (Frankfurt am Main: Lang, 1996).

[27] Hoffmann's promotion of Donna Anna at the expense of other characters in the opera is discussed by, among others, Hartmut Kaiser, "Mozarts *Don Giovanni* und E. T. A. Hoffmanns *Don Juan*: Ein Beitrag zum Verständnis des 'Fantasiestücks,'" *Mitteilungen der E.T.A. Hoffmann-Gesellschaft* 21 (1975), 6–26; for the view that Hoffmann's view of Donna Anna was inflected by his relationship to the thirteen-year-old Julia Marc, see Hans Erich Valentin, "Der reisende Enthusiast: Mozart-Aspekte im Werk E. Th. A. Hoffmanns," in *Deutsches Mozartfest der deutschen Mozart-Gesellschaft in Verbinderung mit der Stadt Augsburg und dem Bayerischen Rundfunk, Augsburg 13.–18. Mai 1972* (Augsburg: Mozart-Gesellschaft, 1972), 11–20.

[28] George Bernard Shaw, *The Intelligent Woman's Guide to Socialism and Capitalism* (London: Constable, 1928).

[29] Shaw, "Don Giovanni Explains," 95.

[30] Ibid., 95–96.

[31] Ibid., 115.

and proves his point and his innocence. Shaw uses the relationship between the two characters to provide the matrix of his narrative.

Donna Anna and the narrator interact similarly in Hoffmann. At the end of the interview in the narrator's box during the interval, Donna Anna claims that he will understand her views on *Don Giovanni*, singing, and the power of music. She says that she understands "the magical frenzy of eternal yearning love"[32] when the narrator wrote the title role in his most recent opera. She continues: "I have understood you; your soul revealed itself to me in song… I have sung *you*, for your melodies are *me*."[33] At this point, Hoffmann's narrator is as deeply embedded in the projection of the character from *Don Giovanni* as is Shaw's young woman.

An important part of the bonding between narrator and interlocutor is the consequent alienation of the narrator from his or her companions. Both tales handle this alienation in exactly the same way: the narrator is surrounded by companions who fail to share his or her view of the opera, or its performance, and is disgusted in consequence. Shaw's disappointed narrator separates herself from her companions by not liking the performance: "Everybody was delighted; and when I said I wasnt, they said, 'Oh! youre so critical and so hard to please. Dont you think youd enjoy yourself far more if your were not so very particular.' The idea of throwing away music like Mozart's on such idiots!"[34] The alienation of Hoffmann's narrator takes place during dinner after the performance but before the writing of the letter. His view is identical to Shaw's:

> There was general praise for the Italians and their gripping performance, but little remarks, dropped rather facetiously here and there, showed that probably no one had the slightest idea of the deeper significance of the opera of all operas [Die Oper aller Opern]. Don Ottavio had been well liked. Donna Anna had been too passionate for people.…The Italian woman, although certainly quite beautiful was too little concerned about her dress and toilette.…A Lady remarked that Don Juan had seemed to her the least satisfactory of the whole cast. The Italian had been much too sinister, too intent, and had failed to play the character with enough levity and frivolity.…Tired of this rubbish I hurried back to my room.[35]

---

[32] "Der zauberische Wahnsinn ewig sehnender Liebe" (Hoffmann, *Fantasie- und Nachtstücke*, 71).

[33] "Ich habe dich verstanden: dein Gemüt hat sich im Gesange mir aufgeschlossen! . . . ich habe *dich* gesungen, so wie deine Melodien *ich* sind" (ibid., 71–72). Hoffmann's opera *Undine* was composed during 1813–14 and premiered at the Königliches Schauspiel, Berlin, in 1816.

[34] Shaw, "Don Giovanni Explains," 97.

[35] "Man pries im allgemeinen die Italiener und das Eingreifende ihres Spiels: doch zeigten kleine Bemerkungen, die hier und da ganz schalkhaft hingeworfen wurden, daß wohl keiner die tiefere Bedeutung der Oper aller Opern auch nur ahnte.—Don Ottavio hatte sehr gefallen. Donna Anna war einem zu leidenschaftlich gewesen. . . . Die Italienerin sei aber übringens eine recht schöne Frau, nur zu wenig besorgt um Kleidung und Putz . . . eine Dame bemerkte, am wenigsten sei sie mit dem Don Juan zufrieden: der Italiener sei viel zu finster, viel zu ernst gewesen, und habe überhaupt den frivolen, luftigen Charakter nicht leicht genug genommen. . . . Des Gewäsches satt eilte ich in mein Zimmer" (Hoffmann, *Fantasie- und Nachtstücke*, 73).

Both authors select Donna Anna's final request to Don Ottavio that she be given a year before she marries him for attention at the end of their stories. The texts are therefore further linked by content, but the comparison again reveals the contrast in their generic modalities.[36] Hoffmann's narrator, in his letter to Theodor, is convinced that only Don Giovanni's destruction can bring peace to Donna Anna's soul, but that this will entail her own death. Donna Anna "will not survive the year. Don Ottavio will never embrace the woman whose pious nature has saved her from remaining Satan's consecrated bride."[37] It is difficult to imagine that Shaw is not referring to Hoffmann directly when he presents his own interpretation of this part of the story: "[Donna Anna] nursed Ottavio through a slight illness with such merciless assiduity that he died of it, a circumstance he did not afterwards regret. She put on fresh mourning, and made a feature of her bereavements until she was past forty, when she married a Scotch presbyterian and left Spain."[38] Both authors invent a death to tie up the loose ends at the conclusion of the opera. In Da Ponte and Mozart's work, Donna Anna only requests a year's grace before marrying Don Ottavio; the idea of her death is introduced by Hoffmann. The romantic logic of Donna Anna's death in Hoffmann is paralleled but reversed in Shaw: Hoffmann's portrayal of Donna Anna as the eternal feminine is changed by Shaw into a caricature of the overprotective widow, and the tragic is transformed into the mundane.

Reading Shaw's story against Hoffmann's, and considering Shaw's as a satirical response to Hoffmann's, gives focus to interpretations of both texts. Both authors execute a generic swerve from *dramma giocoso* to commentaries. These commentaries replace the libretto and music in the case of Shaw and in Hoffmann's case provide an accompaniment to extracts from the libretto shorn of their music. Both authors evoke the supernatural, and exhibit striking similarities in the scenarios that are set up and in the narrative patterns they establish. The aims of the two readings of the libretto are very different, however: Hoffmann presents a romantic reading that sets the opera in the context of the writings of Jean Paul, Wackenroder, and other German romantic authors writing thirty years either side of 1800. Shaw's aim is satirical, and his text quite possibly a lampoon, not just of Hoffmann but of German romanticism in general. The immediate circumstances of publication are not dissimilar: Hoffmann published in a journal that supported the types of text that do more than describe and categorize, and his "Don Juan" found a natural home in the *Allgemeine musikalische Zeitung*. Although Shaw's text was

---

[36] This exchange takes place in the tiny ensemble that precedes the final fugue; part of the *scena ultima*, it demonstrates that both Hoffmann and Shaw—whatever contemporary attitudes were toward how the opera should end—were convinced that the opera should end with the final fugue.

[37] "Wird dieses Jahr nicht überstehen; Don Ottavio wird niemals *die* umarmen, die ein frommes Gemüt davon rettete, des Satans geweihte Braut zu bleiben" (ibid., 77).

[38] Shaw, "Don Giovanni Explains," 114.

also intended for publication in a periodical, it never appeared, and was only approved for public dissemination in the collected works published in 1931; Shaw had not been able to publish it before, although it had clearly been planned as a freestanding essay in the same way Hoffmann's was.[39] To view the text merely as a draft scenario for *Man and Superman*, for example, is to overestimate the relationships between the two texts, and to underestimate the significance of writing and dating a text in the *Don Giovanni* centenary year. If published, it would have been a worthy—if contentious—addition to the other Shavian contributions to the *Don Giovanni* literature of 1887.

The looseness of the relationship between "Don Giovanni Explains" and *Man and Superman* is clear from the most cursory examination of the two texts. In *Man and Superman*, Shaw frames the central scene of "Don Giovanni in Hell" (act 3) with characters and their relationships based on *Don Giovanni*: Octavius, Anne, Jack Tanner, Violet parallel Don Ottavio, Donna Anna, Don Giovanni Tenorio, and Elvira. The narrative has little to do with that of the opera, and uses the frame and the appearance of Mozart's characters themselves in act 3 (at which point their relationship with Shaw's characters is made explicit) as the basis for a comedy of manners intermingled with political and philosophical commentary. "Don Giovanni Explains" is not only a recasting of large parts of Mozart's opera but also one that is viewed through the lens of Hoffmann's 1813 story.

A critical context for Shaw's parody of Hoffmann is Shaw's knowledge of Hoffmann. Shaw's view of his own command of German varied. In his *Sixteen Self Sketches*, published in 1949, he claimed that he could "read French as familiarly as English. . . . I know enough German to guess my way through most of the letters I receive in that language."[40] Shaw was able to translate Siegfried Trebitsch's *Frau Gittas Sühne* as *Jitta's Atonement* in 1923 with relatively little trouble.[41] But Shaw's French was better than his German. He explained that when he had read Marx's *Das Kapital* in 1883 he had read it in a French translation, since no English version was available, and the German was impenetrable.[42] Shaw's linguistic abilities in

---

[39] The autobiographical elements that relate to Shaw's seduction by Mrs Jane (Jenny) Patterson in July 1885 surely made the work unpublishable before it was even written. On 25 July 1887, Shaw wrote: "Began a tale which I shall probably offer to [Henry] Norman if he wants anything from me for *Unwin's Annual*"; on the day of completion, he titled the work "The Truth about Don Giovanni"; on 2 November, Shaw confided to his diary that he had written to the editor of *Longmans* "asking him if he would take the Don Giovanni story." Stanley Weintraub, ed., *Bernard Shaw: The Diaries 1885–1897, with Early Autobiographical Notebooks and Diaries, and an Abortive 1917 Diary*, 2 vols. (University Park and London: Pennsylvania State University Press, 1986), 1:287, 289, and 311. Shaw read the story to William Archer at tea on 30 August 1887 (ibid., 1:295), and as late as 6 December 1889—perhaps in a fit of pique against Mr Patterson—he got the story out again for H. W. Massingham (ibid., 1:566–7). It might be noted that despite its literary pretensions, the *Allgemeine musikalische Zeitung* was a music periodical, whereas *Unwin's Annual* and *Longmans* were more eclectic.

[40] Bernard Shaw, *Sixteen Self Sketches* (London: Constable, 1949), 72.

[41] See translator's note to Bernard Shaw, *Translations and Tomfooleries* (London: Constable, 1926; reprint, 1932), 4–5 (p. nos. refer to 1932 reprint).

[42] *Sixteen Self Sketches*, 39.

French had developed sufficiently to allow him to write *Un petit drame* by October 1884. As far as is possible to determine, no English translation of Hoffmann's "Don Juan" was published before 1887.[43] However, just about all of Hoffmann was available in a French translation, and the works were collected and translated more than once.[44] Shaw might have known Hoffmann's story, if his self-deprecating remarks about his command of German are to be believed, in one of a number of French translations.[45]

Shaw knew his Hoffmann well enough to have his works entirely assimilated and available as a point of critical reference. Shaw even felt able to use Hoffmann as a term of near-abuse. In a review of the London premiere of Gounod's *Mors et Vita*, dated December 1885 (two years before "Don Giovanni Explains"), Shaw digressed on the subject of modern sacred music in general: "And so nowadays religious music means... a legend from scripture, melodramatically treated exactly as a legend from Hoffmann or an opera libretto would be."[46] Shaw is here traducing modern composers of sacred music in a manner predicated on an equal familiarity with opera libretti and Hoffmann's stories. Whether Shaw knew all Hoffmann as well as certain opera libretti is an open question, but the evidence for his working knowledge seems unassailable.[47]

If Shaw was indeed at home with the works of Hoffmann, a second question that arises a propos "Don Giovanni Explains," and its relationship to Hoffmann, is whether Shaw would have been inclined to produce such a satire surrounding *Don*

---

[43] See Gerhard Solomon, *E. T. A. Hoffmann: Bibliographie* (Berlin and Leipzig: Paetel, 1927), where all English translations of Hoffmann, from the 1824 translation of *The Devil's Elixir* to the 1852 translation of *The Strange Child*, are listed. No translation of the Don Juan essay is listed before Solomon's terminal date of 1871. For Hoffmann reception in general, see Brigitte Feldges and Ulrich Stadler, *E. T. A. Hoffmann: Epoche-Werk-Wirkung*, Beck'sche Elementarbücher (Munich: Beck, 1986), 258–282 (especially, for England, 279–281). For older studies of Hoffmann's significance for England, see Henry Zylstra, "E. T. A. Hoffmann in England and America" (Ph.D. diss., Harvard University, 1940), and Erwin G. Gadde, "E. T. A. Hoffmann's Reception in England," *Proceedings of the Modern Languages Association* 41 (1926), 1005–1010.

[44] The two earliest French translations of Hoffmann's complete works were Théodore Toussenel, *Œuvres complètes de E. T. A. Hoffmann*, 12 vols. (Paris: Lefebure, 1830), and François-Adolphe Loève Weimars, *Œuvres complètes de E. T. A. Hoffmann*, 19 vols. (Paris: Renduel, 1830–32). Translations that might have been known to Shaw are too numerous to mention here. See *Ministère de l'Instruction Publique et des Beaux-Arts: Catalogue général des livres imprimés de la Bibliothèque Nationale—Auteurs*, vol. 72, *Hildebrandsson–Holm* (Paris: Catin, 1929), 840–853.

[45] French translations of Hoffmann were known in England from at least the 1830s. See the review of the Loève-Weimars translation of the *Fantasiestücke* in *Literary Gazette* 19 (1835), 164, cited in Bayard Quincy Morgan and Alexander Rudolf Hohlfeld, *German Literature in British Magazines, 1750–1860* (Madison: University of Wisconsin Press, 1949), 229.

[46] *Our Corner*, December 1835 (*Shaw's Music*, 1:300).

[47] There is a question of the impact of Offenbach's 1881 *Les Contes d'Hoffmann* (to a libretto by Jules Barbier, with the orchestration completed by Ernest Guiraud). Whether Shaw knew the score by 1887 is not clear; there is no evidence that he ever mentioned the work in his critical writing (although he did comment on earlier Offenbach). The work was not premiered in London until 1907; Alfred Loewenberg, *Annals of Opera: 1597–1940*, 3rd ed., rev. and corrected (London: Calder, 1978), 1089.

Giovanni, a work that was manifestly central to Shaw's musical existence. Shaw published a good deal on the opera around 1887, its centenary year. Two texts that both, like "Don Giovanni Explains," develop satirical elements are worth investigation alongside it.[48] Two years before writing "Don Giovanni Explains," Shaw had reviewed a Philharmonic Society concert of the world premiere of Dvorak's Symphony in d minor, op. 70, known today as his seventh. The review appeared in the *Dramatic Review* for 25 April 1885.[49] Mozart's *Don Giovanni* overture was among three overtures on the program. Shaw lampoons "the advanced musicians" who would not want to stay and hear the Mozart, most especially the pianist and critic Edward Dannreuther: "There were three overtures in the program: Spohr's to *Faust*, Beethoven's to *Fidelio* (the seldom played one in C, known as [Leonore] no. 1) and an obsolete work formerly admired as the overture to *Don Giovanni*. It appears to have been written by a man named Mozart. It was placed at the end of the concert, in order that advanced musicians should have an opportunity of leaving before it was played. The position was not ill chosen, as it sounded better after the other overtures than the best of them might have sounded after it. Mr Dannreuther would hardly have believed it." The irony in the latter part of this quotation hardly needs to be indicated.

Shaw reviewed the Crystal Palace centenary performance of *Don Giovanni* in the *Pall Mall Gazette* of 31 October 1887, three months after he had completed "Don Giovanni Explains."[50] Here, he developed at greater length the position he had taken in the Dvorak review cited above. The review was presented as a satire of those who viewed Mozart's music as pretty and naïve. Shaw cast himself in the role of one of these individuals: "We are all agreed as to the prettiness of Mozart's melodies, his *naïve* touches of mild fun, and the touch, ingenuity, and grace with which he rang his few stereotyped changes on the old-fashioned forms."[51] Shaw expressed satirical concern that respected musicians—and he cites Wagner by name—did not share this view: "Even Richard Wagner seems to have regarded Mozart as in some respects the greatest of his predecessors. To me it is obvious that Mozart was a mere child in comparison with Schumann, Liszt, or Johannes Brahms [at this point Shaw's irony is explicit, given his public lack of regard for Brahms]; and yet I believe that I could not have expressed myself to that effect in the presence of the great master without considerable risk of contemptuous abuse, if not of bodily violence."[52] And the dénouement of the review is obvious; Shaw goes to the performance and declares Mozart "a master compared to whom Berlioz was a

[48] For an overview of Shaw's criticism, see Helga Hushahn, "George Bernard Shaw and Mozart," *Mozart in Anglophone Cultures*, ed. Sabine Coelsch-Foisner, Dorothea Flothow, and Wolfgang Görtschacher, Salzburg Studies in English Literature and Culture 4 (Frankfurt-am-Main: Lang, 2009), 135–143.

[49] "Dvorak at the Philharmonic," *Dramatic Review*, 25 April 1885 (*Shaw's Music*, 1:237).

[50] "The Don Giovanni Centenary," *Pall Mall Gazette*, 31 October 1887 (*Shaw's Music*, 1:507–509).

[51] Ibid., 1:507.

[52] Ibid., 1:508.

musical pastrycook."[53] In both reviews, Shaw uses satire to produce an indirect eulogy of the work.

Including "Don Giovanni Explains," then, Shaw made reference to *Don Giovanni* no less than three times during two and a half years. All three texts employed a satirical mode of expression. The essays in the *Dramatic Review* and the *Pall Mall Gazette* satirized those whose view of *Don Giovanni*, and Mozart in general, did not agree with Shaw's. The correspondences between "Don Giovanni Explains" and Hoffmann's "Don Juan," coupled with the satirical context for Shaw's other *Don Giovanni* criticism, gives support to the interpretation of "Don Giovanni Explains" as a parody of, and satire on, Hoffmann's story. Despite its overt claim that it is an attempt to exonerate Don Giovanni at one level and to give a reading of the libretto at another, much of its cultural work is accomplished at the level of a critique of Hoffmann's 1813 story.[54]

Shaw's "Don Giovanni Explains," seemingly an essay on *Don Giovanni* with the humorous intent of exonerating the eponym, is in fact a parody of Hoffmann's 1813 essay on the opera. This is a striking instance of a mode of reception that enhances the focus on Mozart's opera, while at the same time adjusting the recipient's gaze toward one of its own generic ancestors.

Focusing on this single example is by no means an attempt to exclude other texts from consideration within the context of such modes of reception. Musset's appropriation of Laclos's *Les Liaisions Dangéreuses*, Grabbe's of *Faust*, and Mörike's reuse of Oulibicheff's *Nouvelle Biographie de Mozart* are three further sets of relationships that call for analysis in exactly the same way as Shaw's 1887 contributions to the literature on *Don Giovanni*. The position Mozart's *Don Giovanni* holds in our cultural matrix of values is colored, not to say determined, by more than two hundred years of reflection on the opera, and on works that in turn are sites of the work's reception. Examination not only of Mozart's opera but of the traces it has left in the works of others can only enhance an understanding of the opera of all operas.

---

[53] Ibid., 1:509.

[54] The association of the music of Mozart with the supernatural, as found in "Don Giovanni Explains," was also present in another story (unpublished at the time but written in 1879): "The St James's Hall Mystery." Here, Mozart appears at a concert in London in 1879 to act as a mouthpiece for Shaw's views on various aspects of contemporary musical culture. Mozart is invited to give an opinion on, among other works, Beethoven's *Pastoral* Symphony; Jerald E. Bringle and Dan H. Laurence, "Bernard Shaw: The St James's Hall Mystery," *Bulletin of Research in the Humanities* 81 (1978), 270–296.

9

The Specter at the Feast

ELVIRA MADIGAN AND ITS LEGACY

Trajectories

This chapter investigates a particular moment in Mozart reception when a relatively little-known composition—or at least a composition not signficantly better known than most of its fellows—was catapulted to fame because of its inclusion in a film, *Elvira Madigan* (1967). Never before used as part of a film's music track, the slow movement of Mozart's Piano Concerto No. 21 in C Major, K. 467, took on a particular status in the subsequent history of classical music in film, and has since been found in science fiction, horror, comedies, romantic comedies, comedies of manners, thrillers, biopics, Disney disasters, and films from the Bond franchise.[1]

Such a trajectory is of great interest to a study such as this book, for it allows not only the identification of a highly charged site of reception (the release of the film in 1967) but also the analysis of its consequences over half a century of cinematographic history. Furthermore, the association of Mozart's slow movement with *Elvira Madigan* gave the work an unparalleled status outside the cinema, as the concerto in concert and in recording both took on the name of the film, as well as some of its ideology and *tinta*. So the concerto is effectively renamed Piano Concerto No. 21 in C Major, K. 467 ("Elvira Madigan"), and this particular quality triggers an enthusiasm for the movement, especially in the domain of compilation CDs that claim various sorts of therapeutic and beneficial attributes for a tiny subset of Mozart's works.

---

[1] For a recent brief but useful introduction to, and typology of, popular novels that engage with the biography or work of Mozart see Milada Franková, "The Magic Sound of *The Magic Flute* in Barbara Trapido's *Temples of Delight*," *Mozart in Anglophone Cultures*, ed. Sabine Coelsch-Foisner, Dorothea Flothow, and Wolfgang Görtschacher, Salzburg Studies in English Literature and Culture 4 (Frankfurt-am-Main: Lang, 2009), 51–57.

What follows, then, is an investigation of *Elvira Madigan*, the origins of its inclusion of the Mozart concerto, and the use of music in the film itself. This is followed by the pursuit of various themes arising out of the film and its music throughout the history of the cinema from 1967 to the present, and the chapter ends with examinations of two highly regarded films from the 1970s and 1980s in which the "Elvira Madigan" Concerto, as it is now indelibly known, plays an important part.

Mozart's Summer of Love

FILM

Bo Widerberg's *Elvira Madigan* was premiered in Sweden in April 1967, in the United States in October the same year, and worldwide during the next few months. Pia Degermark playing the eponymous role won the best actress award at the Cannes Film Festival in 1967 and was nominated as most promising newcomer at the 1968 Golden Globes and at the 1969 British Academy of Film and Television Awards. Bo Widerberg was nominated for the Cannes *Palme d'or*, and the film itself won the National Board of Review award for the best foreign language film of 1967.[2]

The film narrates the doomed love affair of the tightrope walker Hedvig Jensen (a.k.a. Elvira Madigan) and the deserting and adulterous cavalry officer Sixten Sparre. The film charts their elopement, the difficulties of their life on the run, and their eventual joint suicide; it is based on a true story that took place in the summer of 1889 and was well known in Sweden throughout the first half of the twentieth century. The tale has remarkable resemblances to the so-called Mayerling incident of January 1889, when Crown Prince Rudolf of Austria and his lover, Baroness Mary Vetsera, were both found dead at the Mayerling hunting lodge, although theories that the apparent suicide pact was a in fact a political assassination have been in circulation for over a century.[3] No such intrigue surrounds either the 1889 Jensen-Sparre suicide pact or the 1967 film.

Its immediate and medium-term reception focused on the sheer beauty of its color: Roger Ebert could refer to the fact that "somewhere in these pages [of the *Chicago Sun-Times*] there is doubtless an advertisement describing *Elvira Madigan* as the most beautiful film ever made,"[4] and there is no doubt that this was the way

---

[2] The standard source for bibliographical and discographical information on *Elvira Madigan* and all other films discussed in this chapter is the International Movie Database, www.imdb.com/title/tt0061620 (accessed 10 July 2012).

[3] This is a well known and celebrated story; see Emil Franzel, *Crown Prince Rudolph and the Mayerling Tragedy: Fact and Fiction* (Vienna: Herold, 1974), and more recently, Georg Markus, *Crime at Mayerling: The Life and Death of Mary Vetsera: with New Expert Opinions Following the Desecration of Her Grave* (Riverside, Calif.: Ariadne, 1995).

[4] Roger Ebert, "Elvira Madigan," *Chicago Sun-Times*, 22 December 1967.

the film was marketed. On the English-language advertising poster for the film are three quotations:

Perhaps the most beautiful movie in history.

Exquisite is only the first word that surges in my mind as an appropriate description of this exceptional film. Its colour is absolutely gorgeous, the use of music and, equally eloquent, of silences and sounds, is beyond verbal description. The performances are perfect. That is the only word.

May well be the most beautiful film ever made.[5]

Ebert went on to argue that such an account of *Elvira Madigan* failed to do it justice and that Widerberg's triumph was in succeeding in creating a counterpoint between art and reality in the film. Writing with only slightly greater hindsight, Ernest Callenbach pointed to the many techniques borrowed from silent film (and at this point it is worth remembering that the distance that separates *Elvira Madigan* from the present is almost exactly the same as the gap between it and the appearance of the silent *Phantom of the Opera* discussed in chapter 2).[6] But a decade after its first appearance, Bosley Crowther could still point unequivocally to the film's beauty.[7]

Critics could not agree about the music, however. Ebert describes the first scene in the film with Hedvig and Sixten: "Mozart's Piano Concerto No. 21 provides the sound track. The scene, and most of the following ones, are pure romanticism and are intended to be."[8] For Callenbach, however, "Widerberg...has rightly chosen to accompany much of [the film] with a Mozart piano concerto—from which, even chopped up to fit the editing, emerges a pervasive melancholy. Mozart is neither elegiac nor romantic."[9] Crowther would, however, claim that the "music of Mozart was not too frequently or insistently used. It was discreetly slid onto the sound track for tonal emphasis at times and that was all."[10] More important, Crowther pointed to the elision of film and music when he wrote: "Mozart's *Piano Concerto 21*...was so appropriately used to embrace the romance that it is now popularly referred to as the Elvira Madigan Theme."[11]

Time has not been kind to *Elvira Madigan*. The veteran film critic Bert Cardullo contrasted his responses to the film in 1967 and in 2009:

I had remembered...*Elvira Madigan*...as a beautiful, romantic film from a beautiful, romantic period in my own life.... But a film of Beauty—whatever its subject—is a risk forever. And the beauty of...Bo Widerberg's film did

---

[5] The poster consists of a three-quarter view of Pia Degermark wearing her straw hat, shot over the shoulder of her lover. The title "Elvira Madigan" heads the poster.

[6] Ernest Callenbach, untitled review [*Elvira Madigan*], *Film Quarterly* 21 (1968), 49.

[7] Bosley Crowther, *Reruns: Fifty Memorable Films* (New York: Putnam, 1978), 205.

[8] Ebert, "Elvira Madigan."

[9] Callenbach, untitled review, 49.

[10] Crowther, *Reruns*, 207–208.

[11] Ibid., 205.

not age well.... Forty-two years later, *Elvira Madigan* falls short not only through the inevitable tedium—in a sense, the distraction—of the incessantly beautiful, but also because of the very subject on which all that beauty has been lavished.[12]

Cardullo is blind to the paradigm shifts that had taken place between 1967 and 2009 both in filmmaking and in film criticism, and this may have colored his negative view of the inclusion of Mozart's music, although it is difficult to understand how he can argue that "[Widerberg] also begins and ends these quotations abruptly."[13] But modern scholarly views of the use of Mozart's piano concerto in the film—rare though those views are—are shot through with the same ahistorical critique as Cardullo's.

Elvira Madigan has had its day in the scholarly sun, however, because of the interest in issues surrounding the attempts to embed traditional artistic techniques in film. Early commentaries pointed to the "impressionism" that had been imparted to the film, and Crowther wittily played off recollections "of Renoir—not only the great painter, Auguste, but his cinema-artist son, Jean."[14] The film figured large in these discussions simply because of its attempt at a sustained series of "impressionistic" scenes across the duration of the film[15]—an attempt doomed to fail because of the alternation of rural exteriors with essentially rural interiors, for which there were no "impressionistic" models, since most such "interiors are urban (cafés, the opera, nightclubs, etc.)."[16] Charles Tashiro points to the consequences: "*Elvira Madigan* creates an intricately oscillating discourse, moving rapidly from one kind of representation to another, painterly here, cinematic there, Impressionist one moment, photographic the next."[17] Of course, as will be seen, one of the functions of the use of Mozart's slow movement is to elide these "oscillating discourses" as the music moves effortlessly—as it can—from exterior to interior, from imprecise to precise image and back again.

But those who saw the film in San Francisco after its release in October 1967, just as the Summer of Love was coming to its close, took a different view—less critical, perhaps, but a more precise indicator of the film's and the music's significance:

I recall sitting through it several times on a Saturday. Back then, one could pay the price of admission and just—well, never leave the theater all day. That weekend, I was in Elvira Madigan Heaven. The movie also introduced me to Mozart's Piano Concerto #21 in C (K467). The andante movement is played

---

[12] Bert Cardullo, *Screen Writings: Partial Views of a Total Art, Classic to Contemporary*, 2 vols. (New York: Anthem Press, 2010), 1:192.

[13] Ibid., 1:194.

[14] Crowther, *Reruns*, 205.

[15] Allen K. Schwartz, "The Impressionism of 'Elvira Madigan,'" *Cinema Journal* 8 (1969), 25–31.

[16] Charles Tashiro, "When History Films (Try to) Become Paintings," *Cinema Journal* 35 (1996), 26.

[17] Ibid.

as the movie's theme—quite frequently—throughout the entire film. In truth, it really was repeated ad nauseam, but that mattered not to me, who found the music to be magical and mesmerizing. I wasted no time before running out to buy the Deutsche Gramophon *phonograph* recording by Geza Anda. That way, I could listen to it ad nauseam whenever the "Elvira" spirit moved me. That week in 1967, when "Elvira Madigan" played at the Palace Movie Theater in San Francisco, I became completely and hopelessly smitten

with Elvira Madigan aka Hedvig...

with Sixten Sparre...

...with dizzying romance...

...and tragedy.

...I fell in love with the lilting andante of Piano Concerto No. 21, and wanted more more more Mozart...[18]

A desire for "more more more Mozart" was exactly what the inclusion of the slow movement of K. 467 engendered.

MUSIC

The slow movement of Mozart's piano concerto K. 467 was initially tied to Widerberg's *Elvira Madigan* through a single recording. Géza Anda's pathbreaking account of all Mozart's piano concertos with the Camerata Academica des Mozarteums Salzburg took from 1962 to 1971, and was striking not only for the novelty of recording the entire corpus but also because Anda acted as both soloist and director.[19] He was not the first to undertake this type of performance—that honor probably belongs to his teacher Edwin Fischer—but, together with Daniel Barenboim, he established a popular mode of performance for Mozart piano concertos that continues, perhaps less widely spread than in the 1960s and 1970s, to this day.

Anda's earliest involvement with the Salzburg Mozarteum dates back to 1952, when he played under Bernard Paumgartner,[20] but as early as November the same year Ernst von Siemens, the head of Deutsche Gramophon, was suggesting a recording of a series of Mozart concertos with the Berlin Philharmoniker *ohne Dirigenten*, in exactly the same way Anda was to record them a decade later.[21] It

---

[18] Beverly Smith, "Elvira Madigan, *A Little Bit o'dis and a Little Bit o'dat*," 13 June 2010, http://bafflesblog.blogspot.com/2010/06/elvira-madigan.html (accessed 10 July 2012).

[19] The complete series was recorded for Deutsche Gramophon Gesellschaft between 1962 and 1971, and the individual disc, pairing K. 467 with K. 453, was [Wolfgang Amadeus] Mozart, *Klavierkonzert / Piano Concertos G-Dur / in G Major / KV 453 C-Dur / In C Major / KV 467*, Camerata Academica des Mozarteums Salzburg, Geza Anda (Solist und Dirigent) (Hamburg: Deutsche Gramophon Gesllschaft, 138783, [1962]).

[20] Max Kaindl-Hönig, "Salzburg und wie glücklich Mozart gespielt werden kann," in *Geza Anda: Ein Erinnerungsbild*, ed. Karl Schumann et al. (Zurich and Munich: Artemis, 1977), 36.

[21] Hans-Christian Schmidt, ed., *Géza Anda: "Sechzehntel sind auch Musik": Dokumente seines Lebens* (Zürich: Artemis & Winkler, 1991), 214.

may well be that Anda's relationship with Paumgartner had soured by early 1962, thus freeing up the musical space for a complete recording of the Mozart concertos *ohne Dirigenten*, not with the Berlin Philharmoniker but with the Camerata Academica des Mozarteums Salzburg.[22]

The series was complete in 1971, but the recording of the two piano concertos K. 453 and 467 was made in the summer of 1962 in the Großes Festspielhaus in Salzburg. The recording won the 1963 Grand Prix du Disque and would have remained a distinguished component—but nothing more—of the complete recording that was put on sale in 1971, had it not been for the cinematic events of 1967. The cover of the 1971 U.S. release of the two concertos in 1971 brings together both aspects of its celebrity.

The classic understated Deutsche Gramophon black-on-yellow titling is completely undercut by the additional text "Contains theme [*sic*] from Elvira Madigan as played in the motion picture by Geza Anda."[23] The misleading sense that Anda played (diagetically) in the film or at least that the recording was prepared expressly for the film is perhaps the inevitable price of publicity, but the label underneath—elegantly at an angle to give the impression of something added after the artwork had been printed (which is clearly nonsense—the award was the best part of a decade old at that point) in itself brooks no contradiction. And of course the largest image on the cover is of Pia Degermark in a classic pose, shot over her lover's shoulder, the same as the one for the film advertising poster discussed earlier.

Anda himself had no idea that his recording was being used for the film. He wrote to Otto Gerdes on 5 December 1967 in terms that any performer would understand: "I have heard from New York about the movie issue. For now I just want to ask how my recordings have reached a film company, who gave the authorization and at what price?"[24] The absence of any response suggests that the deal was struck by Deutsche Gramophon directly, but it is clear that Anda was not consulted, and that Deutsche Gramophon probably did not think that it was necessary to exercise great caution for a Scandinavian film that they probably thought would have little impact outside northern Europe.

The reality was, of course, very different. In the wake of *Elvira Madigan*'s U.S. release, Anda's recording shot to the top of the classical Billboard charts and remained there for fifty weeks during 1968.[25] Hardly any recording of Mozart's Piano concerto K. 467 was released after 1967 that did not describe the work as Mozart, Piano Concerto No. 21, K. 467, "Elvira Madigan." In Daniel Barenboim's 1968 recording with the English Chamber Orchestra (with Barenboim conducting as

---

[22] Ibid., 70–71.

[23] The recording details are otherwise the same as those given in note 19.

[24] "Von des Filmangelegenheit habe ich aus New York gehört. Für heute möchte ich nur fragen, wie meine Aufnahmen zu einer Filmgesellschaft gekommen sind, wer hat die Autorisation zur Verwendung gegeben und zu welchem Preise" (Schmidt, *Géza Anda*, 89).

[25] Kaindl-Hönig, "Salzburg und wie glücklich Mozart gespielt werden kann," 37, note 3.

well as acting as soloist), for example, the work was titled "The Elvira Madigan," Concerto."[26] The soubriquet "Elvira Madigan" was attached ubiquitously. To take examples from different decades: Stephen Hough's 1987 recording and Peter Lang's 2004 CD both describe the concerto the same way.[27]

Even more remarkable was the way treatment of recordings that predated 1967 but were rereleased after *Elvira Madigan* changed the fortunes of K. 467 so strikingly. So Artur Rubinstein's 1961 recording with Alfred Wallenstein for RCA Victor (paired with the d minor concerto K. 466) was rereleased in 1989 with K. 467 enjoying the status of the "Elvira Madigan" concerto.[28] The same was true when Robert Casadesus's 1965 recording with George Szell and the Cleveland Orchestra was rereleased in 1983.[29] The value of the *Elvira Madigan* "brand" was such that even recordings by artists who had probably never heard the name "Elvira Madigan" were caught up in the enthusiasm for, and profitability of, the work engendered by its success in the film.

It is difficult to assess the relative impact of the film on the concerto's success after 1967. About three times the number of recordings exist of K. 467 than of the work with which it was paired on the key Anda 1962 recording, but only between two and two and a half times more than those of K. 466. Much of this is because of the colossal impact K. 467 has had in the world of CD compilations since the emergence of the format. So the slow movement of K. 467 (and no other movement ever figures) appears on *Mozart 250: A Celebration, The Very Best of Mozart, The Basic Mozart,* and beyond the Mozart canon, in such compilations as *The Essential Collection: Great Classical Highlights, Adagio Chillout, More Classical Passion,* and so on.

K. 467 also figured in compilations claiming a therapeutic or other benefit: *Mozart for Meditation, Perfect Summer Wedding, The Most Relaxing Piano Album in the World—Ever, Bedtime Beats: The Secret to Sleep.* It was also caught up in the later stages of the so-called Mozart Effect, featuring on such compilations as *Maths with Mozart III: Multiplication* and *Build Your Baby's Brain II through the Power of Mozart.*[30] Most of these compilations used material from preexisting recordings under license, but K. 467—in just the same way the "Twelfth Mass" had 150 years earlier—circulated

---

[26] Wolfgang Amadeus Mozart, *Symphony no. 40, in g minor, K. 550, Concerto no. 21 in C, K. 467 (Elvira Madigan Concerto),* English Chamber Orchestra, Daniel Barenboim (soloist and conductor) (London: EMI, 1968).

[27] Wolfgang Amadeus Mozart, *Piano Concerto No. 21 in C Major, K. 467 "Elvira Madigan," Piano Concerto no. 9 in E Flat Major, K. 271,* Hallé Orchestra, Bryden Thomson (conductor), Stephen Hough (soloist) (Hayes, England: EMI, 1987); Wolfgang Amadeus Mozart, *Piano Concertos K. 466 and K. 467,* Capella Istropolitana, Christoph Eberle (conductor), Peter Lang (soloist) (Naxos, 2004).

[28] Wolfgang Amadeus Mozart, *Concerto no. 20 in d minor, K. 466; Concerto No. 21 in C, K. 467 "Elvira Madigan,"* RCA Victor Orchestra, Alfred Wallenstein (conductor), Artur Rubinstein (soloist) (New York: RCA Victor Gold Seal, 1989) (originally issued 1961).

[29] Wolfgang Amadeus Mozart, *Concerto no. 21 in c major for Piano and Orchestra, K. 467 "Elvira Madigan" (cadenzas by Robert Casadesus); Concerto no. 24 in c minor for Piano and ORCHESTRA, K. 491 (Cadenza by Saint-Saëns),* Cleveland Orchestra, George Szell (conductor), Robert Casadesus (soloist) (New York: CBS, 1983) (originally issued 1965).

[30] The "Mozart Effect" is discussed in chapter 10.

in a variety of arrangements: *Heavenly Harp, Finger Picking Mozart,* and *Classics for Tranquillity: Sublime Guitar Performances of Classical Works.*

Given the remarkable effect that the inclusion of the slow movement of K. 467 in *Elvira Madigan* had on the work's subsequent reception, a close reading of the music track to the film may serve as the basis for an examination of the fate of K. 467 in film after *Elvira Madigan.*

MUSIC AND FILM

Despite the enthusiasm for Mozart in the immediate and later reception of the film, the musical elements of *Elvira Madigan* are not limited to the slow movement of K. 467. It is not even true to say that the movement constitutes any sort of "theme"; that distinction probably goes to the seventeenth-century Swedish hymn "Den blomstertid nu kommer," whose sacred qualities are not made evident until the end of the second stanza:

> The summer days of beauty in blessedness are come.
> The flowers are rejoicing to feel the gleaming sun.
> In grace arisen brightly o'er fields of golden grain
> So warm and all restoring, that nature lives again.
>
> The fragrance of the meadows, the planting in the vale,
> The whispers of the forest through branches green and hale,
> These wonders all remind us how great the stores of wealth
> Of Him whose hand has made us, who gives us life and health.[31]

"Den blomstertid nu kommer" appears over the opening and closing credits of the film only, but the congruence between the summer setting of the hymn and that of the film is self-evident, and it could well be argued that the hymn is a closer and more immediate musical parallel to the film than the slow movement from Mozart's piano concerto.[32] Indeed, it points up the importance of the season in the same way as another major musical work used in the film: Vivaldi's *L'estate* from *The Four Seasons.*

While walking in the woods (during one of the episodes using the K. 467 slow movement), Hedvig tells Sixten about walking on a tightrope, and especially an occasion in Venice when she walked on a rope over a canal while an orchestra played on a raft in the lagoon by torchlight. So it is almost inevitable that in the scenes where Hedvig is seen stealing the housekeeper's washing-line and using it as tightrope, the music should be Venetian.[33] The first movement of Vivaldi's Concerto for Violin in E Major, R. 271, possibly chosen for its subtitle, *L'amoroso,* accompanies the two scenes when Hedvig walks the tightrope.[34] The first of these

---

[31] "Den blomstertid nu kommer" is probably best known from Johan Olof Wallin's 1819 hymn collection *Den svenska psalm-boken, af konungen gillad och stadfästad år 1819* (Stockholm: n.p., 1821).

[32] *Elvira Madigan*, dir. Bo Widerberg (AB Svensk Filmindustri, 1967).

[33] Ibid., at 13' 20".

[34] Ibid., at 18' 26" and 26' 55".

also transitions into the first of two al fresco dining scenes, the first of these with the celebrated moment when the wine bottle is overturned, splashing a fateful red onto the predominantly white, yellow, and green palette of the film, a subtle reference also to Vivaldi's fame as *il prete rosso*.[35]

But in the section of the film that concentrates on Vivaldi, another movement is also employed for the lovers' flight from the hotel first on foot and then on horseback: the presto finale of the another violin concerto by Vivaldi, the second of the op. 8 set entitled *Il cimento dell'armonia e dell'inventione*, R. 315, better known as *L'estate* from *The Four Seasons*. This celebrated *agitato* movement undertakes a clear mimetic program as the narrative follows Hedvig and Sixten from the hotel, avoiding the individual who has betrayed them and riding on horseback across the Danish sand dunes.[36] Vivaldi violin concertos, triggered by a reference to Venice, are made to work narratively, and brought back by a reference to the season—and to the elopement—which, like the season, as exemplified in the finale of *L'estate*, is coming rapidly to an end.

But if Vivaldi and the hymn "Den blomstertid nu kommer" play elegant cameo roles, it is Mozart's slow movement that both takes pride of place in the music track to the film and that has acted as the *Wirkungsträger* for both the film and the concerto in the near half century since the former appeared. There are a number of remarkable qualities to the use of the music.

The Mozart is compressed into a single long sequence at the beginning of the film and into three much shorter ones. All the later sequences (48' 15" to 50' 26"; 1:3' 40" to 4' 07"; 1:8' 40" to 8' 58") are short and related to the more frequent quarrels and subsequent forgiveness as the relationship between the two lovers comes under greater and greater strain. This is in direct contrast to, or perhaps in nostalgic reminiscence of, the use of the same music at the very beginning—no more than its first eighteen minutes. Here, the movement is used as a sonic analogue to the film's scenic and corporeal beauty. Accordingly, the nine scenes that make use of Mozart in these eighteen minutes are combined with scenes where Hedvig and Sixten are viewed walking hand in hand in the countryside or engaging in precoital humor, but in many of the scenes the music functions as a nonverbal response to such questions as "Are you happy?" and "Do you love me?"[37]

Given the amount of emphasis this piano concerto movement was to receive in the aftermath of the film's release, it is striking how few of the scenes actually make use of music that uses a piano concerto texture. Almost all the scenes in the first section of the film take their music exclusively from the opening orchestral ritornello, where the piano figures hardly at all. A rare moment is the last Mozart scene in the first part of the film, where a passage from the middle of the movement (bars 88–93) is used, but it lasts for no more than fourteen seconds. Much more extended is the scene where the two lovers engage in a fruitless attempt at catching

---

[35] Ibid., at 22' 40".
[36] Ibid., at 31' 40".
[37] Ibid., at 2' 50"; 4' 22"; 6' 40"; 7' 20"; 9' 45"; 11' 20"; 13' 20"; 14' 57"; 17' 29".

butterflies—a thinly disguised metaphor for their doomed attempts at catching happiness—which is set to the A-flat variation of the main theme (ex. 9.1).

But this is Géza Anda's most foregrounded moment in the entire film, and it is dwarfed by the predominance of the opening orchestral ritornello. Here, Mozart's music is fragmented and combined in a variety of ways. Widerberg and Ulf Björlin take the first twenty-two bars of the movement and break them up into three fragments (see ex. 9.2).

EXAMPLE 9.1: *Mozart, Piano Concerto 21, C Major, second movement, 73–93.*

EXAMPLE 9.1: *continued*

EXAMPLE 9.1: *continued*

EXAMPLE 9.2: *Mozart, Piano Concerto 21, C Major, K. 467, second movement, 1–22 (with segmentations noted).*

In some cases, the complete twenty-two-bar sequence underscores a single scene, as in the scene that follows the telling moment when Elvira/Hedwig instructs Sixten to "Call me Hedvig," and when she effectively renounces her former life by renouncing her former name,[38] or in the forest scene where she tells Sixten about

---

[38] Ibid., 4' 22".

EXAMPLE 9.2: *continued*

EXAMPLE 9.2: *continued*

her life as a tightrope walker and her adventures in Venice.[39] In both these instances, the music suppresses the opening and introductory bar, but presents all three fragments in order.

A preferred permutation of the fragments is a combination of A and the opening bars of B fading out before it ends. This is the way the music is heard for the first time in the film, as it crosscuts from Sixten cutting the buttons off his military jacket to his all too obvious absence at the Christianstad cavalry barracks, and then in two adjacent scenes, the one where Sixten and Hedwig walk out of the forest and the first interior scene in the hotel. The hotel room is also the location of the single occasion where fragments B and C are combined, and a rare occasion when the end of fragment C continues to the repeated piano chords before its first solo.

Far and away the most striking musical feature of the film is the use of the six-bar fragment C. With one exception, this is given in its form from the orchestral introduction (bars 17–22). The exception is just after the scene where the two lovers attempt catching butterflies and makes use of the A-flat variation of the first two fragments followed by the unadorned presentation of C. So while here the final

---

[39] Ibid., 7' 20".

fragment is repeated in its version for piano and orchestra, the other six appearances are for orchestra alone. They are all related to tragedy, and become more intensely so during the course of the action. So the fragment accompanies the scene in which Hedvig shows Sixten a drawing of herself, made—so she says—by "a cripple, in a café in Paris," which she is forced to sell for more or less nothing; the description of the artist and the detail of the signature make it clear that the drawing is by Henri de Toulouse-Lautrec, which, had the drawing's authorship been known, would have largely forestalled the tragic dénouement.[40] But in the second half of the film, fragment C of the ritornello accompanies many of the tensest moments of Sixten's and Hedvig's relationship coming under greater and greater stress as their money and options run out; there are three of these in the scenes running from fifty minutes to an hour into the film: the fragment bears witness to quarrel and forgiveness in a context of increasing desperation.[41] Almost inevitably, this fragment is the final musical sign during the lovers' final meal, just before Sixten picks up the revolver and ends both their lives.[42]

"Elvira Madigan" after *Elvira Madigan*

Between 1967 and the present, around thirty films have made use of the slow movement of K. 467 in a variety of different ways. The absence of any diagetic use of the music in *Elvira Madigan* has had resonances throughout the following half century, with almost no diagetic presence of the music in any film to date. Strangely, other movements of the same concerto have figured, both in thrillers with pretensions to psychological drama. Alan Pakula's *Consenting Adults* (1992) and Bruce Beresford's *Silent Fall* (1994) use extracts from the first movement (in a piano lesson) and the finale (on a car radio) as diagetic context for the action, almost consciously ignoring the much better-known slow movement (the outside movements hardly ever figure in film at all).[43]

Almost perversely, K. 467 seems to be singled out for particular extradiagetic treatment among other uses of classical music in film. A good example is George Hickenlooper's 2007 biopic of the 1960s socialite Edie Sidgwick (Sienna Miller), who was a central figure in Andy Warhol's "Factory" in the 1960s and was also associated with Bob Dylan.[44] Apart from some Bach keyboard music as non-diagetic background in a restaurant toward the end of the film, almost all the classical music is diagetic background music to the events in the Factory itself. During the first hour of its running time, there are three scenes set there with

---

[40] Ibid., 11' 20".

[41] Ibid., 48' 15"; 1:3' 40"; 1:8' 40".

[42] Ibid., 1:23' 15".

[43] *Consenting Adults*, dir. Alan J. Pakula (Hollywood Pictures, 1992), 5' 00"; *Silent Fall*, dir. Bruce Beresford (Morgan Creek, 1994), 1:9' 35".

[44] *Factory Girl*, dir. George Hickenlooper (Weinstein, 2006), 51' 23".

Puccini, Bach, and Gounod playing in the background; the scenes always begin with the elevator rising from the ground floor to the Factory and with the music increasing in volume. But the exception is the slow movement of the Mozart concerto, which is reserved for a scene between Warhol and Chuck Wein that in many respects could be argued is a turning point in the film: Warhol admits to disappointment and doubt about Sidgwick's acting abilities, and from this point the relationship spirals out of control. This remarkable scene is the only one in the film where classical music is used as simple extradiagetic underscore—as it is in *Elvira Madigan*—and it is unlikely to be incidental, as it points up the key exchanges between Warhol and his confidant.

The best known and most recent—and unique—example of the K. 467 slow movement as a diagetic moment is the opening scene of Radu Mihaileanu's 2009 film *Le concert*.[45] A rehearsal of the opening ritornello and the beginning of the first solo (the same section selected for fragmentation in *Elvira Madigan*) underpins the opening credits and the first scene, where Andreï Filipov, the ex-conductor, demoted to janitor for his political beliefs, is present at the rehearsal but hidden in the balcony. The nobility of the scene is entirely undercut by the ringing of Andreï's mobile telephone (with a low-budget ring tone of the *galop* from the overture to Rossini's *Guillaume Tell*). Given that the musical star of the show is Tchaikovsky's violin concerto, it is easy to read the bathetic treatment of K. 467 as a response to its near-ubiquitous use in film and as a foil to a work— the Tchaikovsky—that is deeply embedded in the musical values embodied in the film itself.

Perhaps the most perplexing use of the K. 467 slow movement is in Philip Saville's 1998 *Metroland*, based on Julian Barnes's 1980 novel of the same name. The Mozart simply appears as one of two diagetic examples in the film, emerging from a kitchen radio with no other role or significance.[46] But its meaning might be at least partially discerned by comparison with the other scene involving musical diagesis, which is in a restaurant whose sound system is playing Dire Straits' "Sultans of Swing," originally released as a single and on the album *Dire Straits* in 1978–79.[47] This would be of no great significance were it not for the fact that Mark Knopfler was the music producer for *Metroland*, and by 1998 not only had Dire Straits dissolved but their entire catalog had just been released on CD for the first time.[48] If there is at least the possibility that there is some significance to the inclusion of "Sultans of Swing" in *Metroland*—whether a crude plug for a CD rerelease or some sort of in-joke is unclear—then it is possible that something similar is in play for the K. 467 slow movement.

---

[45] *Le concert*, dir. Radu Mihaileanu (Productions du Trésor, 2009), opening credits.

[46] *Metroland*, dir. Philip Saville (Metrodome, 1998), 29' 35".

[47] Ibid., 17' 35".

[48] "Dire Straits Biography," www.musicianguide.com/biographies/1608000435/Dire-Straits.html (accessed 10 July 2012).

Alternatively, the role played by the Mozart in *Metroland* may be part of a wider use of the music as a display of cultural capital, and in this case the movement may be set alongside other works by Mozart—and other popular classics—that fulfil a similar role.[49] In some cases, these uses serve to point up the social status of individuals in the action. So in *Superman Returns* (2006), all three scenes on Lex Luther's luxury power boat are illustrated with popular classics: the first movement of the first Vivaldi concerto of *The Four Seasons*, arguably his best known work; the *Habañera* from *Carmen*, which enjoys perhaps the same status in Bizet's output; and the slow movement from K. 467 (exactly the same twenty-two bars that were fragmented and permutated in *Elvira Madigan*).[50] This is a strong indicator that by 2006, the K. 467 slow movement held— at least for the music team on *Superman Returns*—the same status in Mozart's oeuvre as the other two works did for Vivaldi and Bizet, respectively. One needs to be careful not to overstate the case, however, since a keyboard might have been deemed essential to the music track in the film at this point: the scene begins with a close-up of a shiny, reflective piano (good product placement for Steinway), which will end up—well after the conclusion of the Mozart extract— smashed in pieces (not such good product placement for Steinway). This may be a parody of, or at least analogous to, a similar suite of scenes in the Bond franchise film *The Spy Who Loved Me* (1977), where the evil protagonist—again in a luxury marine environment (although this time an embryonic submarine city)— enjoys his opulence to the accompaniment of the slow movement of Bach's Third Orchestral Suite (the so-called *Air on a G String*), a string arrangement of a Chopin nocturne, and the slow movement of K. 467.[51] Other examples that simply include K. 467 as part of the musical capital of a particular scene pair the K. 467 slow movement with Gluck (*Janice Beard: 45 Words per Minute*, a 1999 comedy)[52] and with Schubert (*Twelve Monkeys*, Terry Gilliam's 1995 futuristic psychological drama).[53]

Whether or not *Superman Returns* in its use of the K. 467 slow movement parodies *The Spy who Loved Me*, in at least one instance a film returns to *Elvira Madigan* to imitate its colors, its estival nature, and of course its music. Agnès Jaoui's *Le goût des autres* (2001) sets a scene where the wife of the protagonist (who has just left her) has stopped in the countryside and is talking to her

---

[49] For an application of Bourdieu's concept of cultural capital to music in film, see Rick Altman, "Early Film Themes: Roxy, Adorno, and the Problem of Cultural Capital," in *Beyond the Soundtrack: Representing Music in Cinema*, ed. Daniel Goldmark, Lawrence Kramer, and Richard D. Kramer (Berkeley: University of California Press, 2007), 205–224.

[50] *Superman Returns*, dir. Bryan Singer (Warner Brothers, 2006): Vivaldi, 1:3' 8"; Bizet, 1:18' 2"; Mozart, 1:19' 40".

[51] *The Spy Who Loved Me*, dir. Lewis Gilbert (MGM, twentieth Century Fox, 1977): Bach, 15' 15"; Mozart, 16' 40"; Chopin, 1:3' 5".

[52] *Janice Beard 45 WPM*, dir. Clare Kilner (Film Consortium, 1999): Mozart, 25' 00"; Gluck, 1:8' 39".

[53] *Twelve Monkeys*, dir. Terry Gilliam (Universal, 1995): Mozart, 11' 25"; Schubert, 1:10' 10".

driver. She watches her dog scampering around the field and attributes to him all that is good in the world while she claims that all she has is the bad. Against a backdrop of the first twenty-two bars of the Mozart slow movement, the dog runs back and forth against a landscape of exactly the same colors as so many of the scenes in *Elvira Madigan*. Angélique, the wife, wears exactly the same cream shades as does Hedwig, and—to a degree—she faces the same type of collapse of her life. Sixten and Hedvig, cavorting in the field, are wittily parodied as Angélique's dog fulfils the same role in *Le goût des autres*: an irreverent, witty, and a cinematographic trick to which Mozart's music is both the key and the essential component.[54]

Such a position sets up the slow movement of K. 467 as an ideal vehicle for the anempathetic: music that clearly evokes a mood of tranquility that can be used to undercut various sorts of violence. But for this to happen, the essentially tragic qualities with which the movement empathized in *Elvira Madigan* have to be suppressed, and it becomes generic classical music of a serene sort (as the movement's inclusion in the CD compilations of "Music for Mediation" and related recordings discussed earlier in this chapter testifies). The plot of the 1999 teen comedy *Virtual Sexuality* hardly bears repeating, but one of the key comic scenes involves moving a ten-foot-high virtual sexuality machine into a terraced house, for which the solution is simply putting the machine on a truck and driving it through the wall of the house in question (it is best not to ask further).[55] So the visual qualities of the scene involve bricks flying, dust everywhere, breaking glass, and shrieks from observers, passersby, and inhabitants, and this is accompanied by the K. 467 slow movement, as serene as the action is frenetic. The inclusion of the concerto movement is all the more telling, since this is the only classical music in a film that is characterized by high-profile visual chatter on the screen in the form of textual display in curved boxes and other images derived from video games.

Slightly more subtle is the use of K. 467 in the Anglo-Australian film *The Rage in Placid Lake* (2003), where the schoolboy protagonist (named Placid Lake) wins a film prize with a saccharine paean to the established values of his school. When it comes to the formal screening of the prizewinning film, Placid substitutes a reel that includes playground bullying, extortion, protection, the trading of sexual favors, enforced sex, the disclosure of his mother's lesbian proclivities, and the humiliation of his parents. The sound track to this film that brings disgrace to every character depicted is K. 467, used simply to contrast the

---

[54] *Le goût des autres*, dir. Agnès Jaoui (Pathé, 2001), 1:36' 45". The musical component to *Le goût des autres* is complex, with music by Verdi ("Caro nome" from *Rigoletto*) and Schubert (slow movement of the Piano Sonata in a minor, D. 537, Op. Post. 164), but with Mendelssohn's duet "Ich wollt' meine Lieb," op. 63, no. 1 (sung in English translation in a 1945 recording by Isobel Baillie and Kathleen Ferrier) as a recurring and emblematic motif running throughout the work.

[55] *Virtual Sexuality*, dir. Nick Hurran (Columbia TriStar, 1999), 1:13' 30".

various types of violence with the classic serenity that the movement had developed by 2003.[56]

Later in the same decade, K. 467's status as synecdoche for Mozart, and perhaps for classical music *tout court*, alongside *The Four Seasons*, the *Air on a G String*, and *Carmen*, is so assured that it could be used to pivot the empathetic and the anempathetic. In *The Happening* (2008), M. Night Shyamalan's ecodisaster blockbuster, survivors fleeing "airborne toxins" arrive at the home of a horticulturalist, and the two principal characters, Elliot and Alma (Mark Wahlberg and Zooey Deschanel) wander into the greenhouse, accompanied by the C fragment of the K. 467 slow movement that was so celebrated in *Elvira Madigan*.[57] At first glance, this has all the signs of a straightforward empathetic underscore to the scene, but as the orchestral introduction yields to the first piano solo, the nursery owner (Frank Collison) proposes that he knows how the airborne toxins are being spread: it is the plants themselves that are responsible. At this point, the bucolic gives way to the sinister, and the expressive power of the Mozart switches from empathetic to anempathetic. Not a particularly sophisticated move, perhaps, but one that points up the status of the music as a suitable vehicle for such an efficient volte-face.

Armed Robbery, Murder, and Under-age Sex: Mozart as Cinematographic Character

In two instances in cinema in the 1970s and 1980s, the use of the K. 467 slow movement is embedded in a more wide-ranging practice of structuring the sound track to the film around selected works by Mozart. The works in question, both in French, are Bertrand Blier's 1978 *Préparez vos mouchoirs* and Claude Lelouch's 1986 *Attention! Bandits!*[58] Original music sits side by side with the use of Mozart and is composed by two veterans in the field, in the case of *Préparez vos mouchoirs* by Georges Delerue (for which he won a César award; the film itself won an Oscar as Best Foreign Language Film in 1979 and was nominated in the same category for a Golden Globe the same year) and in the case of *Attention! Bandits!* by Francis Lai, well known for his scores to *Un homme et une femme* and, perhaps best known, *Love Story*. It is inconceivable that Delerue and Lai were not involved in the planning of the preexistent music in the films, and Blier claimed credit for one of the central musical scenes in *Préparez vos mouchoirs*.[59]

---

[56] *The Rage in Placid Lake*, dir. Tony McNamara (Guerilla Films, 2003), 17' 46". The original film for which the one with the Mozart sound track is substituted is at 8' 30". The original film's sound track is an amalgam of the diagetic and extradiagetic, as irredeemably saccharine as the film itself.

[57] *The Happening*, dir. M. Night Shyamalan (Spyglass, 2008), 29' 10".

[58] *Préparez vos mouchoirs*, dir. Bertrand Blier (TF1 International, 1978); *Attention! Bandits!*, dir. Claude Lelouch (Warner Brothers, 1986).

[59] Blier claimed in an interview with an anonymous interlocutor that the scene including Depardieu's monologue (see below) was triggered by listening to the slow movement of Mozart's clarinet

In both cases, the K. 467 slow movement is selected for particular attention by its position in the drama, its relationship with dialogue, or its connection with action. Furthermore, in both films, "Mozart" as an abstract concept features extensively, almost as a character in one and embodied in a character in the other. It is not going too far to say that Mozart is written into cinema in these two examples as a principal theme.

Préparez vos mouchoirs obtained a certain notoriety at its appearance in 1978, since it formed part of a campaign by French intellectuals and others between 1977 and 1979 to lower the age of consent from the age of fifteen, as it was then. A petition, according to Michel Foucault, was signed in 1977 by Jacques Derrida, Louis Althusser, Jean-Paul Sartre, Simone de Beauvoir, Roland Barthes, and Alain Robbe-Grillet. A radio program aired on France-Culture in its *Dialogues* slot, on 4 April 1978, eleven weeks after the release date of *Préparez vos mouchoirs*; it featured Foucault, Jean Danet, and Guy Hocquenghem discussing the lowering of the age of consent, and was subsequently published as *La loi de la pudeur* and translated prosaically as *The Danger of Child Sexuality* and then in Foucault's collected writings as *Sexual Morality and the Law*.[60]

This radio debate, and the surrounding public discourse around the question of the age of consent, was a radiophonic reinscription of themes in Blier's *Préparez vos mouchoirs,* which listeners to France-Culture could immediately experience in the Cinema. Raoul (Gérard Depardieu, aged twenty-nine) and Solange (Carole Laure) are a recently but unhappily married couple, and Raoul approaches Stéphane (Patrick Dewaere) for help; Raoul offers Solange to Stéphane in the hopes that he will be able to drag her out of her melancholy. The enterprise is a failure, but Solange meets the thirteen-year-old Christian Belœil (Riton [Henri] Liebman) who succeeds—in all respects including the sexual—where Raoul and Stéphane have failed. The first half of the film is largely dedicated to Raoul and Stéphane's mostly comical and unsuccessful attempts to divert Solange; after the introduction of the character of the thirteen-year-old boy, the film takes a different turn, triggered by a scene in which music plays a key role.

This division of the film into two is reflected in its use of music. In the first half, the musical element of the sound track is exclusively devoted to Mozart, whereas in the second, Mozart is entirely absent and the underscore is entirely Delerue's work. The point of change is a dialogue where Stéphane sings Mozart's praises to the exclusion of all other music: in other words, he produces the sort of uncritical panegyric to the composer that has figured so frequently in this

---

concerto, and that he had thought of having the composer appear in period costume at the end of the monologue. "I didn't have the cheek and I regret it" ("Je n'ai pas eu ce culot et le regrette"). See the full account in "Sonate pour Solange: L'histoire des 'Mouchoirs,'" www.dvdcritiques.com/critiques/dvd_visu.aspx?dvd=834 (accessed 10 July 2012).

[60] Michel Foucault, "Sexual Morality and the Law," in Foucault, *Politics, Philosophy, Culture: Interviews and Other Writings 1977–1984*, ed. Lawrence D. Krizman (New York and London: Routledge, 1990), 275.

book. The thirteen-year-old Christian takes a very dim view of such a position and describes his father's tastes, which leads to the following exchange, supported by Delerue's original music as underscore:

CHRISTIAN: My father only likes Wagner. Wagner bores me, I prefer Schubert.

STÉPHANE: What about Mozart?

CHRISTIAN: Mozart..., Mozart..., Mozart...He's all right, once in a while.

STÉPHANE: Once in a while? Listen to him! Big brain, maybe but no ear definitely!

CHRISTIAN: Not at all! I give Mozart his due but you can't listen only to Mozart.

STÉPHANE: Yes, you can! Mozart is enough for me; it fills my life.

CHRISTIAN: You can't just ignore Haydn, Schumann, Brahms, not to mention Beethoven.

STÉPHANE: Beethoven...come on! Are you out of your mind?

Delerue's pastiche of a piano concerto slow movement stops dead at this point but has productively evoked one of the key moments in the first half of the film, the slow movement of K. 467.[61]

The irony of the thirteen-year-old's contextual view of Mozart coupled to the thirty-year-old's adulation is remarkable, and it not only sets up the absence of Mozart from the second half of the film but also the triumph of youth over experience, and therefore the case—one would imagine—for lowering the age of consent. Not a note of Mozart is heard after this scene, although a final diagetic appearance of Schubert underscores the triumph of Christian over Stéphane, of inexperience over age.

The power of this scene is enhanced by the use of Mozart slow movements in the scenes that precede it. There are three groups of material that are used discretely in this first half: string chamber music, all three movements of the Clarinet Concerto, and the slow movement of K. 467. Each of the three groups undertakes different work: the string chamber music undertakes a scene-setting role, the first two movements of the Clarinet Concerto undertake the set-piece monologue for Depardieu already mentioned, and the slow movement of K. 467 undertakes two further diagetic scenes. These scenes accompanied by Mozart clearly establish Mozart's canonic status in the first fifty minutes of the film, at which point the exchange quoted earlier about Wagner, Schubert, and Mozart undercuts that status and the film—through its avoidance of Mozart—enhances that undercutting.

The music track in *Préparez vos mouchoirs* does not begin until fifteen minutes into the film, at which point there are three scenes in which Raoul and Stéphane are separated out from Solange as their friendship develops and her isolation

---

[61] *Préparez vos mouchoirs*, 52' 30".

increases. Raoul is showing off his apartment to Stéphane, and as the two discuss difficulties with women in general and Solange's gynecological problems in particular, Solange herself pushes open the door of the apartment and enters, to the highly chromatic accompaniment of the slow introduction to Mozart's "Dissonance" Quartet, K. 465 (ex. 9.3).[62]

Solange is sick, takes aspirin, and faints. The ensuing attempts to revive her and to find a doctor, accompanied by very loud sound effects, all but drown out the music, and the effect is one of mock tragedy at Solange's entrance that collapses into bathos.

EXAMPLE 9.3: *Mozart, String Quartet in C Major, "Dissonance," K. 465, slow introduction, opening.*

EXAMPLE 9.3: *continued*

   Similarly bathetic are the two other scenes early in the film where Blier and
Delerue deploy Mozart's string chamber music. Stéphane and Solange's less-than-
satisfactory first attempt in the bedroom, as Raoul waits in a local bar, is set to the
tragic slow introduction to Mozart's g minor string quintet K. 516 (ex. 9.4).
   The music stops as the film cuts from the bedroom to the bar where Raoul
waits.[63] The two men return to the hotel bedroom, where Solange is now asleep,
and Depardieu delivers one of two impassioned monologues (the other is about
Mozart himself, to be discussed below), this one about sleeping women in general
(and not Solange in particular) to the strains of the slow movement of the second
of Mozart's three "Prussian" quartets, K. 590.[64] Raoul and Stéphane are leaning
over the sleeping Solange's bed:

> RAOUL: She looks like an angel. How could you abandon something so fragile?
> Look at that vein [points]; look how it throbs. Have you ever imagined what's
> going on in the body of a woman asleep next to you at night? The blood
> circulating through a thousand canals, some the size of a hair, the heart
> pumping away in slow motion, a whole factory working noiselessly, defense-
> less, at the mercy of the slightest aggression.

---

[63] Ibid., 20' 49".
[64] Ibid., 25' 55".

EXAMPLE 9.4: *Mozart, String Quintet in G Minor, K. 516, slow introduction, opening.*

The music—the first sixteen bars only of the movement—fades out at this point as Raoul strokes Solange and awakens her.

Central to the experience of Mozart in *Préparez vos mouchoirs* is the Concerto for Clarinet in A Major, K. 622. The slow movement, as in the case of the Prussian quartet movement, serves as a pretext for a soliloquy by Depardieu. But this is framed by two scenes in which the first and third movements play clear diagetic roles. In the first, Stéphane arrives with a present for Solange—a recording of the concerto by Gervase de Brumer (a thinly veiled reference to Gervase de Peyer, who recorded the concerto in 1960 and 1969);[65] although the recording begins extradiagetically (the sound begins before Solange has unwrapped the present), the rest of the scene features the disc playing on a record-player, over which Raoul and Stéphane celebrate the virtues of the soloist.[66] Similarly, a concert performance of

---

[65] Both recordings were with the London Symphony Orchestra, the first with Anthony Collins, the second with Peter Maag.

[66] Ibid., 38' 20".

the finale of the concerto serves as the backdrop to another of Solange's public faint-
ing fits, and again the diagetic merges into the extradiagetic as the men carry her
from the concert hall to the taxi.[67]

After the short scene where Stéphane presents Solange with the disc of the
concerto, the music cuts to the beginning of the slow movement, still sounding on
the record-player. After a couple of brief exchanges, Depardieu moves into monologue, this time about Mozart himself (bar numbers in the movement are indicated in square brackets):[68]

> RAOUL: You know... [26]
> STÉPHANE: Yes?
> RAOUL: Listen to this. Imagine he was reincarnated.
> STÉPHANE: Who?
> RAOUL: Your friend, Mozart. Get the picture? Reincarnated, my friend! Do you
> follow me? He's down there in the street. He's walking, in a daze. His clothes
> are shabby [33]. He's lost. Nobody's out, everyone's in bed. And what does he
> hear? Our music. His music! His concerto coming from somewhere. That
> blows old Mozart's mind! He can't believe his ears! He lets the sound guide
> him. He comes closer to our house with tearful eyes. He thinks... "it must be
> coming from that old building." He opens the downstairs door and steps in.
> He hesitates. Now he can hear the music better. It resonates in the hall...
> drawing him on irresistibly. [45] He heads for the stairs. He thinks "there
> can't be a whole orchestra in this dump; who would ever have thought that
> I'd ever be so popular?" He starts up the stairs. He climbs them softly, step by
> step in his court shoes and white stockings. At every step, his concerto
> becomes clearer. First floor, second floor, he gets to our landing. He stops
> and stands still [54]. He stands there trembling, right outside our door. He
> listens holding his breath. His concerto, played as never before! Gervase de
> Brumer, the clarinettist he'd never dared hope for! [59]

The music is suddenly interrupted by the neighbor complaining about the noise.
The impact of this moment is enhanced not only by the sharp contrast with the
preceding music and accompanying soliloquy but by the fact that the neighbor is
played by Michel Serrault. Serrault in 1978 had a career spanning twenty-five years
behind him (*Préparez vos mouchoirs* was his seventieth film) and was to look forward to more than another quarter century in the cinema before his death in 2007;
here he plays a small, exhausted greengrocer who resents disturbance at three
o'clock in the morning. Although the caesura here is abrupt, the music continues
(since it is the sound about which the neighbor—he is never given a name—is
complaining), with Serrault's introduction accompanied by the clarinet cadenza at

---

[67] Ibid., 45 50".
[68] Ibid., 39' 05".

bar 59. Serrault is inducted into the cast of the film by being plied with pastis and mystified by Mozart during the course of the rest of the movement, which continues to its final cadence. Furthermore, this is the scene in which Blier had considered introducing Mozart in period dress. Views might differ on the success of such a move, but the way the end of Depardieu's monologue would have been handled in that case remains unclear.

Raoul's soliloquy effortlessly retreads numbers of Mozartian tropes: the composer walks "in a daze," his clothes are shabby; isolated, he is the only one in the street; the sound of his music reduces him to tearfulness, and his modest ambitions for his music at more than exceeded: "who would ever have thought that I'd ever be so popular?" Raoul's rhapsodic, abstract approach to the music of Mozart contrasts starkly with that of Stéphane (so strongly challenged by Christian, as described above) and has been clearly set out before these Clarinet Concerto scenes in an episode that involves the K. 467 slow movement.

Stéphane's single-minded approach to Mozart is not unlike his literary aspirations. When Solange arrives at his apartment in Béthune for an attempt at cohabiting with him to render her happy for Raoul, the first thing that Stéphane does is to introduce her to his complete collection (five thousand volumes) of *livres de poche*. With great pride he invites her to test him by choosing a volume number, to which he supplies the author and title. His unswerving adherence to the *livres de poche* series mirrors exactly his enthusiasm for Mozart, which is immediately foregrounded as he puts a recording of the slow movement of K. 467 on the record player with as much pride as he shows Solange his books.[69] The music remains diegetic for barely a minute, at which point it serves as an underscore for Stéphane and Solange's less-than-satisfactory life in Béthune; when they finally ring Raoul to explain how badly things are going, the music cuts abruptly, but significantly, at bar 50 and highlights the same melodic fragment singled out for attention in *Elvira Madigan* (ex 9.2). The music eventually fades at bar 81 in the middle of the coda.

Mozart figures not at all in *Préparez vos mouchoirs* after its midpoint. The film ends with Raoul and Stéphane staring from outside into the house where Solange and Christian now live. The music at this point is the Schubert *Mélodie hongroise* that Christian's mother used to play (she has by now absconded) and that his father has requested on hearing the news that Christian and Solange are going to have a child. The music continues and accompanies the closing scene and credits. The closing scene consists of Raoul and Stéphane listening to the Schubert that accompanies the domestic bliss of Christian and the now pregnant Solange:

STÉPHANE: That's not by Mozart.
RAOUL: Who is it by?
STÉPHANE: No idea, but it's not Mozart!

---

[69] Ibid., 30' 05".

The two men trudge away from Schubert as the credits roll.[70]

The rather low-key approach to the K. 467 slow movement in *Préparez vos mouchoirs* contrasts strikingly with its treatment in Claude Lelouch's 1986 *Attention! Bandits!*, where it shares a central role with the overture to *Die Zauberflöte*. And whereas Mozart appears as a thematic element in *Préparez vos mouchoirs*—as part of Stéphane's obsessive character—in *Attention! Bandits!* Mozart functions as both an important element in the music track and as a character in the action. Lelouch sets the early action of his *policier* in the context of the recent death (November 1976) of Jean Gabin and then ten years later, in the present; *Attention Bandits* was released in 1987.[71]

The importance of the actor and singer Gabin to *Attention! Bandits!* is fundamental, since it underpins the casting of Patrick Bruel, who in the mid-1980s was enjoying the beginnings of a similar career.[72] And Bruel, as did Gabin, introduces one of his own songs into the film, in this case the single "Tout l'monde peut s'tromper" from the 1984 album *De Face*. It underscores the opening credits and is used in the scene in the club that belongs to Patrick Bruel later in the film. But the name of the character played by Bruel—Julien Bastide—is never used; instead, because he is a gangster who pulled his first job at age five, he is called "Mozart." "Tout l' monde" is a parallel to the moments when Gabin's song "Maintenant je sais" figures liminally on the sound track.[73]

Mozart is the leader of a young but successful gang who convince Simon Verini to fence jewels for them. However, Verini's housekeeper's husband kidnaps and murders Verini's wife and takes the jewels, whereupon Verini is framed by his housekeeper and serves ten years in prison. Before going to prison, he takes his ten-year-old daughter, Marie-Sophie, to a finishing school in Switzerland; as he describes it, they both inhabit a boarding school. When Verini is released from prison and Marie-Sophie finishes school, Mozart identifies the murderer of Verini's wife and is attracted to Marie-Sophie (who is also at this point engaged to a colorless Swiss named Antoine). Verini is, however, then rearrested for the murder of his own wife and again incarcerated.

Julien Bastide's nickname "Mozart" recurs regularly throughout the film, and on one occasion he plays on it in a purposeful way: after he has extracted a promise from Marie-Sophie that she will forsake Antoine and marry him, and after Mozart has successfully sprung Verini from prison, there is a scene in which Marie-Sophie

---

[70] Ibid., 1:39' 30".

[71] Jean Gabin (1904–76) was one of France's most successful screen actors in the years either side of World War II. In addition to being a war hero (buried with full military honors in 1976) he was Marlene Dietrich's lover and a singer of some note, especially in his early career. See Charles Zigman, *World's Coolest Movie Star: The Complete 95 Films (and Legend) of Jean Gabin* (Los Angeles: Allenwood Press, 2008).

[72] There is no published biography of Bruel, but see "Biographie: Patrick Bruel," www.rfimusique. com/siteen/biographie/biographie_6103.asp (accessed 10 July 2012).

[73] "Maintenant je sais" was first broadcast in 1970, a few years before Gabin's death. It is heard at the very end of *Attention! Bandits!* diagetically from a radio playing as Marie-Sophie and Mozart approach each other as lovers for the first time (1:37' 36").

fantasizes about marrying all three men in her life: Antoine, Mozart, and—bizarrely—her father (the whole scene underscored by Bruel's "Tout l'monde peut s'tromper"). Mozart argues: "You can't marry all three of us. If I'm the lucky winner, instead of the organist playing Mendelssohn, how about a little Mozart?"[74]

Attention! Bandits! is held together by the occasional repetition of a synthesized fragment of original music. This, the only original music that Francis Lai wrote for the score, appears at moments of arrival and departure, so it accompanies the scenes when Verini leaves for Amsterdam before the murder of his wife; as he leaves prison for the first time and meets Marie-Sophie, now a grown woman; their arrival in Switzerland; and—the closing scene—Verini's departure for Germany after escaping from prison.[75] It is developed in almost all cases to cover two or three linked scenes; the longest of these begins with the discovery of the body of Verini's wife and his purchase of a revolver.[76] As the scene shifts to the dining room of the hotel where he is staying with Marie-Sophie, and where Mozart's gang have joined them, Lai's music is transformed into effortless cocktail piano, and then—as Mozart and Marie-Sophie dance—into dance music with a cameo role for the music director, Christian Gaubert, as the participating cocktail pianist.[77] The music continues diagetically in the background, as Verini's housekeeper, Michelle, now separated from her husband, betrays him as the murderer of Verini's wife.

But Lai's composition takes second place to the music that drives two extended scenes in the film. Both are cinematographic settings of Mozart, instances of film being cut so as to coincide exactly with major structural articulations in the music and with smaller scale local moves. Bastide/Mozart's plan for, and execution of, Verini's "escape" is set to a performance of the entire overture to *Die Zauberflöte* K. 620, and Marie-Sophie's time in her Swiss boarding school (the best part of a decade) is captured via the slow movement to K. 467, supplemented by the *romance* from the Piano Concerto in d minor K. 466.

Magic flutes first. During the course of the performance of the overture, Mozart plots Verini's escape, executes it, Verini is released, and the performance ends as Mozart receives confirmation on the telephone.[78] The action is divided between Mozart sprinting around Paris on a motor scooter and Verini's release from the prison at Frêsnes. The opening three chords of the overture are carefully crosscut: the first is accompanied by a shot of Marie-Sophie at the *Salon de cheval* at the Porte de Versailles, the second is accompanied by one of Mozart looking at her through binoculars, and the third is accompanied by one again of Marie-Sophie; the cutting is precise, arriving on the downbeat of each of the three chords. During

---

[74] *Attention! Bandits!*, 1:28' 45".

[75] Ibid., 11' 55"; 38' 13"; 1:7' 58"; 1:9' 28".

[76] Ibid., 55' 16".

[77] I am grateful to Michael Thomas Roe for a discussion of the participants and musical significance of this scene (personal communication, 16 September 2010).

[78] The scene takes as long as the overture, slightly under seven minutes, and begins at 1:20' 31".

the course of the slow introduction, Mozart sees a newspaper headline announcing the presence of the Soviet prime minister at the Paris Opéra and makes his plan. Again, the film is cut precisely to the music as Mozart's phone call threatening to blow up the Opéra yields to a long shot of the Opéra just as the allegro begins. The rest of the scene follows a similar pattern. Mozart's sprint around Paris crosscuts back to the *Salon de cheval* at the tutti subito forte at bar 68; Mozart's second phone call occurs at the reprise of the opening adagio just before the development section (bar 97); and the sudden one-bar silence at 127 enables the cut to Verini's comic release from prison. (The recapitulation of the overture is synchronized perfectly with the arrival of the prison governor.) The overture closes to the accompaniment of Mozart receiving confirmation of Verini's release, an enigmatic smile, a mouthed "putain," and a close-up of the poster on the wall of the telephone booth: "Le Gouvernement aux terroristes: nous ne céderons pas au chantage!" Given that the government has exactly just given into blackmail, the humor is obvious.

Lelouch's and Lai's treatment of the slow movement of K. 467 has much more to do with their treatment of the *Zauberflöte* overture than with the fragmentary treatment of the K. 467 movement in *Elvira Madigan*. As in the case of the *Zauberflöte* overture, *Attention! Bandits!* presents a complete performance of the K. 467 slow movement, and as in the case of the overture, scenes are carefully cut to coincide with the structural articulations of the music.[79] In terms of the action, the K. 467 slow movement orchestrates the first few months that Verini is in prison and Marie-Sophie is at her Swiss boarding school. So, for example, the major change of scene as Marie-Sophie narrates her interest in equestrian pursuits (critical to later scenes in the film) occurs at the beginning of the d minor episode at bar 40, the first of several scenes of walks by the lake is cut to the B-flat major episode at bar 62, and the reprise of the main orchestral tutti in A-flat major introduces the scene with Verini and the spider (ex. 9.5).

The movement ends as the treacherous Michelle arrives with Christmas presents and lies about the life of Marie-Sophie's mother in Brazil.[80] Marie-Sophie is then seen lying in bed staring at the ceiling, and this is how the K. 466 *romance* begins, although now Marie-Sophie is much older, providing a perfect point of symmetry around the intervening years.[81]

Only the first thirty-nine bars of the K. 466 *romance* are employed in this scene (out of a total of 162), but it is handled in exactly the same way as the K. 467 slow movement. Accordingly, a further scene by the lake is cut to the orchestral tutti at bar 9, and the scene of horses in the snow is cut to the orchestral reprise at bar 29. It is difficult to assess the aesthetic impact of the truncated performance of the K. 466 *romance*; it does much less narrative work than the K. 467 slow movement and clearly evokes none of the musico-cinematographic tradition that is so

[79] *Attention! Bandits!*, 25' 48".
[80] ibid., 32' 29".
[81] ibid., 33' 45".

important to K. 467, but it is equally true that the accompanying action to the *romance* is much more compressed; while the two Mozart movements are balanced around Marie-Sophie's change of age, the K. 466 movement also appears relegated to a kind of codicil to the scene rather than as an equal partner.[82] This impression is reinforced by the literary frame given to the entire scene, which begins with Marie-Sophie's English class, where the tutor puts the quotation "If a way to the better be, it lies in

EXAMPLE 9.5 (a): *Mozart, Piano Concerto 21, C major, second movement, 40–48.*

---

[82] The slow movement of K. 467, and therefore the scene, lasts six and a half minutes, whereas the K. 466 extract lasts less than two minutes.

EXAMPLE 9.5 (b): *Mozart, Piano Concerto 21, C major, second movement, 62–70.*

EXAMPLE 9.5 (c): *Mozart, Piano Concerto 21, C major, second movement, 73–93.*

EXAMPLE 9.5 (c): *Mozart, Piano Concerto 21, C major, second movement, 73–93 continued*

EXAMPLE 9.5 (c): *Mozart, Piano Concerto 21, C major, second movement, 73–93 continued*

taking a full look at the worst" on the chalkboard. (This is a slight misquotation from Thomas Hardy's poem "De Profundis": "If way to the Better there be, it exacts a full look at the Worst)."[83] The extended scene then closes with Verini, still in prison, reading Oscar Wilde's text with the same name as Hardy's poem, *De profundis*, with the subtitled text "I want to be able to say without affectation that my two turning points were when Father sent me to Oxford and Society sent me to prison."[84]

The scene of Marie-Sophie growing up in Switzerland and her epistolary relationship with her father employs the slow movements of two Mozart piano concertos composed within weeks of each other in February to March 1785, framed by near-contemporary English poets writing with identical Latin titles. Given this pairing, it is difficult to believe that the specific choices of texts and music were anything other than entirely deliberate, and the highly literate intertextual references between Wilde and Hardy simply reinforce the musically highly literate correlations between music and narrative.

Notwithstanding the fact that it frequently appears alongside other popular works by Mozart, the slow movement of the Piano Concerto No. 21 in C Major, K. 467, is the most widely and extensively employed piece of the composer's music in film of the last half century. Whether screen villains attempt to appropriate the movement as cultural capital, whether the movement is used to empathetic or other ends, or whether the film embodies a character himself called Mozart, the music is used and reused in ways that very few other pieces can match. This renown is a consequence of the single usage in the 1967 film *Elvira Madigan*, whose celebrity provided a springboard for future use.

Deeply embedded in practices from the 1960s that prized direction from the keyboard and complete recordings of such repertories as Mozart's piano concertos, the K. 467 piano concerto rapidly became associated almost exclusively with the film in which it played a part, to the extent that the "Elvira Madigan" concerto took on the same status as the "Moonlight" sonata or the "Rider" string quartet. The concerto movement has moved effortlessly across cinematographic genres, encompassing psychodrama, teenage comedy, comedies of manners, ecodisaster blockbusters, the Bond franchise, and science fiction. In some cases, its use has been so extensive that the movement has either taken on a structural role in the film (*Attention! Bandits!*) or has underpinned complete and extended scenes (*Préparez vos mouchoirs*). While in many respects standing as a synecdoche for Mozart's entire œuvre, the "Elvira Madigan" concerto has traced a genealogy of Mozart in film music from 1967 to the present.

---

[83] *Attention! Bandits!*, 25' 48".
[84] Ibid., 35' 39".

{ 10 }

Conclusion

THE MOZART EFFECT

Technology: Two Moments

1

Getreidegaße 9, Salzburg. The year 2006 saw the 250th anniversary of Mozart's birth, and although it did not witness quite the same frenzy of concerts, festivals, and conferences as the 200th anniversary of his death in 1991, it still represented an important contour on the landscape of modern Mozart reception. I was not immune to the frenzy, with invitations to attend two conferences in London, which did little more than celebrate Mozart's birth, early in 2006. The significance of the anniversary was soon made explicit. Like those of many academics, my evenings free from other obligations are occupied with attending to correspondence, stroking colleagues' egos, and pandering to deans. My work—if that is what it could really be called—was interrupted on the evening of 27 January 2006 by the arrival of an email from the Salzburg Tourist Board with an invitation to consult a link that consisted of a live video feed from Getreidegaße 9, the so-called Mozart Geburthaus.[1] As an alternative to reading yet more dismal email, the link was irresistible. The video recorded an attractive sight: the house lit up with candles in the windows, other buildings along the street similarly illuminated, tourists—pilgrims?—in the street. The overall effect was one of quiet calm with some gentle movement in the foreground.

I am still not sure why I received the message with its enclosed link, but it was as if I was being invited to be present at a reinscription of Mozart's birth, a kind of

---

[1] The video feed has since been taken down, and the link has disappeared. See, however, the website for the Salzburg Tourist Board, http://www.salzburg.info/de/ (accessed 10 July 2012).

global witnessing after the fact. Readers of this book will have little difficulty in identifying an invitation to observe the birth of a baby son as having very obvious New Testament—Nativity—overtones, although Getreidegaße is hardly a stable anymore, and the ox and the ass were barely in evidence. But for the kings and shepherds invited electronically to witness the birth of the musical boy king—albeit 250 years too late—with rather different gifts, no livestock was on offer, nor any myrrh or frankincense. Gold, of course, was central to the endeavor.

The video distributed on 27 January 2006 is no longer available, but the Salzburg tourist office continues to exploit its Mozart capital. Its home page, alongside conventional invitations to fly, book hotels, and visit monuments, places "W. A. Mozart" ahead of the Salzburg Festival, even ahead of *The Sound of Music*, even apparently ahead of the center of the city's UNESCO world heritage status, granted in 1996.[2] "High" art, here, runs ahead of Rogers and Hammerstein and of the culture industry, but high art is embedded in the life and work of a single composer, and the city—as the Tourist Board is quick to stress, "is closely associated with Mozart and his world-famous compositions."

2

The corner of Fifty-third and Broadway. The ubiquitous exchange of links on YouTube means that events are easy and fast to distribute, so only a few months after the invitation to the Salzburg nativity scene, I was sent a link to a now well-known video of what can only be described as a critical, perhaps fundamental, moment in recent Mozart reception.[3] The short (41 seconds) video records a performance by the visual humorist, fantasy artist, and musician Michel Lauzière of the first thirty-two bars of the first movement of Mozart's Symphony in g minor, K. 550 (omitting the opening accompaniment). The performance is generated by placing wine bottles filled with various quantities of water in two rows along a road temporarily closed to traffic. The performer is equipped with rollerblades furnished with flexible extensions to their sides so that they strike the bottles of water, and the performer is moved along the rows of bottles by means of ski poles. Careful placement of the bottles of water, and skilful control of speed produce an identifiable performance of the opening of Mozart's symphony (fig. 10.1).

The date at which this video was posted (November 2006) and its original broadcast on the *Late Show with David Letterman* on CBS (11 May 2006) strongly suggests

---

[2] See Salzburg Tourist Board, http://www.salzburg/info/de/ (accessed 10 July 2012). For the Salzburg Festival, Josef Kaut, *Die Salzburg Festspiele, 1920–1981* (Salzburg: Residenz, 1982), and Stephen Gallup, *A History of the Salzburg Festival* (London: Weidenfeld and Nicolson, 1987), are useful. See also Michael P. Steinberg, *The Meaning of the Salzburg Festival: Austria as Theater and Ideology, 1890–1938* (Ithaca and London: Cornell University Press, 1990).

[3] Available at http://www.youtube.com/watch?v=PxAqzMLIDns (accessed 22 July 2011).

FIGURE 10.1: *Michel Lauzière performing Mozart's Symphony 41, g minor, K. 550, First movement*

that it was a further act of homage on the 250th anniversary of Mozart's birth. The location of the event was Fifty-third Street in New York City, starting at the corner of Fifty-third and Broadway.[4] There is no doubt that the technical means of producing sound were as much grounds for applause as the composition itself, and this is as true of the YouTube video as it must have been for the performance. But although the selection of work was ambitious, given the technology available, the choice of composer was also entirely predictable. Whether the work was in any way determined by the strangely popular cover "Mozart 40" of the album *20 Suosikkia: Oi niitä aikoja* (1971), by Päivi Paunu and Aarno Raninen, which had brought this movement into the domain of popular culture for the first time, albeit with a disco beat, is an open question; it is certainly not one of the more obvious works for this sort of populist treatment.

These two examples serve as a productive way of concluding such a work as *Mozart's Ghosts*, exemplifying as they do the ways technologies continue to evolve and the ways Mozart's reputation and renown continue to evolve with them. They represent fitting pendants to the nineteenth- and twentieth-century tropes that have served as the subjects of this book.

The Mozart Effect™

If my two technological examples demonstrate the modern ubiquity of Mozart, a composer who can stand for classical music as it competes with technology,

---

[4] I am grateful to Michel Lauzière for a discussion of this performance (personal communication, 18 February 2012).

popular culture, and the heritage industry, the Mozart Effect™ is something rather different. The history of the Mozart Effect™ looks simple at first glance: Frances Rauscher and her colleagues at the University of California at Irvine published an article in 1993 entitled "Music and Spatial Task Performance" in the journal *Nature*.[5] They reported on three groups of individuals tasked with performing the same spatial task, the first group listening to Mozart's Sonata for Two Pianos in D major, K. 448, the second group listening to a relaxation tape, and the third group listening in silence.[6] Rauscher and her colleagues found that the group who listened to Mozart reported a less than 10 percent improvement on the two other groups. The research presented in the one-page article in *Nature* was picked up by Richard A. Knox in the *Boston Globe* almost immediately. His article, a less than adulatory account, nevertheless coined the key phrase "the Mozart Effect" for the first time, as follows: "Unfortunately, the researchers found, the Mozart effect wears off after the 10 minutes or so it took to administer the IQ test."[7] Nearly twenty years after the event, Rauscher reminisced that "all of a sudden the term ["the Mozart Effect"] was everywhere,"[8] including, one might add, in her own follow-up study of 1995.[9] As John Sloboda has remarked, the subsequent history of the concept of the "Mozart effect" varied in the scientific and popular domains: the scientific trajectory was characterized by largely failed attempts to replicate the Irvine findings (Rauscher's single attempt in her 1995 follow-up study was a rare exception) and a reluctance to pursue the original research team's attempts to identify the ways in which the research might have been enhanced.[10]

Outside the scientific domain, the term "the Mozart Effect" was trademarked by Don Campbell in April 1996 and served as the title for a key text, *The Mozart Effect: Tapping the Power of Music to Heal the Body, Strengthen the Mind, and Unlock the Creative Spirit*, published in 1997 with a second edition in 2001.[11] This book served as a center of a matrix of books, cassette tapes, CDs, downloads, and web resources that have reinforced Don G. Campbell Inc. as the central market driver for this material.[12] The scientific community was clear about the dubious

---

[5] Frances M. Rauscher, Gordon L. Shaw, and Katherine N. Kym, "Music and Spatial Task Performance," *Nature* 365 (October 1993), 611.

[6] The original Köchel number in the article was incorrect and has been corrected by hand in online versions of the text; the original appears to have had "6" as the central number, with the original erroneous entry probably K. 468, which is the 1785 *Lied zur Gesellenreise*.

[7] Richard A. Knox, "Mozart Makes you Smarter Calif. Researchers Suggest," *Boston Globe*, 14 October 1993.

[8] Frances Rauscher, undated personal communication to John Sloboda, cited in his "Mozart in Psychology," *Music Performance Research* 1 (2007), 72.

[9] Frances H. Rauscher, Gordon L. Shaw, and Katherine N. Ky, "Listening to Mozart Enhances Spatial-Temporal Reasoning: Towards a Neurophysiological Basis," *Neuroscience Letters* 185 (1995), 47.

[10] Sloboda, "Mozart in Psychology," 72.

[11] Don Campbell, *The Mozart Effect: Tapping the Power of Music to Heal the Body, Strengthen the Mind, and Unlock the Creative Spirit* (New York: Avon Books, 1997; 2nd ed. New York: Quill, 2001).

[12] See "The Mozart Effect Resource Center," http://www.mozarteffect.com/ (accessed 10 July 2012), where full listings of all the commercially available material are given.

nature of the claims made in *The Mozart Effect* and in related material. Sloboda summed up the position in 2006: "in the media, the false idea was rapidly promoted that listening to Mozart had long term positive effects on the intellectual development of children";[13] he could well have added adults to the target market for the Mozart Effect™, given the target for much of Campbell's endeavors. The impact of the Mozart Effect™ on children in the United States was immense, however, with some states prescribing classical music for schools and expectant mothers.[14]

This is not the place to engage with the detail of either the experimental findings or the commercial success of the Mozart Effect™ (although in a longer book, an account of its success would have certainly appeared). The key question, which addresses issues raised time and time again in this book, is why the *Mozart* Effect™? In an important series of exchanges between Rauscher and Sloboda in 2005, Rauscher suggests—almost certainly correctly:

> I don't think the term "Couperin Effect" has the same appeal as the term "Mozart Effect." Just about everyone in Western society has heard of Wolfgang Amadeus Mozart, *even those who have never heard a note of his music....* I speculate that had we chosen a different composer, and found the same effects, the media would have publicized a "classical music" effect, rather than an effect named for the composer—unless, of course, the composer were Beethoven or some other musical behemoth [emphasis added].[15]

She goes on to cite such well-known pieces of evidence as the Schaffer/Foreman film *Amadeus* and Mozart's early death. Whether "the Beethoven Effect" would have taken off quite so readily is difficult to judge. But Rauscher's view that Mozart effectively stands for classical music is one this book has been at pains to explore, as well as the phenomenon she speaks of here: that a knowledge of Mozart—or "Mozart" perhaps—does not require a knowledge of a single note of his music.

In the acknowledgements to *The Mozart Effect*, dated 1997, Campbell makes reference to Dr. Alfred Tomatis, "who has researched the use of Mozart's music for nearly thirty years and who introduced me to the Mozart Effect a dozen years ago."[16] If this chronology is correct, Campbell is claiming to have been introduced to the Mozart Effect in 1985, well before Rauscher and her colleagues' experiments or what is thought to be the first public coining of the term in the *Boston Globe* in 1993. This is difficult to confirm or deny, but the importance of Tomatis's theoret-

---

[13] Rauscher, personal communication to Sloboda, 29 December 2005, cited in Sloboda, "Mozart in Psychology," 73.

[14] See Adrian Bangerter and Chip Heath, "The Mozart Effect: Tracking the Evolution of a Scientific Legend," *British Journal of Social Psychology* 43 (2004), 609.

[15] Sloboda, "Mozart in Psychology," 73.

[16] Campbell, *The Mozart Effect*, ix (p. nos. refer to 2001 2nd ed.).

ical work and interest in Mozart specifically is central to the question Rauscher
addresses in the above quotation. Campbell includes a short section in *The Mozart
Effect* entitled "Why Mozart?"[17] Campbell quotes directly from *Pourquoi Mozart?*—
Tomatis's 1991 study: "He has an effect, an impact, which the others do not have.
Exception among exceptions [an echo here of Hoffmann's *Oper aller Opern*], he
has a liberating, curative, I would say, *healing* power. His efficacy exceeds by far
what we observe among his predecessors…his contemporaries, or his succes-
sors."[18]

Despite the reference to Hoffmann's 1813 descriptor of *Don Giovanni*, Tomatis
in fact largely restricts his comments to assertions devoid of nineteenth- and twentieth-century traditions and tropes. Not so Campbell, who, after an outline of Mozart's birth and childhood and a restatement of the view of Mozart as the "Eternal
Child," launches into a series of retreads of nineteenth- and twentieth-century
views of the composer.[19] As part of the conclusion to *Mozart's Ghosts*, these comments are convincing proof not only of the longevity of so many of the tropes of
Mozart reception but also of their continued impact on musical and artistic culture
today. Campbell begins with a comfortable elision of Mozart's "compositional and
performing genius" and "chaos in his personal life" and, after pointing to what may
well be erroneous accounts of his appearance, relationships, and scatological
amusements that readers of this book will now recognize as typical of nineteenth-
and twentieth-century reception, turns to a discursive style that would not have
been out of place 150 years ago:

> Vain and innocent, worldly and naïve, Mozart never tried to understand
> who he was, but his ingenious naïveté was a perfect vessel for his seemingly
> heaven-sent compositions. No matter how absurd and tragic his life (and his
> death, at thirty-five), the channel to celestial harmony was never inter-
> rupted.…His work celebrates the freedom of human thought that was
> beginning to show its colors beneath the pale makeup and powered wigs of
> a feudal caste society in Europe and a colonial empire in America. More
> important, there is an *elegance and deeply felt sympathy* in Mozart's music.
> His art remains serene, never becoming strident [emphasis added].[20]

Certainly typical of the 1860s or before, Campbell's world of Mozart selectively
reads some of the tropes of the past and ignores others—the image of Mozart the
demonic or difficult, for example—in exactly the same way as so many predecessors.

---

[17] Ibid., 27–30.
[18] "Il a un effet, une action que n'ont pas les autres. Exception parmi les exceptions, il détient un
pouvoir libérateur, curatif, j'allais dire *guérisseur*. Son efficacité dépasse de loin ce que nous pouvons
observer tant avec les musiciens qui l'ont précédé …ses contemporains ou ses successeurs"; Alfred A.
Tomatis, *Pourquoi Mozart?* (Paris: Fixot, 1991), 16–17.
[19] Campbell, *The Mozart Effect*, 28–29.
[20] Ibid., 29.

The Mozart Effect

It is entirely possible that much of the antipathy to the Mozart Effect™ in the scientific and musicological community has been animated by the trademarking of two words that seem to belong to all. Effect or "impact" is a direct translation of *Wirkung*, shown to be so important for the theoretical underpinning of work in Mozart reception early on in this book, but this is nothing, perhaps, to the trademarking of the name of the composer who is the subject of this study. But almost everything in this book has been about the Mozart effect: the effect of the composer's life, work, and milieu on the century that immediately followed his death, and the century after that, right up to the present. But it is clearly a very different enterprise from the Mozart Effect™. Whatever view one might take of the commercial success of the latter, its ahistorical, purpose-driven objectives stand at a distance from the aims of *Mozart's Ghosts*.

In this book, the aim has been to identify and examine a number of interrelated sites of Mozart reception: points in the last two and a quarter centuries where Mozart, the legends surrounding him, performances of his music, stories about him and his music, have left an imprint on the history of music, arts, and culture in general. Whether it is performances of a work not even by Mozart in the chapel of the Portuguese Embassy in the 1820s or his deification at the Salzburg Festival in the 1930s, these are points in the history of Europe that can only be correctly understood in the terms set forth in this book. The concept of "site" has always been an attractive one in this context, accompanied as it is by the idea of building or archaeology: work-in-progress, provisionality, untidiness, to say nothing of the constant presence of Dahlhaus's "rubble." And while it would be a foolish ambition to attempt to "tidy up" such a site, to understand the disorder in such an environment, much in the same way an archaeologist seeks to understand the layers of Anglo-Saxon, Roman, and medieval in a single site, has very much been the subject of this book.

But the study of Mozart reception is not archaeology, for despite the doomed attempts to deny the existence of musical works, the history of music and the study of musical reception has to negotiate the cultural artefacts posterity has bequeathed to subsequent generations. Centrally it has to be recognized that all musical works are subject to variability in performance, in transmission, and in any type of use, and this book has been at pains constantly to ground observations on the reception of Mozart in the precise configuration of a particular work at a particular time. This is a process fraught with difficulties, not all of which have been overcome in this book. For example, I have happily compared the 1845 versions of *Mozart und Schikaneder* with Offenbach's 1856 *L'impresario* in the certain, but tacit, knowledge that in all Offenbach's early works, large parts of the spoken dialogue and certainly some of the music were subject to the use of *cascades*—ad lib. improvisations for the sake of enhancing the humor—to which it is almost completely impossible to gain any form of access other than the purely incidental. And although this is a difficulty that could be replicated over and over again, this book has engaged with the problem at every turn, setting out the nature of the difficulties right at the beginning of its first chapter.

This book has moved the study of reception yet further away from the study of the press by the engagement with media of all types: performance and publication, yes—and the press, film, theatre, the novel, travelogue, and material culture in a variety of forms. Other forms contributed in part to my initial view of the subject—tourism, advertising, and television for example—but eventually found no place in the final version of the book, although they, too, emerge incidentally from time to time. But if this book has raised the question of the range of media that might serve as the basis for an investigation into the reception of works of music, then it will in part have served its purpose.

Further scope still remains for an examination of the metanarratives that govern the reception of Mozart's music between 1791 and the present. Many have arisen: the demonic, the naïve, "Back to Mozart," the Olympian, and so on. But in such a work as this book, it has been inevitably difficult to foreground such metanarratives while at the same time interrogating specific sites of Mozart reception. When the time comes for a rewriting of Gruber's *Mozart und die Nachwelt* that can profit from the large numbers of case studies written since it was published nearly thirty years ago, that will be the moment for a systematic review of the ways these metanarratives intertwine, amalgamate, and supplant one another.

It is for readers to decide whether this book has managed to examine what for much of the time is a hagiography of the composer while at the same time resisting the temptation either to collapse into reinscribing the same hagiographies into its text or simply sneering at them as if they had no value at all. I hope that my interest in the sites of Mozart reception as stories that have been told, sometimes in good faith, sometimes perhaps not, has revealed that these stories are precisely that—stories—but also that "history" and "story" are cognates: they share the same etymological root, and both form the basis of the history of music that we continue to value as a central part of our culture.

{BIBLIOGRAPHY}

Primary Sources

PUBLISHED WORKS

A GEORGES BIZET / SCÈNES HONGROISES / *2me Suite d'Orchestre* / . . . / MUSIQUE DE / J. MASSENET / . . . PARIS / G. HARTMANN, Editeur, 60, Rue Neuve-St-Augustin.

AGNUS DEI / 12TH MASS / MOZART / Arr^d^ by E. C. F. HARE / At LAFLEUR and SON, Music Publishers, 15 Green Street, Leicester Sq: London W.C [1873].

AIRS DE BALLETS INTERCALÉS DANS L'OPÉRA / DE / DON JUAN / DE / W. MOZART / À / l'Académie Impériale de Musique / TRANSCRITS POUR LE PIANO PAR / CHARLES MAGNE / PARIS / MAISON ARTISTIQUE, 8 rue Ollivier en face N. D. de Lorette, rue Fléchier, 2, H. L. D'AUBEL EDIT^R^.

Allem, Maurice, ed. *A. de Musset: Théatre Complet: Comédies et proverbes, théâtre complémentaire, théâtre posthume.* Bibliothèque de la Pleiade 17. Paris: Gallimard, 1947.

Allem, Maurice, ed. *Alfred de Musset: Poésies Complètes.* Bibliothèque de la Pleiade 12. Paris: Gallimard, 1957.

A MADEMOISELLE ELISABETH de PRADES / DON JUAN / de / W. MOZART / FANTAISIE BRILLANTE / POUR LE PIANO / PAR / J. LEŸBACH / Paris, COLOMBIER, Editeur, 6, r. Vivienne, au coin de la Galerie Vivienne.

A Mademoiselle / *JOSÉPHINE CUVRU* / DON JUAN / DE MOZART / FANTAISIE pour PIANO / *J. B. DUVERNOY.* / *OP. 284* / *PR 7^f^ 50* / PARIS / G. BRANDUS ET S. DUFOUR Editeurs, 103 rue Richelieu.

A Mademoiselle / MARIE MONTFORT / DON JUAN / de MOZART / VALSE de SALON / POUR PIANO PAR / Fréd. BURGMÜLLER / . . . / Paris, LÉON GRUS, Editeur, 31 Boulev^t^ Bonne Nouvelle. / *Londres et Mayence, Schott.*

à Mademoiselle / Mathilde Sautter / Don Juan / Opéra de MOZART / *FANTAISIE BRILLANTE* / *pour* / LE PIANO PAR / J. RUMMEL / *Paris, LÉON GRUS, Editeur, 31, Boulevart Bonne-Nouvelle.*

à Melle Isabelle VINCHON / Souvenir / de Mozart / . . . / N°. 2 / DON-JUAN / POLKA ESPAGNOLE / 2 / Polkas Brillantes / POUR LE PIANO / PAR / G. WOLFRAMM CARON / . . . / Paris, JOLY, Editeur / Imp^r^. de Musique / *rue Bonaparte, N°. 3, 1–2.*

à Melle Marie Lemaire / DON JUAN / Opéra de Mozart / MÉLANGE / *des plus jolis motifs arrangés* / POUR / PIANO / *PAR* / MAURICE LEE / Prix: 6f / *Paris,* JULES HEINZ *éditeur* / *146 rue de Rivoli.*

A Mlle CAROLINE LÉVY / DON JUAN / DE / MOZART / Souvenirs Mélodiques / POUR LE PIANO / PAR / A. BOULEAU-NELDY / OP: 43 PR: 7^f^ 50 / *Paris, au Magasin de Musique du Bazar de l'Industrie française* / O. LEGOUIX, Edit^r^, Boulev^d^ Poissonnière, 27.

A MONSIEUR / JULES PASDELOUP. / SUITE D'ORCHESTRE / EN 4 PARTIES / PAR / E. GUIRAUD / Arrangé pour Piano à 4 mains par l'Auteur / . . . / Paris, Maison FLAXLAND / DURAND, SCHŒNWERK & Cie.

A Monsieur le Docteur KOPFF / Suite Algérienne / *Impressions pittoresques d'un voyage en Algérie* /…/ PAR / C. SAINT-SAËNS / OP: 60 / PARIS, DURAND, SCHŒNWERK & Cie. / *Ancne Maison G. FLAXLAND* / 4 Place de la Madeleine.

à Mr Michel Bergson / *SCÈNE DU BAL* / DU / DON JUAN / DE / *MOZART* / *MENUET* / Trio des Masques / Air de Don Juan / Transcrits et variés / *PAR* / W. KRÜGER / *Op 140* / AU MÉNESTREL rue Vivienne 2bis, HEUGEL & Cie, / *Editeurs, Fournisseurs du Conservatoire* / *Londres et Mayence Schott.*

Anderson, Emily, ed. *The Letters of Mozart and His Family.* London and New York: Macmillan, 1966. 3rd ed. 1985.

Anthem / "I WILL CRY UNTO GOD WITH MY VOICE," / (MOZART.) / *Adapted expressly for the* / Choir of Durham Cathedral, / (BY A FORMER MEMBER.) / *from the* / 'ET INCARNATUS', & 'ET RESURREXIT," MASS No 12. / *revised, edited, & respectfully dedicated by permission to* / The Honourable George Wingfield Bourke, / PRESIDENT, / *AND THE GENTLEMEN OF THE CHORAL SOCIETY OF UNIVERSITY COLLEGE DURHAM,* / BY / CHARLES ASHTON, / OF THE CATHEDRAL CHOIR. /…/ LONDON / *Published for the Editor, by* / JOSEPH WILLIAMS, 123, CHEAPSIDE. / J SMITH, & T. KAYE, MUSIC SELLERS, DURHAM.

Bauer, Wilhelm A., and Otto Erich Deutsch, eds. *Mozart: Briefe und Aufzeichungen Gesamtausgabe.* 6 vols. Kassel: Bärenreiter, 1962–71.

Blaze, Ange-Henri (Blaze de Bury). *Écrivains et poètes de l'Allemagne.* Paris: Lévy, 1846.

Blaze, Ange-Henri (Blaze de Bury). *Le Faust de Goethe, traduction complète précédée d'un essai sur Goethe, accompagnée de notes et de commentaires et suivie d'une étude sur la mystique du poème.* Paris: Charpentier, 1840.

Blaze, Ange-Henri (Blaze de Bury). *Musiciens contemporains.* Collection Michel Lévy. Paris: Lévy, 1856.

Blaze, Ange-Henri (Blaze de Bury). *Musiciens du passé, du présent et de l'avenir*, Bibliothèque contemporaine. Paris: Calmann-Lévy, 1880.

Bouquet de Mélodies / POUR / PIANO / PAR / CRAMER / 21. DON JUAN, *opéra de Mozart* / Paris, rue St Honoré, chez CHOUDENS, Éditeur.

Cellarius, Henri. *Danses des salons.* Paris: author, 1847. Reprint, with an introduction by Rémi Hess, Grenoble: Millon, 1993.

Cohen, Robert, and Yves Gérard, eds. *Hector Berlioz: La Critique Musicale, 1823–1863.* 10 vols. Paris: Buchet/Castel, 1996–.

Croll, Gerhard, ed. *Der Schauspieldirektor.* Neue Mozart-Ausgabe II/5/15. Kassel: Bärenreiter, 1958; 2nd ed. 1990.

De Bornier, Henri. *Poésies Complètes (1850–1893).* Paris: Dentu, 1894.

Da Ponte, Lorenzo. *Mémoires (1749–1838) suivies de lettres inédites de Lorenzo Da Ponte à Jacques Casanova.* Ed. Raoul Vèze Jadis et Naguère. Paris: Jonquières, 1931.

Der / *Schauspieldirektor* / *Ein* / *Gelegenheitsstück* / *in* / *einem Aufzuge* / *WJEN,* / *bei Joseph Edlen von Kurzbek k.k. Hofbuchdrucker* / *Groß = und Buchhändler.* / 1786.

Der / Schauspieldirektor / — / Komische Operette von L. Schneider. / — / Musik von W. A. Mozart. / — / Officielle Bearbeitung für die Leipziger Bühne / Leipzig, / Druck und Verlag von Breitkopf und Härtel.

Dibdin, Thomas Frognall. *A Bibliographical, Antiquarian and Picturesque Tour in the Northern Counties of England and in Scotland.* 3 vols. London: author, 1838.

DON GIOVANNI / *Dramma Giocoso* / in due Atti / *Messo in Musica dal Signor* / W. A. MOZART / *Edition Dédiée* / *Aux Souscripteurs* / PAR L'ÉDITEUR / No. 2 de la Collection des Opéra[s] de Mozart / *A PARIS* / *Au Mag*in *de J. FREY, Artiste de l'Académie Royale, Editeur de Musique…/ Plce des Victoires No. 8.*

DON GIOVANNI / DRAMMA GIOCOSO IN DUE ATTI / MUSICA / DI W.-MOZART. / — / PARIGI / MICHEL LÉVY FRERES, ÉDITEURS / RUE VIVIENNE, 2 BIS / — / 1856 / DON JUAN / OPÉRA BOUFFON EN DEUX ACTES / MUSIQUE / DE W.-A. MOZART / — / PARIS / MICHEL LÉVY FRERES, ÉDITEURS / RUE VIVIENNE, 2 BIS / — / 1856.

DON JUAN / DE / MOZART / QUADRILLE des Bals de la Cour et de L'OPÉRA / PAR / STRAUSS /…/ Paris, AU MÉNESTREL, 2bis. rue Vivienne HEUGEL & Cie / *Editeurs-Libraires pour la France et l'Étranger.*

DON JUAN / (DON GIOVANNI) / OPÉRA DE / MOZART / *Partition Piano seul complète.* / PRIX NET: 5 FRANCS / Paris, Editeur, LÉON ESCUDIER, 21, r. de Choiseul.

DON JUAN / Fantaisie / pour Piano / PAR / G. REDLER / Op. 110 / *À PARIS CHEZ EMILE CHATOT ÉDITEUR DE MUSIQUE, / 2 rue de la Feuillade Place des Victoires.*

DON JUAN / Opéra de / Mozart / *MOSAÏQUE, / Pour / Le* PIANO *par* / FR. RYSLER /…/ *Paris, LÉON GRUS, Editeur,* 31, *Boulevart Bonne-Nouvelle.*

DON JUAN, / OPÉRA EN CINQ ACTES / DE MOZART, / TRADUCTION FRANCAISE / DE MM. ÉMILE DESCHAMPS ET HENRY BLAZE, / DIVERTISSEMENS DE M. CORALY.—DÉCORS DE MM. CICÉRI, FEUCHÈRE, / DESPLÉCHIN, LÉGER, FILASTRE ET CAMBON. / Représenté pour la premère fois, à Paris, sur le théâtre de l'Académie / Royale de Musique, le 10 mars 1834, et repris sur le même théâtre, / le 26 mars 1841 / NOUVELLE ÉDITION, / Conforme à la Repésentation. / PARIS. / MICHEL FRÈRES, LIBRAIRES, / RUE ET TERRASSE VIVIENNE, 1, ET RUE MARIE-STUART, 6. / C. TRESSE, / LIBRAIRE AU PALAIS-ROYAL, / Me Ve JONAS, / LIBRAIRE DE L'OPÉRA. / 1841.

THE DUKE of YORK'S / NEW MARCH *as performed by* / HIS ROYAL HIGHNESS'S NEW BAND / *in the Coldstream Reg*t. *of Guards* / *Composed, and Arranged for the* / PIANO FORTE or HARPSICHORD / *by C. H. Eley* /…/ LONDON / Printed by Longman and Broderip No. 26 Cheapside and No. 13 Hay Market.

ECOLES FRANCAISE, ALLEMANDE, ITALIENNE. / CHEFS D'ŒUVRE / DES / GRANDS MAITRES / TRANSCRIPTIONS / POUR PIANO PAR / LEO MARESSE / Paris chez FÉLIX JANET, EDITR Boulevart Poissonnière, 5.

Ella, John. *Musical Sketches, Abroad and at Home with Original Music by Mozart, Czerny, Graun etc.* London: Ridgway, 1869.

FAUST / Opéra en cinq Actes / DE / Jules BARBIER et Michel CARRÉ / Musique de / CH. GOUNOD / — / Partition Chant et Piano / Transcrite par LÉO DELIBES / — / Paris, CHOUDENS, Editeur / 30 Boulevard des Capucines, 30. / — Belgique: Vve MU-RAILLE.

Fétis, François-Joseph. *Biographie universelle des musiciens et bibliographie générale de la musique.* 2nd ed. 8 vols. With supp. in 2 vols. Paris: Firmin Didot, 1860–65.

FORMAT LEMOINE / POLYEUCTE / OPÉRA EN CINQ ACTES / PAROLES DE / JULES BARBER ET MICHEL CARRÉ / MUSIQUE DE / CH. GOUNOD / DE L'INSTITUT /…/ PARIS / HENRY LEMOINE, ÉDITEUR, RUE PIGALLE, 17.

GLORIA IN EXCELSIS DEO / FROM / Mozart's 12ᵗʰ Mass / ARRANGED FOR THE / Pianoforte / *and Dedicated to* / The Misses Musters, / *(of Colwick, near Nottingham[)]* / BY / HENRY FARMER / LONDON / JOSEPH WILLIAMS, 123, CHEAPSIDE; MOZART'S / GLORIA IN EXCELSIS / *from his* 12ᵗʰ *Mass,* / Arranged expressly / FOR THE / Piano Forte / BY / H. G. NIXON / *LONDON* / HARRY MAY, / MUSIC PUBLISHER AND PIANO FORTE MANUFACTURER, 11 HOLBORN BARS.

Grande / *FANTAISIE* / POUR LE PIANO / *Sur* / La Sérénade et Le Menuet. / *DE* / DON JUAN / *Par* / S. THALBERG / *Paris chez E Troupenas & Cⁱᵉ Rue NᵛᵉᵛVivienne,* 40.

Grangé, Eugène, and Philippe Gilles. *Le carnaval des revues: Revue de carnaval en 2 actes et 9 tableaux; Les souper de mardi-gras, prologue, Paris, Bouffes-parisiens, le 10 février 1860...Musique de Jacques Offenbach.* [Paris]: Michel Lévy frères, [1860].

G. Schirmer's Octavo Church Music / General / Anthems / No. 7212 / Gloria in Excelsis / From / W. A Mozart's Twelfth Mass / Arranged / For Three-Part Chorus / Of Women's Voices / By / W. G. Owst / G Schirmer Inc., New York.

Gugler, Bernhard, ed. *Mozart's Don Giovanni: Partitur erstmals nach dem Autograph herausgegeben unter Beifügung einer neuen Textverdeutschung.* Breslau: Leuckart, 1868.

Hirsch, Rudolf. *Mozart's "Schauspieldirektor": Musikalische Reminiscenzen.* Leipzig: Heinrich Matthes, 1859.

Hoffmann, Ernst Theodor Amadeus. "Don Juan: Eine fabelhafte Begebenheit, die sich mit einem reisendem Enthusiasten zugetragen." *Allgemeine musikalische Zeitung,* 31 March 1813; reprinted in Hoffmann, *Fantasie-Stücke in Callot's Manier mit einer Vorrede von Jean Paul.* 2 vols. Bamberg: Kunz, 1814. Modern ed. in *E. T. A. Hoffmann: Fantasie- und Nachtstücke: Fantasie-Stücke in Callots Manier, Nachtstücke, Seltsame Leiden eines Theater-Direktors,* ed. Georg von Maassen and Georg Ellinger, 6th ed., 67–78. Düsseldorf and Zurich: Artemis-Winkler, 1996.

Holmes, Edward. *A Critical Notice of Mozart's Twelfth Mass, Extracted from the Papers on Mozart's Masses in the "Musical Times."* London: Novello, s.d.

Holmes, Edward. *The Life of Mozart.* London: Chapman and Hall, 1845.

Holmes, Edward. *The Life of Mozart.* Ed. Ebenezer Prout. London: Novello, Ewer & Co., 1878.

Holmes, Edward. *The Life of Mozart.* Ed. Ernest Newman. Everyman's Library. London: Dent, 1912.

Holl, Monika, and Karl-Heinz Köhler, eds. *Wolfgang Amadeus Mozart: Messe c-moll KV 427 (417a): Faksimile der autgraphen Partitur.* Documenta musicologica 2:9. Kassel: Bärenreiter, 1983.

Hommage à Madame Tarpet-Leclercq / *Professeur au Conservatoire* / DON JUAN / *Opéra de Mozart* / *Souvenirs Mélodiques* / POUR LE PIANO / *PAR* / E. KETTERER / *A PARIS,* / E & A. GIROD *EDITEURS.*

IL DON GIOVANNI / DRAMMA GIOCOSO IN DUE ATTI. / — / DON JUAN / OPERA BOUFFON EN DEXU ACTES, / Représenté, pour la première fois, à Paris, sur le / Théâtre royal Italien, Salle de Louvois, le 3 / Octobre 1820. / PARIS, / AU THÉÂTRE LOUVOIS / — / De l'Imprimerie de HOCQUET, rue du Faubourg Montmartre / — / 1820.

IL DON GIOVANNI, / DRAMMA GIOCOSO IN DUE ATTI. /.../ DON JUAN / OPERA COMIQIUE EN DEUX ACTES, / Représenté, pour la première fois, à Paris, sur le / Théâtre de l'IMPÉRATRICE, le [ ] Octobre 1811 / DE L'IMPRIMERIE DE HOCQUET ET Cⁱᵉ / RUE DU FAUBOURG MONTMARTRE, Nᵒ. 4 / PARIS / AU THÉÂTRE DE L'IMPÉRATRICE / — / 1811.

IN THREE BOOKS / Mozart's Service / N⁰ 12. / ARRANGED EXPRESSLY FOR / TWO PERFORMERS / ON THE / PIANO FORTE / *With ad lib. Accomp*ᵗˢ *for Flute, Violin, & Violoncelli* / BY / WILLIAM HUTCHINS CALLICOTT. / *London, Published by LEADER & COCK, 63, New Bond Street.*

Jahn, Otto. *W. A. Mozart.* 4 vols. Leipzig: Breitkopf und Härtel, 1856–59. Trans. Pauline D. Townsend. 3 vols. London: Novello, Ewer, 1882.

Joyce, James. *Ulysses: A Critical and Synoptic Edition.* Ed. Hans Walter Gabler, Wolfhard Steppe, and Claus Melchior. 3 vols. New York and London: Garland, 1984.

J. R. LAFLEUR & SON'S FIFE & DRUM JOURNAL. / SACRED MARCH / GLORIA / From Mozart's 12ᵗʰ Mass. / EDWIN HARE.

Kierkegaard, Søren. *Either/Or.* Trans. David F. Swenson and Lillian Marvin Swenson. Princeton, N.J.: Princeton University Press, 1971.

Köchel, Ludwig Ritter von. *Chronologisch-thematisches Verzeichnis sämtlicher Tonwerke Wolfgang Amadé Mozarts.* Leipzig: Breitkopf und Härtel, 1862. 8th ed. Ed. Franz Giegling, Alexander Weinmann, and Gerd Sievers. Wiesbaden: Breitkopf und Härtel, 1983.

KYRIE ELEISON / FROM / MOZART'S 12ᵀᴴ MASS / *Arranged as a* / PIANOFORTE TRIO / BY / GEORGE FREDERICK WEST / PR: 5/- / LONDON: ROBERT COCKS & C⁰ / NEW BURLINGTON ST, REGENT ST W.

Leroux, Gaston. *Le fantôme de l'Opéra.* Paris: Livre de Poche, 1983.

Liszt, Franz. "Pauline Viardot-Garcia 1859." *Neue Zeitschrift für Musik,* 28 January 1859. Reprinted in Franz Liszt, *Dramaturgische Blätter: Essays über musikalische Bühnenwerke und Bühnenfragen, Komponisten und Darsteller,* Gesammelte Schriften von Franz Liszt 3/1. Leipzig: Breitkopf und Härtel, 1881.

Lodge, David. *Small World: An Academic Romance.* London: Secker & Warburg, 1984. Reprint, Harmondsworth, England: Penguin, 1985.

London, Jack. *Burning Daylight.* New York: Macmillan, 1910. Reprint, 1961.

Lubin, Georges, ed. *George Sand: Correspondance.* Paris: Garnier, 1972.

Missa / aux C moll / von / W. A. MOZART / Partitur / *Nach der* / hinterlassenen Original=Handschrift herausgegeben / und / *mit einem* VORBERICHT *begleitet* / *von* / A. André. / *Eigenthum des Verlegens und eingetragen in das Vereins-Archiv* / Offenbach ᵃ/ₘ, bei Johann André.

Mörike, Eduard. *Sämtliche Werke.* 2 vols. Ed. Helmut Koopman. Düsseldorf and Zurich: Artemis-Winkler, 1996–97.

Morley, Henry. *The Journal of a London Playgoer.* London: Routledge, 1866.

MOSAÏQUE / SUR / DON JUAN / DE / *MOZART* / POUR PIANO / *PAR* / E. CRAMER / *PARIS,* EUG. MATHEIU, *ÉDIT.* / 30 rue Bonaparte.

MOZART / DON JUAN / OPÉRA EN CINQ ACTES / TRADUCTION FRANÇAISE DE MM. ÉMILE DESCHAMPS ET HENRI BLAZE / REPRÉSENTÉ POUR LA PREMIÈRE FOIS, A PARIS, SUR LE THÉÂTRE DE L'ACADÉMIE ROYALE DE MUSIQUE, / LE 10 MARS 1834, ET REPRIS SUR LE MÊME THÉATRE, L2 2 AVRIL 1866 / NOUVELLE ÉDITION / PARIS / MICHEL LÉVY FRÈRES, LIBRAIRES ÉDITEURS / RUE VIVIENNE, 2 BIS, ET BOULEVARD DES ITALIENS, 15 / A LA LIBRAIRIE NOUVELLE / — / 1866.

Mozart, Wolfgang Amadeus. *Die Zauberflöte.* Ed. Gernot Gruber and Alfred Orel. Neue Ausgabe sämtlicher Werke II/5/19. Kassel: Bärenreiter, 1970.

Mozart, Wolfgang Amadeus. *Don Giovanni.* Ed. Wolfgang Plath and Wolfgang Rehm. Neue Ausgabe sämtlicher Werke II/5/17. Kassel: Bärenreiter, 1968.

Mozart, Wolfgang Amadeus. *KlavierKonzerte*. Vol. 6. Ed. Hans Engel and Horst Heussner. Neue Ausgabe sämtlicher Werke V/15/6. Kassel: Bärenreiter, 1961.

Mozart, Wolfgang Amadeus. *Lieder*. Ed. Ernst August Ballin. Neue Ausgabe sämtlicher Werke III/8. Kassel: Bärenreiter, 1963. 2nd ed. 1987. 3rd ed. 2003.

Mozart, Wolfgang Amadeus. *Messe / à 4 Voix / avec accompagnement de / 2 Violons, 2 Altos, Violoncelle et Basse / 2 Hautbois, 2 Cors, 2 Trompettes, Timballes / et Orgue / Composée par / W. A. MOZART / Partition / Prix 20 Fr*. N°. VII / BONN et cologne chez N. SIM-ROCK. / Propriété de l'éditeur. / 1815.

Mozart, Wolfgang Amadeus. *Missa in c KV 427 (417a)*. Ed. Monika Holl and Karl-Heinz Köhler. Neue Ausgabe sämtlicher Werke I/1/5. Kassel: Bärenreiter, 1983.

Mozart, Wolfgang Amadeus. *MOZART'S MASSES / WITH / an Accompaniment for / THE / Organ, / arranged from the Full Score / BY / VINCENT NOVELLO / Organist to the Portuguese Embassy in London. / No. [1–18] / London. Published b W. Gallaway at his Music and Musical Instrument Warehouse / No. 21 Wigmore Street. Cavendish Square.*

Mozart, Wolfgang Amadeus. MOZART'S TWELFTH MASS "CHORUSES."—NO. 1. / Kyrie Eleison. / J. CURWEN & SONS LTD., 24 BERNERS STREET, W. Price 1d.

Mozart, Wolfgang Amadeus. *Sinfonien*. Vol. 8. Ed. Friedrich Snapp and László Somfai. Neue Ausgabe sämtlicher Werke IV/11/8. Kassel: Bärenreiter, 1971.

Mozart, Wolfgang Amadeus. *Streichquartette*. Vol. 3. Ed. Ludwig Finscher. Neue Ausgabe sämtlicher Werke VIII/20/1/3. Kassel: Bärenreiter, 1961.

Mozart, Wolfgang Amadeus. *Streichquintette*. Ed. Ernst Hess and Ernst Fritz Schmid. Neue Ausgabe sämtlicher Werke VIII/19/1. Kassel: Bärenreiter, 1967.

MUSICAL BOUQUET / GRAND PARADE MARCH / ON ENGLISH NATIONAL MEL-ODIES. / HEARTS OF OAK, RULE BRITANNIA / GOD SAVE THE QUEEN / Arranged for the Piano-Forte / BY / J. SIDNEY JONES / ... / LONDON: / MUSICAL BOUQUET OFFICE, 192 HIGH HOLBORN; / & J. ALLEN, 20, WARWICK LANE, PATERNOSTER ROW.

The Musical Bouquet 4161 / Hear us when we call, O Lord / ("DONA NOBIS PACEM.") / Written and Arranged by / J. A. WADE, / from the / 12TH MASS / composed by / Mozart. / LONDON: PUBLISHED BY C. SHEARD, MUSICAL BOUQUET OFFICE; 129 HIGH HOLBORN.

Nectoux, Jean-Michel, ed. Gabriel Fauré, *Correspondance*. Harmoniques. Paris: Flammarion, 1980.

Niemetschek, Franz Xaver. *Leben des K. K. Kapellmeisters Wolfgang Gottlieb Mozart, nach Originalquellen beschrieben*. Prague: Herrlisch, 1798.

NOUVELLE BIBLIOTHÈQUE DRAMATIQUE / ÉDITION DU THÉÂTRE LYRIQUE / — / DON JUAN / OPÉRA / EN DEUX ACTES ET TREIZE TABLEAUX / MUSIQUE DE MOZART / (T. G. C.) / *Deuxième Édition* / — / PARIS / LIBRAIRIE INTERNATION-ALE / 15, BOULEVARD MONTMARTRE / A. LACROIX, VERBROECKHOVEN & Cᵉ, ÉDITEURS / *à Bruxelles, à Leipzig et à Livourne*.

ŒUVRES / DE / RÉNÉ FAVARGER / OP. B. Don Juan, 1ʳᵉ fantaisie / PARIS / ALFRED IKELMER ET Cⁱᵉ, EDITEURS-COMMISIONNAIRES / 4, BOULEVARD POSSON-NIÈRE.

Oulibicheff, Alexander. *Nouvelle biographie de Mozart suivie d'un aperçu sur l'histoire générale de la musique et de l'analyse des principales œuvres de Mozart*. Moscow: n.p., 1843. Reprint, with an introduction by Jean-Victor Hocquard, Paris: Séguier, 1991.

PARTITION COMPLÈTE / DU / DON JUAN / DE / MOZART / D'APRÈS L'ÉDITION ORIGINALE / TRANSCRITE POUR / PIANO SOLO / PAR / GEORGES BIZET / — / PARTITION SOIGNEUSEMENT REVUE, DOIGTÉE / AVEC / LES INDICATIONS D'ORCHESTRE ET DE CHANT / Prix Net: 8 francs / — / PARIS, AU MÉNESTREL, 2 BIS, RUE VIVIENNE / HEUGEL & Cie / ÉDITEURS-FOURNISSEURS DU CONSERVATOIRE.

PENSÉES DRAMATIQUES / SIX FANTAISIES TRANSCRIPTIONS / POUR LE / PIANO /…/ PAR / J. B. DUVERNOY / OP. 294 / 3 Don Juan…MOZART /…/ Paris, LÉON GRUS Editeur, 31, Boulev^t Bonne Nouvelle.

PETITE FANTAISIE / SUR / DON JUAN / de MOZART / Pour le Piano / PAR / A. [*sic*] CROISEZ / Paris, COLOMBIER, Editeur, 6, r. Vivienne, au coin de la Galerie Vivienne.

"THE PHANTOM OF THE OPERA" / BY / GASTON LEROUX / ADAPTATION AND SCENARIO / BY / RAYMOND L. SCHROCK / AND / ELLIOT CLAWSON. Facsimile in Philip J. Riley, *The Making of "The Phantom of the Opera."* Classic Silents series 1. Absecon, N.J.: MagicImage Filmbooks, 1999, 80–175.

PIANO / MUSIC SCORE / Compiled by / G. HINRICHS and M. WINKLER / Original Compositions (except Love Theme) by G. Hinrichs / for / PHANTOM OF THE OPERA /…/ BELWIN INC. / NEW YORK, U.S.A.

POLKA / *sur les motifs de* / *DON JUAN* / *DE* / W. MOZART / Pour LE PIANO PAR / CARLO MICHELI / PARIS / MAISON ARTISTIQUE, 8 rue Ollivier en face N. D. de Lorette, rue Fléchier, 2, H. L. D'AUBEL EDIT^R.

PUBLICITY SECTION / 2nd edition / CARL LAEMMLE / presents / The / Phantom of the Opera /…/ A UNIVERSAL Production. Facsimile in Philip J. Riley, *The Making of "The Phantom of the Opera."* Classic Silents Series 1. Absecon, N.J.: MagicImage Filmbooks, 1999, 211–254.

Pushkin, Aleksandr. "Kamennïy gost'" [The stone guest]. *Sto rousskikh literatorov* [A hundred Russian authors]. Ed. Aleksandr Filippovich Smirdin. 3 vols. Saint Petersburg: Smirdin, 1839–45.

RÉPERTOIRE DES BOUFFES-PARISIENS / L'IMPRESARIO / Opérette bouffe / PAR / MM. LÉON BATTU ET LUDOVIC HALÉVY / MUSIQUE DE / MOZART / — / REPRÉSENTÉE POUR LA PREMIÈRE FOIS SUR LE THÉÂTRE DES BOUFFES-PA-RISIENS, LE 20 MAI 1856 /…/ PARIS / G. BRANDUS, DUFOUR ET Ce, ÉDITEURS…/ MICHEL LÉVY FRÈRES ÉDITEURS…/ 1856.

RÉPERTOIRE DU THÉÂTRE IMPÉRIAL DE L'OPÉRA à Monsieur EMILE PERRIN / *DON JUAN* / DE MOZART / QUADRILLE / POUR PIANO / PAR / HENRI MARX / — / Paris: en dépot chez BBandus [*sic*] et Cie. 103 r. de Richelieu / *Propriété de l'Editeur*.

ROMEO AND JULIET / Opera in Five Acts / Libretto by / J. BARBIER and M. CARRÉ / Music by / CHARLES GOUNOD / The English Version by / DR. THEO. BAKER / With an Essay on / Story of the Opera by / W. J. HENDERSON / G. SCHIRMER, Inc., NEW YORK.

Sacred Series / N° 1 / Gloria in Excelsis / FROM / MOZART'S 12TH MASS / FOR / Violin and Pianoforte / *with Second Violin & Violoncello, (ad. lib.)* / BY / BENJAMIN BARROW / London, / S. WHITE, 37, BOOKSELLERS ROW, STRAND, W.C.

Scharf, Thomas. *The Chronicles of Baltimore; Being a Complete History of "Baltimore Town" and Baltimore City from the Earliest Period to the Present Time.* Baltimore: Turnbull, 1874. Reprint, Port Washington and London: Kennikat, 1972 [Middle Atlantic States Historical Publications 15].

Schmitt, Georg Alois, ed. *Grosse Messe in C moll...-Werk 427-Nach Mozartschen Vorlagen vervollständigt von A. Schmitt.* Wolfgang Amadeus Mozart's Werke: Kritische durchgesehene Gesamtausgabe 24:29. Leipzig: Breitkopf und Härtel, 1901.

Seule Edition conforme à l'exécution de l'Opéra / — / OTHELLO / *Grand Opéra en trois Actes* / *Paroles de MM* / Alphonse Royer et Gustave Waez / *Musique* / DE / G. ROSSINI / PRIX 10[f]. net / *PARIS* / AU MÉNESTREL, 2 bis rue Vivienne, HEUGEL et FILS / Editeurs-Propriétaires pour tous Pays.

SEULE ÉDITION / CONFORME à L'INTERPRÉTATION DU THÉÂTRE LYRIQUE / DON / JUAN / Opéra en 2 Actes et 12 Tableaux / MUSIQUE DE / MOZART / *Partition Chant & Piano* / A PARIS, CHOUDENS / EDITEUR, Rue St Honoré, 265, Près de l'Assomption / *Propriété* / p[r]. tous Pays.

Simrock, N. "Erklärung der Verlagshandlung von N. Simrock betreffend *die Echtheit der Mozartischen Messe Nr. 7.*" *Caecila: Ein Zeitschrfit für die musikalische Welt, herausgegeben von einem Vereine von Gelehrten, Kunstverständigen und Künstler* 6 [vol. 21] (1827), 129–131.

Tchaikovsky, Peter Illych. *The Diaries of Tchaikovsky.* Trans. Wladimir Lakond. New York: Norton, 1945. Reprint, Westport, Conn.: Greenwood, 1973.

THÉÂTRE LYRIQUE IMPÉRIAL / DON JUAN / *OPÉRA EN DEUX ACTES* / *et douze Tableaux* / TRADUCTION française de H. TRIANON et *** / MOZART / *Catalogue des Morceaux de Chant séparés avec accompagn[t] de Piano* /.../ Paris rue St Honoré, 265 chez CHOUDENS, Éditeur, (près de l'Assomption).

THÉATRE-LYRIQUE IMPÉRIAL / LA FLÛTE ENCHANTÉE / DE / MOZART / OPÉRA EN QUATRE ACTES / REPRÉSENTÉ AU THÉÂTRE-LYRIQUE IMPÉRIAL LE 23 FÉVRIER 1865 / TRADUCTION FRANÇAISE / DE / MM. NUITTER & BEAUMONT /.../ PARIS / Au MÉNESTREL, 2 bis, rue Vivienne / HEUGEL ET Cie.

THE THREE / FAVORITE MASSES, / COMPOSED BY / MOZART, HAYDN, / AND / BEETHOVEN, / IN VOCAL SCORE, / WITH AN ACCOMPANIMENT FOR THE ORGAN OR PIANO FORTE, / BY / VINCENT NOVELLO. / — / MOZART'S TWELFTH MASS [HAYDN'S THIRD (OR IMPERIAL) MASS; BEETHOVEN'S MASS, IN C]. / — / In addition to the original Latin Words, an adaptation to English Words has been added by R. G. Lorraine, Esq. / — / LONDON SACRED MUSIC WAREHOUSE: / J. ALFRED NOVELLO, MUSIC SELLER (BY APPOINTMENT) TO HER MAJESTY, / 69, DEAN STREET, SOHO, AND 24, POULTRY; / SIMPKIN, MARSHALL, & Co., STATIONERS' HALL COURT.

THE THREE / FAVORITE MASSES, / COMPOSED BY / MOZART, HAYDN, / AND / BEETHOVEN, / IN VOCAL SCORE, / WITH AN ACCOMPANIMENT FOR THE ORGAN OR PIANO FORTE, / BY VINCENT NOVELLO. / — / MOZART'S TWELFTH MASS. / — / In addition to the original Latin Words, an adaptation to English Words has been added by R. G. Lorraine, Esq. / To this Edition is added Mr E. HOLMES' Critical Essay, extracted from the "Musical Times". / — / LONDON SACRED MUSIC WAREHOUSE: / NOVELLO & CO., MUSIC SELLERS (BY APPOINTMENT) TO HER MAJESTY, 69, DEAN STREET, SOHO, / AND 35, POULTRY; ALSO IN NEW YORK, AT 1, CLINTON HALL, ASTOR PLACE.

THREE MOVEMENTS / from / MOZART'S MASS, N° 12, / VIZ. / GLORIA IN EXCELSIS DEO / BENEDICTUS QUI VENIT, / CUM SANCTO SPIRITU, / *Arranged for the Two Performers* / on the / Piano Forte, / WITH ACCOMPANIMENTS (AB LIBITUM) FOR

/ FLUTE, VIOLIN & VIOLONCELLO / *By* / W. WATTS. / LONDON, / C. LONSDALE, 26, OLD BOND STREET.

Toussnenel, Théodore. *Œuvres complètes de E. T. A. Hoffmann.* 12 vols. Paris: Lefebure, 1830.

Trois / *Grandes Simphonies* / Composées / *par W. M Mozart* / Arrangées pour / *Deux Violons, Deux Altos, Basse, Contrebasse et Flûte* / La Flûte Obligato ou Ad-libitum / ou *Deux Violons, Deux Altos, Deux Basses et Flûte* / La Flûte toujours Obligato ou Ad-libitum. / par / J. B. Cimador / N.B. *La Contradiction apparente dans les mots Obbligato et Ad-libitum vient de ce que la partie* / *de Flûte quoique fort belle, n'est pas absolument nécessaire* / [1] Suite. *Enregistré à la Bibliothèque Nationale.* Prix 18 fr. / à Paris / *Chez* IMBAULT, *Professeur & Editeur de Musique, au Mont d'Or Rue St Honoré N° 200, près celle des Poulies* / Et Péristile du Théâtre Italien Rue Favart N°. 461.

Vasari, Giorgio. *Le Vite de' piu eccellenti pittori, scultori, e architettori...di nuouo...riuiste et ampliate con i ritratti loro et con l'aggiunta delle Vite de' viui, & de' morti dall'anno 1550 insino al 1567...Con le tauole in ciascun volume, delle cose piu notabili, de' ritratti, delle vite degli artefici, et dei luoghi doue sono l'opere loro.* 3 vols. Florence: Giunti, 1568. Trans. by George Bull as *Lives of the Artists.* London: Penguin, 1987. Reprint, 2003.

Viardot, Pauline. "Mes Premiers Souvenirs." *Les Annales politiques et littéraires*, 29 May 1910.

Weimars, François-Adolphe Loève. *Œuvres complètes de E. T. A. Hoffmann.* 19 vols. Paris: Renduel, 1830–32.

XXX Gesänge mit Begleitung des Pianoforte von W. A. Mozart. Œuvres complettes de Wofgang Amadeus Mozart 5. Leipzig: Breitkopf und Härtel, 1798–1806.

PERIODICALS

Allgemeine musikalische Zeitung

All the Year Round

Australasian Sketcher

Caecilia: Ein Zeitschrfit für die musikalische Welt, herausgegeben von einem Vereine von Gelehrten, Kunstverständigen und Künstler

Caecilia: Monthly Magazine of Catholic Church and School Music

Chicago Sun-Times

Cinema Journal

Dramatic Review

Dwight's Journal of Music: A Paper of Art and Literature

Film Quarterly

Galignani's Messenger

Graham's Magazine

Journal des Débats

La France musicale

La gazette de France

La Patrie

La revue contemporaine

La revue française

L' artiste

L'art musical

Le Carillon Théâtral
Le Figaro
Le Ménestrel
Le messager des théâtres
Le messager des théâtres
Le moniteur universel
Le Temps
Longman's Magazine
L'union
Manchester Guardian
Musical Time and Singing Class Circular
Musical World
National Democrat
Neue Zeitschrift für Musik
New York Musical World
New York Times
Our Corner
Pall Mall Gazette
Quarterly Musical Magazine and Review
Revue des deux mondes
Revue et gazette musicale de Paris
Revue musicale
Unwin's Annual

DISCOGRAPHY

Wolfgang Amadeus Mozart. *Concerto No. 20 in a Minor, K. 466; Concerto No. 21 in C, K. 467 "Elvira Madigan."* RCA Victor Orchestra, Alfred Wallenstein (conductor), Artur Rubinstein (soloist). New York: RCA Victor Gold Seal, 1989. (Originally issued 1961).

Wolfgang Amadeus Mozart. *Concerto No. 21 in C Major for Piano and Orchestra, K. 467 "Elvira Madigan" (Cadenzas by Robert Casadesus); Concerto No. 24 in c Minor for Piano and Orchestra, K. 491 (Cadenza by Saint-Saëns).* Cleveland Orchestra, George Szell (conductor), Robert Casadesus (soloist). New York: CBS, 1983. (Originally issued 1965).

Wolfgang Amadeus Mozart. *Klavierkonzert: Piano Concertos G-Dur in G Major, KV 453; C-Dur in C Major, KV 467.* Camerata Academica des Mozarteums Salzburg, Geza Anda (Solist und Dirigent). Hamburg: Deutsche Gramophon Gesellschaft, 138783, [1962].

Wolfgang Amadeus Mozart. *Piano Concerto No. 21 in C Major, K. 467 "Elvira Madigan." Piano Concerto No. 9 in E-Flat Major, K. 271.* Hallé Orchestra, Bryden Thomson (conductor), Stephen Hough (soloist). Hayes, England: EMI, 1987.

Wolfgang Amadeus Mozart. *Piano Concertos K. 466 and K. 467.* Capella Istropolitana, Christoph Eberle (conductor). Peter Lang (soloist). Naxos, 2004.

Wolfgang Amadeus Mozart. *Symphony No. 40 in g Minor, K. 550. Concerto No. 21 in C, K. 467 (The Elvira Madigan concerto).* English Chamber Orchestra, Daniel Barenboim (soloist and conductor). London: EMI, 1968.

FILMS

Attention! Bandits! Dir. Claude Lelouch. Warner Brothers, 1986.

Consenting Adults. Dir. Alan J. Pakula. Hollywood Pictures, 1992.

Elvira Madigan. Dir. Bo Widerberg. AB Svensk Filmindustri, 1967.

Factory Girl. Dir. George Hickenlooper. Weinstein, 2006.

Janice Beard 45 WPM. Dir. Clare Kilner. Film Consortium, 1999.

The Happening. Dir. M. Night Shyamalan. Spyglass, 2008.

Le concert. Dir. Radu Mihaileanu. Productions du Trésor, 2009.

Le goût des autres. Dir. Agnès Jaoui. Pathé, 2001.

Metroland. Dir. Philip Saville. Metrodome, 1998.

Préparez vos mouchoirs. Dir. Bertrand Blier. TF1 International, 1978.

The Rage in Placid Lake. Dir. Tony McNamara. Guerilla Films, 2003.

Silent Fall. Dir. Bruce Beresford. Morgan Creek, 1994.

The Spy who Loved Me. Dir. Lewis Gilbert. MGM, 20th Century Fox, 1977.

Superman Returns. Dir. Bryan Singer. Warner Brothers, 2006.

Twelve Monkeys. Dir. Terry Gilliam. Universal, 1995.

Virtual Sexuality. Dir. Nick Hurran. Columbia TriStar, 1999.

WEB RESOURCES

Biographie: Patrick Bruel. www.rfimusique.com/siteen/biographie/biographie_6103.asp.

Dire Straits Biography. www.musicianguide.com/biographies/1608000435/Dire-Straits. html (accessed 10 July 2012).

Elvira Madigan: A Little Bit o'dis and a Little Bit o'dat. http://bafflesblog.blogspot. com/2010/06/elvira-madigan.html (accessed 10 July 2012).

Feedbooks. www.ebooksgratuits.com (accessed 10 July 2012).

Francophone Music Criticism, 1789–1914, Collection 1. www.music.sas.ac.uk/fmc (accessed 10 July 2012).

Grove Music Online-Oxford Music Online. www.oxfordmusiconline.com/subscriber/article/ grove/music/ (accessed 10 July 2012).

Guernsey Weekly Press. www.thisisguernsey.com (no longer extant).

Illustrious and Unknown Compositions. http://peyot.com/page2.html (accessed 20 March 2006; since taken down).

International Movie Database. www.imdb.com/title/tt0061620 (accessed 10 July 2012).

Mozart Effect Resource Center. www.mozarteffect.com/ (accessed 10 July 2012).

Mozart's Twelfth Mass; Chester-Novello. www.chesternovello.com/default.aspx?TabId=2432 &State_3041=2&WorkId_3041=10783 (accessed 30 June 2012).

Mozart Symphony in g minor K. 550. www.youtube.com/watch?v=PxAqzMLIDns (accessed 10 July 2012).

Patterns of Mozart Reception in the Nineteenth Century. www.soton.ac.uk/~me/pmr/pmr. html (accessed 30 June 2012).

Retrospective Index of Music Periodicals. www.ripmfulltext.org (accessed 10 July 2012).

Salzburg Tourist Board. www.salzburg.info/de/ (accessed 10 July 2012).

Sonate pour Solange: L'histoire des 'Mouchoirs.' www.dvdcritiques.com/critiques/dvd_visu. aspx?dvd=834 (accessed 10 July 2012).

Secondary Sources

Agulhon, Maurice. *Marianne au combat: L'imagerie et la symbolique républicaines de 1789 à 1880*. Bibliothèque d'ethnologie historique. Paris: Flammarion, 1979.

Ahlquist, Karen Ethel. *Democracy at the Opera: Music, Theater, and Culture in New York City, 1815–60*. Music in American Life. Urbana: University of Illinois Press, 1997.

Alexandre, Arsène-Pierre-Urbain. *Jean Carriès, imagier et potier: Étude d'une œuvre et d'une vie*. Paris: Librairies-imprimeries réunies, 1895.

Altman, Rick. "Early Film Themes: Roxy, Adorno, and the Problem of Cultural Capital." In *Beyond the Soundtrack: Representing Music in Cinema*, ed. Daniel Goldmark, Lawrence Kramer, and Richard D. Kramer, 205–224. Berkeley: University of California Press, 2007.

Amalric, Jean-Claude. "Shaw: *Man and Superman*." Cahiers Victoriennes et Edouardiennes 24 (1986), 153–160.

Amalric, Jean-Claude. "Shaw's *Man and Superman* and the Myth of Don Juan: Intertextuality and Irony." *Cahiers Victoriennes et Edouardiennes* 33 (1991), 103–114.

Angermüller, Rudolph. *Das Salzburg Mozart-Denkmal: Eine Dokumentation (bis (1845)' zur 150-Jahre-Enthüllungsfeier*. Salzburg: Internationale Stiftung Mozarteum, 1992.

Bericht über den Internationalen Mozart-Kongreß, Salzburg, 1991, 2 vols [paginated consecutively], ed. Rudolph Angermüller, Dietrich Berke, Ulrike Hofmann and Wolfgang Rehm. *Mozart-Jahrbuch 1991 des Zentralinstitutes für Mozartforschung der Internationalen Stiftung Mozarteum Salzburg* (Kassel, Basel and London: Bärenreiter, 1992).

Baker, Theodore, trans. "Pauline Viardot-Garcia to Julius Rietz (Letters of Friendship)." *Musical Quarterly* 1 (1915), 556–557.

Bangerter, Adrian, and Chip Heath. "The Mozart Effect: Tracking the Evolution of a Scientific Legend." *British Journal of Social Psychology* 43/4 (2004), 605–623.

Barzun, Jacques, ed. *Pleasures of Music*. London: Michael Joseph, 1952.

Battersby, Christine. *Gender and Genius: Towards a Feminist Aesthetics*. London: Women's Press, 1989.

Blanch, Robert L. "The Myth of Don Juan in *Man and Superman*." *Revue des langues vivantes* 33 (1967), 158–163.

Bogdanov-Berezovskogo, Valerian Mikhailovich, ed. *Mikhail Ivanovich Glinka, Literaturnoe nasledie*. 2 vols. Leningrad and Moscow: Gos. muzykalnoe izd-vo, 1952–53.

Böhme, Erdmann Werner. "Mozart in der schönen Literatur (Drama, Roman, Novelle, Lyrik)." In *Bericht über die musikwissenschaftlicheTagung der Internationalen Stiftung Mozarteum in Salzburg vom 2. bis 5. August 1931*, 179–297. Leipzig: Breitkopf und Härtel, 1931.

Böhme, Erdmann Werner. "Mozart in der schönen Literatur: Ergänzungen und Fortsetzung." In *Mozart-Jahrbuch 1959 des Zentralinstitutes für Mozartforschung der Internationalen Stiftung Mozarteum Salzburg*, 165–187. Kassel, Basel and London: Bärenreiter, 1959.

Borchard, Beatrix. "'Ma chère petite Clara—Pauline de mon cœur': Clara Schumann et Pauline Viardot, une amitié d'artistes franco-allemande." *Cahiers Ivan Tourguéniev, Pauline Viardot, Maria Malibran* 20 (1996), 127–143.

Borchard, Beatrix. "Zwei Musikerinnen—zwei Kulturen: Unveröffentlichte Briefe von Clara Schumann und Pauline Viardot-Garcia." In *Pauline Viardot in Baden-Baden und Karlsruhe*, ed. Ute Lange-Brachmann and Joachim Draheim, Baden-Badener Beiträge zur Musikgeschichte 4, 71–80. Baden-Baden: Nomos, 1999.

Bosch, Ingrid, and Horst Hallensleben, eds. *Monument für Beethoven: Zur Geschichte des Beethoven-Denkmals (1845) und der frühen Beethoven-Rezeption in Bonn.* (Catalog of an exhibition at the Ernst-Moritz-Arndt-Haus, Bonn, 1995.) Bonn: Stadtmuseum, 1995.

Brandstetter, Gabriele, and Gerhard Neumann. "Mozart auf der Reise ins 20. Jahrhundert: Mörikes Novelle und Schaffer's Amadeus." *Freiburger Universitätsblätter* 27 (1988), 85–105.

Braun, Joseph. *Die Reliquiare des christlichen Kultes und ihre Entwicklung.* Freiburg im Breisgau: Herder, 1971.

Bringle, Jerald E., and Dan H. Laurence. "Bernard Shaw: The St James's Hall Mystery." *Bulletin of Research in the Humanities* 81 (1978), 270–296.

Bromber, Beth Archer. *Cristina: Portraits of a Princess.* New York: Knopf, 1977. Reprint, Chicago: University of Chicago Press, 1983.

Brooks, Jeanice. "Noble et grande servante de la musique: Telling the Story of Nadia Boulanger's Conducting Career." *Journal of Musicology* 14 (1996), 92–116.

Broyles, Michael. "Art Music from 1860 to 1920." In *The Cambridge History of American Music*, ed. David Nicholls, 214–254. Cambridge: Cambridge University Press, 1998.

Burnham, Scott. *Beethoven Hero.* Princeton, N.J.: Princeton University Press, 1995.

Cadot, Michel. "Turgenev und Louis Viardot als Mittler russischer Literatur in Frankreich." *Zeitschrift für Slavistik* 32 (1987), 442–444.

Campbell, Don. *The Mozart Effect: Tapping the Power of Music to Heal the Body, Strengthen the Mind, and Unlock the Creative Spirit.* New York: Avon Books, 1997.

Cannone, Belinda. *La Réception des opéras de Mozart dans la presse parisienne (1793–1829).* Paris: Klincksieck, 1991.

Cardullo, Bert. *Screen Writings: Partial Views of a Total Art, Classic to Contemporary.* 2 vols. New York: Anthem Press, 2010.

Casta-Husson, Isabelle. "Les fortunes paraculturelles du *Fantôme de l'Opéra*." In *De l'écrit à l'écran: Littératures populaires—mutations génériques, mutations médiatiques*, ed. Jacques Migozzi, 695–704. Limoges: Presses Universitaires de Limoges, 2000.

Casta-Husson, Isabelle. *Le travail de l'obscure clarté' dans "Le fantôme de l'Opéra."* Archives des lettres modernes 268. Paris: Lettres Modernes, 1997.

Chinn, Genevieve. "The Académie Impériale de Musique: A Study of Its Administration and Repertory from 1862–1870." Ph.D. diss., Columbia University, 1969.

Coelsch-Foisner, Sabine, Dorothea Flothow, and Wolfgang Görtschacher, eds. *Mozart in Anglophone Cultures.* Salzburg Studies in English Literature and Culture 4. Frankfurt-am-Main: Lang, 2009.

Comini, Alessandro. *The Changing Image of Beethoven: A Study in Mythmaking.* New York: Rizzoli, 1987.

Connolly, Thomas. *Mourning into Joy: Music, Raphael and Saint Cecilia.* New Haven and London: Yale University Press, 1994.

Constant, Pierre. *Le Conservatoire National de Musique et de Déclamation: Documents historiques et administratives.* Paris: Imprimerie Nationale, 1900.

Crowther, Bosley. *Reruns: Fifty Memorable Films.* New York: Putnam, 1978.

Csobádi, Peter, Gernot Gruber, Jürgen Kühnel, Ulrich Müller, and Oswald Panagl, eds. *Das Phänomen Mozart im 20. Jahrhundert: Wirkung, Verarbeitung und Vermarktung in Literatur, bildender Kunst und den Medien.* Wort und Musik: Salzburg Akademische Beiträge 10. Anif and Salzburg: Müller-Speiser, 1991.

Dahlhaus, Carl. *Grundlagen der Musikgeschichte*. Musiktaschenbücher: Theoretica 13. Cologne: Hans Gerig, 1977. Trans. by J. R. Robinson as Foundations of Music History. Cambridge: Cambridge University Press, 1983.

Daverio, John. "Mozart in the Nineteenth Century." In *The Cambridge Companion to Mozart*, ed. Simon P. Keefe, 171–184. Cambridge: Cambridge University Press, 2003.

Deathridge, John, Martin Geck, and Egon Voss. *Wagner Werk-Verzeichnis (WWV): Verzeichnis der musikalischen Werke Richard Wagners und ihrer Quellen*. Mainz: Schott, 1986.

De Bévotte, Georges Gendarme. *La Légende de Don Juan*. 2 vols. Paris: Hachette, 1911.

De Broglie, Gabriel. *Histoire politique de la Revue des deux mondes de 1829 à 1979*. Paris: Perrin, 1979.

De Cossart, Michael. *The Food of Love: Princesse Edmond de Polignac (1865–1943) and Her Salon*. London: Hamish Hamilton, 1978.

De Curzon, Henri. *Mozart, Les maîtres de la musique*. Paris: Alcan, 1914.

Dent, Edward J. *Mozart's Operas: A Critical Study*. London: Chatto and Windus, 1913. 2nd ed. London: Oxford University Press, 1947.

De Voragine, Jacobus. *The Golden Legend: Readings on the Saints*. Trans. William Granger Ryan. 2 vols. Princeton, N.J.: Princeton University Press, 1993.

Devriès, Anik, and François Lesure. *Dictionnaire des éditeurs de musique française*. 2 vols. Vol. 1 in 2 parts. Archives de l'édition musicale française 4. Geneva: Minkoff, 1979–88.

Diezmann, Johann August. *Goethe-Schiller-Museum*. Leipzig: Baumgärtner, 1858.

Döhring, Sieghart. "Réminiscences: Liszts Konzeption der Klavierparaphrase." In *Festschrift Heinz Becker zum 60. Geburtstag am 26. Juni 1982*, ed. Jürgen Schläder and Reinhold Quandt, 131–151. Laaber: Laaber, 1982.

Donoghue, Denis. "Approaching Mozart." In *On Mozart*, ed. James M. Morris, 15–35. New York: Cambridge University Press; Washington, D.C.: Woodrow Wilson Center for Scholars, 1994.

Dubois, Jacques, and Jean-Loup Lemaitre. *Sources et méthodes de l'hagiographie médiévale*. Paris: Cerf, 1993.

Dutronc, Jean-Louis. "Un siècle de représentations au Palais Garnier." *Gounod: Faust*, L'Avant-Scène Opéra 2 (March-April 1976), 83–85.

Eggebrecht, Hans Heinrich. *Zur Geschichte der Beethoven-Rezeption: Beethoven 1970*. Akademie der Wissenschaften und der Literatur: Abhandlungen der Geistes- und Sozialwissenschaftlichen Klasse, Jahrgang 1972, 3. Wiesbaden: Steiner, 1972.

Einstein, Alfred. *Mozart: His Character and His Work*. Trans. Arthur Mendel. London: Kassel, 1944.

Eldridge, Richard. "'Hidden Secrets of the Self': E. T. A. Hoffmann's Reading of Don Giovanni." In *The Don Giovanni Moment: Essays on the Legacy of an Opera*, ed. Lydia Goehr and Daniel Herwitz, 33–46. New York: Columbia University Press, 2006.

Ellis, Katharine. "Female Pianists and Their Male Critics in Nineteenth-Century Paris." *Journal of the American Musicological Society* 50 (1997), 353–385.

Ellis, Katharine. *Music Criticism in Nineteenth-Century France: La Revue et gazette musicale de Paris, 1834–80*. Cambridge: Cambridge University Press, 1995.

Ellis, Katharine. "Rewriting Don Giovanni, or 'The Thieving Magpies.'" *Journal of the Royal Musical Association* 119 (1994), 212–250.

Everist, Mark. "Gluck, Berlioz and Castil-Blaze." In *Reading Critics Reading: French Music Criticism, 1789–1848,* ed. Mary Ann Smart and Roger Parker, 86–108. Oxford: Oxford University Press, 2001.

Everist, Mark. "Grand Opéra—Petit Opéra: Parisian Opera and Ballet from the Restoration to the Second Empire." *19th-Century Music* 33 (2010), 195–231.

Everist, Mark. "'Il n'y a qu'un Paris au monde, et j'y reviendrai planter mon drapeau!': Rossini's Second grand opera." *Music & Letters* 90 (2009), 636–672.

Everist, Mark. "Jacques Offenbach: The Music of the Past and the Image of the Present." In *Music, Theater and Cultural Transfer: Paris, 1830–1914,* ed. Mark Everist and Annegret Fauser, 72–98. Chicago: Chicago University Press, 2009.

Everist, Mark. *Music Drama at the Paris Odéon, 1824–1828.* (Berkeley: University of California Press, 2002.

Everist, Mark. "Partners in Rhyme: Alphonse Royer, Gustave Vaëz, and Foreign Opera in Paris during the July Monarchy." In *Fashions and Legacies in Nineteenth-Century Italian Opera,* ed. Roberta Montemarra Marvin and Hilary Poriss, 30–52. Cambridge: Cambridge University Press, 2009.

Everist, Mark. "Reception Theories, Canonic Discourses and Musical Value." In *Rethinking Music,* ed. Nicholas Cook and Mark Everist, 378–402. Oxford: Oxford University Press, 1999.

Everist, Mark. "Rossini at the Paris Opéra, 1843–1847: Translation, Arrangement, Pasticcio." In *Librettoübersetzung: Interkulturalität im europäischen Musiktheater,* ed. Herbert Schneider and Rainer Schmusch, Musikwissenschaftliche Publikationen 32, 131–163. Hildesheim: Olms, 2009.

Everist, Mark. "Theatres of Litigation: Stage Music at the Théâtre de la Renaissance, 1838–1840." *Cambridge Opera Journal* 16 (2004), 133–162.

Fauquet, Joël-Marie, and Antoine Hennion. *La Grandeur de Bach: L'amour de la musique en France au xixe siècle.* Les Chemins de la Musique. Paris: Fayard, 2000.

Fauquet, Joël-Marie, and Laure Schnapper. "Salle de Concert." In *Dictionnaire de la musique en France au xixe siècle,* ed. Joël-Marie Fauquet, 1113–1114. Paris: Fayard, 2003.

Feldges, Brigitte, and Ulrich Stadler. *E. T. A. Hoffmann: Epoche-Werk-Wirkung, Beck'sche Elementarbücher.* Munich: Beck, 1986.

Fellerer, Imogen. "Brahms's View of Mozart." In *Brahms: Biographical, Documentary and Analytical Studies,* ed. Robert Pascall, 41–57. Cambridge: Cambridge University Press, 1983.

Fitzlyon, April. *Maria Malibran: Diva of the Romantic Age.* London: Souvenir, 1987.

Fitzlyon, April. *The Price of Genius: A Life of Pauline Viardot.* London: Calder, 1964.

Föhrenbach, Elisabeth, ed. *Der Schauspieldirektor: Kritische Berichte.* Neue Mozart-Ausgabe II/5/15. Kassel: Bärenreiter, 2001.

Ford, George. *Dickens and His Readers: Aspects of Novel Criticism since 1836.* Princeton, N.J.: Princeton University Press, 1955. Reprint, New York: Norton, 1965.

Fort, Ilene Susan, and Michael Quick. *American Art: A Catalogue of the Los Angeles County Museum of Art Collection.* Los Angeles: Museum Associates, 1991.

Foucault, Michel. "Sexual Morality and the Law." *Politics, Philosophy, Culture—Interviews and Other Writings* 1977–1984, ed. Lawrence D. Krizman, 271–285. New York and London: Routledge, 1990.

Franzel, Emil. *Crown Prince Rudolph and the Mayerling Tragedy: Fact and Fiction.* Vienna: Herold, 1974.

Fuchs, Ingrid, ed. *Internationaler Musikwissenschaftlicher Kongress zum Mozartjahr 1991, Baden-Wien.* 2 vols. Tützing: Schneider, 1993.

Furman, Nelly. *La Revue des deux mondes et le romantisme (1831–1848).* Histoire des idées et critique littéraire 149. Geneva: Droz, 1975.

Gadde, Erwin G. "E. T. A. Hoffmann's Reception in England." *Proceedings of the Modern Languages Association* 41 (1926), 1005–1010.

Gallup, Stephen. *A History of the Salzburg Festival.* London: Weidenfeld and Nicolson, 1987.

Gifford, Don, and Robert J. Seidman. *"Ulysses" Annotated: Notes for James Joyce's "Ulysses."* 2nd ed. Berkeley: University of California Press, 1988.

Giraud, Jean. "E. T. A. Hoffmann (1776–1822) ou Est-ce Mozart qu'on mythifie?" In *Mozart: Origines et transformations d'une mythe: Actes du colloque international organise dans le cadre du Bicentaire del la mort de Mozart, Clemont-Ferrand, décembre 1991,* ed. Jean-Louis Jam, 185–205. Berne: Lang, 1994.

Gislason, Donald Garth. "Castil-Blaze, De l'Opéra in France and the Feuilletons of the Journal des Débats (1820–1832)." Ph.D. diss., University of British Columbia, 1992.

Gorner, Rudiger. *"Die Zauberflöte* in Kierkegaards *Entweder-Oder."* In *Mozart-Jahrbuch 1980–83 des Zentralinstitutes für Mozartforschung der Internationalen Stiftung Mozarteum Salzburg,* 247–257. Kassel: Bärenreiter, 1983.

Gorner, Rudiger. "Zu Kierkegaards Verstandnis der *Zauberflöte."* *Miteillungen der internationalen Stiftung Mozarteum* 28 (1980), 25–31.

Graevenitz, Gerhard von. "Don Juan oder die Liebe zur Hausmusik: Wagner-Kritik in Edouard Mörikes Erzählung Mozart auf der Reise nach Prag." *Neophilologus* 65 (1981): 247–262.

Grey, Thomas. "Metaphorical Modes in Nineteenth-Century Music Criticism: Image, Narrative and Idea." In *Music and Text: Critical Inquiries,* ed. Steven Paul Scher, 93–117. Cambridge: Cambridge University Press, 1992.

Gribenski, Jean. *Catalogue des éditions françaises de Mozart, 1764–1825.* Musica Antiquomoderna: Collection du Centre de Musique Baroque de Versailles 1. Hildesheim: Olms, 2006.

Gribenski, Jean, and Patrick Taïeb, eds. *Mozart et la France: De l'enfant prodige au génie (1764–1830).* Lyon: Symétrie, forthcoming.

Grover-Friedlander, Michael. "'The Phantom of the Opera': The Lost Voice of Opera in Silent Film." *Cambridge Opera Journal* 11 (1999), 179–192.

Gruber, Gernot. *Mozart und die Nachwelt.* Salzburg: Residenz Verlag, 1985. Trans. by R. S. Furness as *Mozart and Posterity.* London: Quartet, 1991.

Guillaiss, Joëlle. *La Chair de l'autre.* Paris: Olivier Orban, 1986. Trans. by Jane Dunnett as *Crimes of Passion: Dramas of Private Life in Nineteenth-Century France.* Cambridge: Polity, 1990.

Haberkamp, Gertaut. *Die Erstdrucke der Werke von Wolfgang Amadeus Mozart.* 2 vols. Musikbibliographisches Arbeiten 10. Tützing: Schneider, 1986.

Hamilton, Kenneth Lawrie. *After the Golden Age: Romantic Pianism and Modern Performance.* New York: Oxford University Press, 2008.

Hamilton, Kenneth Lawrie. "The Opera Fantasias and Transcriptions of Franz Liszt: A Critical Study." D.Phil. diss., University of Oxford, 1989.

Harbsmeier, Gotz. *Unmittelbares Leben: Mozart und Kierkegaard.* Göttingen: Vandenhoeck und Ruprecht, 1980.

Head, Matthew. "Music with 'No Past'? Archeologies of Joseph Haydn and *The Creation.*" *19th-Century Music* 23 (2000), 191–217.

Heilbrun, Carolyn G. *Writing a Woman's Life.* New York: Ballantine, 1988.

Heinich, Nathalie. *The Glory of Van Gogh: An Anthropology of Admiration.* Trans. Paul Leduc Browne. Princeton, N.J.: Princeton University Press, 1996.

Henze-Döhring, Sabine. "E. T. A. Hoffmann-'Kult' und 'Don Giovanni'-Rezeption im Paris des 19. Jahrhunderts: Castil-Blazes 'Don Juan' im Théâtre de l'Académie Royale de Musique [*sic*] am 10 März 1834." In *Mozart-Jahrbuch 1984/5 des Zentralinstitutes für Mozartforschung der Internationalen Stiftung Mozarteum Salzburg,* 39–51. Kassel: Bärenreiter, 1986.

Héritte de la Tour, Louise. *Une grande famille de musiciens: notes et souvenirs anecdotiques sur Garcia, Pauline Viardot, La Malibran, Louise Héritte Viardot et leur entourage.* Paris: Stock, 1922.

Herttrich, Ernst, and Hans Wolfgang Schneider, eds. *Festschrift Rudolf Elvers zum 60. Geburtstag.* Tützing: Schneider, 1985.

Hogle, Jerrold E. *The Undergrounds of "The Phantom of the Opera": Sublimation and the Gothic in Leroux's Novel and Its Progeny.* New York and Basingstoke: Palgrave, 2002.

Holub, Robert C. *Reception Theory: A Critical Introduction.* New Accents. London and New York: Routledge, 1984.

Huebner, Steven. *The Operas of Charles Gounod.* Oxford: Clarendon Press, 1990.

Jam, Jean-Louis, ed. *Mozart: Origines et transformations d'une mythe: Actes du colloque international organisé dans le cadre du Bicentaire de la mort de Mozart, Clemont-Ferrand, décembre 1991.* Berne: Lang, 1994.

Jauss, Hans Robert. "Horizon Structure and Dialogicity." In *Question and Answer: Forms of Dialogic Understanding,* ed. and trans. Michael Hays, Theory and History of Literature 68, 197–231. Minneapolis: University of Minnesota Press, 1989.

Joubin, André, ed. *Journal de Delacroix.* 3 vols. Paris: Plon, 1932.

Jung, Hermann, and Imogen Fellerer, eds. *Mozart: Aspekte des 19. Jahrhunderts.* Mannheimer Hochschulschriften 1. Mannheim: Palatium, 1995.

Kaindl-Hönig, Max. "Salzburg und wie glücklich Mozart gespielt werden kann." In *Geza Anda: Ein Erinnerungsbild,* ed. Karl Schumann et al., 35–38. Zurich and Munich: Artemis, 1977.

Kaiser, Harmut. "Mörike's Use of Sonata Form in Mozart's Tale of the Neapolitan Water Games." *A Yearbook of Interdisciplinary Studies in the Fine Arts* 2 (1990), 607–625.

Kaiser, Harmut. "Mozarts Don Giovanni und E. T. A. Hoffmanns Don Juan: Ein Beitrag zum Verstandnis des Fantasiestucks." *Mitteilungen der E. T. A. Hoffmann-Gesellschaft* 21 (1975), 6–26.

Kalbeck, Max. *Johannes Brahms.* 4 vols. Berlin: Deutsche Brahms-Gesellschaft, 1921. Reprint, Tützing: Schneider, 1976.

Kaut, Josef. *Die Salzburg Festspiele, 1920–1981.* Salzburg: Residenz, 1982.

Keefe, Simon. Introduction to *The Cambridge Companion to Mozart.* Cambridge: Cambridge University Press, 2003.

Keys, Ivor. *Mozart: His Music in His Life.* St. Albans: Holmes & Meier, 1980.

King, Alec Hyatt. *Mozart in Retrospect: Studies in Criticism and Bibliography.* London: Geoffrey Cumberledge; Oxford: Oxford University Press, 1955.

Kirk, Geoffrey Stephen. "On Defining Myths." In *Sacred Narrative: Readings in the Theory of Myth*, ed. Alan Dundes, 53–61. Berkeley: University of California Press, 1984.

Knox, Richard A. "Mozart Makes You Smarter Calif. Researchers Suggest." *Boston Globe*, 14 October 1993.

Kobbé, Gustav. *Complete Opera Book*. 10th ed. London: Bodley Head, 1987.

Konrad, Ulrich. "Friedrich Rochlitz und die Entstehung des Mozart-Bildes um 1800." In *Mozart: Aspekte des* 19. *Jahrhunderts*, ed. Hermann Jung and Imogen Fellerer, Mannheimer Hochschulschriften 1, 1–22. Mannheim: Palatium, 1995.

Kregor, Jonathan. "Franz Liszt and the Vocabularies of Transcription, 1833–1865." Ph.D. diss., Harvard University, 2007.

Kreutzer, Hans Joachim. "Die Zeit und der Tod: Über Eduard Mörikes Mozart-Novelle." In *Obertöne: Literatur und Musik, neun Abhandlungen*, ed. Hans Joachim Kreutzer, 196–216. Würzburg: Königshausen & Neumann, 1994.

Kreutzer, Hans Joachim. "Ein Tag aus Mozarts Jugendleben: Die neapolitanische Pantomime in Mörikes Mozart-Novelle." In *Bericht über den Internationalen Mozart-Kongreß, Salzburg, 1991*. 2 vols. *Mozart-Jahrbuch 1991 des Zentralinstitutes für Mozartforschung der Internationalen Stiftung Mozarteum Salzburg*, 248–253. Kassel: Bärenreiter, 1992.

Kunze, Stefan. *Mozarts Opern*. Stuttgart: Reclam, 1984.

Kutsch, Karl-Josef, and Leo Riemens. *Großes Sängerlexikon*. 4 vols. Bern and Stuttgart: Francke, 1987–94. 4th ed. 7 vols. Munich: Saur, 2003.

Landon, H. C. Robbins. *The Mozart Compendium: A Guide to Mozart's Life and Music*. London: Thames and Hudson, 1990.

Langley, Leanne. "The English Musical Journal in the Early Nineteenth Century." 2 vols. Ph.D. diss., University of North Carolina at Chapel Hill, 1983.

Langley, Robin. "Weber in England." *Musical Times* 117 (1976): 479.

Larousse, Pierre. "Blaze de Bury." In *Grand Dictionnaire universel du xixe siècle français, historique, géographique, biographique, mythologique, bibliographique, littéraire, artistique, scientifique, etc.* 17 vols., 2:813. Paris: Grand Dictionnaire Universel, 1866.

Lecomte, Louis-Henry. *Les Folies-Nouvelles*. Histoire des théâtres de Paris 4. Paris: Daragon, 1909.

Ledout, Annie. "Le théâtre des Bouffes-Parisiens, historique et programmes, 1855–1880." Ph.D. diss., Université de Paris IV, 2001.

Lesure, François, René Dumesnil, and Jacques Duron, eds. "Le Manuscrit de *Don Giovanni*." In *Edition Princeps: W. A. Mozart, Don Giovanni, opéra en deux actes: Fac-similé in extenso du manuscrit autographe conservé à la Bibliothèque Nationale*. Paris: La Revue Musicale; Maisonneuve, n.d.

Lewicki, Ernst. "Die vervollständigung von Mozarts grosser c-moll Messe durch Alois Schmitt in ihrem Werdegang nach authentischen Quellen dargestellt." *Die Musik* (January-February 1906), 2–12.

Lieberman, Lisa. "Crimes of Reason, Crimes of Passion: Suicide and the Adulterous Woman in Nineteenth-Century France." *Journal of Family History* 24/2 (1999), 131–147.

Lipsius, Ida Marie Lipsius [La Mara]. *Liszt und die Frauen*. Breitkopf und Härtels Musikbücher. Leipzig: Breitkopf und Härtel, 1911.

Litzmann, Berthold, ed. *Clara Schumann–Johannes Brahms: Briefe aus dem Jahren 1853–1896*, 2 vols. Leipzig: Breitkopf und Härtel, 1927. Reprint, Hildesheim: Olms, 1970.

Loewenberg, Alfred. *Annals of Opera:* 1597–1940. 3rd ed. rev. and corrected. London: Calder, 1978.

Loubinoux, Gerard. "Le chercheur d'esprit, ou Offenbach et la mémoire du xviiie." In *Retour au xviiie siècle,* ed. Roland Morier and Hervé Hasquin, Études sur le xviiie siècle 22, 63–76. Brussels: Éditions de l'Université de Bruxelles, 1994.

Loué, Thomas. "L'inévidence de la distinction: *La Revue des Deux Mondes* face à la presse à la fin du XIXe siècle." *Romantisme* 33 (2003), 41–48.

MacDonald, Hugh. "Berlioz and Mozart." In *The Cambridge Companion to Berlioz,* ed. Peter Bloom, 211–22. Cambridge: Cambridge University Press, 2000.

MacDonald, Hugh, and François Lesure, eds. *Hector Berlioz: Correspondence Générale V:* 1855–1859. Nouvelle Bibliothèque Romantique. Paris: Flammarion, 1989.

MacIntyre, Bruce. "Mass." In *The Cambridge Mozart Encyclopedia,* ed. Cliff Eisen and Simon P. Keefe, 271–280. Cambridge: Cambridge University Press, 2006.

MacQueen, Scott. "The 1926 Phantom of the Opera." *American Cinematographer* 70/9 (September 1989), 34–40.

MacQueen, Scott. "Phantom of the Opera." *American Cinematographer* 70/10 (October 1989), 34–40.

Mandel, Oscar. *The Theatre of Don Juan: A Collection of Plays and Views,* 1630–1963. Lincoln: University of Nebraska Press, 1963.

Mandelkow, Karl Robert. "Probleme der Wirkungsgeschichte." *Jahrbuch für internationale Germanistik* 2 (1970), 71–84.

Marix-Spire, Thérèse. "Gounod and His First Interpreter." *Musical Quarterly* 31/2 (1945), 193–211.

Markus, Georg. *Crime at Mayerling: The Life and Death of Mary Vetsera: With New Expert Opinions Following the Desecration of Her Grave.* Riverside, Calif.: Ariadne, 1995.

Marshall, Robert L. "Mozart and *Amadeus.*" *Sonus* 4 (1983), 1–15.

Marty, Laurent. *1805: La création de Don Juan à l'Opéra de Paris.* Univers musical. Paris: L'Harmattan, 2005.

Massin, Jean. *Don Juan: Myth littéraire et musical.* Paris: Éditions Complexe, 1993.

Massip, Catherine. *Le Chant d'Euterpe.* Paris: Hervas, 1991.

McFarland, Carlyle A. "*Man and Superman:* Shaw's Statement on Creative Evolution—A Modern Analysis." *Panjab-University Research Bulletin* 18 (1987), 75–80.

Menascé, Esther. *Il labirinto delle ombre: L'immagine di Don Giovanni nella letteratura britannica.* Florence: La Nuova Italia, 1986.

Menascé, Esther. *Minor Don Juans in British Literature.* Testi e studi de letterature moderne 2. Milan: Cisalpino-Goliardica, 1986.

Meyer, Herbert. "Das Fortleben Mozarts bei Mörike und seinen Freunden." *Acta Mozartiana* 32 (1985), 29–40.

Michaud, Stéphane. *Muse et madone: Visages de la femme de la révolution française aux apparitions de Lourdes.* Paris: Seuil, 1985.

Mills, Carl H. "Man and Superman and the Don Juan Legend." *Comparative Literature* 19 (1967), 216–225.

Mongrédien, Jean. "A propos du manuscrit autographe de *Don Giovanni.*" *Cahiers Ivan Tourguéniev, Pauline Viardot, Maria Malibran* 2 (1978), 39–45.

Moraldo, Sandro M. *Wandlungen des Doppelgängers: Shakespeare, E. T. A. Hoffmann, Pirandello.* Frankfurt am Main: Lang, 1996.

Morgan, Bayard Quincy, and Alexander Rudolf Hohlfeld. *German Literature in British Magazines, 1750–1860.* Madison: University of Wisconsin Press, 1949.

Moser, Walter. "Writing (about) Music: The Case of E. T. A. Hoffmann." In *The Romantic Tradition: German Literature and Music in the Nineteenth Century,* ed. Gerald Chapple, Frederick Hall, and Hans Schulte, McMaster Colloquium on German Studies 4,209–226. Lanham, Md.: University Press of America, 1992.

Nelson, Molly. "The First Italian Opera Season in New York City: 1825–1826." Ph.D. diss., University of North Carolina at Chapel Hill, 1976.

Newark, Cormac. "'Vous qui faites l'endormie': The Phantom and the Buried Voices of the Paris Opéra." *19th-Century Music* 33 (2009), 62–78.

Oldman, Cecil. "Mozart and Modern Research." *Proceedings of the Musical Association* 58 (1931–32): 58.

Oppenlander, Ella Ann. *Dickens' "All the Year Round": Descriptive Index and Contributor List.* Troy, N.Y.: Whitston, 1984.

Orlova, Alexandra. *Tchaikovsky: A Self-Portrait.* Oxford: Oxford University Press, 1990.

Osborne, Linda-Payne. "Shaw and Mozart: Dramaturgy and the Life Force." *Journal of Irish Literature* 11 (1982), 96–110.

Osolsobe, Petr. "Kierkegaard's Aethetics of Music: A Concept of the Musical Erotic." *Sborník prací Filozofické Fakulty Brnenské Univerzity. H. Rada hudebnevedná* 27–28 (1992–93), 97–106.

Pailleron, Marie-Louise. "Les Blaze de Bury et l'Autriche." *Revue de Paris,* 1 July 1922, 126–148.

Pailleron, Marie-Louise. *Les derniers romantiques.* François Buloz et ses amis [3]. Paris: Perrin, 1923.

Panagl, Oswald. "Direct and Indirect Routes to the Sketch of a Music Drama: The Victors and *Parsifal.*" In *Bayreuther Festspiele* 1994, 97–104. Bayreuth: n.p., 1994.

Perry, Nicholas, and Loreto Echeverría. *Under the Heel of Mary.* London: Routledge, 1988.

Pfannhauser, Karl. "Epilogomena Mozartiana." In *Mozart-Jahrbuch 1971–72 des Zentralinstitutes für Mozartforschung der Internationalen Stiftung Mozarteum Salzburg,* 268–312. Kassel: Bärenreiter, 1973.

Pollak, Paulina Salz. "Master to the Masters: Mozart's Influence on Bernard Shaw's *Don Juan in Hell.*" *Shaw: The Annual Review of Shaw Studies* 8 (1988), 39–68.

Potter, Dorothy Turner. "The Cultural Infuences of W. A. Mozart's Music in Philadelphia, 1786–1861." Ph.D. diss., University of Virginia, 2000.

Prévost, Michel. "Blaze de Bury (Ange-Henri)." In *Dictionnaire de biographie française,* ed. Michel-Prévost and Jean-Charles Roman d'Amat, 6:659–660. Paris: Letouzey et Ané, 1933–.

Pustovalova, Margarita. "Mocart I Gofman." *Sovetskaja muzyka* 12 (1991): 81–84.

Rachmanova, Olga. *L'Amour d'une vie: Ivan Tourgueniev—Pauline Viardot Garcia.* Trans. Pierette Viardot. Paris: author, 1996.

Radomski, James. *Manuel García (1775–1832): Chronicle of the Life of a Bel Canto Tenor at the Dawn of Romanticism.* Oxford: Oxford University Press, 2000.

Rank, Otto. *Der Doppelgänger: A Psychological Study.* Trans. and ed. Harry Tucker Jr. Chapel Hill: University of North Carolina Press, 1971.

Rauscher, Frances M., Gordon L. Shaw, and Katherine N. Kym. "Music and Spatial Task Performance." *Nature* 365 (October 1993), 611.

Reames, L. Sherry. *The Legenda Aurea: A Reexamination of Its Paradoxical History.* Madison: University of Wisconsin Press, 1985.

Rigaud, Yvette Sieffert. "Pauline Viardot: Mythe et Réalité." Thèse d'État, Université de Rouen, 1991.

Riley, Philip. *The Making of "The Phantom of the Opera."* Hollywood Archives Series. Absecon, N.J.: Magicimage Filmbooks, 1999.

Robinson, William. "Conceptions of Mozart in German Criticism and Biography 1791–1828: Changing Images of a Musical Genius." Ph.D. diss., Yale University, 1974.

Rosenberg, Alfons. "Mozart in Kierkegaards Deutung." *Österreichische Musikzeitschrift* 23 (1968), 409–412.

Rousset, Jean. *Le Myth de Don Juan.* Paris: Armand Colin, 1976. Reprint, Prismes Littéraires 1994.

Rozanov, Aleksandr Semoenovitch. *Polina Viardo Garsia.* Leningrad: Editio Muzika, 1969.

Rushton, Julian. *W. A. Mozart: "Don Giovanni."* Cambridge Opera Handbooks. Cambridge: Cambridge University Press, 1981. Reprint, 1994.

Saint-Saëns, Camille. *École Buissonnière: Notes et souvenirs.* Paris: Lafitte, 1913.

Schafer, R. Murray. *E. T. A. Hoffmann and Music.* Toronto and Buffalo: University of Toronto Press, 1975.

Schmidt, Hans-Christian, ed. *Géza Anda: "Sechzehntel sind auch Musik": Dokumente seines Lebens.* Zürich: Artemis & Winkler, 1991.

Schneider, Herbert. "Die Bearbeitung des *Pardon der Ploërmel* von G. Meyerbeer im Jahre der Uraufführung." In *Festschrift Heinz Becker zum 60. Geburtstag am 26. Juni 1982*, ed. Jürgen Schläder and Reinhold Quandt, 152–161. Laaber: Laaber, 1982.

Schrade, Leo. *Beethoven in France: The Growth of an Idea.* New Haven: Yale University Press; London: Humphrey Milford and Oxford University Press, 1942.

Schuster-Fournier, Carolyn. "Les Orgues de salon d'Aristide Cavaillé-Coll." *L'Orgue: Cahiers et Mémoires* (1997): 57–58.

Scudo, Paul. *Critique et littérature musicales.* Paris: Amyot, 1850.

Seidel, Wilhelm. "Absolute Musik und Kunstreligion um 1800." In *Musik und Religion*, ed. Helga de La Motte-Haber, 89–114. Laaber: Laaber, 1995.

Shaw, George Bernard. *The Complete Plays of Bernard Shaw.* London: Odham, 1934.

Shaw, George Bernard. *The Intelligent Woman's Guide to Socialism and Capitalism.* London: Constable, 1928.

Shaw, George Bernard. "Short Stories, Scraps and Shavings." In *The Works of Bernard Shaw* 6, 95–116. London: Constable, 1932.

Shaw, George Bernard. *Sixteen Self Sketches.* London: Constable, 1949.

Shaw, George Bernard. *Translations and Tomfooleries.* London: Constable, 1926. Reprint, 1932.

Slatford, Rodney. "Cimador, *Cimadoro*, Giambattista, *Giovanni Battista, Gian Battista.*" In *Die Musik in Geschichte und Gegenwart: Allgemeine Enzyklopädie der Musik*, 1125–1127. Kassel: Bärenreiter; Stuttgart and Weimar: Metzler, 2000.

Slatford, Rodney, and Marita P. McClymonds. "Cimador, Giambattista." In *Grove Music Online. Oxford Music Online.* www.oxfordmusiconline.com/subscriber/article/grove/music/05784. Accessed 20 April 2011.

Sloboda, John. "Mozart in Psychology." *Music Performance Research* 1 (2007): 66–75.

Smeed, John William. *Don Juan: Variations on a Theme.* London: Routledge, 1990.

Sohn, Anne-Marie. "The Golden Age of Male Adultery: The Third Republic." *Journal of Social History* 28 (1995), 469–490.

Solie, Ruth. "Changing the Subject." *Current Musicology* 53 (1993), 55–65.

Solomon, Gerhard. *E. T. A. Hoffmann: Bibliographie*. Berlin and Leipzig: Paetel, 1927.

Soubies, Albert. *Le Théâtre-Italien de 1801 à 1913*. Paris: Fischbacher, 1913.

Soubies, Albert. *Soixante-sept ans à l'Opéra en une page du "Siège de Corinthe" à "La Walky-rie" (1826–1893)*. Paris: Fischbacher, 1893.

Staehelin, Martin. "Mozart auf der Reise nach Prag: Musikhistorisches zu Mörikes Novelle." *Neue Zürcher Zeitung*, 26–27 May, 1990.

Stafford, William. "The Evolution of Mozartian Biography." In *The Cambridge Companion to Mozart*, ed. Simon P. Keefe, 200–211. Cambridge: Cambridge University Press, 2003.

Stafford, William. *The Mozart Myths: A Critical Reassessment*. Stanford: Stanford University Press, 1991.

Steinberg, Michael P. *The Meaning of the Salzburg Festival: Austria as Theater and Ideology, 1890–1938*. Ithaca and London: Cornell University Press, 1990.

Stocker, Arnold. *La Double: L'homme à la rencontre de soi-même*. Geneva: Éditions de Rhône, 1946.

Suleiman, Susan R. "Introduction: Varieties of Audience-Oriented Criticism." In Suleiman, *The Reader in the Text: Essays on Audience and Interpretation*, 3–45. Princeton, N.J., and Oxford: Princeton University Press, 1980.

Taruskin, Richard. *Text and Act: Essays on Music and Performance*. New York and Oxford: Oxford University Press, 1995.

Taruskin, Richard. "Why Mozart Has Become an Icon for Today." *New York Times*, September 9, 1990.

Tauber, Abraham, ed. *George Bernard Shaw on Language*. London: Peter Owen, 1965.

Taylor, Gary. *Reinventing Shakespeare: A Cultural History from the Restoration to the Present*. London: Hogarth, 1990.

Tiersot, Julien. *Don Juan de Mozart: Étude historique et critique, analyse musicale*, Les chefs d'œuvre de la musique expliqués. Paris: Mellottée, 1930.

Tomatis, Alfred A. *Pourquoi Mozart?* Paris: Fixot, 1991.

Troubetzkoy, Wladimir. "Pouchkine, Alexandre (1799–1837)." In *Dictionnaire de Don Juan*, ed. Pierre Bunel, Bouquins 752. Paris: Laffont, 1999.

Tschuggnall, Peter. "Sören Kierkegaards Mozart-Rezeption: Analyse einer philosophisch-literarische Deutung von Musik." Ph.D. diss., Universität Innsbruck, 1991.

Valentin, Hans Erich. "Der reisende Enthusiast: Mozart-Aspekte im Werk E. Th. A. Hoffmanns." In *Deutsches Mozartfest der deutschen Mozart-Gesellschaft in Verbinderung mit der Stadt Augsburg und dem Bayerischen Rundfunk, Augsburg 13.–18. Mai 1972*, 11–20. Augsburg: Mozart-Gesellschaft, 1972.

Veeser, H. Aram, ed. *The New Historicism*. New York and London: Routledge, 1989.

Vertrees, Julie-Anne. "Mozart's String Quartet K. 465: The History of a Controversy." *Current Musicology* 17 (1974), 96–114.

Viardot, Louis. "Un Souvenir du Don Juan de Mozart." In *Espagne et Beaux Arts: Mélanges*, 439–446. Paris: Hachette, 1866. Reprinted in *Le Ménestrel* 46 (1879–80), 65–67. Reprinted in *Cahiers Ivan Tourguéniev, Pauline Viardot, Maria Malibran* 2 (1978), 64–71.

Viardot, Louis, and Ivan Turgenev, trans. "L'Invité de Pierre." In *Poèmes dramatiques d'Alexandre Pouchkine*, 237–279. Paris: Hachette, 1862.

Voerster, Jürgen. *160 Jahre E. T. A. Hoffmann-Forschung, 1805–1965: Eine Bibliographie mit Inhaltserfassung und Erläuterungen*. Bibliographien des Antiquariats Fritz Eggert 3. Stuttgart: Eggert, 1967.

Voss, Egon, and Martin Geck. *Richard Wagner: Parsifal.* 3 vols. Sämtliche Werke 14. Mainz: Schott, 1972–73.

Waddington, Patrick. "Turgenev and Pauline Viardot: An Unofficial Marriage." *Canadian Slavonic Papers* 26 (1984), 42–64.

Walker, Alan. *Franz Liszt: The Virtuoso Years, 1811–1847.* New York: Knopf, 1983.

Walsh, Thomas Joseph. *Second Empire Opera: The Théâtre Lyrique, Paris, 1851–1870.* The History of Opera. London: Calder; New York: Riverrun, 1981.

Waschek, Matthias. "Zum Wagnérisme in den bildenden Künsten." In *Von Wagner zum Wagnérisme: Musik, Literatur, Kunst, Politik*, ed. Annegret Fauser and Manuela Schwartz, Deutsch-Französisiche Kulturbibliothek 12, 535–546. Leipzig: Universitätsverlag, 1999.

Wates, Roye E. "Eduard Mörike, Alexander Ulibishev and the 'Ghost Scene' in *"Don Giovanni."* In Wates, *The Creative Process*, 31–48. New York: Broude, 1992.

Webber, Andrew J. *The Doppelgänger: Double Visions in German Literature.* Oxford: Clarendon, 1996.

Webster, James. "To Understand Verdi and Wagner We Must Understand Mozart." *19th-Century Music* 11 (1987), 175–193.

Weick, Karl E., David P. Gilfillan, and Thomas A. Keith. "The Effect of Composer Credibility on Orchestra Performance." *Sociometry* 36 (1973), 435–462.

Weinreb, Ruth Plant. "In Defense of Don Juan: Deceit and Hypocrisy in Tirso de Molina, Molière and G. B. Shaw." *Romanic Review* 74 (1983), 425–440.

Weintraub, Stanley. *Bernard Shaw: A Guide to Research.* University Park: Pennsylvania University Press, 1992.

Weintraub, Stanley, ed. *Bernard Shaw: The Diaries 1885–1897, with Early Autobiographical Notebooks and Diaries, and an Abortive 1917 Diary.* 2 vols. University Park and London: Pennsylvania State University Press, 1986.

Weintraub, Stanley. "Genesis of a Play: Two Early Approaches to *Man and Superman."* In *Shaw: Seven Critical Essays*, ed. Norman Rosenblood, 25–35. Toronto: Toronto University Press, 1971.

Werner, Elmar. "Der 'gottliche' Mozart: Die Mozart-Kritiken Ludwig Bornes." *Acta Mozartiana* 32 (1985): 13–17.

Wild, Nicole. *Dictionnaire des théâtres parisiens au xixe siècle: Les théâtres et la musique.* Paris: Amateurs des Livres, 1989.

Wilder, Victor. *Mozart, l'homme et L' artiste: Histoire de sa vie d'après les documents authentiques et les travaux les plus récents.* Paris: Le Ménestrel, 1880.

Wiora, Walter. "Zu Kierkegaards Ideen über Mozarts *Don Giovanni."* In *Beiträge zur Musikgeschichte Nordeuropas: Kurt Gudewill zum 65. Geburtstag*, ed. Uwe Haensel, 39–50. Wolfenbüttel and Zurich: Möseler, 1978.

Wirth, Julia, ed. *Julius Stockhausen: der Sänger des deutschen Liedes nach Dokumenten seiner Zeit.* Frankfurt am Main: Englert und Schlosser, 1927.

Woestyn, Eugène, and Eugène Moreau. *Les Folies-Nouvelles.* Les théâtres de Paris. Paris: Martinon, 1855.

Wolff, Christoph. *Mozarts Requiem: Geschichte, Musik, Dokumente, Partitur des Fragments.* Munich: Deutscher Taschenbuch Verlag; Kassel: Bärenreiter, 1991. Trans. by Mary Whittall as *Mozart's Requiem: Historical and Analytical Studies, Documents, Score.* Oxford: Clarendon, 1994.

Wood, Elizabeth. "Lesbian Fugue: Ethel Smyth's Contrapuntal Arts." In *Musicology and Difference: Gender and Sexuality in Music Scholarship*, ed. Ruth A. Solie, 164–183. Berkeley: University of California Press, 1993.

Yon, Jean-Claude. *Jacques Offenbach*. Paris: Gallimard, 2000.

Yon, Jean-Claude. "La création du Théâtre des Bouffes-Parisiens (1855–1862) ou La difficile naissance de l'opérette." *Revue d'histoire moderne et contemporaine* 39 (1992), 575–600.

Zaslaw, Neal, ed. *Köchelverzeichnis: Chronologisch-thematisches Verzeichnis sämtlicher Tonwerke Wolfgang Amadé Mozarts—Neuausgabe in Zusammenarbeit mit der Internationalen Stiftung Mozarteum*. Leipzig and Wiesbaden: Breitkopf und Härtel, forthcoming.

Zhdanov, V. A., ed. *P. I. Tchaikovsky, S. I. Taneyev, Pis'ma*. Moscow: Gosudarstvennïy Literaturnïy Muzey, 1951.

Zhdanov, V. A., and I. T. Zhegin, eds. *Pyotr Il'yich Tchaikovsky, Perepiska s N.F. fon-Mekk*. 3 vols. Moscow and Leningrad: Academia, 1934–36.

Zigman, Charles. *World's Coolest Movie Star: The Complete 95 Films (and Legend) of Jean Gabin*. Los Angeles: Allenwood Press, 2008.

Zimmermann, Jörg. "Philosophische Musikrezeption im Zeichen des spekulativ-erotischen Ohrs: Sören Kierkegaard hört Mozarts *Don Juan*." In *Rezeptionsästhetik und Rezeptionsgeschichte in der Musikwissenschaft*, Publikationen der Hochschule für Musik und Theater Hannover 3, 73–103. Laaber: Laaber, 1991.

Zylstra, Henry. "E. T. A. Hoffmann in England and America." Ph.D. diss., Harvard University, 1940.

{ INDEX }